Ulrich Broich, H. T. Dickinson,
Eckhart Hellmuth, Martin Schmidt

Reactions to Revolutions

Kulturgeschichtliche Perspektiven

herausgegeben von

Martin Baumeister
und
Eckhart Hellmuth

Band 2

LIT

Ulrich Broich, H. T. Dickinson,
Eckhart Hellmuth, Martin Schmidt

Reactions to Revolutions

The 1790s and their Aftermath

LIT

Cover Picture: Isaac Cruikshank, The Royal Extinguisher, 1795
(British Museum)

Bibliographic information published by the Deutsche Nationalbibliothek
The Deutsche Nationalbibliothek lists this publication in the Deutsche Nationalbibliografie; detailed bibliographic data are available in the Internet at http://dnb.d-nb.de.

ISBN 978-3-8258-7427-8

A catalogue record for this book is available from the British Library

Ziegelstr. 30
D-10117 Berlin

Auslieferung:

LIT Verlag Fresnostr. 2, D-48159 Münster
Tel. +49 (0) 2 51/620 32 - 22, Fax +49 (0) 2 51/922 60 99, e-Mail: lit@lit-verlag.de

Distributed in the UK by: Global Book Marketing, 99B Wallis Rd, London, E9 5LN
Phone: +44 (0) 20 8533 5800 – Fax: +44 (0) 1600 775 663
http://www.centralbooks.co.uk/acatalog/search.html

Distributed in North America by:

Transaction Publishers
New Brunswick (U.S.A.) and London (U.K.)

Transaction Publishers
Rutgers University
35 Berrue Circle
Piscataway, NJ 08854

Phone: +1 (732) 445 - 2280
Fax: + 1 (732) 445 - 3138
for orders (U. S. only):
toll free (888) 999 - 6778
e-mail:
orders@transactionspub.com

Preface

This collection of essays is the result of a joint collaborative enterprise undertaken between the Modern History Department at the University of Edinburgh and the Departments of History and English Studies at the University of Munich. The collaboration itself culminated in a series of interdisciplinary workshops in intellectual history and the history of political thought held between the years 1998-2002. These workshops were attended by faculty members and doctoral students from a number of academic institutions, including the universities of De Montfort, Leicester, Northwestern, and Leeds. Nicholas Phillipson and Christoph von Ehrenstein deserve special thanks for their major contribution both to organisation and to academic debate.

This collaboration would not have been possible without generous financial help from both the British Council and the *Deutscher Akademischer Auslandsdienst* (DAAD). The publication itself has been subsidised by the University of Edinburgh, the Moray Fund and the Verein der Förderer und Freunde des Historicums. The editors would like to express their gratitude to each of these bodies for their support.

The majority of contributions published here were completed and submitted in 2003. Publication has been delayed by the difficulty involved in coordinating a collaborative enterprise of this kind, and by the intervention of competing academic schedules. The editors would like to thank the contributors for their forbearance.

H. T. Dickinson
Eckhart Hellmuth

List of Contributors

Ulrich Broich studied at the universities of Köln, Freiburg, and Bonn. He held positions at the universities of Göttingen and Erlangen and became full professor of English literature at the university of Bochum in 1967. From 1976 to 2000 he held a chair of English literature at the university of Munich. He published books on Thackeray, literary patronage in the Middle Ages and the eighteenth-century mock-heroic poem and coedited books on intertextuality, the 1920s and Britain at the turn of the 21st century.

Marianne Czisnik has gained two degrees in law in Germany and a Masters degree in history from the University of Edinburgh and has finished her doctoral thesis at the University of Edinburgh on the image of Admiral Nelson. Her book on *Horatio Nelson: A Controversial Hero* has been published in 2005. She has written articles for the *Mariner's Mirror* and *The Trafalgar Chronicle*, and is the author of an article on Nelson in the journal *History* (2006).

H. T. Dickinson is emeritus Professor of British History at the University of Edinburgh and a Concurrent Professor of History at the University of Nanjing in China. Formerly the editor of the journal *History* (1993-2000), he is at present the President of the Historical Association of Great Britain, a Vice-President of the Royal Historical Society, and Convener of the History Research Panel of the UK's Arts and Humanities Research Board. He has written many articles and essays, and he is the author or editor of thirteen books, including *Bolingbroke*, *Walpole and the Whig Supremacy*, *Liberty and Property: Political Ideology in Eighteenth-Century Britain*, *The Politics of the People in Eighteenth-Century Britain*, and *A Companion to Eighteenth-Century Britain*.

M. O. Grenby received his degree in History and English, and then his PhD, from the University of Edinburgh. His first book, *The Anti-Jacobin Novel*, was published by Cambridge University Press in 2001 and he is currently editing several of the novels it discussed for publication by Pickering and Chatto and the Broadview Press. His next book will explore the early history of British children's literature. Having returned to Britain from the USA, where he was Fulbright-Robertson visiting professor of British history, he is now a Senior Research Fellow in the English Department at De Montfort University, Leicester.

Eckhart Hellmuth is Professor of Modern History at the University of Munich. His has specialized in the history of eighteenth-century Britain and Germany, and focusses on the history of the state and the intellectual and cultural history of the bureaucracy. His authored and edited publications include: *Naturrechtsphilosophie und bürokratischer Werthorizont* (1985), *The Transformation of Political Culture: England and Germany in the Late Eighteenth Century* (1990), and *Rethinking Leviathan: The Eighteenth-Century State in Britain and Germany* (1999, co-edited with John Brewer).

Anton Kirchhofer taught English Literature at the University of Munich, where he took his Ph.D. and his *Habilitation* (a post-doctoral thesis on Victorian criticism and critical journals). His publications include a monograph on types of sexual knowledge in eighteenth-century novels (*Strategie und Wahrheit*, 1995), a number of essays on nineteenth and twentieth-century literature and theory, and a co-edited collection (*Psychoanalyticism: Uses of Psychoanalysis in Novels, Poems, Plays and Films*, 2000). He is now Professor for English Literature at Oldenburg, Germany.

Kai Merten finished his PhD in 2002 with a thesis on classical culture and ancient myth in contemporary poetry in English. He is now a Lecturer in English Literature at the University of Kiel, Germany. Currently he focusses on theatre and theatricality in first-generation British Romantic writing. Publications inlcude work on contemporary poetry in English, on William Wordsworth, Walter Scott, and on the Medusa myth in nineteenth-century British and German poetry and painting. He has jointly edited with Hansjörg Bay *Die Ordnung der Kulturen* (2005).

Benjamin Pauley is an Assistant Professor of English at Eastern Connecticut State University. He received his PhD in English from Northwestern University (Evanston, Illinois). He is currently revising his dissertation, a study of the ways in which the consolidation of the legal profession provoked a rethinking of the meanings of lay status in eighteenth-century Britain. Moreover, he is beginning a new project exploring representations of eighteenth-century London as a world city located at the heart of an increasingly global system of commerce.

Gordon Pentland graduated in Modern History from Oxford University, and then completed an MSc by Research degree in History at the University of Edinburgh on British radicalism in the 1790s. After receiving his doctorate from Edinburgh University with a thesis on the movement for political reform in Scotland in the 1820s and 1830s, he now holds a post as Lecturer in History at the University of York. He has published several articles on Scottish radicalism and reform politics in journals such as *History*, the *Historical Journal*, and the *Scottish Historical Review*.

Katharina Rennhak has been teaching English Literature at Munich since 1997. She was a Visiting Assistant Professor at University of Texas in 2004 (spring term). She is the author of *Sprachkonzeptionen im metahistorischen Roman* (2002). With Virginia Richter she has co-edited *Revolution und Emanzipation: Geschlechterordnungen in Europa um 1800* (2004), an essay collection on gender and politics around 1800. With Christoph Bode she has co-edited *Romantic Voices, Romantic Poetics* (2005). She is currently working on narrative cross-gendering and constructions of masculinity in women writers' fiction around 1800.

Martin Schmidt studied Modern History, Art History, and Social and Economic History at the universities of Freiburg, Edinburgh, and Munich. He is Assistant Lecturer in the Department of History at Munich and works on British cultural and intellectual history from ca. 1750 to 1914. He is currently finishing a PhD thesis on the political thought of John Ruskin. Together with Eckhart Hellmuth, he has authored articles on British political thought around 1800 and on the Cambridge School. Further articles on Ruskin's aesthetics and Prince Albert's legal studies at Bonn are forthcoming.

Atle Wold studied for his Cand Mag degree at the University of Oslo and spent one of his four years as an undergraduate studying at the University of Dundee in Scotland. In 2003, he completed his PhD degree at the University of Edinburgh with a dissertation on the Scottish response to the war with Revolutionary France. He has worked as a Lecturer in British History in the University of Stavanger and is now Associate Professor for British Culture at Oslo University. His publications include an essay on 'A Union of Arms: Scottish Attitudes to the French Revolutionary War'.

Contents

H. T. Dickinson and Ulrich Broich

Introduction

The outbreak of revolution in Paris in 1789 began a long chain of events that was to have the most profound effect on the history of France. Europe did not escape the consequences either. The attachment of French revolutionaries to the principles of liberty, equality and fraternity, and their desire to secure the natural and inalienable rights of all men and to create a state in which the people were sovereign, both inspired reformers and alarmed the governing elite across the whole of Europe. The subsequent French efforts to export their revolutionary principles to the rest of Europe provoked wars that involved almost every country in Europe. The impact on Britain was both profound and prolonged.[1] The French threat forced Britain into a long and bitter conflict that compelled the British people to make unprecedented sacrifices in blood and treasure. To win this war Britain had to suffer economic dislocation, find new sources of revenue, expand her navy, overhaul her army and repeatedly seek armed coalitions with the other great powers of Europe. The French wars, lasting almost uninterrupted for more than twenty years, were unprecedented in their scale, duration and consequences. What was particularly remarkable about the impact of the French Revolution and the French wars on Britain, however, was the deep and abiding influence that they had on the intellectual climate and the ideological discourse of the age. Throughout the British Isles French revolutionary principles, French political practices, and the French wars, became the most important subjects of public comment and political debate – inside and outside parliament, in sermons delivered in churches of all denominations, in the London and provincial press, and in a very remarkable number of poems, novels, plays and graphic prints. This vast range and wealth of political comment and political propaganda emerged from a society excited, alarmed and perplexed by the nature and consequences of the French Revolution. While a few people tried to stand aloof and rather more changed their view of the French Revolution, the majority of those engaged in this public debate were sharply polarized. The intense and prolonged British debate on French revolutionary principles and on the French wars re-shaped the domestic scene within the British Isles. It greatly stimu-

1 See, for example, the essays in *Britain and the French Revolution 1789-1815*, ed. H.T. Dickinson (Basingstoke, 1989).

lated the demand for radical reform while, paradoxically, developing a conservative ideology of considerable intellectual sophistication and wide appeal. It significantly altered the alignments within the governing elite, eventually transforming the supporters of William Pitt into a new Tory party and condemning Charles James Fox's Whig opposition to minority status for nearly forty years. It provoked ideological divisions within both Scotland and Ireland of an intensity not seen for decades and yet it also led to closer relations between England and Scotland and to an attempt to unite the whole British Isles into a single state for the first time. And last, but not least, it greatly influenced the writings of almost every imaginative and creative author of poems, novels and plays.

I.

The dramatic first months of the French Revolution inspired most Britons of liberal views. Veteran British reformers of all shades of opinion were galvanized into action. Demands for parliamentary reforms, first made during the American Revolution but languishing in the later 1780s, were revived. The French Revolution also helped to give birth to more radical reformers, soon known as British Jacobins because of their support for French revolutionary principles.[2] Many of these reformers adopted the political programme of the more extreme British radicals of the early 1780s, including the demand for universal manhood suffrage, annual general elections and equal-sized constituencies, but they also used different arguments to justify their demands. Some radicals still appealed to the historic rights of Britons and to the ancient constitution, but others followed the French in putting more stress on natural rights and the sovereignty of the people. In his widely-read *Rights of Man* (1791-92), Thomas Paine contemptuously dismissed Britain's much-praised constitution and advocated a democratic republic.[3] Few other British reformers were prepared to go so far, although they did wish to democratize the electoral processes. Almost none of them demanded votes for women (not even Mary Wollstonecraft, the leading feminist of the age) and very few showed

2 Among the many works on the British radicals of the 1790s, see Albert Goodwin, *The Friends of Liberty: The English Democratic Movement in the Age of the French Revolution* (London, 1979); H.T. Dickinson, *British Radicalism and the French Revolution 1789-1815* (Oxford, 1985); *The French Revolution and British Popular Politics*, ed. Mark Philp (Cambridge, 1991); and Jenny Graham, *The Nation, the Law and the King, Reform Politics in England, 1789-1799* (2 vols., Lanham, MD, 2000).

3 Gregory Claeys, *Thomas Paine: Social and Political Thought* (London, 1989).

much interest in the economic plight of the poor. Most expected a reformed parliament to reduce government expenditure and hence to reduce the tax burden on the poor. Paine did go further and, in the second part of the *Rights of Man*, he did set out the outlines of a welfare state, including old age pensions, child allowances, and maternity benefits for the poor. In *Agrarian Justice* (1796), Paine also suggested a tax on the propertied elite in order to raise sufficient revenue to give each man a grant of fifty pounds at the age of 21, in order to set him out on life. Thomas Spence went even further, proposing the abolition of all private property. He suggested that each parish should take control of and then lease out the land, water and mines within its boundaries. The money raised would be spent first on the expenses of the government and of local amenities, such as schools, libraries and hospitals, before the remainder was shared equally between every man, woman and child in the parish.[4]

To disseminate their political views far and wide the radicals established dozens of new political clubs and societies in many of the larger urban centres in Britain. By far the most important of these new radical clubs was the London Corresponding Society, which enlisted several thousand members drawn from the lower middles classes and the ranks of the craftsmen and artisans who were so numerous in the capital. Similar, but smaller, societies sprang up in a great many provincial towns such as Sheffield, Manchester, Norwich, Leicester, Nottingham and Edinburgh. Although they failed to attract truly massive support, and they failed in particular to enlist large numbers of the labouring poor, these radical societies did raise the political consciousness of many ordinary people. They offered a political education by employing a variety of tactics to put pressure on the governing elite in order to achieve political reform. Nearly all the radicals favoured an appeal to reason and they urged a massive propaganda campaign designed to expose the abuses of the existing political system. Addresses, petitions and resolutions were submitted to king and parliament. Pamphlets, broadsheets, periodicals and newspapers were all deployed to spread radical propaganda far and wide. Some radicals also decided to emulate the French by calling conventions to unite the numerous radical societies behind an agreed political programme. Conventions of this kind met in Edinburgh in 1792 and 1793, before they were forcibly closed by the alarmed local magistrates.

---

4 *The Political Works of Thomas Spence*, ed. H.T. Dickinson (Newcastle-upon-Tyne, 1982).

As the French Revolution degenerated into violence and anarchy, the government sought to suppress the activities of their radical admirers in Britain. Faced by government repression, most radicals were at a loss how best to respond. The majority lost heart or at least moderated their conduct. As a last desperate resort a militant minority turned to conspiracy and violence as the only means of achieving their political objectives. This minority assumed the violent, subversive and revolutionary character that the majority of British radicals had always repudiated. Groups of United Englishmen were formed in London, Lancashire and West Yorkshire, and bands of United Scotsmen appeared in central Scotland.[5] Links were forged with the even more revolutionary United Irishmen, arms were gathered and some military drilling took place between 1796 and 1798. Lacking numbers, cohesion, military experience and a clear strategy, they had little prospect of success without a French invasion to assist them. Once the government had gained sufficient evidence of their clandestine plotting, it struck hard and arrested most of the leaders in 1798. The treason of a few radicals helped to justify retrospectively the earlier repressive measures of government and parliament.

II.

The propertied elite in Britain had long recognized that their privileged social, economic and political position owed much to the nature of the British constitution that had defeated royal absolutism while denying the vote to the poor masses. Ingrained admiration for this constitution, combined with growing alarm for its safety in the face of French revolutionary principles and French military aggression, led in the 1790s to the articulation of a conservative ideology of considerable appeal, resilience and intellectual power.[6] Edmund Burke, once one of the more liberal MPs at Westminster, was the first close observer of the astonishing events in France to take serious alarm at the development of a revolutionary ideology there. As early as November 1790 he launched his *Reflections on the Revolution in France* upon a surprised public. This was the first impassioned and sophisticated attack on the moral and intellectual claims being advanced by the French revolutionaries and supported

5 Roger Wells, *Insurrection: The British Experience 1795-1803* (Gloucester, 1983).

6 H.T. Dickinson, *Liberty and Property: Political Ideology in Eighteenth-Century Britain* (London, 1977), pp. 270-318.

by British radicals.[7] While Burke acknowledged that all men possessed a common humanity and they all deserved justice, he insisted that men did not have an equal claim to a share of political power in the state. Power of this kind was not a natural and inalienable right belonging to all adult men, but a legal right which any civil society was free to confer or deny as it saw fit. Civil government was created not to convert natural rights into civil liberties, as Paine was shortly afterwards to claim, but to protect private property, to preserve the natural distinctions in society, and to restrain man's selfish and passionate nature. The best constitutions, such as that of Britain, were not created by the rational decisions of a body of men at a particular point in time, but were prescriptive in the sense that they were the product of long experience and the result of trial and error over centuries. It was dangerously conceited for even the wisest and shrewdest of men to presume that they could elevate their rational political construct above a system that had stood the judgement of many generations and the test of time. A reverence for the past and an acceptance of the authority of the positive laws of society were to be admired more than the rash efforts to create a new political and social order on the basis of abstract principles and speculative theories.

In his *Reflections*, Burke warned his readers that, if such dangerous men as the French revolutionaries abroad and the British radicals at home were not firmly resisted, they would destroy justice, social harmony and the rule of law. In the end, they would incite the impoverished masses to pillage the propertied elite. At first, Burke's fears were regarded as alarmist, even unbalanced, but the slide into terror and violence in France and the outbreak of a large-scale European war soon encouraged other conservative thinkers to follow where he had led. Burke himself became a war crusader determined to meet the Jacobin menace by force of arms. He was one of the first to recognize that the war against revolutionary France was no typical eighteenth-century war for territorial gain but was a war of ideas, in which either the British or the French political and social order would be overthrown. Convinced now by the arguments in Burke's *Reflections* and in his later writings, a host of writers, including William Paley, John Bowles, Arthur Young, Robert Nares, Samuel Horsley, John Reeves and Hannah More, contributed to a truly massive campaign that endeavoured to warn the British people of the dire threat posed by French

---

7 F.P. Lock, *Burke's Reflections on the Revolution in France* (London, 1985); and Michael Freeman, *Edmund Burke and the Critique of Political Radicalism* (Oxford, 1980).

revolutionary principles and by the determination of the French to export these principles abroad by force of arms.[8]

Popular conservatism absorbed and simplified the essential principles of Burke's reflections, but did even more to instil a hatred of French principles and an unquestioning pride in the British constitution in church and state. Great care was taken to inform the poor that God had created both rich and poor as a way of rewarding the industrious and punishing the lazy. The pursuit of equality would inevitably lead to social anarchy that would destroy justice and the rule of law, and put everyone's freedom and possessions at risk. In their search for liberty the French were lurching from crisis to crisis, from mob rule to military dictatorship, while the British were seeking to preserve a tried and trusted constitution which achieved an enviable balance between the stability of the state and the liberty of the individual. Radical appeals to popular sovereignty risked unleashing the will of the impoverished and uneducated masses, so that in the end all would suffer. For their moral guides the French had abandoned Christian principles and chivalric virtues in favour of atheism, the worship of human reason and the unrestrained will of man. Crude propaganda, often reprehensible in tone, blackened the character of honourable British radicals and created a hideous caricature of the anarchic, rapacious and bloodthirsty French revolutionaries. British radicals were invariably condemned as men with weak heads and bad hearts. They were depicted as traitors to their own country and as dupes of a foreign enemy. The atheistical, immoral and wilful French were accused of spreading anarchy, oppression and desolation across large areas of Europe. The British needed to remember all the benefits they reaped under the existing political and social order and should unite to preserve their liberty, property and religion from the scourge of French principles and the violence of French practices.

The variety, the sheer volume, and the social and geographical spread of this militantly loyalist propaganda were more impressive than that dis-

---

8 Robert Hole, 'British Counter-Revolutionary Popular Propaganda in the 1790s', in *Britain and Revolutionary France: Conflict, Subversion and Propaganda*, ed. Colin Jones (Exeter, 1983), pp. 53-69; Emily Lorraine de Montluzin, *The Anti-Jacobins 1798-1800* (Basingstoke, 1988); Thomas Philip Schofield, 'Conservative Political Thought in Britain in response to the French Revolution', *Historical Journal*, 29 (1986), 601-22; and Emma Vincent, '"The Real Grounds for the Present War": John Bowles and the French Revolutionary Wars, 1792-1802', *History*, 78 (1993), 393-420.

seminated by the radicals.[9] It was reinforced by a vast number of sermons delivered, and often printed, by the clergy of all religious denominations. Apart from a few Rational Dissenters, most ministers of religion rallied to the defence of the existing constitution in church and state. A majority of British subjects were exposed to this loyalist propaganda and large numbers were persuaded, or possibly intimidated, into declaring their support for the British constitution and their loyalty to the existing regime. Hundreds of loyal addresses to the king testified to the widespread sense of loyalty pervading all levels of British society. Perhaps as many as two thousand loyalist associations were formed in late 1792 and early 1793.[10] Although there was some government encouragement to set up these societies, their rapid spread demonstrates that popular loyalism was not entirely a political reaction manufactured by the elite. While most of the more active loyalists were drawn from the propertied classes, the sheer number of loyal addresses, clubs and anti-radical crowd demonstrations show a considerable degree of support for the existing regime and hostility towards those who sought its overthrow. When it was faced with the threat of a French invasion, the government set about raising a part-time defence force, the Volunteers. Tens of thousands of ordinary British subjects rushed to enlist. Loyalists also raised subscriptions to pay for extra warm clothing for the troops wintering in Europe and they rushed to express their admiration for the admirals and ordinary seamen who saved the country from possible invasion.

III.

In the 1790s British parliamentary politics was also re-shaped as a result of the French Revolution and the outbreak of war. At first the government of William Pitt was content to be a mere observer of the astonishing events in France and it was only very reluctantly dragged into war.[11] Pitt was not an early convert to Burke's *Reflections*, but the French slide into terror and anarchy, and the outbreak of war in Europe helped to

---

9 H.T. Dickinson, 'Popular Conservatism and Militant Loyalism 1789-1815' in *Britain and the French Revolution 1789-1815*, ed. H.T. Dickinson, pp. 103-25; and H.T. Dickinson, 'Popular Loyalism in Britain in the 1790s', in *The Transformation of Political Culture: England and Germany in the Late Eighteenth Century*, ed. Eckhart Hellmuth (Oxford, 1990), pp. 503-33.

10 Robert R. Dozier, *For King, Constitution and Country: The English Loyalists and the French Revolution* (Lexington, KY, 1983).

11 Jennifer Mori, *William Pitt and the French Revolution 1785-1795* (Edinburgh, 1997).

change his mind about adopting a policy of strict neutrality. Events in France and the alarming spread of radical societies in Britain persuaded Pitt to encourage the king to issue two royal proclamations, in May and December 1792, that requested magistrates to suppress the spread of radical propaganda. This action was followed in December 1792 with clandestine support for John Reeves's efforts to establish a nationwide loyalist association to counter the activities of British radicals. War finally convinced Pitt that even sterner measures must be taken with both French revolutionaries and British radicals. Pitt, unlike Burke, did not see the war as an ideological crusade, but as a defensive war against French aggression in the Low Countries, but he did recognize that he needed to meet the French military threat abroad and the British radical threat at home. Pitt, and to a greater degree Henry Dundas, his closest cabinet colleague, sought to fight the war as a territorial campaign with gains to be made in overseas trade and colonies. The king and the foreign secretary, Lord Grenville, were more influenced by Burke and saw the war as a crusade against French revolutionary principles.[12] At home Pitt did see the radicals as an ideological threat that must be crushed. He abandoned his earlier liberal stance and brought before parliament a series of repressive measures sometimes referred to as 'Pitt's reign of terror'.[13] Habeas corpus was twice suspended for lengthy periods so that leading radicals could be imprisoned without trial. The radical press was harassed and all but closed down completely. Leading radicals were charged with treason or seditious libel. Though some were acquitted, others were sentenced, transported or exiled. Radical meetings were declared illegal, radical societies were forcibly closed and combinations of workers were outlawed. While these repressive policies were not on the scale of the French terror, Pitt's staunch defence of the existing constitution in church and state, and his willingness to infringe the subject's civil liberties, led him to be condemned as a 'Tory'. Although he always regarded himself as an 'independent Whig', his political disciples gradually accommodated themselves in the early nineteenth century to a party label originally foisted upon them by their political opponents.

---

12 On different British reactions to the war against Revolutionary France, see Emma Vincent Macleod, *A War of Ideas: British Attitudes to the Wars against Revolutionary France, 1792-1802* (Aldershot, 1998).

13 Clive Emsley, 'An Aspect of Pitt's "Terror": prosecutions for sedition during the 1790s', Social History, 6 (1981), 155-84; and Clive Emsley, 'Repression, ''terror' and the rule of law in England during the decade of the French Revolution', *English Historical Review*, 100 (1985), 801-25.

The French Revolution and the French wars not only turned Pitt into a 'Tory'. They also did much to destroy the political fortunes and the political credibility of his leading opponents in parliament. The disintegration of the opposition to Pitt that was led by Charles James Fox was not entirely due to events abroad, since this political group had lost popularity during the regency crisis of 1788-89 and had long forfeited the support of the king. But the problems facing this Whig opposition were undoubtedly exacerbated by Fox's response to the French Revolution and the French wars.[14] Fox's understanding of what was happening in France was shaped very much by his understanding of the British political system and by his hostility to George III, whom he saw as a threat to the constitution. Fox and his closest allies mistakenly believed that the French were seeking to establish a constitutional monarchy on the British model and that they were advancing similar principles to those Whig principles that underlay so much of Britain's Glorious Revolution of 1688-89. Even when the French revolutionaries turned to violence, and France witnessed anarchy and terror, the Foxites blamed this on the intervention of Austria and Prussia, aided and abetted by the reactionary government of Pitt, into the internal political affairs of France. The war against France, even when France seemed most obviously the aggressor against smaller, neighbouring countries, was blamed more on Pitt than on the revolutionaries in France. The war was repeatedly condemned as both unjust and unnecessary.[15] Fox seems to have genuinely believed that a satisfactory peace could have been achieved at almost any time if only Pitt would refrain from seeking to intervene in the internal affairs of France. This astonishing misjudgement of the real situation led to Fox and his dwindling band of supporters being regarded as at least the dupes of France and as near traitors to their own country.

These attitudes, maintained in the teeth of the evidence, ensured that the Whig opposition would fragment as the radical movement grew at home, terror spread in France, and the war widened inexorably. Edmund Burke was one of the first to desert and eventually to rally to Pitt. A trickle of other desertions between 1792 and 1793 led to a near flood in 1794, when the Duke of Portland, the nominal leader of the opposition, at last formally broke with Fox and his remaining allies and led a large

---

14 Frank O'Gorman, *The Whig Party and the French Revolution* (London, 1967); and L.G. Mitchell, *Charles James Fox and the Disintegration of the Whig Party 1782-1794* (Oxford, 1971).

15 Emma Vincent Macleod, *The War of Ideas*, pp. 90-113.

body of the opposition into an alliance with Pitt. Portland and others who had long opposed Pitt actually took office in a new coalition government. The parliamentary elite, alarmed by the threat to the political and social order posed by French principles and French arms, rallied behind Pitt and his policies at home and abroad. Increasingly, any young politician with serious ambitions to hold public office attached himself to Pitt and the party of government that he was now seen to lead. Although the war with France went badly – a disastrous situation that normally destroyed a government's majority in the eighteenth century – Pitt's majority in parliament actually increased and the Foxite opposition was reduced to 50-60 members in the House of Commons. For the Foxite Whigs the 1790s were years of protracted agony as familiar loyalties were shattered, longstanding friendships were ruptured, conventional assumptions were undermined, and political expectations were repeatedly thwarted. The Foxite Whigs lost a great deal of support among the propertied elite and yet were unable, as yet, to increase their support among the middling orders because of their ambivalent and lukewarm support for parliamentary reform. Although the Foxite Whigs continued to argue the case for peace with France and bravely opposed the repressive policies of Pitt's government, their efforts were condemned by the vast majority of the political elite as defeatist and unpatriotic and were rejected by the radicals as half-hearted and insincere. For decades the Foxites remained a minority party desperately seeking a role in a world dominated by the fear of French principles and French military power.

IV.

Many historians of late eighteenth-century Britain have been interested in the rapid expansion of popular radicalism in the early 1790s, in the even more rapid development of a conservative ideology and a popular loyalist movement, and in the rallying of the propertied elite against French principles and French arms. Most of this research has centred on events in England. As shown in the essays below, by Gordon Pentland and Atle Wold, the situation in Scotland, however, was very similar. There too the 1790s witnessed the rise of a radical movement with distinctive local features, but with many features in common with the radical movement in

England.[16] In Scotland, too, the descent of the French Revolution into anarchy and terror, and the outbreak of war, led to a loyalist backlash which encouraged most men of property to rally behind the government of the day. With regard to parliamentary politics Henry Dundas had even more success than Pitt in England in rallying the political elite behind the party of government and in casting the Foxite opposition into the political wilderness.[17] Almost the whole political elite in Scotland supported Pitt's policies at home and abroad. All these developments in Scotland in the 1790s offer support for Linda Colley's influential thesis that a succession of wars with Catholic France, culminating in the epic conflict with Revolutionary and Napoleonic France, did much to unite the English and the Scots as 'Britons'.[18]

If we turn to Ireland in the 1790s, however, the situation is very different. Linda Colley's thesis has never been able to embrace the Irish question, since the Catholic majority in Ireland did not fit comfortably into an essentially Protestant constitution and state and it was never as enthusiastic about fighting Catholic France. Developments in the 1790s helped Scotland to assimilate itself more closely with its more populous and powerful southern neighbour, England. On the other hand, this decade of revolution and war did much to prove how difficult it was to absorb the Catholic Irish into a state dominated by a political elite based in Westminster. Moreover, the impact of the French Revolution and the French wars on Ireland were markedly different from their influence on either England or Scotland.[19] The political polarization in Ireland was very different. There the radicals enlisted truly massive support for extensive reforms and there the propertied elite never rallied a clear loyal majority in defence of the *status quo*. Without the intervention of British forces, Ireland might have become an ally of France. Whereas in Britain, the government could contrast the political stability largely prevailing at home during the 1790s with the anarchy, violence and terror in France, it could not make the same claims about Ireland. In Ireland there was a large-scale rebellion against the existing political and social order, and the casualties that ensued were probably proportionately greater

---

16 See, for example, Henry W. Meikle, *Scotland and the French Revolution* (London, 1912); E.W. McFarland, *Ireland and Scotland in the Age of Revolution* (Edinburgh, 1994); and John Brims, 'The Scottish Democratic Movement in the Age of the French Revolution', unpublished PhD thesis (University of Edinburgh, 1983).

17 Michael Fry, *The Dundas Despotism* (Edinburgh, 1992).

18 Linda Colley, *Britons: Forging the Nation 1707-1837* (New Haven and London, 1992).

19 Hugh Gough and David Dickson, *Ireland and the French Revolution* (Dublin, 1990).

than the number who suffered in the far more populous France during the years of the Jacobin Terror.

In 1782, as a result of the American crisis, the Irish parliament in Dublin had achieved legislative independence that meant that it could no longer be so easily controlled by either the British government or the Westminster parliament. This had done little to solve the longstanding 'Irish problem'. The British government still controlled appointments to the Irish executive, however, and the vast majority of the population had no influence on the composition of the Irish parliament. Moreover, the granting of legislative independence had merely served to entrench the political influence of the Protestant Ascendancy in Ireland, a small minority of rich landowners of largely English ancestry and Protestant Episcopalian religion. They owned most of the land of Ireland, dominated the Irish parliament and filled most of the posts in the Irish administration. Nothing had been done to conciliate the Catholics beyond a few relief acts that allowed them to worship freely, to inherit some land and to hold minor posts in the law. Tensions between the impoverished, largely Catholic masses, who were excluded from the franchise, from parliament and from public office in the state, and the Protestant Episcopalian ruling elite and the Protestant Dissenters (who sought to dominate Ulster) led to a bitterly-torn sectarian society. These essential features of the 'Irish problem' existed before 1789, but there can be no doubt that the French Revolution made a difficult situation very much worse.

The outbreak of revolution in Catholic and absolutist France had a profound effect on the minority of reformers and on the Catholic majority in Ireland. The reformers were enormously stimulated by the news of events in France and were soon seeking to spread French principles. The Catholics were encouraged by evidence that liberty could be achieved in a Catholic country and stimulated by proof that there was no necessary connection between Catholicism and absolutism. The early 1790s saw the rise, at first in Belfast and then in Dublin and other towns, of radical reformers who set up societies of United Irishmen with the aim of extending political liberty to Irishmen of all denominations.[20] At first the United Irishmen adopted a parliamentary reform programme very much on the lines of the reform movements in England and Scotland. They also used similar tactics to achieve their ends and reached out to similar

20 *The United Irishmen: Republicanism, Radicalism and Rebellion*, ed. David Dickson, Daire Keogh and Kevin Whelan (Dublin, 1993); and Nancy J. Curtin, *The United Irishmen: Popular Politics in Ulster and Dublin 1791-1798* (Oxford, 1994).

social groups in the larger urban centres. Their most radical objective was to extend the franchise to Catholics, a policy that the British government favoured – so long as the franchise was possessed by men of property only – as it strove to ensure that the Catholic majority in Ireland would not look to France for support. Pitt's government ensured that the Protestant Ascendancy in Ireland passed this reform measure through the Irish parliament. Although forced to concede this measure, the Protestant Ascendancy, aided by many of the Protestant Dissenters of Ulster, reacted against all other attempts to grant further concessions to the Catholics. The outbreak of war with France and the need to rally the propertied elite against the French threat, persuaded Pitt that further reforms of a political nature were now off the agenda. Pitt, under pressure from the Protestant Ascendancy, recalled the liberal viceroy, Earl Fitzwilliam, from Dublin and endorsed a policy of suppressing the United Irishmen. The Protestants in Ulster formed the Orange Order in order to safeguard their position against their Catholic neighbours. Sectarian violence became widespread, especially though not exclusively in Ulster.

The United Irishmen faced the prospect of political extinction, like the radicals in England and Scotland. The constitutional moderates left the movement, but the more militant members decided to re-constitute themselves as a revolutionary underground movement ready to achieve their aims by force of arms. This objective drove them to seek military assistance from France and this strategy, in turn, persuaded them to plan for a democratic republic along French lines. To expand their base of support in Ireland, the United Irishmen, although still including many Protestants in their ranks, sought out support among the oppressed and resentful Catholic majority. For some years those Catholics engaged in sectarian clashes with their Protestant neighbours had looked to a shadowy force, the Defenders, to protect them. The United Irishmen forged a loose alliance with the Defenders and together they enlisted a huge number of recruits interested in the cause of reform and ready to welcome a French invasion. A French invasion attempt narrowly failed to land a significant force in the south-west of Ireland in December 1796 due to severe weather conditions. The United Irishmen had been unprepared to welcome them with an effective force and this failure convinced the French not to intervene again until a rebellion had first broken out in Ireland.[21] The United Irishmen prepared for rebellion, but their organization was soon infiltrated by informers. This

---

21 Marianne Elliott, *Partners in Revolution: The United Irishmen and France* (New Haven and London, 1982).

led to the arrest many of their leaders early in 1798. This did not prevent the army continuing to disarm all Catholics by draconian policies and it only served to encourage the Orange Order to indulge in more sectarian attacks on their Catholic neighbours. Provoked beyond endurance, United Irishmen, Defenders and ordinary Catholics still turned to rebellion. When rebellion did break out in Ireland in May-June 1798, it was only partly a political rebellion. Never in full control of the rebellion, the United Irishmen did however try to give the rebels a political lead. Faced with superior forces, rushed over from Britain, and receiving only very limited French assistance, too late and in the wrong place, the rebellion was crushed with horrific loss of life.[22]

Thoroughly alarmed by this crisis the British government exerted all its powers of persuasion, patronage and influence to convince the Protestant Ascendancy to give up its legislative independence, to abandon the separate Irish parliament in Dublin, and to accept a fully incorporating union with the Westminster parliament.[23] The Act of Union of 1800 created the United Kingdom of Great Britain and Ireland, which came into existence on 1 January 1801, the first day of the nineteenth century. The act significantly increased the size and altered the composition of the united parliament, but it failed to solve the Irish problem. Pitt had hoped, and had virtually promised the Catholics, that union would allow the new parliament to make greater concessions to the Catholic majority in Ireland. This strategy could be risked because the members of the Protestant Ascendancy, who had dominated the Dublin parliament, were now a clear minority in the Westminster parliament. At the same time, the Catholic majority in the Irish population posed less of a threat to an essentially Protestant constitution now that they formed a minority of the population of the whole United Kingdom. Unfortunately, the king himself, his resolve stiffened by many leading politicians, refused to concede Catholic emancipation which would allow Catholics to sit in the Westminster parliament and to hold public office in the new state. The king regarded such a concession as a betrayal of his coronation oath that had required him to swear to defend the Protestant constitution. This decision left the Catholics deprived of the full rights of citizenship and in a markedly inferior so-

---

22 The best narrative accounts of the rebellion are in Daniel Gahan, *The People's Rising: Wexford 1798* (Dublin, 1995); and A.T.Q. Stewart, *The Summer Soldiers: The 1798 Rebellion in Antrim and Down* (Belfast, 1995).

23 G.C. Bolton, *The Passing of the Irish Act of Union* (Oxford, 1966); and Patrick M. Geoghegan, *The Irish act of Union* (Dublin, 1999).

cial and economic position compared to the vast majority of Protestant Irishmen. The Union got off to a bad start, and Pitt himself felt obliged to resign in 1801.

V.

It is long ago that a study of the impact of political events and ideas on literature would have been called 'extrinsic' to the study of literature. And yet, long after René Wellek established his seminal distinction between 'intrinsic' and 'extrinsic' subjects for literary studies,[24] the relationship between the French Revolution and British literature remained a rather neglected field. This has become different in the last few decades, but above all in the wake of the bicentenary of the French Revolution in 1989. Various academic conferences took place in Britain to mark this bicentenary, and a number of monographs and collections of essays duly appeared in print.[25] However, there were far more substantial reasons for this change. There has lately been a considerable opening up of literary history into the history of culture, and this led to a historicist reinterpretation and revaluation of English literature in the 1790s and in Romanticism. At the same time, there has been an increasing interest by historians in the history of culture. As a result, the common ground between historians and literary critics has become larger.

One of the consequences of this recent trend is that the perspectives on the literature of the period have changed. It is now seen more clearly than before that the term 'literature' in the period had a much wider sense than nowadays and that, consequently, the literary landscape has to be seen as much broader than before. In the eighteenth century and even more decidedly in the 1790s the term 'literature' was seen as to include not only poetry, drama and fiction but also political, religious, economic and social writings, and indeed the numerous literary journals of the period reviewed texts and discussed topics from all these different fields. Moreover, literature was not regarded as a private affair but as part of the 'public sphere' (Habermas). In the wake of the Enlightenment and the French Revolution literature was considered 'to be the basis of an infor-

---

24 René Wellek and Austin Warren, *Theory of Literature* (New York, 1949).

25 Two of these collections which were based on academic conferences that marked the bicentenary are *Revolution in Writing: British Literary Responses to the French Revolution*, ed. Kelvin Everest (Milton Keynes, 1991) and *Representing the French Revolution: Literature, Historiography and Art*, ed. James A.W. Heffernan (Hanover, 1992).

mation revolution with far-reaching political consequences'.[26] Some regarded literature as a medium for further enlightenment and as an engine of social and intellectual progress, whereas more conservative authors, particularly when the political climate in Britain changed towards the end of the 1790s, saw literature also as something potentially subversive or dangerous. There was an ongoing and heated discussion of the nature and function of literature, which took place in texts such as the preface to the *Lyrical Ballads* or *The Pursuits of Literature* (1797) by T.J. Mathias but above all in the literary journals of the period, whose number increased considerably towards the end of the eighteenth and at the beginning of the nineteenth century.[27] There has lately been an increase of research on the periodicals of this time, and in this volume the essay by Anton Kirchhofer is devoted to one of the leading journals.

Another recent trend of the research by literary historians is a growing interest in writers outside the traditional canon of 'great writers'. As a consequence of this, much more attention has been paid to the publications of the female writers of the period.[28] An ever-increasing number of women published fiction, poetry, travel literature and essays in the 1790s, and they even wrote texts in genres such as history writing that had traditionally been regarded as reserved for men. Some women among the radicals such as Catherine Macaulay, Mary Wollstonecraft and Mary Hays propagated the equality of women, though in general the British and French radicals did not favour this demand, while others such as Hannah More defended the traditional role of woman. This discussion was another part of the political discourse of the period that had a strong influence on literature.

VI.

Part of the impact of the French Revolution on Britain was that literature – in the widest sense of the word – was politicized to a degree that had been rare in the earlier eighteenth century. This means that even if writers told the story of love affairs, intrigues or travels of individuals they tended to refer these stories to the political structure of the state, to society as a whole with its class structure, to the legal system or to the position of

---

26 Paul Keen, *The Crisis of Literature in the 1790s: Print Culture and the Public Sphere* (Cambridge, 1999), p. 236.

27 See Keen, *The Crisis of Literature*, pp. 121f.

28 See Gary Kelly's *Women, Writing and Revolution, 1790-1827* (Oxford, 1993) as well as Eleanor Ty's *Unsex'd Revolutionaries: Five Women Novelists of the 1790s* (Toronto etc., 1993) and many others.

women in society. Thus their texts very often became a critique of 'things as they are' (this is the characteristic subtitle of William Godwin's novel *Caleb Williams*, 1794) and, at the same time, a vision of things as they should be. Of course, earlier texts from the eighteenth century also had such a critical intention. But if one compares, let us say, Daniel Defoe's *Moll Flanders* with a novel from the 1790s such as Godwin's *Caleb Williams* one can easily see how much more political and how much more strongly critical a considerable part of British literature in the 1790s had become and how much more the demand for a change of the status quo became evident in these works.

'Political', however, does not necessarily mean 'in favour of the ideas behind the French Revolution'. Those who opposed the Revolution had an influential spokesman in Edmund Burke, and Burke found an increasing number of supporters. In this way, not only politicization but also polarization became characteristic of the 1790s in Britain. This polarization became particularly evident in the controversy caused by Burke's *Reflections on the Revolution in France* (1790). Many writers took part in this controversy, and Mary Wollstonecraft wrote her treatise *Vindication of the Rights of Man* (1790) explicitly as a critique of Burke's *Reflections*, while in other texts of the period the references to Burke – or Thomas Paine – were more implicit. Nevertheless it would be wrong to draw a clear-cut division between radicals and conservative writers, between 'left' and 'right', in this period. As Eckart Hellmuth in his article in the present volume has shown, the dividing line between the two camps often became blurred.

In any case, the French Revolution had a deep impact on all textual genres in Britain. To begin with drama, the action of a play could be located far away in the past and yet be intended to refer to contemporary political events and ideas. This was for instance the case in William Wordsworth's *The Borderers* (1795/6), in Robert Southey's *Wat Tyler* (1794), a drama of an attempted revolution of the lower classes in the Middle Ages that resembled the French Revolution so much that the play could not be published for a long time.[29] It goes without saying that a mythological play like Shelley's closet drama *Prometheus Unbound* (1820) cannot be understood if the French Revolution is not seen as the subtext of the conflict between Prometheus and Jupiter. The same applies to his

---

29 It was published only in 1817, and not by the author, who had become ultraconservative in the mean time, but by his opponents who wanted to damage his reputation.

historical tragedy *The Cenci*.[30] Because of these political implications there has recently been a growing interest in English drama from the 1790s to the end of Romanticism.[31] In this volume, the essay by Katharina Rennhak is devoted to a political reading of Shelley's two plays.

There was a similar politicization in the fiction of the 1790s.[32] A novel such as Robert Bage's *Hermsprong* (1796) – by the way one of the many texts outside the traditional canon that has become of interest to literary historians in recent times – tells the traditional love story in which the union of the lovers is for a long time prevented by the tyrannical father of the girl, but in which this traditional story is characteristically used to criticize the present class system, power structure and legal system. In a similar way, the structure of the gothic novel is at the same time used and politicized in Godwin's *Caleb Williams*. Godwin tells the story of a servant who is persecuted by his master, and he is bent on showing that this persecution is only made possible by a class structure and by a legal system that is made to serve the ruling class. Moreover, it seems to me characteristic of the 1790s that so many novels do not have a happy ending. This applies not only to both the endings Godwin wrote for *Caleb Williams* and to his novel *St. Leon* (1799), but also to other novels of the period such as Mary Wollstonecraft's *Mary, A Fiction* (1788) and *The Wrongs of Woman: or, Maria* (1798) as well as Mary Hays's *Memoirs of Emma Courtney* (1796). The British eighteenth-century novel in most cases ended happily, Richardson's *Clarissa* being one of the few exceptions. When novelists of the 1790s broke this convention they tried to show that 'things as they are' have gone wrong to such an extent that a happy ending would give a lie to their critical analyses of contemporary society.

Lyrical poetry, which is traditionally at a greater distance from politics, was politicized in this period, too. There was a spate of minor poems that were directly concerned with the French Revolution and the debate about

---

30 See e.g. Michael Rossington, 'Shelley, *The Cenci* and the French Revolution', in *Revolution in Writing*, ed. K. Everest , pp. 138-57.

31 See e.g. Gillian Russell, *The Theatres of War: Performance, Politics, and Society* (Oxford, 1995) as well as *British Romantic Drama: Historical and Critical Essays*, ed. Terence Allan Hoagwood and Daniel P. Watkins (Madison and London, 1998); George Taylor, *The French Revolution and the London Stage*, 1789-1805 (Cambridge, 2000).

32 See e.g. Gary Kelly, *The English Jacobin Novel 1780-1805* (Oxford, 1976) and Matthew O. Grenby, *The Anti-Jacobin Novel: British Conservatism and the French Revolution* (Cambridge, 2001) and 'Politicized Fiction in Britain 1790-1810: An Annotated Checklist', in *The European English Messenger*, 9 (2000), 47-53.

it, such as Helen Maria Williams's highly sentimental 'The Bastille. A Vision' (1790), but also poems by 'canonical authors' were strongly influenced by the debate on the French Revolution. William Wordsworth's *Descriptive Sketches* (1793/1836) and his 'long poem' *The Prelude*, which was never published in his lifetime and the extant manuscript versions of which were written in later years though Wordsworth began to write it much earlier, may serve as examples.

It goes without saying that other textual genres were politicized as well – even the sermon and the travelogue. Thus, the dissenting minister Richard Price delivered a sermon in 1789 which was entitled 'A Discourse on the Love of our Country' and in which he praised the Revolution in France – a sermon which was harshly criticized by loyalists such as Edmund Burke. Travelogues in the eighteenth century had been characterized either by the attempt at a scientific description of a country or by a rendering of highly subjective experiences in the manner of Sterne's fictional *Sentimental Journey*. When British writers travelled to France after 1789, however, they tended to leave out all those experiences which had nothing to do with the political events and the political and social structure of the country in which they travelled and thus politicized their travelogues.[33]

Indeed, most of the leading authors published texts in many different textual genres – theoretical treatises and fiction, poetry and travelogues, dramas and sermons, essays and reviews – and all these texts form part of the political discourse of the period. This, however, does not mean that the ideological or political stance is the same in all genres. Thus, treatises like Godwin's *Political Justice* or Wollstonecraft's *Vindication of the Rights of Woman* (1792) tend to place their hope of political progress exclusively in their belief in reason and in the final victory of reason, at the same time devaluing passion, whereas their novels are far more aware of the enormous power of the passions and are accordingly far less optimistic.[34] In this volume, the essay by Ben Pauley will discuss the fact that Godwin's novel *Caleb Williams* is more pessimistic than his earlier utterances.

---

33 See the last chapter in Katherine Turner, *British Travel Writers in Europe 1750-1800: Authorship, Gender and National Identity* (Aldershot etc., 2001) and Ulrich Broich, 'Revolutionstouristen? Britische Literaten besichtigen die Französische Revolution', forthcoming.

34 See Ulrich Broich, 'British Radical Thought and the Radical Novel of the 1790s', in *English Studies Today*, 1 (2002), 16-60.

Toward the end of the century, however, some authors turned their backs on overtly political subjects and preferred to write about nature or their own individuality. But even such seemingly non-political texts are reactions to the political developments of the period and may be subjected to a political interpretation.

VII.

Some time ago, in British literary history the eighteenth century and Romanticism were seen as two clearly distinguished literary periods, with Wordsworth's and Coleridge's *Lyrical Ballads* marking the watershed. According to the influential book by Meyer Howard Abrams, *The Mirror and the Lamp* (1953), the literature of the earlier period could be characterized by the symbol of the mirror, meaning imitation, whereas the literature of Romanticism was based on an entirely different concept, that of expression, which he symbolized by the lamp. In recent times, the historians were first in problematizing the binary opposition between Enlightenment and Romanticism and in emphasizing the continuity between the eighteenth century and the beginning of the next one. 'The long eighteenth century' – lasting from the Glorious Revolution in 1688 to the first Reform Bill in 1832 – became a frequently used concept in new books on British history.[35] Also in British literary history it is rewarding to see not only the differences between the literature of Romanticism and that of the previous century but also the continuities. In this case, the 1790s and their aftermath – see the title of this volume – would form a bridge crossing the gap between the two centuries and thus could be regarded as a *Sattelzeit* between earlier periods and modernity.

Indeed, there is a continuing presence of the political ideas of the Enlightenment and the French Revolution in English literature after 1800, in particular a continuing presence of the ideas of Rousseau and Burke. This is true even of the first generation of the romantic poets – Wordsworth, Coleridge and Southey – who, after a period of enthusiastic belief in the ideas of the French Revolution, became conservative towards the turn of the century. And yet, when Wordsworth praised the imagination of the child as superior to that of the man and called 'the child the father of the man', he was evidently influenced by Rousseau. Even stronger was the impact of Burke's praise of custom and tradition on Wordsworth, which induced him to add a praise of Burke to a later version of his *Prel-*

[35] See e.g. Frank O'Gorman, *The Long Eighteenth Century* (London, 1997).

ude. In fiction, we find a similar Burkean approach to the past in Scott's historical novels. Wordsworth's praise of liberty and his criticism of slavery and of Napoleon in his later 'Poems dedicated to liberty and independence', however, betray the continuing impact of ideas of the French Revolution although in a conservative context.

The second generation of the English romantic writers – Byron, Shelley, Keats, Leigh Hunt and Hazlitt – even remained radicals in a period of a conservative backlash. They wrote political texts which criticized the present political order in Britain and propagated a belief in liberty as the French Revolution had defined it. When they attacked Napoleon they did so not from a British patriotic point of view but because he had betrayed the ideals of the French Revolution (though, paradoxically, some of them admired Napoleon at the same time).

This certainly does not mean that there was nothing new in the romantic conception of literature and that there were no new themes, forms and ideas in this literature. There is no space here even to attempt an overview of these innovations. Instead, three – out of many – new concepts shall be mentioned. On the one hand, the concept of nature changed from the eighteenth century to the Romantic period. Nature became much more important, perhaps owing to the progress of industrialization. It was no longer general but individual nature, no longer civilized but wild nature which became the main subject of writers, and some romantics even came close to a pantheistic view in which nature was part of the divine being. On the other hand, myth became much more central to romantic thought, whereas the eighteenth century with its belief in reason had been skeptical of myth. Thus, Prometheus became a leading figure in romantic thought and literature. Finally, there was a new view of heroes. As Carlyle correctly said: 'The Eighteenth was a *Sceptical* Century; . . . not an age of Faith, an age of Heroes'.[36] This changed at the turn of the century. It was perhaps owing to the great changes and the threat of even greater changes that the general public but also writers came to regard great men or heroes as an antidote against chaos and disorder. Thus, the general public in Britain idolized Lord Nelson, and some of the leading writers felt a fascination for Napoleon though he was the national enemy and though he was believed to have betrayed the French Revolution. In this volume, the essay by Marianne Czisnik discusses the cult of Lord Nelson.

---

36 Thomas Carlyle, *On Heroes and Hero Worship*, in: Carlyle, *Sartor Resartus, On Heroes and Hero Worship* (London, 1908), p. 298.

VIII.

The 1790s and their aftermath were characterized by a tremendous conflict of ideas and nations and frequent and radical changes of the political situation. It is therefore not surprising that many leading writers of the period were hardly able to maintain a consistent and permanent political stance. Many of their writings are full of faultlines and contradictions, and, moreover, many of the writers changed their political positions, often more than once. For the understanding of a particular text it is accordingly often important to know if it was written in the heyday of the Revolution, in the period after the execution of the French king and queen and during the reign of terror or during the rise of Napoleon.

The leading conservative writer of the period, Edmund Burke, had been a 'liberal' before 1789, and had supported the grievances of the American colonists that led to the Declaration of Independence. After 1789, however, he soon became uncompromisingly opposed to the Revolution and the ideas behind it. Other writers who had held radical ideas before 1789, however, became admirers of the Revolution and used their writings to support its ideas. But even William Godwin and Mary Wollstonecraft were not able to maintain this position without revisions. Godwin toned down the radical position of *Political Justice* in later editions, and though he never gave up his belief in liberty, equality and fraternity he voiced his belief with much more reserve in later publications and made them less openly political. For Mary Wollstonecraft the period of the *terreur*, which she witnessed when living in Paris, was a deeply shocking experience, and in her writings during this time the contradictory feelings of belief in progress and pessimism often stand side by side. Towards the end of her life she did not abandon her belief in the ideals of the Revolution but 'was able to admit – as she had been unable to do two years earlier – that violent upheavals, such as had taken place in France, were never to be desired'.[37]

Wordsworth, Coleridge and Southey were deeply shaken by the degeneration of the Revolution but strangely it was not before the end of the century that they definitely turned their backs on it. It is still a more or less open question when and why this change took place. Some attribute it to the general change of the political climate in Britain and to the

---

37 Harriet Devine Jump, '"The Cool Eye of Observation": Mary Wollstonecraft and the French Revolution', in *Revolution in Writing*, ed. K. Everest, pp. 101-20, this quote p. 117.

increasing attacks on radical writers, others to the progress of Napoleon and the growing threat of Napoleon to Britain's independence. In any case, even after their change from the radical to the loyalist camp, these authors did not maintain an unchanged position. This can be seen for instance in Wordsworth's later revisions to his earlier works, which were made apparently not only from aesthetic but also from political reasons. In this volume, the essay by Kai Merten discusses the implications of the later revisions in Wordsworth's *Descriptive Sketches.*

The writers of the second generation were radicals at a time when Wordsworth, Coleridge and Southey had become conservative, and they remained so throughout their lives. Living at a greater temporal distance from the French Revolution they reacted more strongly to later events such as the rise of Napoleon or the increasing suppression of radical ideas in Britain. Their political stance was also characterized, however, by inconsistencies and contradictions. Thus, Byron wrote his highly critical 'Ode to Napoleon Buonaparte', in which he called the Emperor 'All Evil Spirit'[38], in 1814 but was overjoyed when shortly afterwards Napoleon escaped from Elba.[39]

These were highly political times, times in which great changes were taking place. No wonder then that the writers were highly political, too, that they were well informed about recent political events and – different from Goethe – that they were not willing to keep their political commitment out of their literary texts. It was therefore high time that the literature of the period was more strongly linked to its historical and political contexts. The articles on literature in the present volume are part of this ongoing effort.

---

[38] Stanza ix.

[39] Ulrich Broich, 'Prometheus oder Satan? Zur Mythisierung von Napoleon im Deutschland und England des frühen 19. Jahrhunderts', in *Komparatistik als Arbeit am Mythos*, ed. Monika Schmitz-Emans and Uwe Lindemann (Heidelberg, 2004).

H.T. Dickinson

The Irish Rebellion of 1798

History and Memory

Introduction

The Irish rebellion of 1798 was one of the most dramatic, alarming and tragic events in the British Isles during the whole eighteenth century. It produced the fiercest fighting by the largest forces contesting for power on British soil throughout the century. It led to the last foreign invasion of, and the last battles in, the British Isles. It resulted in many thousands of casualties (killed, wounded and punished), over £1 million of damage to private property, and a most alarming breakdown of law and order and social relations. It led to a significant Irish diaspora – to the USA, Australia and Europe – and to an Act of Union that ended the existence of the separate Irish parliament. These attempted solutions to the Irish question however simply created pockets of Irish resentment against Britain across the world and utterly failed to solve the sectarian and social tensions within Ireland, because nothing was done to grant Catholics full political rights or to solve the land question.

There are therefore many good reasons for taking an interest in the events of 1798. Not surprisingly, the recent 200th anniversary of the Irish rebellion inspired a positive flood of scholarly and popular studies of Irish radicalism in the 1790s in general and the nature of the great rebellion of 1798 in particular. This wealth of material has not however solved all the controversies surrounding the rebellion. It is still possible to dispute when the rebellion started and when it ended, and even where it took place. It is also far from certain how many people were slain or how much property was damaged in the rebellion.[1] Finally, there is still considerable controversy over whether the events of 1798 were a failed rebellion or a potential revolution, and whether the causes were primarily agrarian, sectarian or political.

---

[1] Thomas Bartlett, 'Why the history of the 1798 rebellion has yet to be written', *Eighteenth-Century Ireland*, 15 (2000), 181-90. Casualties in the rebellion are frequently given as up to 30,000, but Bartlett puts the number killed at 10,000 (though there were other casualties) in 'Clemency and compensation: the treatment of defeated rebels and suffering loyalists after the 1798 rebellion', in *Revolution, Counter-Revolution and Union*, ed. Jim Smyth (Cambridge, 2000), p. 100 and note 6.

This essay does not seek to present another history of the rebellion. What it offers is an exploration of various interpretations of the rebellion, both those current today and those offered over the last two centuries. It will explore whether the rebellion can best be described as an agrarian revolt by oppressed peasantry, as a sectarian conflict between Protestant loyalists and Catholic rebels, or as a largely political revolution planned and conducted by the democratic and non-sectarian United Irishmen. It will then outline how interpretations of the Irish rebellion have changed over the two centuries since 1798, largely in order to serve the political purposes of those who wrote on this controversial subject. It will demonstrate that the rebellion has never retreated into being an historical event that can be examined in an impartial and dispassionate manner. It has long been and still remains a live political issue. There have been widely differing interpretations offered of the Irish rebellion, from 1798 to the present day, and all of these have been influenced by, and have had an influence on, the political climate of their day.

I. The Nature of the Irish Rebellion

A profound and massive event such as the Irish rebellion of 1798 undoubtedly has many causes and, not surprisingly, historians are divided in their attempts to rank these causes according to their importance. Some scholars – starting with James Anthony Froude and William Lecky in the nineteenth century – have stressed the deep structural fissures in Irish society that stretched back for many decades.[2] They have concluded that the deep divisions and severe tensions in Irish society, as well as the failings of the governing elite in Ireland and in Britain, made a rebellion very likely, if not inevitable. Other scholars, such as J.C. Beckett and R.B. McDowell believe that there were important developments in eighteenth-century Ireland – demographic change, economic progress, cultural improvements, enlightened religious attitudes, and political reforms – that might have healed the deep divisions in Irish society had not the French Revolution re-opened these wounds and poisoned the whole political, religious and social climate in Ireland.[3] Perhaps the most convincing interpretation of

---

2 James Anthony Froude, *The English in Ireland in the Eighteenth Century* (3 vols., 1872-74; new impression, London, 1906) and William Edward Hartpole Lecky, *A History of Ireland in the Eighteenth Century* (5 vols., new ed., New York, 1898).

3 J. C. Beckett, *The Anglo-Irish Tradition* (London, 1976), pp. 82-3, and R. B. McDowell, *Ireland in the Age of Imperialism and Revolution* (Oxford, 1979).

the causes of the rebellion, however, is that offered by those scholars who argue that the developments just referred to did no more than paper over the deep fissures in Irish society while the dramatic events in France in the 1790s did much to tear away this thin facade.[4]

Historians have differed sharply not only over the causes of the Irish rebellion, but in their interpretation of what kind of insurrection it was. Three fundamentally different interpretations have been presented. It has been argued that the rebellion was essentially a spontaneous agrarian revolt by an oppressed and impoverished Catholic peasantry; that it was a sectarian war between the dominant Protestant minority and the oppressed Catholic majority; and that it was essentially a political revolution planned and largely led and fought by United Irishmen who were primarily interested in radical reform and political independence. Evidence can be provided for and against each of these interpretations.

1. A Peasants' Revolt?

One of the most substantial modern studies of the Irish rebellion – Thomas Pakenham's *The Year of Liberty* (first published in 1969 and often reissued since) – lays considerable stress on the agrarian aspects of the Irish rebellion. Pakenham describes the rebellion as 'the old agrarian war under a new name' and 'a noisy jacquerie of the local peasantry'. He refers to the rebels 'as a half disciplined mob with little idea beyond plunder' and 'the primitive force of the countryside'. He claims that 'the disaffected had no serious political aims' and were 'aimless and leaderless men'.[5] Before this, R. B. McDowell has claimed that 'the great bulk of the people were restricted by poverty and persecution to political speculations of the simplest kind'.[6] Later he insisted that the Defenders, who were so active in the rebellion, were 'rural rioters' whose 'aims were agrarian' and he has described the rebellion in county Wexford as 'a rural riot on an enormous scale'.[7] The bi-centenary of the rebellion in 1998, however, produced a veritable flood of studies of the events of 1798 and nearly all of these reject this emphasis on the agrarian aspects of the Irish rebellion. While undoubtedly impressive, this body of work should not lead us to conclude that there were no agrarian aspects to the rebellion.

---

4 *Revolution, Counter-Revolution and Union*, ed. Smyth, pp. 1-9.

5 Thomas Pakenham, *The Year of Liberty: The Great Irish Rebellion of 1798* (London, 1969), pp. 66, 87, 101, 130, 150.

6 R. B. McDowell, *Irish Public Opinion 1750-1800* (London, 1944), p. 4.

7 R. B. McDowell, *Ireland in the Age of Imperialism and Revolution*, pp. 462, 473.

There are obvious reasons why some historians have advanced an agrarian interpretation of the Irish rebellion. Ireland was a largely rural country with a mainly agrarian economy. A large proportion of the Catholic poor lived near the margin of subsistence and it did not take much to plunge them into destitution. A sudden collapse in grain prices in 1797 devastated Wexford farming and provided the suddenly depressed economic circumstances that may have persuaded those hardest hit to resort to revolutionary violence.[8] Later eighteenth-century Ireland certainly had a history of persistent rural disorder and agrarian revolt. Protestant landlords were often resented because of their religion, the fact that they often owed their land to conquest and confiscation, and they were sometimes non-resident, and abused or neglected their duties as civil magistrates.[9] A succession of Catholic rural protest movements – from the Whiteboys of the 1760s through to the Defenders of the 1790s – used violent methods to oppose enclosures, high rents, tithes and local taxes. Economic grievances continued to inspire Defender agitation throughout the 1790s and Defender propaganda encouraged the dispossessed Catholics to hope that they might yet recover their lost status and their confiscated lands. There was a strong millenarian streak in Defender ideology that raised Catholic expectations that the world might be turned upside down once more and the dispossessed Catholics might yet recover their lost rights and their lost lands.[10] The desire to protect traditional Catholic territory from Protestant incursions led to violent clashes between the Defenders and Protestant protest groups. A major conflict in Armagh in 1795-96 saw militant Protestants (led by the Peep O' Day Boys and encouraged by the Orange Order) drive out thousands of Catholic families who had relied upon the Catholic Defenders for protection.

---

8 Thomas Powell, 'An economic factor in the Wexford rebellion of 1798', *Studia Hibernica*, 16 (1976), 140-57.

9 Froude, *The English in Ireland*, iii, 5, 400, 523.

10 On the Defenders see Deirdre Lindsay, 'The Defenders: The other great movement of the late eighteenth century', in *1798: 200 Years of Resonance*, ed. Mary Cullen (Dublin, 1998), pp. 15-25; Marianne Elliott, *Partners in Revolution: The United Irishmen and France* (London, 1982), pp. 40-42; Marianne Elliott, 'The Defenders of Ulster', in *The United Irishmen: Republicanism, Radicalism and Rebellion*, ed. David Dickson, Daire Keogh and Kevin Whelan (Dublin, 1993), pp. 222-33; Jim Smyth, *The Men of No Property: Irish Radicals and Popular Politics in the late Eighteenth Century* (London, 1992), pp. 26, 112-15; L.M. Cullen, 'The Political Structures of the Defenders' in *Ireland and the French Revolution*, ed. Hugh Gough and David Dickson (Dublin, 1990), pp. 117-38; and Thomas Bartlett, 'Select documents XXXVIII: Defenders and Defenderism in 1795', *Irish Historical Studies*, 24 (1985), 373-94.

Given the fact that Ireland, and especially county Wexford, was largely rural, it was inevitable that many rebels would be peasants and agricultural workers. When the United Irishmen sought mass support in rural areas they did stress their political aims, but they also indicated that they had some sympathy for the economic grievances of the peasantry and the landless labourers. While it is true that many of the leading United Irishmen were socially conservative and were primarily interested in achieving political reforms, some of them were concerned with social and economic reforms. Thomas Russell, Henry Joy McCracken and James Coigly strongly identified with the plight of the poor and wanted a more equal distribution of material benefits. Some local leaders of the United Irishmen, especially when they forged an alliance with the Defenders, not only took an interest in abolishing tithes and lowering rents and taxes, but even held out the prospect of confiscating the great estates of the landed elite.[11] William Lecky believed that hostility to tithes became a major issue among the Catholic rebels in Wexford and that 'hopes of a lowering of rents, and, still more, of a great agrarian revolution, or confiscation of lands . . . were abroad.'[12] More recently, James Donnelly has concluded: 'If the rebellion had somehow succeeded, nothing, I think, was more certain than the dissolution of the great estates.'[13]

While there were agrarian aspects to the rebellion of 1798, no recent historian of the rising has endorsed Thomas Pakenham's view that it was *essentially* a peasants' revolt. There are strong grounds for rejecting his thesis that the Irish rebellion was primarily an agrarian revolt. As we shall see below, many of the leaders of the United Irishmen were not peasants and the rebellion was a planned rising not a spontaneous eruption. Moreover, the Catholic Defenders, who were also active in the rebellion, were not simply a peasant secret society interested solely in agrarian issues. Many of the Defenders were not farmers or agricultural workers, but publicans, shopkeepers, schoolteachers, blacksmiths, canal workers, and a wide range of textile workers. Their main centre in Armagh was experi-

---

11 Jim Smyth, *The Men of No Property*, pp. 112-20, 161-73; James Quinn, 'The United Irishmen and social reform', *Irish Historical Studies*, 31 (1998), 188-201; Ian McBride, 'The harp without the crown: nationalism and republicanism in the 1790s', in *Political Ideas in Eighteenth-Century Ireland*, ed. S.J. Connolly (Dublin, 2000), pp. 174-77; and James S. Donnelly, 'Propagating the cause of the United Irishmen', *Studies*, 69 (1980), 5-23.

12 Lecky, *Ireland in the Eighteenth Century*, iv, 123.

13 Donnelly, 'Propagating the cause of the United Irishmen', *Studies*, 69 (1980), 21 and note 28.

encing intense commercialization at this time. The Defenders were interested in protesting about enclosures, tithes and rents, and were also active in opposing a range of innovations and in defending customary rights. In 1792-3 they had campaigned for the franchise for Catholics and in 1793 they had been active in opposing the new Militia Act. While never entirely fused with their allies, the United Irishmen, they did adopt some of the latter's political aims. They bitterly opposed the draconian methods of the Irish government to disarm the Catholic population and they resented British interference in Irish affairs.

Finally, the location of the Irish rebellion suggests that it was not primarily an agrarian revolt. The rebellion occurred largely in the eastern counties of Ireland, the most economically advanced, outward-looking and anglophone areas, where there were many small towns and where most of Ireland's commerce and manufacture was based. There was very little rebel activity in the west and south, where the most predominantly agrarian and backward counties were located. Tipperary was perhaps the most class-ridden county in Ireland and it had witnessed more agrarian disturbances than any other county before the rebellion broke out, but it remained quiet in 1798. Wexford had experienced few agrarian outrages before 1798, but it put more rebels into the field than any other county in Ireland.[14]

2. A Sectarian Revolt?

There is stronger evidence for regarding the Irish rebellion as a sectarian conflict between Protestants and Catholics. Without denying the political ambitions of the United Irishmen, who desired and planned the rebellion, both Froude and Lecky believed that the rebellion in Wexford in particular was largely a Catholic rising. Froude claimed of the Wexford rebellion that 'Conceived originally by Jacobins, it had become a struggle of the Irish Catholics to get possession of the county'. He went on to maintain that 'the rebellion, like every other rising since the Reformation, assumed a Catholic aspect, and was regarded as a holy war.'[15] Lecky showed much greater sympathy with the Catholic rebels in Wexford, putting much of the blame for the rising on the harsh treatment which the Catholics received

---

14 David Dickson, 'The state of Ireland before 1798', in *The Great Irish Rebellion of 1798*, ed. Cathal Poirteir (Dublin, 1998), p. 16; and Kevin Whelan, 'Reinterpreting the 1798 rebellion in County Wexford', in *The Mighty Wave*, ed. Daire Keogh and Nicholas Furlong (Dublin, 1996), pp. 30, 33.

15 Froude, *The English in Ireland*, iii, 434, 521.

from the military seeking to disarm them. While he admitted the role of the United Irishmen in fomenting rebellion, Lecky concluded:

> ... what little fanaticism existed was almost entirely religious. There was no question of nationality or parliamentary reform. The feeling of the people was not primarily directed against England, or against monarchy, or against landlords. The natural spontaneous division was between Catholics and Protestants; and a disarming of the Protestants, the confiscation of their property, and their expulsion from power and from Ireland, were frequently threatened.[16]

In sharp contrast, most recent studies of the Irish rebellion have denied that it was essentially or mainly a religious war. While these studies have conceded that the catastrophe of 1798 was provoked to some extent by the oppressive policies of a sectarian state, in association with vindictive Orangemen and terrified Protestant loyalists, their authors have been reluctant to go any further than this and they have endeavoured to play down the sectarian nature of the rebellion. They have stressed that the rebels did not take up arms solely or even mainly in pursuit of religious objectives or to wreak sectarian revenge, but to support a revolutionary political campaign led by the United Irishmen. The role of Catholic priests in the rebellion – so much stressed by Froude and Lecky – has been much reduced in recent studies. It has been argued, for example, that, while eleven Catholic priests – most notably John Murphy, Philip Roche and Mogus Kearns – were involved in the rebellion in Wexford, none was an accredited parish priest and six of these priests had been suspended or were unemployed at the time.[17] James Caulfield, the Catholic Bishop of Ferns, who was in Wexford throughout the rebellion, was bitterly critical of those priests who joined the rebels. He denounced them as 'excommunicated priests, drunken and profligate couple-beggars, the very faeces of the church'.[18] Moreover, these priests were a small minority in a county where there was a total of 85 Catholic priests.[19] In county Mayo only sixteen out of 314 Catholic priests supported the French when they landed in that part of Ireland.[20] In Ireland as a whole there were about 1800

---

16 Lecky, *Ireland in the Eighteenth Century*, v, 55-56.

17 Kevin Whelan, 'The Wexford Priests in 1798' in *Protestant, Catholic and Dissenter: The Clergy and 1798*, ed. Liam Swords (Dublin, 1997), pp. 65-85.

18 Daire Keogh, *'The French Disease': The Catholic Church and Radicalism in Ireland 1790-1800* (Dublin, 1993), p. 205.

19 Kevin Whelan, 'The Role of the Catholic Priest in the 1798 Rebellion in Wexford' in *Wexford: History and Society*, ed. Kevin Whelan and William Nolan (Dublin, 1987), pp. 296-315.

20 Daire Keogh, *'The French Disease'*, p. 186.

Catholic priests, but only about 70 had any connection with the rebellion and many of these had relatives among the United Irishmen.[21] On 24 May 1798 Archbishop Troy of Dublin denounced the rebellion in a pastoral letter sent to every Catholic priest.[22]

There is undoubtedly substantial evidence of both Protestant and Catholic involvement in the rebel cause and clear signs of a determined effort by some leading rebels to curb any sectarian tendency among their followers. A very significant number of leading members of the United Irishmen, throughout their existence, were Protestants: including such luminaries as Wolfe Tone, Lord Edward Fitzgerald, Arthur O'Connor and William Drennan. In preparing for the rebellion however seven of the fifteen Dublin-based leaders of the United Irishmen were Catholics.[23] The United Irishmen were explicitly non-sectarian. Indeed, Protestant United Irishmen such as William Drennan and Henry Joy McCracken were greatly influenced by the way French Catholics had overthrown priestcraft and despotism and had promoted radical reform.[24] In Ulster some 71 Presbyterian ministers, six Church of Ireland ministers, and twelve Catholic priests were involved with the United Irishmen prior to the outbreak of the rebellion.[25] When the rebellion in Ulster did occur, it was primarily, though not exclusively, a Presbyterian rebellion.[26] Even in Wexford, where the Catholics were in a clear majority, many Protestants played a significant part in the rebellion. The Wexford provisional council, which sought to control the rebellion in that area, was made up of four Protestants and four Catholics. Beauchamp Bagenal Harvey, the president of the council, was a member of the Church of Ireland, while Nicholas Grey, the secretary of the council, was a Presbyterian. Matthew Keugh, the governor of Wexford town throughout the rebellion, was another Protestant, while the committee of public safety in the town included such Protestants as Cornelius Grogan. Bagenal Harvey also led one of the

---

21 *Ibid.*, p. 199.

22 *Ibid.*, pp. 136-7, 152.

23 *Revolution, Counter-Revolution and Union*, ed. Jim Smyth, p. 64.

24 I. R. McBride, '"When Ulster joined Ireland": Anti-Popery, Presbyterian Radicalism and Irish Republicanism in the 1790s', *Past & Present*, 157 (1997), 86.

25 Ibid., 66; and Nancy Curtin, *The United Irishmen: Popular Politics in Ulster and Dublin, 1791-1798* (Oxford, 1994), p. 127.

26 William McMillan, 'Presbyterian ministers and the Ulster rising', in *Protestant, Catholic and Dissenter*, ed. Liam Swords, pp. 81-117; and *1798 Rebellion in County Down*, ed. Myrtle Hill, Brian Turner and Kenneth Dawson (Newtownards, 1998), pp. 162-86.

major rebel field armies in Wexford and commanded it during the abortive assault on New Ross on 5 June.[27] In Wicklow one of the most determined and able rebel commanders, Joseph Holt, was also a Protestant.[28]

Recent studies of the rebellion in Wexford have stressed how the leading United Irishmen strove hard to maintain political control over events and to prevent sectarian divisions and outrages – despite the provocation offered by ill-disciplined loyalist forces. Edward Roche, a Catholic commander of the northern Wexford army, declared on 7 June:

> To promote an union of brotherhood and affection amongst our countrymen of all religious persuasions, has been our principal object; . . . To my Protestant soldiers I feel much indebted, for their gallant behaviour in the field, where they exhibited proofs of bravery in the cause. . . . In the moment of triumph, my countrymen, let not your victories be tarnished with any wanton act of cruelty: . . . neither let a difference in religious sentiments cause a difference among the people.[29]

On 9 June the Wexford provisional council proclaimed its determination 'to protect the persons and properties of those of all religious persuasions who have not oppressed us, and are willing, with heart and mind, to join our glorious cause'.[30] There were only a few rebel attacks on Protestant churches in county Wexford and when sectarian outrages did occur, the rebel leadership condemned or at least never sanctioned these attacks on Protestants. Several Catholic priests in Wexford also strove hard to save Protestants from attack. Father John Corrin tried to halt the murder of Protestant prisoners on Wexford bridge, for example, while others pretended that Protestants had converted to Catholicism in an effort to protect them.[31] It should also be added that, after the rebellion, the more liberal Protestant landlords sought to help some of the rebels escape execution and tried to re-establish cordial relations with their Catholic neighbours.

---

27 Kevin Whelan, 'Reinterpreting the 1798 Rebellion in County Wexford', in *The Mighty Wave*, ed. Keogh and Furlong, p. 25; Brian Cleary, 'Wexford in 1798: A Republic before its Time', in *The Great Irish Rebellion of 1798*, ed. Cathal Poirteir, pp. 101-4; and Patrick Comerford, 'Church of Ireland Clergy and the 1798 Rising', in *Protestant, Catholic and Dissenter*, ed. Liam Swords, p. 240.

28 Ruan O'Donnell, *The Rebellion in Wicklow 1798* (Dublin, 1998).

29 Kevin Whelan, *Fellowship of Freedom: The United Irishmen and 1798* (Cork, 1998), p. 73.

30 Charles Dickson, *The Wexford Rising in 1798: Its Causes and Course* (reprinted, London, 1997), p. 150.

31 James S. Donnelly, 'Sectarianism in 1798 and in Catholic nationalist memory', in *Rebellion and remembrance in modern Ireland*, ed. Laurence M. Geary (Dublin, 2000), pp. 33-34.

Recent scholars have also stressed that no rebellion occurred in the most heavily Catholic counties which lay in Munster, and there was no rebellion in south Ulster or north Leinster, where sectarian divisions were as great as in Wexford. Armagh witnessed the worst sectarian clashes prior to the rebellion, but remained quiet during it. In the massacre at Scullabogue – usually cited as the worst example of sectarian violence during the rebellion – some of those who were murdered were Catholics and at least three Protestants helped to commit the crime.[32]

Finally, it must not be forgotten that large numbers of Catholics actually served with the government forces in opposing and ultimately suppressing the rebellion. When the North Cork militia were defeated by the rebels at Oulart Hill, the force included Catholics and they were shown no more mercy than their Protestant comrades.[33] When Bagenal Harvey led the abortive rebel attack on New Ross, his force included many Protestants, while the town's defenders included many Catholics who fought heroically in the Dublin, Donegal and Clare militias.[34] In the battle of Ballynahinch on 13 June many loyal Catholics served in the Monaghan militia which played a major role in defeating the Protestant rebels.[35] In county Mayo loyal Catholics serving with the Kerry militia helped to recover Killala from Catholic rebels.[36] When attacked by Catholic rebels the defence of Borris, on the border of Wexford and Carlow, was led by Thomas Kavanagh, a Catholic landlord from one of the great Gaelic families of Ireland.[37]

Despite this weight of evidence to show that both Catholics and Protestants joined the rebel cause and also fought together to suppress the rebellion, it can still be argued that many recent studies have been too anxious to play down the sectarian nature of the Irish rebellion. Religious tensions had existed in Ireland for centuries and sectarian violence had broken out in many parts of the country prior to the outbreak of the rebellion. It is hardly surprising that the chaotic circumstances of the rebellion allowed oppressed religious groups to settle old grievances. It is almost certainly going too far to claim that religious grievances had been

---

32 Daniel Gahan, *The People's Rising: Wexford 1798* (Dublin, 1995), pp. 26-27.

33 *A Military History of Ireland*, ed. Thomas Bartlett and Keith Jeffrey (Cambridge, 1996), pp. 247-49.

34 Daniel Gahan, *The People's Rising*, pp. 121-35.

35 Lecky, *Ireland in the Eighteenth Century*, iv, 423.

36 *Ibid.*, v, 65.

37 Gahan, *The People's Rising*, pp. 165-7.

entirely replaced by radical political sentiments by the late1790s. The leaders of the United Irishmen may have been explicitly non-sectarian, but many of these men had been arrested just prior to the outbreak of the rebellion or were in exile. It was impossible for these men fully to control the rebellion or to ensure that sectarian hatred never raised its ugly head.

Some of these recent efforts to deny the sectarian nature of the rebellion do not carry complete conviction. Kevin Whelan, for example, is now at the forefront of those scholars determined to describe the Irish rebellion as a political event, but, in 1987, he wrote an impressive and highly regarded essay, which stressed the sectarian divisions in Wexford just prior to the outbreak of the rebellion.[38] Louis Cullen too wrote some years back that north Wexford and south Wicklow had witnessed a rise in the socio-economic status of Catholic farmers and a decline in that of the middling Protestant farmers, and he claimed that this had fuelled ethno-religious tensions between the two groups. Now, he wishes to stress the political dimensions of the rebellion in Wexford.[39]

Despite some signs of a more enlightened attitude towards religious differences, Ireland remained a deeply sectarian state in the later eighteenth century. The Protestants still regarded themselves as a beleaguered minority throughout the 1790s and they made great efforts to strengthen and entrench the 'Protestant Ascendancy'. In 1795 the new lord lieutenant, Earl Camden, who was appointed to replace the more liberal Earl Fitzwilliam, was given explicit instructions to defend the Protestant interest.[40] The government virtually sanctioned the creation of the Orange Order in 1795 and it subsequently commended its efforts to disarm Catholic Defenders in Ulster. From 1796 to 1798 the Irish government passed legislation to impose martial law and to raise a staunchly Protestant yeomanry. In 1797 and 1798

---

38 Compare his essay in *The Mighty Wave*, ed. Keogh and Furlong, pp. 9-36 and his 'Politicisation in County Wexford and the origins of the 1798 Rebellion', in *Ireland and the French Revolution*, ed. Gough and Dickson, pp. 156-78, with 'The religious factor in the 1798 rebellion in county Wexford' in *Rural Ireland 1600-1900: Modernisation and Change*, ed. Patrick O'Flanagan, Paul Ferguson and Kevin Whelan (Cork, 1987), pp. 62-85 and 'The Role of the Catholic Priest in the 1798 Rebellion in County Wexford' in *Wexford: History and Society*, ed. Whelan and Nolan, pp. 296-315.

39 Compare L.M. Cullen, *The Emergence of Modern Ireland* (London, 1981), pp. 210-33 with L.M. Cullen, 'The 1798 Rebellion in Wexford: United Irishman organisation, membership, leadership', in *Wexford: History and Society*, ed. Whelan and Nolan, pp. 248-95 and "The United Irishmen in Wexford', in *The Mighty Wave*, ed. Keogh and Furlong, pp. 48-64.

40 Daire Keogh, 'Sectarianism in the Rebellion of 1798: The Eighteenth-Century Context', in *The Mighty Wave*, ed. Keogh and Furlong, p. 43.

the government explicitly instructed General Lake to disarm anyone suspected of being disaffected. Many innocent people suffered in the process, but Earl Camden made no effort to halt this reign of terror. Indeed, he commented: 'If the great body of Protestants can exert themselves in the contest, I am authorised to give them the most decided and unreserved support'.[41] Many loyalists were very willing to condemn the rebellion, when it did break out, as a sectarian revolt. On 7 June 1798 the Dublin *Freeman's Journal* fabricated a rebel oath in these terms: 'I, A.B., do solemnly swear by our Lord Jesus Christ, who suffered on the cross, and by the Blessed Virgin Mary, that I will burn, destroy and murder all heretics, up to my knees in blood. So help me God.'[42] While this was a fabrication, genuine Protestant violence certainly did terrify many Catholics and helped to provoke a sectarian reaction. The North Cork militia under Lord Kingsborough marched into Wexford in April 1798 and earned public infamy by its violent efforts to disarm all suspected rebels.[43] On 24 May more than 30 Catholic yeomen were summarily executed at Dunlavin, in west Wicklow, by regular British troops convinced that they were United Irishmen. The next day some 28 prisoners, suspected of being rebels, were shot at Carnew on the Wexford-Wicklow border. Such events undoubtedly helped to spark off a sectarian response from the majority Catholic population.[44]

The sectarian nature of the Irish state and the savage response to the rebellion among fearful Protestant loyalists cannot be denied. What remains a matter of controversy is whether the rebels who took up arms against this state were motivated by fears and hopes that were shaped by sectarian attitudes. There is certainly some evidence that Catholicism fuelled the resentment of the rebels, but this evidence may not be sufficient to support the claim that the rebellion was primarily motivated by religious hatred.[45] Irish-language ballads and poems of the period reveal that many Catholic rebels still conceived of their political and military opponents in sectarian terms.[46] In the1790s the Defenders were undoubtedly a Catholic organization seeking to protect the interests of the Catholics and the promotion of sectarian designs were never entirely absent from their

41 Kevin Whelan, *The Tree of Liberty* (Cork, 1996), p. 112.

42 Jim Smyth, *The Men of No Property*, p. 179.

43 Kevin Whelan, in *The Mighty Wave*, ed. Keogh and Furlong, pp. 20-21.

44 James S. Donnelly, 'Sectarianism in 1798 and in Catholic nationalist memory', pp. 18-20.

45 Daniel Gahan, 'Class, religion and rebellion: Wexford in 1798', in *Revolution, Counter-Revolution and Union*, ed. Smyth, pp. 83-98.

46 James S. Donnelly, 'Sectarianism in 1798', p. 24.

wider aims. While there is considerable evidence to suggest that the United Irishmen were explicitly non-sectarian, they did sometimes play the 'Orange card' in order to forge an alliance with the Defenders and to secure mass support among the Catholics. In Ulster, by contrast, the Presbyterian leaders of the United Irishmen promoted a political ideology that was suffused with religious inspiration. They attacked the penal laws and promoted political reforms, but these objectives were predicated upon millenarian hopes for the withering away of 'popery' and for the final triumph of rational, reformed Christianity.[47]

It is true that during the rebellion in Wexford the political leaders of the rebels did try to restrain sectarian passions, but they had to admit the difficulty of protecting Protestants from popular retribution. The sectarian desire for revenge was so strong among some rebel rank-and-file that their leaders could not prevent some notorious sectarian outrages: the murder of 300-400 Protestants in the rebel camp on Vinegar Hill; the killing of unarmed Protestants at Rathangan on 26 May; the brutal slaughter of over one hundred Protestants (including some women and children) burned to death in a barn at Scullabogue on 5 June 1798; and the savage piking to death of Protestant prisoners on Wexford bridge on 20 June. While it has been acknowledged by recent scholars that these killings were undoubtedly sectarian to some degree, it has also been argued that they were not committed solely because the victims were Protestants. Protestant clergy and landowners were sometimes attacked because they were magistrates or oppressors of poor Catholics. Some Protestant prisoners were killed because they had previously killed rebels or in revenge for Catholic rebels murdered by government forces. Moreover, sectarian violence occurred, so the argument runs, mainly when the firm discipline previously exercised by the political leaders of the rebellion broke down.[48] It is also maintained that many Protestants went unmolested in rebel-held territory – particularly the Quaker community in Wexford itself.[49]

These efforts to minimize the sectarian dimension to the Irish rebellion have not convinced all recent scholars. Kevin Whelan, who has done much

---

47 I. R. McBride, '"When Ulster joined Ireland"', *Past & Present*, 157 (1997), 93.

48 James S. Donnelly, 'Sectarianism in 1798', pp. 23-25, 32; Daire Keogh, 'Sectarianism in the Rebellion of 1798' in *The Mighty Wave*, ed. Keogh and Furlong, p. 45; and Kevin Whelan, in *Rural Ireland 1600-1900*, p. 75. But see Tom Dunne, '1798: Memory, History, Commemoration', *Journal of the Wexford Historical Society*, 16 (1996-7), 22-25.

49 William McMillan in *Protestant, Catholic and Dissenter*, ed. Liam Swords, p. 83.

in some of his writings to stress the political dimensions of the rebellion, has admitted elsewhere: 'The rebels tried, or claimed to try, to distinguish between "Orangemen" and "Protestants:" in general but a purely sectarian motive was evident in many of the killings.'[50] Tom Dunne has concluded that it is difficult to see sectarianism as the major explanation for the rebellion, but hard to dismiss it as one of the causes.[51] James Donnelly has admitted that anti-Protestant sectarianism was rife among ordinary Catholics and it could not have been excluded from the rebel ranks.[52]

3. A Political Rebellion?

While many contemporaries in 1798 sought to make political capital by denouncing the rebellion as a Catholic revolt against a beleaguered Protestant state, others believed that the rebellion was in fact a political revolt. Lord Cornwallis, the new Lord Lieutenant appointed to subdue the rebellion, informed the Home Secretary in London of 'the folly which has been too prevalent in this quarter of substituting the word Catholicism for Jacobinism as the foundation of the present rebellion.'[53] He was not alone in seeing the rebellion in political terms. Lord Castlereagh claimed that the rebellion was a 'jacobinical' or French-inspired rising, pursuing its objectives with 'Popish instruments'.[54] Over the last decade or so many historians have argued that the rebellion was politically-motivated, was planned and led by the non-sectarian United Irishmen, and sought to achieve primarily political objectives.

There is certainly much evidence to support such conclusions. Louis Cullen and Kevin Whelan have drawn attention to the split among the Wexford elite between the liberal and reactionary Protestant gentry and they have shown how this division, greatly intensified as it was in the 1790s, gave the United Irishmen an opportunity to gain support among the former.[55] Both of these historians have retreated from their former emphasis on the sectarian nature of the Irish rebellion in Wexford and now stress the political involvement of the United Irishmen. Nearly all

---

50 *Rural Ireland 1600-1900*, p. 75.

51 Tom Dunne, '1798: Memory, History, Commemoration', *Journal of the Wexford Historical Society*, 16 (1996-7), 14-15.

52 James S. Donnelly, 'Sectarianism in 1798', pp. 27, 30.

53 Daire Keogh, '*The French Disease*', p. 202.

54 Thomas Bartlett, *The Fall and Rise of the Irish Nation* (Dublin, 1992), p. 237.

55 L.M. Cullen, *The Emergence of Modern Ireland 1600-1900* (London, 1981), pp. 210-33 and Kevin Whelan, in *Rural Ireland 1600-1900*, pp. 62-85.

recent studies of the rebellion have highlighted the fact that the United Irishmen were politically motivated, and that they planned the rebellion, enlisted French support, initiated the rising, and played a major role in it. Wolfe Tone's *Argument on behalf of the Catholics of Ireland* explicitly sought to end sectarian divisions in Ireland and to submerge all denominational distinctions under the common name of 'Irishman'. He continued to strive to convince Protestants that Catholics could be trusted with political rights. When the leaders of the United Irishmen agreed their first programme in 1794, they came out in support of a set of political aims. When the United Irishmen later became a secret, insurrectionary movement, they sought similar political aims by more militant means, but added a desire for greater political independence from Britain. Throughout their existence the United Irishmen believed in politicizing the Irish population by propaganda, debates, rituals, ceremonies, and festivities. Thomas Russell declared that it was 'not only the right but the *essential duty* of every man to interest himself in the conduct of government'.[56] When they recognized that political success might require French support, the United Irishmen sent a series of missionaries to Paris. By 1795 the United Irishmen had decided that political reform in Ireland required a severing of the connection with Britain. In 1796 Tone declared in the name of the United Irishmen:

> To subvert the tyranny of our execrable governance, to break the connection with England, the never-failing source of all our political evils, and to assert the independence of my country – these were my objectives. To unite the whole people of Ireland, to abolish the memory of past dissensions, and to substitute the common name of Irishman, in place of the denominations of Protestant, Catholic and Dissenter – these were my means.[57]

Finally, it is quite clear that the leaders of the United Irishmen supported the French invasion efforts of 1796-98, laid plans for the rebellion of May 1798, led most of the forces which took up arms throughout the rebellion, and endeavoured to create an independent, republican and democratic Ireland. Tens of thousands of those who took up arms in support of these political objectives were sworn members of the United Irishmen.

Despite the wealth of evidence supporting the claim that the Irish rebellion was *primarily* a political rising inspired, planned, and fought by the United Irishmen, it has to be conceded that the rebellion was neither

---

[56] Jim Smyth, *The Men of No Property*, p. 5.

[57] Tone, *Memoirs*, in *Life of Theobald Wolfe Tone*, ed. Thomas Bartlett (Dublin, 1998), p. 46.

solely nor entirely a political event. In the first place, it is clear that the United Irishmen – despite all their efforts – were never fully in control of the rebellion. In the months prior to the rebellion the United Irishmen had established a formal, though rather loose, alliance with the Catholic Defenders, an organization with a much more sectarian ethos and with a programme with wider socio-economic aims.[58] The United Irishmen hoped they could give a political lead to, and maintain control over, these allies, but it is far from clear that they achieved these objectives. They certainly did not incorporate all the Defenders into their own organization and they did not persuade them all to abandon their religious and economic aims. In the rebellion in County Down, for example, it is clear that the Presbyterian United Irishmen did not share the same aims as the Catholic Defenders and these differences undoubtedly weakened their military alliance.[59]

It is also apparent that the United Irishmen themselves were divided. When the movement was transformed into a secret, mass-based and militant organization, some members left the movement and there were disputes within the new structure about how much violence might be needed to achieve their political objectives. There were also disputes about whether to rise only after the French had arrived or to start a rebellion even if it were uncertain how much assistance might be secured from France.[60] Whereas it is true that the programme of the United Irishmen was very largely a political one – they were largely what might be described as bourgeois radicals – the members of the movement were not all devoid of religious and social objectives. On the night before the battle of Ballynahinch the rebel commanders, the Presbyterian Henry Munro and the Catholic John Magennis disputed its overall command. Munro allegedly 'did declare aloud his intentions was to establish a presbiterian independent government after the begun revolution would become compleated'. Not surprisingly, Magennis and his men stole away in the middle of the night.[61] We have already seen that there were several outbreaks of violent sectarianism among the Catholic rebels in Wexford.

Finally, it needs to be acknowledged that the United Irishmen never established full control even over the rebellion that they had planned. This

58 *A Military History of Ireland*, ed. Bartlett and Jeffery, p. 260.

59 Nancy Curtin, 'The transformation of the Society of United Irishmen into a mass-based revolutionary organisation, 1794-96', *Irish Historical Studies*, 24 (1985), 48-92.

60 This theme runs throughout Marianne Elliott, *Partners in Revolution*.

61 *A Military History of Ireland*, ed. Bartlett and Jeffery, p. 282.

is hardly surprising given the number of leading United Irishmen who were arrested over several years prior to the rebellion and the number who were driven into involuntary exile. Once the rebellion had been planned, the arrest of Lord Edward Fitzgerald, the most aristocratic, charismatic leader and the nominated commander of military operations, was a bitter blow. This was then followed by the arrest of almost the entire Leinster Directory very shortly before the rebellion was due to start. The rebellion began with hardly a single major leader in his place to command the rebels to coordinate operations. The initial plan for a rising in Dublin did not materialize and there was never a coordinated campaign thereafter. Instead of a coordinated campaign, with counties rising in succession to support those who had just risen before them, different counties rose almost haphazardly and sometimes just as the rebellion was being crushed elsewhere. The leadership of the movement devolved upon local commanders, some of whom were quite junior figures among the United Irishmen, or upon natural leaders in the local community who were not necessarily disciplined and committed United Irishmen. The United Irishmen were in serious disarray just before the rebellion broke out and hence, in the words of Marianne Elliott: 'The rebellion was not a United Irish one as it would have been a year earlier, but a protective popular uprising which a spent United Irish leadership failed to harness.'[62]

Once government forces began to inflict heavy casualties upon the rebels, the rebellion lost all cohesion and direction. With dozens of engagements across several counties, discipline broke down at times. In such circumstances it is hardly surprising that sectarian passions, social resentment and economic grievances sometimes took precedence over political objectives. As we have seen elements of an agrarian revolt were not entirely absent in 1798 and sectarian outrages did take place. The wonder is that these were the exceptions. The Irish rebellion may have remained largely – but it was not *exclusively* – a political revolt. Recent scholars have gone too far in asserting the absolute primacy of its political dimensions. James Donnelly has rightly tried to scale back this undue emphasis on the political aspects of the Irish rebellion:

> By all means let us continue to seek to know the full extent of the United Irishmen's ideological and organisational presence in Wexford and everywhere else. But at the same time let us gauge accurately the central sectarian component of popular politics and culture in the 1790s – in all its harshness, crudeness, and repulsiveness.[63]

---

62 Marianne Elliott, *Partners in Revolution*, p. 166.

63 Donnelly, 'Sectarianism in 1798', p. 37.

II. Remembering '98

It has proved difficult for modern scholars to reach a consensus on the nature of the Irish rebellion because it is not an event that has passed safely into history. The Irish rebellion has had such a profound effect on subsequent Irish history that it has never become a subject that can be examined and interpreted in an impartial or dispassionate manner. It was a major political issue in its own day, it profoundly affected the Union debates of 1798-1800, and it has remained a subject of deep political significance ever since. It was the subject of major commemorative efforts in both 1898 and 1998 in which contemporary political issues played a major role in determining how the rebellion would be interpreted. The nature of the Irish rebellion has been a matter of great significance in Irish politics over the entire two centuries since it occurred.

Immediately after the rebellion conservative Protestant loyalists promptly exploited the situation in order to defeat any new proposal to grant Catholic emancipation. The first major study of the rebellion – Sir Richard Musgrave's *Memoirs of the Different Rebellions in Ireland* (1801) – linked the events of 1798 with those of 1641 and 1688-91 and deliberately stressed that the rebellion was a popish plot to destroy the Irish Protestants: 'It is not what is erroneously and ridiculously called emancipation that the masses of the Irish Roman Catholics want; it is the extirpation or expulsion of the Protestants, the exclusive occupation of the island for themselves and its separation from England.'[64] Musgrave sought to depoliticize the Ulster rebellion in order to erase links with the rebellion in Leinster. He accused the Presbyterians of being foolishly misled into joining a popish plot, and he claimed that the privileged position of the Church of Ireland needed to be maintained because its adherents had been the most loyal denomination during the rebellion. The Irish Catholics were portrayed as the enemy of the state from within, while the French Catholics were the enemy of the state from without. To protect Irish Protestants it was therefore sensible to support union with Britain.[65]

This sectarian interpretation of the rebellion embarrassed both those who had some sympathy for the Catholics and the Catholic hierarchy itself. Bishop Stock, a liberal episcopalian, wrote an account of the rebellion in Connaught that played down the violence and the political aspects of the

---

64 Thomas Bartlett, Kevin Dawson and Daire Keogh, *Rebellion: A Television History of 1798* (Dublin, 1998), p. 161.

65 Kevin Whelan, *The Tree of Liberty*, pp. 136-40.

rebellion compared to the events in Wexford, and also stressed the essential loyalty of the Catholics. He argued that the rebellion had been largely provoked by the attacks on the Catholics launched by the ill-disciplined military and the militant members of the Orange Order.[66] For their part the Catholic bishops recognized the problem created for their church by the prominent part played in the rebellion by a number of Catholic priests. They therefore embarked on a damage limitation exercise to depict these priests as an entirely unrepresentative minority.[67] They were portrayed as men of disgraceful character, with no real standing in the Catholic church, whereas the mass of the Catholic clergy, and particularly the church hierarchy, had been decidedly loyal during the rebellion. While it had to be admitted that large numbers of Catholics did rebel, the Catholic hierarchy insisted that this had been due to the severe provocation given by the military and the Orange Order.[68] The Catholic church could therefore argue that Catholic emancipation was the best way of preventing such sectarian outrages in the future and of cementing the loyalty of the Catholic majority to the state.

Curiously, but understandably, it suited the United Irishmen to depict the rebellion in primarily sectarian terms. Some prominent leaders of the United Irishmen tried to save their lives and their reputation by absolving themselves of responsibility for the rebellion. They endeavoured to represent the rebellion as a spontaneous rising, which broke out only after unrelenting persecution by government forces and militant loyalists. In August 1798 three imprisoned United Irish leaders – Thomas Addis Emmet, Arthur O'Connor and William James MacNeven – produced a detailed *Memoir* for the government that put just such a case. This *Memoir* stressed the violence in Armagh – provoked by the Orange Order, the Catholic Defenders, and the military – that had spiralled out of control into rebellion. The United Irishmen were reasonable men caught in the crossfire between an intransigent government and an infuriated peasantry. They had been drawn into the rebellion as the reluctant leaders of reluctant rebels. This 'confession' helped to save the lives of its authors and other United Irishmen. It also suited the government's purposes, since government ministers were anxious to diminish the political aspects of the

---

66 *Ibid.*, p. 146; and *Bishop Stock's 'Narrative' of the Year of the French: 1798*, ed. Grattan Freyer (Ballina, 1982).

67 Bartlett *et al*, *Rebellion*, p. 163.

68 Kevin Whelan, *The Tree of Liberty*, pp. 148-50.

rebellion as this might help to dissuade staunch Presbyterians from any future flirtation with peasant or Catholic rebels.[69]

Other United Irishmen joined in this damage limitation exercise in an effort to distance themselves from responsibility for a bloody armed rebellion. Edward Hay, a former rebel, played down the involvement of the United Irishmen in the rebellion and obscured its political aspects, in his *History of the Insurrection of the County of Wexford* (1803). His *History* was a personal vindication of his own conduct, produced to conceal as well as clarify his role in the rebellion. He denied that there were any premeditated plans for a rebellion in Wexford. Instead, he claimed that the rising had been provoked by Ascendancy bigots and violent Orangemen. Hay rejected the claim that the rebels were religious fanatics. He downplayed Catholic lay involvement in the rebellion, though he did admit the role of a few Catholic priests in leading the rebels in the field.[70] Thomas Cloney, another rebel, in *A Personal Narrative of those Transactions in the County of Wexford . . . 1798*, was also ready to claim that the militant loyalists provoked the rebellion in Wexford, which was led by Catholic priests rather than by the United Irishmen. He insisted that he was not himself a United Irishman and he asserted that 'no organised political conspiracy [existed] in that county even to a limited extent'.[71] Joseph Holt's *Memoirs*, dictated in 1818, were heavily edited by Thomas Crofton Croker when they finally appeared in 1838. Croker's fictitious additions to the original manuscript were designed to de-politicize the rebellion and to rehabilitate Holt's reputation among loyalists following his return to Ireland after thirteen years of exile in Australia. Holt insisted that he, like many others, was driven to rebel to revenge private wrongs and individual oppression.[72]

From the 1820s to the early 1840s Daniel O'Connell and his supporters deliberately sought to dissociate their own respectable and constitutional activities from the oath-based organizations and violent actions of the rebels of 1798. In 1841 O'Connell declared:

---

69 *Ibid.*, pp. 156-57; and Bartlett *et al.*, *Rebellion*, pp. 163-64.

70 *Ibid.*, p. 164; Margaret O hOGartaigh, 'Edward Hay: Historian of 1798', *Eighteenth-Century Ireland*, 13 (1998), 121-34; James S. Donnelly, 'Sectarianism in 1798', pp. 23, 34; L.M. Cullen, 'The 1798 rebellion in Wexford', in *Wexford: History and Society*, ed. Whelan and Nolan, pp. 252-53.

71 *Ibid.*, p. 252 and also 256, 258, 279, 280; and Bartlett *et al.*, *Rebellion*, p. 165.

72 *Ibid.*, *Rebellion*, p. 165; Ruan O'Donnell, *The Rebellion in Wicklow 1798* (Dublin, 1998), p. 76; Ruan O'Donnell, '"Keeping up the flame": General Joseph Holt', *History Ireland*, 6 (1998), 39-43; and *Memoirs of Joseph Holt*, ed. T. C. Croker (2 vols., London, 1838).

> As to 1798, we leave the weak and wicked men who considered sanguinary violence as part of their resources for ameliorating our institutions and the equally wicked and villainous designing wretches who fomented the rebellion ... to the contempt and indignation of mankind.[73]

Throughout the 1840s O'Connell emphasized the extent of the death and destruction caused by the rebellion of 1798 and the renewed sectarian hatred which its repression engendered.[74] It was in the 1840s however, in opposition to O'Connell, that the Young Ireland movement began to advance a nationalist case and a distinct Irish cultural identity. Its leaders demonstrated a greater readiness to acknowledge the revolutionary and republican principles of the United Irishmen and their crucial role in organizing the rebellion. Thomas Davis, a leader of the Young Ireland movement, became a great admirer of Wolfe Tone and erected a memorial stone at Tone's burial place in 1844. He admired Tone's personal character and courage, praised his nationalism, but passed over his later republicanism. He moulded an image of Tone as the founder of Irish nationalism – an image that went on to become a part of the collective Irish memory. It was not until 1848 however that John Mitchel began to praise the political views of the United Irishmen in general. He deliberately titled his radical newspaper, the *United Irishman*, and he printed the French revolutionary slogan, 'Liberty-Equality-Fraternity' across the title page. The cult of Tone continued with the Fenians and nurtured their nationalism. They were inspired by Tone's plea for political independence and his readiness to employ physical force in order to achieve a republican regime.[75]

This new interest in the United Irishmen was fostered by contemporary historians and by the publication of the memoirs of United Irishmen. Luke Cullen and R.R. Madden set about collecting evidence from surviving United Irishmen and other witnesses of events in 1798 about what had really happened during the rebellion. The personal testimonies collected by Cullen gave no hint of sectarian hatred, while Madden, in particular, not only rejected the sectarian interpretation of 1798, but blamed the Wexford rebellion on the violent oppression of the Protestants. Madden placed the rebellion planned by the United Irishmen back in its French revolutionary context and presented the rebels as politically conscious freedom fighters.

---

73 Kevin Whelan, *The Tree of Liberty*, p. 151.

74 Sean Ryder, 'Young Ireland and the 1798 rebellion' in *Rebellion and remembrance in modern Ireland*, ed. Laurence M. Geary, p. 138.

75 *Ibid.*, pp. 135-47; and Sophie Ollivier, 'Presence and absence of Wolfe Tone during the centenary commemoration of the 1798 rebellion, in *ibid.*, pp. 175-84.

Both Cullen and Madden ignored the surviving ballads written in the Irish language that clearly referred to the rebels' bitter sectarian hatred for Protestants in general and Orangemen in particular.[76] This attempt to recover and restore the crucial role of the United Irishmen in the rebellion was boosted by the publication of the *Memoirs of Miles Byrne* in 1863. Byrne, who had fought in the rebellion, was contemptuous of Edward Hay's earlier account and he deliberately ignored that of Thomas Cloney. He maintained that the rebellion had been waged by the United Irishmen, an organized secret society with leaders drawn from both the Catholic and the Protestant middle classes, and with mass popular support, in order to secure the political independence of Ireland. While he defended the reputations of the few Catholic priests who had been active in the rebellion, he insisted that they had enrolled in a political not a sectarian or agrarian cause.[77]

This much more political interpretation of the rebellion began to embarrass the Catholic hierarchy because the clergy were seriously at odds in the 1860s with the Fenians, who had similarities with the United Irishmen in being another secret, oath-bound conspiracy seeking to establish an Irish republic by militant means. The leaders of the church were anxious to prove to the Irish people that the latter should place their trust in the Catholic clergy – just as they had done in1798 when it was the priests who had led the people in their hour of need. Cardinal Cullen, who had been attacking the Fenians since 1864, insisted that the moral law could not condone an oath-bound society which demanded blind obedience to unknown leaders. He successfully petitioned Rome for an explicit condemnation of the Fenians. Nearer home he found his campaign against the Fenians given a boost from Father Patrick Kavanagh's *Popular History of the Insurrection of 1798*, published in 1870 and reissued in 1874, 1884, 1898 and several times thereafter.[78] Father Kavanagh made no reference to the earlier work on the United Irishmen by Luke Cullen or Dr Madden, and he rejected Miles Byrne's comments on the role of the United Irish-

---

[76] Maura Cronin, 'Memory, story and balladry: 1798 and its place in popular memory in pre-Famine Ireland', in *Rebellion and remembrance in modern Ireland*, ed. Geary, pp. 120-22, 132-33. See also *Insurgent Wicklow, 1798: the story as written by Luke Cullen*, ed. Ruan O'Donnell (Bray, 1998).

[77] Kevin Whelan, *The Tree of Liberty*, pp. 168-69; L. M. Cullen, 'The 1798 Rebellion in Wexford', in *Wexford: History and Society*, ed. Whelan and Nolan, pp. 260-62; and Thomas Bartlett, 'Miles Byrne: United Irishman, Irish Exile and Beau Sabreur', in *The Mighty Wave*, ed. Keogh and Furlong, pp. 118-38.

[78] Kevin Whelan, *The Tree of Liberty*, p. 170.

men. In his history the United Irishmen were blamed for creating a climate of political intrigue which exposed innocent Catholics to the violence of the Orange Order. He maintained that the United Irishmen had made little progress in Wexford because of the superior influence of the Catholic priests and because of popular hostility to secret societies. Kavanagh accepted the earlier Catholic interpretation of the origins of the 1798 rebellion, seeing it principally as a spontaneous response to state persecution and Orange Order terror, as provoked not organized, and as spontaneous not planned. He went further and claimed that the United Irishmen – a dangerous and unreliable secret, oath-bound society – had not led this doomed rebellion, but had helped to provoke it by creating a climate of fear. According to Kavanagh, the United Irishmen had provided little leadership or organization, particularly in Wexford, and it was brave and dedicated Catholic priests who endeavoured to fill the leadership vacuum.[79] Kavanagh ignored the condemnation of such priests by the Catholic hierarchy in 1798, and flatly denied the sectarian motives of the Wexford rebels. In his view, the violence of the rebels was aimed not against Protestants as such, but against Orangemen. Above all, his book endeavoured to prove that there was no conflict between Irish nationalism and Catholicism, and that in their hour of need it was the Catholic priests who stood by the Irish people. His account of the rebellion helped to fuse the two claims – 'faith and fatherland' – in the popular imagination in Catholic Ireland.[80]

Father Kavanagh's account created a new, orthodox interpretation of the rebellion. He went on to become the vice-president of the Ancient Order of Hibernians, the Catholic equivalent of the Orange Order. Meanwhile, Catholic Ireland accepted responsibility for the whole rebellion and the role of the Presbyterians in the United Irishmen and especially in 1798 was largely ignored and all but forgotten. The Presbyterians of Ulster were not averse to this because they were becoming increasingly alarmed by the Catholic Irish efforts to break the Union. In 1859 Ogle Robert Gowan had produced an account of the rebellion, *Murder without Sin*, which had depicted the rebellion as primarily a Wexford rising in which Catholic rebels had sought to destroy the constitution and murder all Protestants. He

79 L. M. Cullen, 'The 1798 Rebellion in Wexford', in *Wexford: History and Society*, ed. Whelan and Nolan, pp. 259-62; and Thomas Bartlett *et al.*, *Rebellion*, pp. 168-69.

80 Anna Kinsella, '1798 Claimed for Catholics: Father Kavanagh, Fenians and the Centenary Celebrations', in *The Mighty Wave*, ed. Keogh and Furlong, pp. 139-55; and James S. Donnelly, 'Sectarianism in 1798', p. 35.

stressed the role of the Catholic priests in the rebellion and highlighted the brutal murders of Protestants at Scullabogue and on Wexford bridge. In his account the Protestant rebels in Wexford are ignored and the rebellion was put down by the valour of Orange Order troops, who deserved to be remembered as the saviours of their country.[81]

As the centenary of the 1798 rebellion approached the more advanced Irish nationalist groups planned to commemorate the aims and achievements of the rebels. Plans to commemorate the rebellion began with the Dublin chapter of the Young Ireland League, but it was John O'Leary and the Irish Republican Brotherhood who established an executive committee in Dublin to promote a wide range of commemorative activities.[82] More visionary republicans such as W.B. Yeats and Maud Gonne, and socialist republicans such as James Connolly, soon got in on the act and numerous local clubs, often named after rebel leaders of 1798, were established across the country. Widespread popular interest in the centenary however only served to reveal the profound divisions within the ranks of Irish nationalists as others tried to play a leading role in these commemorative activities. It was soon clear that the 1898 commemorative efforts were motivated as much by contemporary political concerns as by a desire to memorialize the 1798 rebellion and to praise its brave participants. The Irish Republican Brotherhood had no respect for the constitutional tactics of the nationalist MPs in the Irish Parliamentary Party and they often criticized the Catholic clergy as lackeys of Ireland's English oppressors. They wanted to use the rebellion to support their style of nationalist politics. But, determined to play a major part in the commemoration of 1798, both the Parnellite and anti-Parnellite wings of the Irish Parliamentary Party, led by John Redmond and John Dillon, respectively, put pressure on the executive committee to allow them a public role in the planned celebrations. Supporters of Redmond's group were soon active in the executive committee's work, though MPs were still officially excluded from the committee, but Dillon's group had to establish a rival organization in order to capitalize on the widespread desire to celebrate the centenary of 1798.

---

81 This astonishly biased account was reprinted by the Orange Order in Ulster as recently as 1996.

82 For the 1898 commemorations see Timothy J. O'Keefe, 'The 1898 efforts to celebrate the United Irishmen: The '98 Centennial', *Eire-Ireland*, 23 (1988), 51-73; Timothy J. O'Keefe, '"Who fears to speak of '98?": The rhetoric and ritual of the United Irishman centennial, 1898', *Eire-Ireland*, 27 (1992), 67-91; and Senia Paseta, '1798 in 1898: The Politics of Commemoration', *Irish Studies*, 22 (1998), 46-53.

By early in 1898 there were two distinct nationwide centennial organizations, each claiming to honour the spirit and memory of the United Irishmen. While each claimed to desire unity above all else, they tried, in practice, to undermine the efforts of the other. These divisions among Irish nationalists began to alienate the Catholic clergy in particular and nationalist public opinion in general. Conscious of this, the rival organizations at last sought a compromise in April 1898. It was not until mid-May 1898, however, that a new amalgamated body met for the first time. The constitutional nationalists thus usurped more than their fair share of glory for the commemorative activities initiated by the Irish Republican Brotherhood. The newly amalgamated commemorative body started to coordinate local celebrations across the country. On 15 August John O'Leary, John Dillon and John Redmond joined together in an open-air ceremony in Dublin to lay the foundation stone to a monument to Wolfe Tone and the other leaders of the United Irishmen. The different Irish nationalist groups did not stay united for very long, but the commemorative activities of 1898 did help to re-unite the Irish Parliamentary Party under the leadership of John Redmond. For all the interminable squabbling and intrigue, the ceremony had helped to pave the way for this reconciliation. But the parliamentary politicians, having reaped more than their fair share of glory from the commemorations initiated by the Irish Republican Brotherhood, soon returned to their own affairs. Without the support of the constitutionalists and their more prosperous supporters, the republicans could not afford to raise the money needed to complete the monument to Wolfe Tone and the United Irishmen.

Although the 1898 centenary was marred by factionalism, almost from its inception, the divisions within the Irish nationalist movement did not prevent very large numbers of Irish people from commemorating the rebellion of 1798. Not surprisingly, their various celebrations in 1898 showed that there was no single interpretation of the events of 1798. Local clubs and national societies did organize similar celebrations: processions, meetings and dinners, addresses and speeches, theatrical and musical activities, the erecting of memorials to the rebels, and the distribution of innumerable publications. But different groups stressed different aspects of 1798. The Irish Republican Brotherhood stressed the fact that the United Irishmen had been an oath-bound society ready to use violent means to achieve an independent Irish republic. The constitutional nationalists praised the constitutional aims of the United Irishmen during their earlier constitutional phase, and were even ready to praise Henry Grattan and his parliament.

John Redmond exploited those aspects of 1798 that most suited the interests of the Irish Parliamentary Party. He declared that Irishmen of all shades of nationalist opinion were uniting as one man to celebrate the centenary of the rebellion, but he also stressed that the United Irishmen had been an open and constitutional society seeking parliamentary reform and Catholic emancipation by peaceful means.[83] This strategy had some success in re-uniting the Irish Parliamentary Party, but this political benefit should not obscure the fact that the dominant nationalist interpretation in 1898 of the events of 1798 maintained that the rebellion was the direct result of the savage persecution of the Catholic peasantry by loyalists encouraged by the Protestant state.

The views of Father Kavanagh still held sway and his *Popular History* was reprinted in Cork in 1898. The Catholic clergy in 1898 increasingly ignored the political principles of the United Irishmen and stressed that the rebellion had been a Catholic and a nationalist undertaking, in which the Catholic clergy had played a leading role. They successfully imposed their interpretation of 1798 on the Irish nationalist community. In 1898 Father Kavanagh condemned the limited role of the United Irishmen in 1798 and that of secret societies ever since: 'They promise much but when the hour comes to act they do little or nothing.'[84] When laying the foundation stone for the commemorative monument erected at Wexford, he declared: 'The men, whose memory we honour today, died for a persecuted creed as well as an oppressed country.'[85] The celebrations at St Mullins, county Wexford, were led by the parish priest, who praised 'the brave men . . . who died fighting for the cause of Faith and Fatherland'.[86] The passionate rhetoric of numerous Catholic priests co-opted the revolutionary past for the Catholic church and identified Irish nationalism with the Catholic religion. The commemorative events of 1898 thus did much to keep alive the grievances of Catholics and nationalists, and to reaffirm their aspirations for independence. Rarely has the history of an event been written so exclusively by the defeated as in these centenary celebrations of 1798. They contributed to the resurgence of national feeling among Irish Catholics, to the reunification of the Irish Parliamentary Party, and even-

83 Paseta, *Irish Studies*, 22 (1998), 48.

84 Anna Kinsella, in *The Mighty Wave*, ed. Keogh and Furlong, p. 154.

85 R. F. Foster, 'Remembering 1798', in *The Irish Story: Telling tales and making it up in Ireland* (London, 2001), p. 219. This essay was also published in *History and Memory in Modern Ireland*, ed. Ian McBride (Cambridge, 2001), pp. 67-94.

86 Timothy J. O'Keefe, in *Eire-Ireland*, 28 (1992), 88.

tually to the emergence of Sinn Fein. They persuaded large numbers of Irish Catholics to link a mythical vision of the past to a vision of the future independence of Ireland.

Although Catholic Ireland strove – with incomplete success[87] – to present a united front in the celebrations in Dublin and Wexford in 1898, the role of the Presbyterians in the rebellion was largely ignored. The *Irish Times* and the *Daily Express*, Unionist newspapers in Dublin, even voiced surprise that the Irish Catholic nationalists wished to celebrate the disasters of 1798 at all.[88] John Fowler, at an Orange Order meeting in Dublin, blamed the 1898 commemorations on a popish conspiracy against the liberties of mankind. The Unionist community in Ulster did its best to hand the centenary commemoration of 1898 over to the Catholics. The Ulster Unionists feared the contemporary efforts to secure Home Rule for Ireland and did not wish to promote nationalist triumphalism. Protestant loyalists, wearing Orange sashes, attacked some nationalist attempts to commemorate the rebellion in Ulster. The Grand Master of the Orange Order condemned a commemoration that was planned for Belfast as 'a flagitious display of sympathy with an armed insurrection which, above all things, was characterised by a series of most foul and cowardly murders and massacres of innocent men and women whose only offence was their Protestantism'.[89] He stressed the sectarian excesses of the rebellion and saw it in religious terms. The *Belfast News-Letter* also took a hostile stance towards the 1898 commemorative celebrations. It opposed the proposal for a memorial to Wolfe Tone, while Protestant loyalists in Ulster smashed the gravestone of Betsy Grey, a young woman who had died with her brother and lover at the battle of Ballynahinch in 1798.[90]

Bronze monuments to the rebels of 1798 were erected in Wexford in 1905 and in Enniscorthy in 1908, when thousands attended the unveilings. On both occasions the Irish Parliamentary Party exploited the ceremonies to enlist support for the cause of Home Rule. At the Enniscorthy ceremony William Redmond gave full credit to the United Irishmen, but Father FitzHenry reiterated the Catholic church's long-established view of the rebellion. Referring to the two-figure statue he claimed: 'It was particu-

---

87 Kevin Whelan, *The Tree of Liberty*, p. 172; and Timothy J. O'Keefe, in *Eire-Ireland*, 23 (1988), 68-73.

88 Timothy J. O'Keefe, in *Eire-Ireland*, 27 (1992), 82-83.

89 Anna Kinsella, in *The Mighty Wave*, p. 152; and Thomas Bartlett *et al.*, *Rebellion*, pp. 170, 172.

90 Timothy J. O'Keefe, in *Eire-Ireland*, 27 (1992), pp. 83-84.

larly fitting that a priest and a peasant should stand together united as they stood . . . when they fought side-by-side for faith and fatherland.'[91] The rebellion was commemorated again in 1938 and 1948, and on both occasions Father Patrick Murphy, a Wexford parish priest, did much of the organizing, while Father Kavanagh's interpretation of the rebellion still prevailed.[92] The new Irish state openly adopted what was clearly the orthodox Catholic and nationalist interpretation of the rebellion. In November 1967 de Valera, president of the Irish Republic, accompanied by the Protestant archbishop of Dublin, unveiled a monument to the United Irishmen at the north-east corner of St Stephen's Green in Dublin. Three years later it was blown to pieces by Protestant militants from Ulster.[93] The unity sought for by the United Irishmen remained as elusive as ever, and attempts to evoke their memory still excited political divisions.

As the bi-centenary of the rebellion approached, however, Irish politicians desired to commemorate it on a vast scale, but they were most anxious not to irritate the British or to exacerbate sectarian tensions within Northern Ireland. Peace negotiations were then at a very delicate stage and there was an understandable reluctance not to arouse Protestant sensibilities in Ulster. When, on 24 November 1995, Avril Doyle, a Fine Gael minister, announced plans to commemorate the bi-centenary of the rebellion, she declared:

> Firstly, we must discard the now discredited sectarian version of '98, which was merely a polemical post-rebellion falsification. Secondly, we must stress the modernity of the United Irish project, its forward-looking, democratic dimension, and abandon the outdated agrarian and peasant interpretation. Thirdly, we must emphasize the essential unity of the 1798 insurrection: what happened in Wexford was of a piece with what happened in Antrim and Down.[94]

Two and a half years later, the same points were made by Sile de Valera, a member of Fianna Fail.[95] When the Irish government established a '1798 Commemoration Commission', it issued a mission statement on 10 April 1997 in the following terms:

> 1. To commemorate the ideals of the United Irishmen and the 'fellowship of freedom' that inspired them in 1798.

---

91 John Turpin, '1798, 1898 & the political implications of Sheppard's monuments', *History Ireland*, 6 (1998), 47.

92 Kevin Whelan, *The Tree of Liberty*, p. 172.

93 Timothy J. O'Keefe, in *Eire-Ireland*, 23 (1988), 71-72.

94 Roy Foster, *The Irish Story*, p. 229.

95 *Ibid.*

2. The recognition of the 1798 rebellion as a forward-looking, popular movement aspiring to unity; acknowledging that what happened in Dublin and Wexford was part of what happened in Antrim and Down.
3. Attention should shift from the military aspects of 1798 and be directed towards the principles of democracy and pluralism which the United Irishmen advocated.
4. A focus on the international perspective of the United Irishmen and the enduring links which 1798 forged with America, France and Australia.
5. To acknowledge the Ulster dimension and particularly the contribution of the Presbyterian tradition, with its emphasis on justice, equality and civil liberty.
6. To focus attention on the ideals of the leaders of 1798 which still live in Irish history.[96]

The Irish government retained the services of various historians and they were sent forth on this mission to stress that the rebellion of 1798 had been pluralistic, inclusive, secular and progressive.

The bi-centenary of the rebellion in 1998 undoubtedly presented an opportunity for many scholars to restore the United Irishmen to centre stage, to remind readers of the impact on Irish events of the French Revolution, and to give credit once more to the Protestant rebels of 1798. A flood of scholarly and more popular publications, national and local celebrations, exhibitions, television shows, radio programmes, conferences and touring lecturers sponsored by the Irish government attempted to do full justice to the complex events of 1798. There was an admirable effort to understand the pain as well as the heroism of 1798. There was a commendable determination not to allow the bi-centenary celebrations to be captured by one political and religious tradition in Ireland, as had been the case in 1898. While deeply admiring of this recent scholarly work on Ireland in the 1790s – and while confessing that this essay depends almost entirely on the efforts of modern scholars – I believe that in 1998 contemporary events were still influencing how the rebellion should be interpreted. Liberal-minded Irish Catholic nationalists were, perhaps unconsciously, influenced by the desire to reduce the continuing deep divisions between Ireland and Ulster, between Irish Catholics and Irish Protestants. This laudable ambition has perhaps encouraged some recent scholars to play down the agrarian, sectarian and violent aspects of the rebellion of 1798 and to overstress its political dimensions, and most especially the modernity of the United Irishmen and their forward-looking, pluralistic and democratic aims. Recent scholarship has rescued the rebellion from some of its earlier traducers, but present concerns about the situation in Ulster and satisfaction with recent changes in Ireland have led some historians to allow their admirable political senti-

---

[96] *Ibid.*, pp. 225-26.

ments about present issues to distort their views of the past. Too many of those celebrating the bi-centenary of the Irish rebellion were reverting to a romantic, celebratory style of history in which heroes and villains are identified and lessons for the future are deduced. Surely we must, as historians rather than as political actors, have some qualms when we are told in a recent work of history:

> We must stress the modernity of the United Irish project, its forward looking, democratic dimension, and abandon the outdated agrarian or peasant interpretation. . . . We can use the 1790s as a vision and inspiration for the 1990s. . . . By recovering the real history of the Wexford Republic, we reappropriate a profoundly democratic symbol, and an inspiring example of an effort to construct a representative, secular and pluralistic politics in the island of Ireland. Two hundred years later, it can again serve to encourage us towards that imaginative inclusiveness which the United Irish had identified as being essential to unite Catholic, Protestant and Dissenter.[97]

This may be worthy politics, but it is bad history. We need to remember that the rebellion of 1798 'involved a lethal mixture of idealism, sectarianism, agrarianism, revolutionary organisation, state terrorism, mayhem and massacre'.[98] As historians we need to hear those in the past 'speak', but we must be careful not to place our words and our contemporary concerns into the mouths of those who lived and died more than two hundred years ago.

---

97 Kevin Whelan, in *The Mighty Wave*, ed. Keogh and Furlong, pp. 34-36.

98 Tom Dunne, '1798: Memory, history, commemoration', *Journal of the Wexford Historical Society*, 16 (1996-7), 36. See also Tom Dunne, 'Wexford's Comoradh '98: politics, heritage and history', *History Ireland*, 6 (1998), 49-53.

M. O. Grenby

Rebels Denied a Cause

Fiction, Anti-Jacobinism and the Irish Rebellion

The long-planned Irish rebellion finally broke out in May 1798. Within three months it had been successfully suppressed. Within three years, it had begun to appear in fiction. Over the century that followed, the rebellion became a mainstay of what can loosely be called 'Irish fiction': that is to say, those novels dealing with Irish subjects, whoever may have written them and wherever they may have been published. Certainly, this is how Stephen J. Brown defined the genre in his *Reader's Guide to Irish Fiction* published in 1910, in which are to be found a great many of these novels of the rebellion. They tend to have highly descriptive titles such as *The United Irishman; or, The Fatal Effects of Credulity* (1819) or *The Island of Sorrow* (1903). Brown's concise, if somewhat hasty, summaries of these novels reveal overt political alignments and, sometimes, what Brown considers to be manifest literary failings. In M. L. O'Byrne's uncompromisingly titled *Ill-won Peerages; or, An Unhallowed Union* (1884), for instance, Brown tells us that 'The bias is ultra-nationalist'. D. P. Conyngham's *The O'Mahony, Chief of the Comeraghs* (1879) is 'A vivid picture, though obviously partisan, and marred by some inartistic melodrama.' Mary Damant's *Peggy* (1887) is 'Favourable to "poor deluded peasants"' and 'Thinks little of United Irishmen who are "imbued with the poison of revolutionary principles."'[1] In fact, Brown's discovery of forty-three novels of the Irish rebellion published before 1910 is something of an underestimate. His bibliography is skewed to the decades immediately before its publication, and, for the period before 1829, it has now been superseded by Jacqueline Belanger's internet checklist.[2] Even Belanger's list, though it adds a further ten or so titles, is not absolutely exhaustive.

Essentially, the books listed by Brown, and most of those by Belanger, are of interest primarily to students of the historical novel or of the particu-

---

1 Stephen J. Brown, *A Reader's Guide to Irish Fiction* (London, 1910), pp. 204, 33 and 30.

2 J. Belanger, 'Some Preliminary Remarks on the Production and Reception of Fiction Relating to Ireland, 1800-1829', *Cardiff Corvey: Reading the Romantic Text*, 4 (May 2000). Online: Internet (27 March 2003): <http://www.cf.ac.uk/encap/corvey/articles/cc04_n02.html>

lar authors who wrote them. Lady Caroline Lamb's *Glenarvon*, for example – surely the most notorious novel set amidst the events of 1798, though unaccountably omitted by Brown – remains a fascinating document for anyone interested in Romanticism. Thinly veiling the history of Lamb's relationship with Lord Byron behind a narrative of the rebellion, the novel became an immediate *succès de scandale* when it appeared in 1816. It went through three editions within a matter of weeks, and its remorseless exposé of the author's brief love affair was enough to banish Lamb from polite society for the rest of her short life.[3] But like almost all of the novels listed by Brown and Belanger, *Glenarvon* tells us little about the reaction to the Irish rebellion itself. The narrative revolves around a love-triangle encompassing the leader of the rebels (Byron, as 'Glenarvon'), the leader of the force sent to subdue the rebels (Sir William Lamb, later Viscount Melbourne, Lamb's husband, as 'Lord Avondale'), and – torn between the two – 'Calantha', representing the author. The rebellion fades in and out of the action as required by the love-plot. Lamb's chief desire in *Glenarvon* was to disgrace Byron. Casting him as the leader of the insurgents was a strategy designed simply to attach a deeper opprobrium to him. While Lamb used the rebellion merely as scenery, other novels could enlist it for comic purposes. Brown labelled Frank Mathew's *The Wood of the Brambles* (1896), for example, 'a burlesque '98', with the rebels as 'comic savages', their leaders 'little better than buffoons'.[4] The point is that these are novels which provide the historian with, at best, evidence about how the rebellion was understood and mythologized by the generations which came after, particularly in England. But they offer little to the historian of the rebellion itself, and tell us little of its immediate impact on the British and Irish public.

The same cannot be said, however, of the very first novels of the rebellion. Both *The Infernal Quixote. A Tale of the Day* and *Dorothea; or, A Ray of the New Light* were set extensively, though not exclusively, in the midst of the rebellion. Both were published in London in 1801. They differed from those that would come afterwards on two major counts. First, they described events which were still in the public eye. When they appeared, the ink was scarcely dry on the Act of Union, the legislative response to the rebellion which created the Union parliament from January 1801. The novels were in print even before the conspiracies of Edward Despard and Robert Emmet had begun, and had failed, in 1802 and 1803 respectively.

---

3 See Cy Frost, 'Lady Caroline Lamb', in *The Dictionary of Literary Biography*, 116: 'British Romantic Novelists, 1789-1832', ed. Bradford K. Mudge (Detroit, 1992), pp. 170-76.

4 Brown, *Reader's Guide to Irish Fiction*, p. 29.

These novels, in other words, might almost be thought of as journalism, or a contribution to a public debate, rather than fiction. Second, *The Infernal Quixote* and *Dorothea* did not relegate 'the 1798 uprising to mere background action, come and gone in the space between chapters' as Katie Trumpener wrote of *Glenarvon*, and as was the case with the great majority of the subsequent historical novels of the rebellion.[5] Rather, *Dorothea* and *The Infernal Quixote* were deeply enmeshed in their political context. It is these two characteristics – of contemporaneity and political involvement – which also distinguish them from the Irish 'national tales' which were just coming into vogue as these first novels of the rebellion were appearing. *Castle Rackrent, an Hibernian Tale* (1800), by Maria Edgeworth, and *The Wild Irish Girl; A National Tale* (1806), by Sydney Owenson, Lady Morgan, are generally credited with beginning this new genre. These 'national tales' dealt with Irish nationalism (Owenson's *Wild Irish Girl* and *O'Donnel*, 1814), with contemporary Irish abuses (Edgeworth's *Castle Rackrent* and *The Absentee*, 1809), and even with rebellions (Scott's *Waverley*, 1814, set during the 1745-46 Jacobite uprising, and directly influenced by Edgeworth and Morgan[6]). They did not however match the level of opportune political comment to be found in *The Infernal Quixote* and *Dorothea*. Both of these were novels were written in the immediate aftermath of the rebellion, when writers and readers in Britain were trying to make sense of it, and were still deciding what should be done to rectify the situation.

I.

The Infernal Quixote was written by Charles Lucas (1769-1854), an unremarkable Church of England curate – unremarkable, that is, except for his steady literary output: two long poems, four novels, and a number of pamphlets on various religious questions.[7] While the pamphlets concerned

---

5 Katie Trumpener, *Bardic Nationalism: The Romantic Novel and the British Empire* (Princeton, New Jersey, 1997), p. 333n.61. For an alternative assessment of *Glenarvon*, see Malcolm Kelsall, 'The Byronic Hero and Revolution in Ireland: The Politics of *Glenarvon*', *The Byron Journal*, 9 (1981), 4-19.

6 See Peter Garside, 'Popular Fiction and National Tale: The Hidden Origins of Scott's *Waverley*', *Nineteenth-Century Literature*, 46 (1991), 30-53.

7 Most of what little is known of Lucas's life is to be found in *The Dictionary of National Biography*, although one or two more details will become available in the 'Introduction' to a forthcoming edition of *The Infernal Quixote*, ed. M. O. Grenby (Peterborough, 2004).

themselves with refuting the 'Romish doctrine of Transubstantiation' and with other such theological controversies, the poems roamed a larger territory. The first, Lucas's earliest published work, appearing in 1795, was entitled *The Old Serpentine Temple of the Druids*. It sought to elucidate the purpose of the huge neolithic-era complex of standing stones and artificial earthworks in the midst of which Lucas lived as curate of Avebury, Wiltshire. In verse form, Lucas assented to the opinions of the pioneering antiquarian, William Stukeley, that the Avebury complex had been constructed for the 'druids', priests of a primitive Christian faith. A faith which could have brought into being such an immense stone circle must have been strong indeed, he reasoned, and British Christianity had sadly declined since. Lucas's novels were distinctly more populist. Both *The Castle of St. Donats; or, the History of Jack Smith* (1798) and *The Infernal Quixote* were published by William Lane's Minerva Press, the most famous, most fashionable, and most disreputable publishing house for fiction of its day. Neither novel was especially successful. Although there were French editions in 1803 and 1801 respectively, neither achieved a second London edition, although it should be noted that second editions were rare for the ephemeral, popular novels which were churned out at the rate of about thirty per year from the Minerva Press.[8] Neither *The Castle of St. Donats*, nor Lucas's two last novels – *The Abissinian Reformer, or the Bible and Sabre* (1808) and *Gwelygordd; or, the Child of Sin. A Tale of Welsh Origin* (1820) – shared the Irish theme which loomed so large in *The Infernal Quixote*. Lucas wrote his novel of the 1798 rebellion because it was current, and because he had pressing points to make, not because he was consistently interested in the question of Anglo-Irish relations.

The Infernal Quixote begins with the simultaneous birth of two boys, Lord James Marauder, the nephew of the duke of Silsbury, and Wilson Wilson, the son of a humble village carpenter, his name the result of a slip-up by the vicar (an incident signalling Lucas's desire to be thought of as a novelist in the comic manner of Laurence Sterne). As both grow up, they become rivals, first in country sporting pursuits, then for the favour of the duke, and, most fatally, for the affections of Miss Emily Bellaire. Marauder wins this contest for her love, using the works of Mary Wollstonecraft and other 'new philosophers' to undermine her chastity. Then he cruelly deserts her. The crux of the novel comes when the duke dies and, in contradiction of all expectations, is found to have had a legitimate son. Disappointed of his inheritance of his uncle's title and estate, Marauder

8 See Dorothy Blakey, *The Minerva Press, 1790-1820* (London, 1939).

vows to pursue wealth and power by other means. With Milton's Satan he argues that it is 'Better to reign in hell than serve in heaven', and he allies himself to the cause of the British 'Jacobins', those reformers and radicals who are intent, says Lucas, on bringing revolution to the world.[9] It is Marauder's career as the infernal Quixote, mixing with radicals and planning schemes of political sedition and personal gain, which forms the framework for the remainder of the plot. Wilson, meanwhile, fades from the narrative, only to re-emerge, in the nick of time, to foil Marauder's schemes of rape and insurrection.

It is towards the beginning of the second of *The Infernal Quixote's* four volumes, shortly after his conversion to the Jacobin cause, that one of Marauder's friends 'unfolded to him the plan in agitation to separate Ireland from this country' – Great Britain – 'and the glory, wealth, and power which must necessarily accrue to the daring leaders of the multitude'.[10] Marauder is nominally a Roman Catholic, though he despises religion, and he has large estates in county Tipperary. Tempted by the promise of financial gain, he raises mortgages in London on his Irish estates, certain that 'when we have freed St. Patrick's noble country, we'll wipe out the mortgage, both interest and principal, at the same time'. He then journeys to Ireland.[11] Becoming a captain of the government militia, Marauder also takes the assumed name of M'Ginnis and joins the United Irishmen, the organization behind the rebellion, becoming a colonel in the rebels' underground army. Lucas devoted almost the whole of his third volume to the progress of the rebellion, and his anti-hero's part in it.

The fusion of history and fiction in *The Infernal Quixote* is an impressive feat, and it required a substantial amount of research on Lucas's part. In the introductory chapter of his final novel, *Gwelygordd* (1820), he suggested the principal source he had used. He recalled that he had taken 'the political facts' of the rebellion as they appeared in *The Infernal Quixote* from 'state-papers'.[12] The papers in question were almost certainly the *Report of the Secret Committee of the House of Commons in Ireland*, an account of the rebellion composed from the confessions of some of its leaders made before the Irish parliament in August 1798. On several occasions in *The Infernal Quixote*, Lucas quoted from this publication, or at least from the

9 Charles Lucas, *The Infernal Quixote. A Tale of the Day* (4 vols., London, 1801), ii, 29.

10 Lucas, *Infernal Quixote*, ii, 95-96.

11 Lucas, *Infernal Quixote*, ii, 98.

12 Lucas, *Gwelygordd; or, the Child of Sin. A Tale of Welsh Origin* (3 vols., London, 1820), i, 5.

selection of United Irishmen handbills and pamphlets which were included as an appendix to the report. For instance, when he mocked as ludicrously impracticable a directive that every member of the United Irishmen should wear around his neck a symbolic amulet composed of white silk and multi-coloured ribbons, and adorned with gold lettering, he was directly quoting from a United Irishmen declaration.[13] This said, it is not impossible that Lucas came across this material through an intermediate source. Much of the *Report of the Secret Committee* was repeated in a 'Note' at the end of the final volume of the English translation of the Abbé Augustin Barruel's *Memoirs, Illustrating the History of Jacobinism* (1797-98), an exposé of the conspiracy supposed to lie behind the French Revolution. Ideas from Barruel's treatise certainly crop up repeatedly in *The Infernal Quixote*.

Whatever the publication in which Lucas came across the government account of the rebellion, he apparently accepted it uncritically. Confessions, made to save the deponents from trial and execution, are usually treated with scepticism by many historians. The central theme of the *Report*, repeatedly stressed in the rebels' affidavits, is that the United Irishmen leaders had merely used the constitutional campaign for political reform as a cover for their real, revolutionary and levelling aims. Lucas chose not to disregard such depositions, or at the least did not admit to any doubts, but included them wholesale in his novel:

> The *real intentions* of the Union were only known to the leading members; and, *by their own confessions*, have at length appeared to be (what every rational man from the first supposed) the introduction of that no-principle of the French, which seeks the gratification of its own interest, without any regard to the laws of God or man, and which has already been so fully defined under the term DIABOLISM.[14]

The 'Diabolism' mentioned here was Lucas's own invention. He had previously coined the term to describe all the various categories of reformism and radicalism that he had rather idiosyncratically taxonomized at great length earlier in the novel. But essentially his characterization of the rebellion's motivations came straight from this official, if rather tainted, source.

If Lucas was guilty of taking at face value a very prejudiced construction of the Irish rebellion, and then of contorting it further to fit in with his own rather curious taxonomy of Jacobinism, his appropriation of many of the events, ideas and even the technicalities of the rebellion was surprisingly

---

[13] Lucas, *Infernal Quixote*, iii, 170-75 and note.

[14] Lucas, *Infernal Quixote*, iii, 182.

accurate, both historically and geographically. He went to great pains, for instance, to describe the United Irishmen's 'affiliating system', that is to say its civil and military chain of command, from the Lower Baronial Committees to the General Executive Directory (although it should be noted, once again, that this hierarchical structure was cited in the English editions of Barruel's *Memoirs, Illustrating the History of Jacobinism* as a strong indication of the affinity of the United Irishmen to the Illuminati and freemasons whom Barruel thought were behind the French Revolution).[15] Similarly, he powerfully dramatized the debate at the core of the rebellion: whether the United Irishmen should rise without French assistance, or whether they should wait until the French had effected a landing. In the councils of the United Irishmen, Marauder is the most fiery supporter of an immediate uprising. 'Why should we wait the uncertain coming of the French?', he asks. 'Delay cools our ardour – delay encourages the traitor – delay opens our intentions to the enemy – delay adds to the bulwarks of tyranny – brings with every wind fresh troops from England, and raises more and more obstacles to our success.'[16] Although he receives support from the delegates from Ulster, his views are opposed by the delegates from Leinster and Connaught, and the committee votes for delay. After all, one of Marauder's opponents argues, 'A trusty citizen . . . is about to be sent to France to nogociate [*sic*] a second treaty, and hasten the promised succours' (to which Lucas adds, in parentheses, that 'Edward John Lewins was again sent in April, 1797'). Such a meticulous entwinement of fact and fiction is characteristic of *The Infernal Quixote*. Lucas even boasted, on occasion, that he had provided 'a *literal* and *correct* specimen of the *language*, *sentiments*, and *conduct* of some of the more prominent characters from among the members of the Society of United Irishmen'.[17]

Lucas's description of the events of the rebellion was just as convincing. The presence of Marauder as a rebel leader is often the only detail which reminds us that we are reading fiction, not history. Here, for instance, is an account of the storming of the town of Cahir in southern Tipperary from the historical account of the rebellion written by Thomas Pakenham in 1969:

---

15 Lucas, *Infernal Quixote*, iii, 177-82 and Augustin Barruel, *Memoirs, Illustrating the History of Jacobinism. A Translation from the French of the Abbe Barruel* (4 vols., London, 1797-98), iv, unpaginated 'Note'.

16 Lucas, *Infernal Quixote*, iii, 160.

17 Lucas, *The Infernal Quixote*, iii, 166-67, 161 and 167.

> About one o'clock in the afternoon of March 28th, a body of nearly a thousand country people led by officers dressed in blue and scarlet regimentals, marched into the town of Cahir in Tipperary and, having posted guards at the avenues, proceeded from house to house disarming the inhabitants. They surrounded the house of the local magnate, Lord Cahir, and stripped this too of all its arms. And then, after an address by their commander, warning his men against any deeds of violence, they marched peacefully away again.[18]

The chronology of Lucas's novel tallies perfectly with Pakenham's dating of the attack. Pakenham's suggestion that the officers leading the rebels were commissioned by the government – evidenced by their official uniforms – also conforms to Marauder's treacherous membership of both the militia and the United Irishmen forces. Indeed, Pakenham's account matches in all important regards the description given by Lucas:

> In a little time M'Ginnis [i.e. Marauder] had above a hundred horse under his command, and infantry to a very large amount, armed promiscuously. So strong did he consider himself, that, having arranged his plans with some of his neighbouring Officers, he joined them early in the month of March with a respectable body of cavalry, and invested the town of Cahir, in the county of Tipperary. This he boldly did in the open day; and, with the utmost order and discipline, searched every house for arms and ammunition, and carried the whole away with him.
> In this expedition they mustered a thousand men, well armed, and chiefly horse.[19]

Even the number of rebels matches in these two accounts (although it has been disputed by other historians[20]). It seems unlikely that Lucas had access to the same sources as Pakenham – a letter from Lord Camden to Lord Portland now preserved in the Home Office records – but what is clear is that the novel was firmly based on genuine historical events.

The raid on Cahir notwithstanding, county Tipperary was one of the quietest areas of Ireland during the rebellion. This was not because there was no sympathy for the United Irishmen in the county, but rather because there was too much. Dissent had manifested itself in 1797 and early 1798. Tipperary had consequently been 'proclaimed' on 2 April 1798, that is to say it had been made subject to government legislation against insur-

---

[18] Thomas Pakenham, *The Year of Liberty. The History of the Great Irish Rebellion of 1798* (London, 1969; rpt., 1992), pp. 56-57.

[19] Lucas, *Infernal Quixote*, iii, 265-66.

[20] Contemporary estimates put the figure at between 300 and 800: Thomas P. Power, *Land, Politics and Society in Eighteenth-Century Tipperary* (Oxford, 1993), p. 313. According to William J. Hayes, the raid on Cahir was organized by the Clonmel branch of the United Irishmen, possibly led by one Philip Cunningham. Hayes, *Tipperary In The Year Of Rebellion 1798* (Roscrea, 1998), pp. 36-37.

rection (36 *George III*, c.20). This imposed a curfew and arms searches, and authorized the death penalty for those found guilty of administering illegal oaths. A further notice was issued on 6 April, requiring all stolen arms to be handed in within ten days, or troops would be freely quartered on the population. These decrees had been ruthlessly enforced by Tipperary's sheriff, the notorious Thomas Judkin 'Flogger' Fitzgerald, which is why, historians agree, 'no rebellion of serious proportions manifested itself there in 1798'.[21] This raises the question of why Lucas, who was free to set his novel anywhere in Ireland, chose Tipperary. Two answers seem possible. Either Lucas believed that the recent history of the main sites of rebel activity – Kildare and Wexford – would have been too well known by his readers for him to be able convincingly to introduce Marauder as a fictional rebel leader. Or Lucas may have genuinely believed Tipperary to have been one of the hot-beds of revolt. This impression might have come from the testimony of Thomas Judkin Fitzgerald, who was called on several times during 1799, 1800 and 1801 to defend the extremely severe methods of suppression he had used there. As Thomas Power writes, Fitzgerald 'found it necessary to construe retrospectively the existence of a rebellion in Tipperary in 1798 as a cover for his actions'.[22] Reading accounts of these trials in the newspapers, while he was writing *The Infernal Quixote*, Lucas may have thought Tipperary the perfect setting for his depiction of the rebels' most energetic activities. In either case, Lucas's version of Tipperary history accords very well with the historical reality. Although he introduces Marauder into historical events at the time of the attempted French landing at Bantry Bay in 1796, which Marauder proposed to assist, and keeps him there until the actual French landing, almost two years later, at Killala Bay in August 1798, most of the outrages perpetrated by Marauder occur in the months before the outbreak of the rebellion proper. Although it might have been accomplished with ease, Lucas prevented Marauder from becoming a supreme leader of the rebellion, perpetrating revolutionary outrages throughout 1798. Thus, unlike Lamb's *Glenarvon*, the novel remained within the bounds of historical probability. It was perhaps necessary that this should be the case if Lucas wanted to retain the credence of readers, who might have known these recent events well, and if he wished to persuade them that his interpreta-

21 Power, *Land, Politics and Society*, p. 302. See also Hayes, *Tipperary In The Year Of Rebellion*, p. i.

22 Power, *Land, Politics and Society*, p. 318.

tion of the rebellion was correct. The success of his propaganda rested on his verisimilitude.

Lucas's very firm location of Marauder's activities in Tipperary also serves to distance the character of Marauder from that of the real-life United Irishman leader, Lord Edward Fitzgerald. Otherwise, it would certainly have been natural for readers to associate the two for there were some glaring similarities. Fitzgerald was the son of the duke of Leinster while Marauder was nephew to the fictional duke of Silsbury. Fitzgerald had fought as a loyalist during the American Revolution before being dismissed from the army in 1792 for his vocal support of the French Revolution, and he joined the United Irishmen in 1796. Marauder had converted from the cause of 'aristocracy' to 'democracy' at about the same point in time. Long after publication, Lucas boasted that his characters in *The Infernal Quixote* 'were almost all drawn from the etchings of real life'.[23] He cannot have been unaware of the parallels between Marauder and Fitzgerald, and perhaps he even sought to capitalize on the glamour that might attach itself to a novel which included an anti-hero reminiscent of one of the most notorious characters of the age. On the other hand, the care he took to distinguish between Fitzgerald in Dublin and Marauder in Tipperary argues the opposite: that he was anxious to prevent the admiration which many contemporaries felt for the gallant, charismatic and glamorous Fitzgerald, from attaching itself to Marauder.[24]

II.

In contrast, there could have been no danger that Thomas Williams, Marauder's equivalent in *Dorothea; or, A Ray of the New Light*, would be regarded as glamorous by any of the novel's readers. While Lucas endowed his anti-hero with a certain urbanity and élan, *Dorothea*'s anonymous au-

---

23 Lucas, *Gwelygordd*, i. 5.

24 It is possible that Lucas had another real-life model for Marauder, namely Hervey Montmorency Morres, or Morris (1767-1839), the United Irishmen representative for Tipperary from May 1796 and the commander of a group of rebels in Nenagh, a town in the north-west of the County – precisely where Marauder is reported to have had his estate. Morres had initially fought with the Austrian army against the French Revolution, but switched in 1796 – like Fitzgerald and Marauder – to the rebel cause in Ireland. Like Marauder, he was attached to the United Irishmen general military committee and appointed adjutant-general for the Munster region. Unlike Marauder, he was then put in charge of the assault on Dublin. See Martin O'Dwyer, *A Biographical Dictionary of Tipperary* (Folk Village, Cashel, 1999), pp. 276-77.

thor – probably a Mrs. Bullock[25] – presented Williams as a far more grubby and repugnant villain. Except in the matter of personal charisma, however, Williams is the exact counterpart of Marauder. Precisely like Marauder, Williams adopts the fashionable 'new philosophy' of William Godwin, Mary Wollstonecraft and others, to further his own avaricious and lustful ambitions. Also like Marauder, Williams works towards a revolution on the French model only for reasons of self-aggrandisement:

> An epoch of confusion is, perhaps, the only one in which, circumstanced as I am, I can expect to reach my proper sphere: to me then it is most desirable, and it is a *duty* I owe myself, to lend a hand to the cause which alone is likely to place me where I ought to be.[26]

Inevitably, just as Marauder had done, Williams crosses the Irish Sea to take advantage of the growing spirit of rebellion in Ireland. As Bullock explains, the United Irishmen (though she prefers the terms 'the party' or 'the society') share his rationale exactly:

> These active spirits, with a very few exceptions, were composed of a certain set, who having neither name, fortune, or principles to lose, were willing to take the chance of a scene of confusion; in the belief, that where property is exposed to the scramble, the most agile will be the greatest gainers; more particularly if they are wholly careless through what channel it comes, they laboured, therefore, indefatigably planting the tree of liberty in the mould of discontent, and waiting with impatience the signal to moisten it with human blood . . .[27]

In such company Williams was perfectly at home. Like Marauder, he is quickly admitted to the inner councils of the United Irishmen, advancing to secretary and treasurer so that 'nothing could be done without his concurrence'.[28] In contrast to Marauder, however, he urges delay. Were the

---

25 There is no indication of the authorship of *Dorothea* in the novel itself, although by the pronouns used, it appears that the *narrator* was a woman. A tentative attribution to Mrs. Bullock comes from the first internet update of *The English Novel, 1770-1829: A Bibliographical Survey of Prose Fiction Published in the British Isles*, ed. Peter Garside, James Raven and Rainer Schöwerling (2 vols., Oxford, 2000), the update being by Peter Garside, with Jacqueline Belanger and Anthony Mandal, dated April 2000-May 2001, and available online at:
<http://www.cf.ac.uk/encap/corvey/articles.engov1.html>.
The evidence for Bullock's authorship is a catalogue from the London publishing firm of A. K. Newman from 1814 which ascribes *Dorothea*, along with *Susanna; or, Traits of a Modern Miss*, to this otherwise unknown writer.

26 Mrs. Bullock, *Dorothea; or, A Ray of the New Light* (3 vols., London, 1801), i, 32-33.

27 Bullock, *Dorothea*, ii, 134.

28 Bullock, *Dorothea*, ii, 133.

crisis to be brought to a head, he fears, not only would his personal safety be jeopardized, but the profiteering that has been made so easy under the cover of insurgency would be impossible.

To have an omniscient narrator condemn the rebels as self-serving rogues, and to exhibit the hypocrisy and cowardice of the rebel leaders, were both effective way of denying the rebellion any political legitimacy. The author's use of plot to denigrate the rebellion was also as successful as Lucas's had been, though it adhered less to the historical reality. After having stayed long enough in Dublin to find, marry and abandon a rich heiress, Williams moves to Kilkenny, arriving there sometime in late 1797 or early 1798 (as far as can be discerned from Bullock's rather loose chronology). Political dissatisfaction having 'obtained some footing in Kilkenny', Bullock informs us, 'Williams hoped now to turn to his own benefit'.[29] He achieves this through his discovery that one of the rebels awaiting execution in the gaol at Kilkenny is the son of a wealthy Dublin merchant, who, Williams speculates, will pay handsomely for the boy's deliverance from the gallows. When the rebels are brought onto the scaffold, Williams exerts all his oratorical skills to whip up the crowd into a frenzy. Because they have not suffered as much as other parts of Ireland from the campaigns of the rebels (Bullock is careful to tell us) the crowd responds, demolishing the prison and liberating its inmates. Once free, the convicts embark on a career of destruction and murder. They kill the only man among them who urges them to abandon their radical views and their criminality. Then, aroused further by their leader's Godwinian rhetoric about the evils of inequality and the desirability of the common ownership of property, they pillage a cottage and massacre the happy family which lives there.[30]

Ultimately, it is the chain of events which Williams began at Kilkenny which results in his death. After freeing the convicts, Williams escapes to London. In the early summer of 1798 he returns to Ireland, landing at Waterford. In his absence, he finds that the 'secret committee' of the rebels has also re-located there (because the 'police' are 'less vigilant'), and that the 'society' has become '*completely organised*, and a day actually fixed for a general insurrection'. It is not long before the rising begins, oddly, in Bullock's account, in Waterford rather than neighbouring Wexford, where the principal rebel activity was actually concentrated. 'Misled

29 Bullock, *Dorothea*, ii, 39.

30 Bullock, *Dorothea*, ii, 40-55.

by the terrors which their rising had inspired' and 'intoxicated with the success' of the early stages of the rebellion, Williams forgets his usual caution and 'like the demon of the storm, directed its violence'. Within a very short time, two regiments of English guards arrive, quell the rising and cause the wholesale flight of the rebels. Williams flees with them, taking care to appropriate for himself the remaining funds of the 'society'. Ironically, he is robbed of his money by a party of fleeing rebels, who think he is a government spy. He is only saved from death at the hands of these '*sons of liberty*' by a party of government soldiers which happens by. Williams is left to wander aimlessly in the 'the unwholesome bogs of the country', eating berries, until finally he repents of his rashness. But Bullock has one final ironic plot-twist. Eventually, he is taken in by an old woman who lives alone with her insane daughter who, we learn, is the only remaining member of the family which had been slaughtered by the convicts who had escaped from Kilkenny gaol. Having painfully witnessed the grief he has indirectly caused her, Williams dies when she plunges a knife into his breast, believing him, in her madness, to be about to murder her family.[31]

The rebellion itself, then, receives limited treatment in *Dorothea*. Bullock's commentary on the events of 1798 concentrates on the Kilkenny episode and its consequences. Contemporary prison reports reveal that Kilkenny was notorious for its miserable, dungeon-like prison, but there is no evidence that any such incident as Bullock describes actually took place there during the 1790s.[32] The whole of the county was, in fact, quiet throughout 1798, and was never proclaimed.[33] It seems most likely, in fact, that Bullock borrowed the incident from an account of the escape of six felons from Kilkenny gaol on 16 November 1800, and their subsequent attack on a number of homes. It was an event reported in *The Times* of London, a week later, precisely when we might expect Bullock to have been writing her novel.[34] But Bullock was more concerned with

---

31 Bullock, *Dorothea*, iii, 114, 115-16, 120, 123 and 131.

32 Rev. F. Archer's prison report (BL Add. Mss. 35,920, ff.1-6), quoted in Pakenham, *Year of Liberty*, p. 279.

33 The only hint of rebellion came in July, at the tail-end of the rising, when some miners from Castlecomer briefly joined rebels fleeing from their defeat in neighbouring County Wexford. L. M. Cullen, 'The Social and Economic Evolution of Kilkenny in the seventeenth and eighteenth centuries', pp.273-88 in *Kilkenny: History and Society. Interdisciplinary Essays on the History of an Irish County*, ed. William Nolan and Kevin Whelan (Dublin, 1990), pp.273-88.

34 *The Times*, 24 Nov. 1800, p. 3b.

the emblematic significance of these events than with their historical authenticity. This is why a more important source is probably William Godwin's 1794 novel *Things as They Are; or, the Adventures of Caleb Williams*. In Godwin's politically radical novel, the eponymous hero (who, it might be noted, shares his surname with the anti-hero of *Dorothea*) escapes from a prison in which he has been unjustly confined and finds refuge with a gang of thieves. Godwin used these outlaws as mouthpieces for the debate on political justice that he conducts throughout the novel. The thieves justify their crimes on the basis of the inequality of society, for instance, and rationally discuss and decide on a new set of moral rules for their behaviour in a world where justice is always subordinate to power. Bullock subtly mimics this in *Dorothea*. As in Godwin's novel, Bullock's escapees rationally debate what course of action they should take. Their leader, whose eloquence and deployment of Godwinian ideas identifies him to be a travesty of Mr. Raymond, the leader of the bandits in *Caleb Williams*, carries the day with these arguments:

> Are we not taught as a first principle, that human beings are partakers of a common nature? what conduces to the good and benefit of one man, will conduce to the good and benefit of another; hence it follows, upon the rules of impartial justice, that the good things of the world are a common stock, upon which one man has as valid a title as another, to draw for what he wants: I have a right to the means of subsistence, *and the commencement of my right should be the limit of his*. Look around ye, then, are there not at that house evident marks of the barbarous and unjust system of accumulation; mark the swelling pride of the corn-rick, the cattle, the poultry; carry your ideas to his loaded granaries; is not the possessor glutted with abundance, whilst we faint with hunger? can all these things be necessary for individual consumption? assuredly not; and public justice demands that we should participate![35]

The first part of this speech is drawn almost verbatim from the *Enquiry Concerning Political Justice* (1793), Godwin's great philosophical treatise which *Caleb Williams* was designed to dramatize through its fiction. What Bullock has artfully done is silently to alter the lesson drawn from the proposition that 'the good things of the world are a common stock'. Whereas the convict in *Dorothea* uses Godwin's philosophical position as the justification for theft and murder, Godwin himself had been careful to acknowledge that each individual had the right to partake in life's goods and pleasures only if this did not cause injury to himself (or her-

[35] Bullock, *Dorothea*, ii, 50-51.

self) or to others.[36] The massacre that derives from the convicts' sophistry in *Dorothea*, 'too revolting' to be described, amply proves the wickedness of Williams' rabble-rousing, and, by extension Bullock hopes, the iniquity of Godwin's political philosophy.

III.

This blood-spattered episode from *Dorothea* was clearly designed to prevent any possibility of sympathy for the rebel cause. What it also demonstrates is that Bullock's novel, however closely intertwined it was with recent events in Ireland, was also an anti-Jacobin novel of the sort which was flourishing in Britain in the late 1790s and early 1800s. As many as fifty of these novels were published in Britain during the crisis engendered by the French Revolution.[37] Very few of these loyalist novels made direct reference to Irish affairs, even though the greater number of them appeared in the years immediately after the rebellion. The majority of authors preferred to set their fiction in the revolutionary events in France, or to depict the agents, and effects, of Paineite, Wollstonecraftian or Godwinian 'new philosophy' in mainland Britain (as had been the case with Lucas's earlier, and more prototypical anti-Jacobin novel, *The Castle of St. Donats*). *Dorothea* – and *The Infernal Quixote* – did this too. Large parts of both novels were set in England, Williams and Marauder both beginning and ending their careers of radicalism there. Indeed, in *The Infernal Quixote*, Lucas gleefully opened up to inspection the workings of a radical debating society, probably meant to represent the London Corresponding Society, and a secret organization, meant to stand for the 'Illuminati', as well as the United Irishmen.[38] *Doro-*

36 The full passage from *Political Justice* runs thus: 'Human beings are partakers of a common nature; what conduces to the benefit or pleasure of one man will conduce to the benefit or pleasure of another. Hence it follows, upon the principles of equal and impartial justice, that the good things of the world are a common stock, upon which one man has as valid a title as another to draw for what he wants. It appears in this respect, as formerly it appeared in the case of our claim to the forbearance of each other, that each man has a sphere the limit and termination of which is marked out be the equal sphere of his neighbour. I have the right to the means of subsistence; he has an equal right. I have a right to every pleasure I can participate without injury to myself or others; his title in this respect is of similar extent.' William Godwin, *An Enquiry Concerning Political Justice*, ed. Isaac Kramnick (Harmondsworth, 1985), p. 703.

37 For more on anti-Jacobin novels see Marilyn Butler, *Jane Austen and the War of Ideas* (1975; rpt. Oxford, 1987), pp. 88-123; and M. O. Grenby, *The Anti-Jacobin Novel. British Conservatism and the French Revolution* (Cambridge, 2001).

38 Lucas, *Infernal Quixote*, ii, 194-208 and 335-44.

thea and *The Infernal Quixote* were, in other words, fairly standard anti-Jacobin novels which stand out mainly for their recitation and invalidation of the proceedings of the Irish rebellion.

It is possible to view Bullock's and Lucas's incorporation of the Irish rebellion into mainstream anti-Jacobin fiction simply as an attempt to inject some variety into the form, to find a fresh theatre for the standard denigration of radicalism. After all, these were novels as well as propaganda, and the demand of the proverbial patrons of the circulating library for the new and the evermore shocking was something which most writers of fiction (and especially of gothic novels) openly admitted and attempted to satisfy.[39] The weaving together of the Irish and anti-Jacobin strands however was also a more deliberately strategic act. In essence, what the anti-Jacobin campaign as a whole was attempting to do was to unify into one single entity all forms of radicalism, no matter how disparate they actually were. The idea was to combine the insurgency of the French revolutionaries, the political and religious iconoclasm of Paine, the supposed sedition of the corresponding and constitutional reform societies, the rational utopianism of Godwin, the sexual license of Wollstonecraft (primarily as transmitted through Godwin's *Memoirs of the Author of the Rights of Woman*), and even sometimes the parliamentary opposition of the Foxites and the religious enthusiasm of Methodists and Evangelicals, all into one giant, hydra-headed conspiracy. Barruel's outlandish conspiracy theory, bringing together freemasons, *philosophes*, the Illuminati and the French revolutionaries into an unlikely axis of iniquity, was only the most blatant manifestation of the anti-Jacobin determination to create unity of purpose out of the almost infinitely ramified reform campaign. The reasons for such a tactic are clear. First, it made the threat to the *status quo* seem that much more dangerous. An underground and concerted conspiracy has always been a more worrying prospect than any number of lone individuals or isolated groupings. Second, to argue that all these radical causes were aligned, and centrally organized with the single aim of undermining all legitimate government, hierarchy and religion, was to invalidate each of their separate campaigns – for fairer political representation, improved education for women, the abolition of the Test and Corporation Acts, and all the other individual radical causes.

---

39 For the connection between anti-Jacobinism and the gothic see James Watt, *Contesting the Gothic. Fiction, Genre and Cultural Conflict, 1764-1832* (Cambridge, 1999), especially pp. 42-69.

In *Dorothea* and *The Infernal Quixote*, Bullock and Lucas were deliberately drawing the Irish rebels into this Jacobin consortium. This effectively undermined the validity of the rebellion as a political movement with its own agenda, making it just another manifestation of the overall Jacobin conspiracy. It was, of course, a travesty of the actual nature of the Rebellion. The Society of United Irishmen could, perhaps, be considered as a product of an international community of radicals. They embarked, at least initially, upon a campaign for constitutional reform which paralleled that taking place in England; they developed links with the French revolutionaries through Theobald Wolfe Tone, Edward John Lewins and others; and they had certainly been inspired in the early 1790s by the writings of Thomas Paine, whose rhetoric was often echoed in their early manifestos. By the middle of the decade, however, the campaign of political radicalism had been augmented by other discontented groups, notably the older bands of Defenders. As a result, long-standing religious, economic and localized grievances had become alloyed with the original non-sectarian United Irishmen campaign, and by 1795 it could hardly be said that the rebels were following a fixed, pre-mediated and internationalist Jacobin agenda. Indeed, when the rebellion broke out, it was characterized more by 'petty-Jacquerie' than any attempt to instigate revolution on the French model. And yet, Lucas and Bullock steadfastly portrayed the rebellion as another manifestation of the Jacobinism infesting France and Britain.

Moreover, however Paineite the early manifestos of the United Irishmen might have been, nowhere did the United Irishmen pamphlets and proclamations use Godwinian rhetoric or propose a programme of Godwinian social, economic or sexual reform. Yet as we have seen, Bullock happily made her escaped convicts in *Dorothea* thoroughgoing adherents of *Political Justice*. She even has Williams construct the rebellion in Rousseauist terms. He only supports the United Irishmen, he explains, because he has 'beheld with anguish how much men must endure before they can return to that blissful state of nature and equality from which their steps have been so widely perverted'.[40] Viewed in this light, the Rerellion became the result of the 'new philosophy', not the United Irishmen's earlier reformist programme nor even of the Defenders' sectarian and socio-economic protests. As we have already seen, the Irish rebels also became just another manifestation of Jacobinism in *The Infernal Quixote*. Lucas characterized them as 'diabolists', seeking only 'the introduc-

---

40 Bullock, *Dorothea*, ii, 160-61.

tion of that no-principle of the French'.[41] Marauder and Williams, gliding smoothly back and forth between the English new philosophers and the Irish rebels, make the point very clear. For Lucas and Bullock, the Jacobins on either side of the Irish Sea are indistinguishable, all of them being out simply to further their own ambitions and desires. It was a strategy cleverly designed to nullify the specific grievances of the Irish rebels, and to reconstruct the rebellion in a form that was more vulnerable to British derision and disdain.

The second reason for showing the Irish rebellion as having been rooted in a 'new philosophy' which could be found equally as easily in London as Dublin was to emphasize the immediacy of the Jacobin threat to the novels' readers. By preventing British readers from thinking that the rebellion had been the result of specifically Irish grievances, and by showing that the same forces which had brought revolution to Ireland were also active in England, Lucas and Bullock were warning that insurrection was a very real prospect for the mainland too. Almost all anti-Jacobin novels sought to make this very point. What Lucas and Bullock had hit upon, however, was a new way of showing that the 'new philosophy' of Godwin, was far from being a harmless set of opinions, and that it actually posed a grave danger to state and society. In their version of events, it was precisely this kind of radical thought which lay behind an insurrection which had almost been successful in Ireland. If unchecked, this 'new philosophy' could precipitate a similar catastrophe on the mainland. It matters little that, with hindsight, we can see that the Jacobin danger had largely passed by 1801, with the radical societies having collapsed under pressure from government legislation and loyalist sentiment, and from the major radical figures having died or been forced into either exile or silence. What is important is that many writers still believed that there was a pressing need for conservative propaganda, and that Lucas and Bullock had found a way of bringing a sense of urgency to their novels which was lacking from those produced by many of their anti-Jacobin allies.

Indeed, when read in the context of other anti-Jacobin novels, what distinguishes both *Dorothea* and *The Infernal Quixote* is their anxiety to demonstrate the immediacy of the Jacobin threat. Bullock justified the politicization of her novel on the basis that it was very timely. She wrote at the beginning of *Dorothea*:

---

41 Lucas, *Infernal Quixote*, iii, 182.

> When our reformers of the present day set out in the career of destruction, overturning all those barriers which experience and wisdom have been for ages erecting and repairing is it not time to shew the deluded victims of modern philosophy, that whilst they open the door to the *new light*, conjugal peace, filial affection, retiring grace, and every feminine virtue shrinking from the blaze, take that moment to depart, never more, alas! to return.[42]

Lucas also sought to alarm his readers. His inclusion of detailed descriptions of a meeting of the Illuminati and of a radical debating society, although they were partly comic in intent, was surely supposed to make his readers ask themselves what was going on behind closed doors in London. In just the same way, his minute description of the United Irishmen, and his inclusion of so many quotations from genuine rebel documents, seemed perfectly designed to blur the boundary between fiction and reality, and to alert his readers that he was describing a rebellion which had only just fallen short of success.

Lucas's determination to alarm his readers about the proximity of insurrection even drove him to veer away from the impression of historical reality, which he was generally so anxious to cultivate. He ends his third volume by having his hero, Wilson, suddenly appear, after an absence of a volume and a half, at the head of a troop of government soldiers, to confront Marauder at the head of a body of rebels. Their personal combat is won by Wilson, against the odds. Defeated, Marauder flees Ireland. If not entirely swept along by the action, one notices that Lucas has silently reordered events here so that Wilson's victory over Marauder in Ireland can become emblematic of the turn of the tide in the war between the insurgents and the state. Their duel, Lucas tells us, occurs just after the French had landed at Killala Bay, which happened on 22 August 1798.[43] In fact, by the time the French landed at Killala in the north-west, the rebellion was all but over, not only in Tipperary and the south, but throughout the country. To all intents and purposes, the battle of Vinegar Hill, west of Wexford, on 21 July, had been the rebels' last stand, and the government had won a comprehensive victory. Lucas makes no mention of this state of affairs. He presents Marauder as confident that the victory of his rebel group will precede a rendezvous with the French, and the certain victory of the uprising. Lucas doubtlessly telescoped events partly for literary reasons. The duel between Wilson and Marauder on the field of battle would provide an even more fitting climax to volume three if the fate of the re-

---

42 Bullock, *Dorothea*, i, 1-2.

43 Lucas, *Infernal Quixote*, iii, 337.

bellion were still in the balance. But there was also a propagandistic purpose to be served by reshuffling events like this. Suggesting that a successful rebellion had been averted only at the eleventh hour, and by the heroism of an individual, emphasized the lucky escape Ireland had had. By extension, it showed Lucas's readers how easily Britain might succumb to revolution too. This was writing designed to provoke readers into action. Even if a rebellion had been defeated this time, Lucas was suggesting, the nation still had to be on its guard against the Jacobin menace, for the timely intervention of a hero such as Wilson could not always be relied upon.

Although anti-Jacobin fiction aimed to alarm the readers, it could be counter-productive, in propaganda terms, to exaggerate the strength of the Jacobins and to overestimate the threat to Britain. Both Lucas and Bullock knew this and used their novels to reassure their readers at the same time as they warned them of their danger. Simply to show Godwinian 'new philosophy' and the Irish rebellion to be nothing more than a cover for the conventional lechery, covetousness and malice of men like Marauder and Williams was to comfort readers with the knowledge that they were not facing a legitimate political threat. But both Lucas and Bullock went further, dissecting the Jacobin menace, laying it open to inspection, and thereby reassuring their readers that it was not inevitable that the nation would succumb to the danger. The most celebrated example of this is Lucas's 83-page taxonomy of Jacobinism, an exhaustive, sardonic analysis of all the many classifications and sub-classifications of radicalism which he thought were present in Britain in the 1790s. To describe and explain all the manifestations of Jacobinism, Lucas evidently thought, was to disable it. This was a strategy which also underpinned much of the rest of the anti-Jacobin campaign, notably the new conservative periodicals such as the *British Critic* (from 1793) and the *Anti-Jacobin Review* (from 1798). Lucas was using the same technique when he laid bare in all its detail the organizational structure of the United Irishmen. The intention was simultaneously to shock and to soothe, to expose the extent of the danger but to avoid dismay by showing that the danger had been perceived, exposed, anatomized and therefore neutralized.

This same intention, simultaneously to frighten and comfort the reader, explains what was perhaps the most surprising part of Lucas's description of the rebellion: his apparent criticism of the United Irishmen leadership for not organizing the rising as well as might have been expected. He has Marauder criticize the United Irishmen's tactics on several occasions. Why are rebel newspapers such as the *Union Star* and *The Press* used to publicize the cause, he demands, complaining that 'They betray the public cause, by alarming the Government . . . anticipate our measures, and put our adversaries on their guard'.[44] And why, he asks, in the run up to the general rising, have 'fears for the fate of their imprisoned friends' – United Irishmen captured by the government – 'prevented any bold stroke', when it is known that there must be sacrifices made if the rebellion is to succeed?[45] This disclosure of the strategic miscalculations and pusillanimity of the rebels was meant to hearten panicky readers. But the author's commiseration with his anti-hero about the shortcomings of the rebel leadership was concurrently designed to show just how narrow an escape Ireland had had, and that it was the rebels themselves who had scuppered their own chances of success. If Marauder's ambitions 'seemed to meet with no check but from the timidity of his own party', and if neither the government nor the army could take credit for having prevented a revolution, then there was real cause for concern.[46]

Bullock faced the same problem of how to de-legitimize the rebellion at the same time as showing it to be a pressing danger. In specific terms, she had to answer the question of why the rebellion had been able to attract so many supporters that it posed a significant threat, and yet was not a legitimate outburst of popular discontent. She came up with several solutions. One tactic was simply to profess amazement that the Irish could be so senseless as to join with the rebels. 'When future ages shall look back with unprejudiced eyes' on the benevolent monarch, the prosperity, and the exemplary judicial system, of the age, Bullock wrote rather archly, 'will they not think the historian is relating an improbable fiction, who adds to these annals the history of that mad and republican spirit which roamed amongst the multitude in the years 1794 and 1795?'[47] A second tactic was to suggest that the crowd could not help itself, having been stirred-up by a rabble-rouser such as Williams.[48] Her third, and most subtle tactic was to blame the United Irishmen for manufacturing their own support-base by insidious and underhand means. Every so often, she re-

---

44 Lucas, *Infernal Quixote*, iii, 164.

45 Lucas, *Infernal Quixote*, iii, 312.

46 Lucas, *Infernal Quixote*, iii, 267.

47 Bullock, *Dorothea*, ii, 154-55.

48 William's rabble-rousing speech, which incites the Kilkenny crowd to storm the gaol, is once again silently lifted almost word-for-word from Godwin's *Enquiry Concerning Political Justice*. Bullock, *Dorothea*, ii, 40-43.

vealed, the United Irishmen executive would send a member of the movement on an embassy, bearing 'sealed documents sufficient for his conviction'. The oblivious agent would then be informed upon by his superiors, who would 'make use of his seizure, trial, and execution, to open the way for a torrent of declamation' and would spread 'Pamphlets and paragraphs . . . with unceasing assiduity', so that amongst the susceptible population 'a spirit of murmuring was often thus engendered by the very means taken to crush it; means, to which government had been driven by the manoeuvres of the party itself'.[49] By pointing out these devious attempts to inspire anti-authoritarian rancour, Bullock was warning her readers to be on their guard against the cunning deceits of the opponents of good order. At the same time, she was offering reassurance, since the fact that the rebellion could only garner support through the use of such furtive tactics testified to the weakness of their cause.

Above all, what Bullock, and Lucas, were trying to do was to minimize the role of ordinary people, with their material distress, in the rebellion. As Bullock and Lucas interpreted events, those who flocked to the rebels' standard were merely dupes, roused into rebellion by the artful oratory and strategies of leaders like Marauder and Williams. For a British audience reading these novels, the lesson was clear. The rebellion was not the genuine expression of popular suffering, but simply the work of a few selfish, licentious and avaricious individuals who were using the language of international Jacobinism to mask their vices and to trick a susceptible population into discontent and mutiny. Beyond this, both writers developed several rather sophisticated means of solving a significant anti-Jacobin dilemma: how to alarm Britons about the possibility of insurrection without admitting that the rebel cause had the cogency or committed support which could ever lead to a successful revolution. The 'Irishness' of these two novels was a key part of this strategy. Ireland was close enough, in both geographical and cultural terms, to alarm Britons about their danger, but far enough away to buoy up patriotic convictions that the institutions and affluence of the mainland must always preclude the frenzy of revolution. Given that many argued that a union of the three kingdoms would enable Ireland to benefit from British institutions and would foster wealth there, these two novels might also be seen as quiet advocates for the Act of Union. Viewed from one perspective, then, *The Infernal Quixote* and *Dorothea* were the first of a long series of historical novels depicting the Irish rebellion. From another, they are an important

---

[49] Bullock, *Dorothea*, ii, 136.

part of the 'war of ideas', carefully crafted reactions to the events of 1798 which sought to construct the rebellion in the way that would most surely prevent its repetition on the mainland.

Gordon Pentland

The French Revolution, Scottish Radicalism and the 'People Who Were Called Jacobins'

Henry Cockburn's *Memorials* contain one of the best-known and oft-quoted characterizations of the impact on Scotland of revolution in France: 'Everything rung, and was connected with the Revolution in France'.[1] Cockburn went on, however, to illustrate the complexity of this impact, suggesting that the notion that the revolution had created many Scottish Jacobins was largely the result of the rhetorical tactic of the government that was designed to stifle all opposition:

> Jacobinism was a term denoting everything alarming and hateful, and every political objector was a Jacobin. No innovation, whether practical or speculative, consequently no political or economic reformer, and no religious dissenter, from the Irish Papist to our own native Protestant Seceder, could escape from this fatal word.[2]

Cockburn, therefore, highlighted both the diversity of reformist opinion which existed in Scotland in the 1790s and the inadequacy of following loyalist propaganda in trying to label reformers of every hue as creatures of an imported French ideology.

The subsequent historiography has gone a long way to delineate the real nature of Scottish radicalism in the 1790s. Whig historians such as W. L. Mathieson and Henry Meikle echoed Cockburn's lofty claims for the impact of revolution and interpreted it as an indispensable catalyst in the political 'awakening' of Scotland. Mathieson described those artisans 'whose long and wholesome slumbers had been broken by the Tocsin of Paris'. He did, however, add a caveat, suggesting that the idea that 'democracy in Scotland was an importation from France' was true only insofar as investigation was limited to politics, conventionally understood.[3] It was the publication of E. P. Thompson's monumental *The Making of the English Working Class* that encouraged historians to investigate the indigenous traditions and ideologies that might have informed Scottish radicalism.[4] The Scottish story,

---

1 Henry Cockburn, *Memorials of his Time* (Edinburgh, 1856), p. 80.

2 *Ibid.*, p. 82.

3 Henry Meikle, *Scotland and the French Revolution* (Glasgow, 1912); W. L. Mathieson, *Church and Reform in Scotland: A History from 1797 to 1843* (Glasgow, 1916), pp. 2, 125.

4 E. P. Thompson, *The Making of the English Working Class* (London, 1963).

for which Thompson appealed in his preface, was told by John Brims, who, while still investigating the British context and wider universalist aims of Scottish radicals, emphasized the indigenous nature of their experience. In particular, Brims identified a radical discourse in the Scottish traditions of Covenanting and religious dissent.[5]

The primacy of this religious basis for Scottish radicalism has received recent and eloquent support in a study of the politics of Robert Burns. In seeking to return Burns to his proper 'contexts' and to prove that there was 'more to his political writings than either lower-class spleen or fashionable French extremism', Liam McIlvanney has emphasized the role of both rational 'New Licht' Presbyterianism and a culture of Covenanting and Buchananite civic humanism in Burns's political education.[6] Such detailed case studies confirm the point made by Mark Philp, that the diversity of ideologies and the dynamic nature of events in the 1790s meant radicals tended to proffer 'highly individual and eclectic responses, rather than a pattern of simple conformity to a creed'.[7]

Another prominent language used by Burns when expressing political sentiments was the pan-British discourse of Whig constitutionalism, the eighteenth-century critique of 'Old Corruption' and the betrayal of the principles of 1688.[8] It is the prominence of this language which should perhaps prompt historians to look more closely at the British context of Scottish radicalism. One approach to this can be found in Elaine McFarland's comparative study of the Scottish and Irish experiences that makes a case for an 'ideological community' between the two and the subsequent impact on the Scottish movement of ideological and organizational imports from Ireland and the continent.[9] The wider British context can help to shed light on Scottish radicalism. In the 1790s radicalism existed throughout the British Isles for the first time. Crucially, contact between Scottish, English and

---

5 J. D. Brims, 'The Scottish Democratic Movement in the Age of the French Revolution', unpublished Ph.D. thesis (University of Edinburgh, 1983); J. D. Brims, 'The Covenanting Tradition and Scottish Radicalism in the 1790s' in *Covenant, Charter and Party: Traditions of Revolt and Protest in Modern Scottish History*, ed. Terry Brotherstone (Aberdeen, 1989), pp. 50-62.

6 Liam McIlvanney, *Burns the Radical: Poetry and Politics in Late Eighteenth-Century Scotland* (East Linton, 2002), p. 7.

7 Mark Philp, 'The fragmented ideology of reform' in *The French Revolution and British Popular Politics*, ed. Mark Philp (Cambridge, 1991), p. 54.

8 McIlvanney, *Burns the Radical*, pp. 24-8.

9 E. W. McFarland, *Ireland and Scotland in the Age of Revolution: Planting the Green Bough* (Edinburgh, 1994).

Irish radicals was close, if a little erratic, and it is not difficult to discern a British dynamic to radicalism in the 1790s, the various 'national' movements having their particular considerations, ideologies and agendas shaped, to an extent, by the British situation. In this context British radicals appealed most prominently to a common language, a 'constitutional idiom' largely based on interpretations of the Glorious Revolution of 1688-89 and earlier periods of British history; an idiom which has been explored by historians such as James Epstein when working on the English context. Less a coherent ideology than a reservoir of concepts and practices, the appeal to popular constitutionalism allowed radicals to claim an alternative British patriotism to that espoused by the government and found in loyalist propaganda.[10]

The historiography thus makes it clear that those 'people who were called Jacobins' appealed to a number of different languages and ideologies, a fact which makes simple characterizations of the movement impossible. This essay will seek first to provide an overview of Scottish radicalism in the 1790s in the form of a narrative which will highlight the dynamic nature of the Scottish, British and international political contexts in which radicals operated. It will then investigate the ideological bases of Scottish radicalism and suggest how different justifications for political reform interacted with one another to create idiosyncratic syntheses.

I.

In investigating the origins of Scottish radicalism a necessary distinction must be made between popular political activity and genuine radical politics. The existence and vitality of the former in eighteenth-century Scotland has been established by Christopher Whatley and Kenneth Logue, who have successfully questioned the 'orthodoxy of passivity' previously applied to the period. Much of the social discontent they identify was of an essentially conservative type, based on communitarian notions of the 'moral economy'.[11] Within traditions of religious protest and dissent, however, we can detect ideologies which could have directly informed radicals in the 1790s.

---

10 J. A. Epstein, 'The Constitutional Idiom: Radical Reasoning, Rhetoric and Action in Early Nineteenth-Century England', *Journal of Social History*, 23 (1990), 553-74.

11 Kenneth J. Logue, *Popular Disturbances in Scotland, 1780-1815* (Edinburgh, 1979); C. A. Whatley, 'How Tame were the Scottish Lowlanders during the Eighteenth Century?' in *Conflict and Stability in Scottish Society, 1700-1850*, ed. T. M. Devine (Edinburgh, 1989), pp. 1-30.

The issue of lay patronage in particular has been conceived of as an indigenous tradition of crucial importance. Patronage was, of course, a theological concern, but it comprehended important social and political issues as well. Calls for the popular election of ministers had broad support not only within the Church of Scotland, but also among the members of the various Secession churches which had left the establishment during the eighteenth century mainly over the issue of lay patronage. Implicit in opposition to the practice was the idea of the people questioning from below decisions taken by the elite, and, as such, Brims has suggested that the right to elect both church ministers and MPs was determined by answers given to the same questions.[12] The conceptual link between the two issues is rendered more apparent by the fact that, especially after 1780, some writers were combining arguments for the popular election of ministers and for the reform of the electoral system in the same pamphlets and letters. It is significant that, in the context of the American Revolution and the writings of Thomas Paine, pastoral election was also increasingly being invoked as a natural right rather than one divinely held by the people.[13]

Church patronage was not the only religious issue with important socio-political ramifications – the notion of Covenanting as a basis for reformist claims has also received some attention. The idea that the godly community could associate to further objectives that might challenge the state and the political elite is clearly a political theology with important implications for a study of radicalism. The Moderate movement's preoccupation with order led to a rejection of the practice of Covenanting as disruptive and chaotic, but such elite disapproval could not eradicate its potency among the people. Richard Finlay has suggested that the popular currency of Covenanting ideas ensured the perpetuation of the concept of an elect nation as an aspect of Scottish identity throughout the eighteenth century.[14] In literature, Covenanters retained an important presence, and the evangelical revival from the second half of the eighteenth century was accompanied by the publishing and reprinting of large numbers of Covenanting texts. Most prominent and popular among these was John Howie's *Biographia Scoticana* (or *Scots Worthies*) which first appeared in

---

12 Brims, 'The Scottish Democratic Movement', pp. 42-5.

13 Dalphy I. Fagerstrom, 'Scottish Opinion and the American Revolution', *William and Mary Quarterly*, 3rd series, 11 (1954), 268.

14 R. J. Finlay, 'Keeping the Covenant: Scottish National Identity' in *Eighteenth Century Scotland: New Perspectives*, ed. T. M. Devine and J. R. Young (East Linton, 1999), pp. 121-33.

1775. Such ventures were supported by an oral and folk culture which transmitted an understanding of Covenanting that would be exploited by Burns and Scott well into the nineteenth century. As an ideology, Covenanting had a strong historical basis from which it could draw its lessons and its martyrs, and a developed political theology in the works of Buchanan, Rutherford and Shields, which, most alarmingly for the authorities, delineated a theory of justified resistance. Institutionally, Covenanting was kept alive by the Secessionist churches and was conceptually linked to the patronage issue, since patronage was always apt to be denounced as a betrayal of the Covenanting heritage. Within these churches, a debate had been raging since the 1740s over the issue of Covenanting allegiance to the British government. According to Colin Kidd, this initiated 'a newer breed of radicals who emerged in the wake of the French Revolution to a deep-laid indigenous critique of the British state'. [15] Certainly, Seceders would figure prominently among the radicals of the 1790s, but we should remain wary of oversimplifying the link between religious and political dissent, especially given the fact that both of the Secession churches and the Reformed Presbytery openly repudiated the link.

Whereas Scottish religion promoted ideas that might inform a radical critique of the state, Scotland had little in the way of a tradition of reform or radical politics on which to draw. Undoubtedly, there had been a political element to the successful resistance offered to a limited measure of Catholic relief in 1778.[16] Scots, however, had been necessarily hostile to John Wilkes's xenophobic defence of English liberties, and were lukewarm when approached by Christopher Wyvill to join his campaign for economical reform. Scotland did, however, develop something of a domestic reform movement after 1782 based on the opposition politics which had been evident, if not prominent, in Scotland's response to the American Revolution.[17]

A moderate case for reform of Scotland's royal burghs was eloquently advanced by Thomas McGrugar's pseudonymous *Letters of Zeno*, which

15 Colin Kidd, 'Conditional Britons: The Scots Covenanting Tradition and the Eighteenth-century British State', *English Historical Review*, 117 (2002), 1168.

16 R. K. Donovan, *No Popery and Radicalism: Opposition to Roman Catholic Relief in Scotland, 1778-82* (London, 1987); E. C. Black, 'The Tumultuous Petitioners: The Protestant Associations in Scotland 1778-1780', *Review of Politics*, 25 (1963), 83-211.

17 W. Hamish Fraser, *Scottish Popular Politics: From Radicalism to Labour* (Edinburgh, 2000), pp. 7-8.

appeared in the *Caledonian Mercury* at the end of 1782.[18] By 1784 a committee of Edinburgh citizens had organized a national convention of burgh reformers which initially attracted delegates from half of Scotland's sixty-six royal burghs, and by 1785 could boast representatives from fifty-three.[19] The movement was moderate, advocating the political participation in municipal affairs by propertied and intelligent citizens, and pointedly excluding what McGrugar termed 'the dregs of the populace'. The convention prepared two bills to reform the peculiar problems of the Scottish burghs. The first aimed at reforming abuses in the internal government of the burghs, particularly the near ubiquitous practice of self-election which had been introduced by a statute of 1469. The fact that town councils elected their successors and thus perpetuated power in the hands of a small oligarchy was seen as the cause of much of the financial mismanagement and peculation that was carried on at the expense of the rest of the burgh communities. It was also the chief foundation of the reformers' other complaint, the manner in which the royal burghs returned MPs. This was done by the self-elected town councils themselves, all, with the exception of Edinburgh, being grouped into 'districts' of several burghs to return a single MP. In anticipation of Pitt's promised reform motion in 1785, the burgh reformers chose to pursue only their first object. A measure of the anti-reform sentiments of Scotland's MPs was that the movement eventually had to appeal to Richard Brinsley Sheridan, the Irish playwright and politician, sitting for an English constituency, to become the parliamentary spokesman for the movement. He presented petitions and motions for reform between 1787 and 1792, all of which were easily defeated in parliament, not least by the skilful management of Henry Dundas.[20]

A movement similarly influenced by the demand for redress of grievances in England was that which aimed at amending Scotland's county franchise. The franchise itself had been fixed by an act of 1681 which conferred it upon those 'enfeft in property or superiority' to a certain value. It was this crucial phrase which allowed lawyers, by a variety of means, to create votes on the basis of superiority over land alone, and convey this superiority and the vote it conferred, without the real property attached.[21] Con-

---

18 *Letters of Zeno to the Citizens of Edinburgh on the Present Mode of Electing a Member of Parliament for that City* (Edinburgh, 1783).

19 Fagerstrom, 'Scottish Opinion and the American Revolution', 255.

20 For Dundas see Michael Fry, *The Dundas Despotism* (Edinburgh, 1992).

21 William Ferguson, 'The Electoral System in the Scottish Counties before 1832', *Stair Society Miscellany*, 2 (1984), 261-94.

sequently, holders of these 'fictitious' or 'faggot' votes, could vote in counties where they did not own an acre of land. In 1782 a meeting of delegates from Scotland's twenty-three counties was held in Edinburgh to consider the issue. The delegates, however, came up with a variety of remedies, and it was this lack of unanimity that, in part, explains the failure of the movement to exert any effective pressure on parliament.[22]

The rejection of these initial attempts to amend the peculiarities of Scottish representation needs to be seen in a wider political context. Parliament at this stage was promptly rejecting many popular claims. It gave short shrift both to the broad and vocal movement for the abolition of the slave trade and the demands of English Dissenters, supported by a similar but distinct Scottish campaign, for the repeal of those penal statutes which enshrined the civil disabilities under which English Dissenters and, significantly, all conscientious members of the Church of Scotland, laboured. It also initiated unpopular legislation, especially the 1791 corn law, which seemed symptomatic of a parliament of landed aristocrats legislating in its own interest.[23]

Scotland, therefore, was discussing reform before the French Revolution, albeit along strictly moderate and constitutional lines, and had traditions of religious dissent that might directly inform a radical critique of Scottish society and British institutions. And it was into the immediate political context of burgeoning reformism and parliamentary intransigence that news of events in France intruded. The rapidly expanding Scottish press kept a very close eye on events in France and throughout Europe, and readers of a newspaper such as the *Caledonian Mercury* could be remarkably well informed about French politics and the ideological issues which underpinned them.[24] In its initial stages, the French Revolution was seen in a largely positive light, a tardy but bloodless replica of the British Revolution of 1688-89. Such was the basis of John Millar's pseudonymous *Letters of Crito*, which explained his early support for the reform movement and a revolution which 'was not hostile to Kingly government' and 'went no further than to establish a limited constitutional monarchy'. He was turned against it only when its prosecutors started to 'equalise the different ranks, to expel or extinguish the superior class of

---

22 Meikle, *Scotland and the French Revolution*, chs. 1-2.

23 Brims, 'The Scottish Democratic Movement', pp. 126-58; G. M. Ditchfield, 'The Scottish Campaign against the Test Act, 1790-1791', *Historical Journal*, 23 (1980), 37-61.

24 R. M. W. Cowan, *The Newspaper in Scotland: A Study of its First Expansion, 1815-1860* (Glasgow, 1946), pp. 8-14.

inhabitants, and to annihilate every monument or vestige of the ancient distinctions'.[25] Millar was certainly not alone. It was only as the revolution progressed and became more radical and more violent that public opinion became polarized.

The political situation was further galvanized by the publication in February 1791 of the first part of Thomas Paine's *Rights of Man*, one of a number of refutations of Burke's attack on the French Revolution and its principles. Paine sought to contrast his own simple, unadorned and rational writing and ideas with the mystification and emotional appeal of Burke, and he delivered a searing radical critique of the British state and a robust defence of events in France. At 3s 6d his work was initially too expensive for most Scottish artisans. Quickly, however, it appeared in cheap and abridged versions and gained a mass readership throughout Britain.[26] When meetings were held in Scotland in July 1791 to commemorate the storming of the Bastille, the government took an interest in the proceedings. When disturbances on the King's birthday in June 1792 included not only the burning of effigies of Scotland's political manager, Henry Dundas, but also the planting of trees of liberty, the authorities laid the blame squarely at the door of the French Revolution and Paine's exposition of its principles.[27]

It was on the back of this popular agitation that an organized reform movement was built in Scotland. In England, in April, reformist Whigs had formed the Association of the Friends of the People, with the aim of establishing a constitutional and moderate body of reformers in Britain who might provide responsible leadership and discourage Paineite approaches to political reform. This society provided a model that was embraced by the diverse assembly of reformers that met at Fortune's tavern in Edinburgh on 26 July and established Scotland's first Association of the Friends of the People. During the remainder of the year similar societies were rapidly established across Scotland, while sporadic disturbances continued in such places as Dundee and Perth. At this point, according to Brims, the reform movement was a broad church, comprehending dissident burgh and county reformers and Foxite Whigs as well as artisans and plebeian radicals. The very pace of reform, however, provoked a strong

---

25 Quoted in James D. Young, *The Very Bastards of Creation: Scottish-International Radicalism; A Biographical Study, 1707-1995* (Glasgow, 1996), p. 79.

26 Brims, 'The Scottish Democratic Movement', pp. 161-2.

27 Henry Meikle, 'The King's Birthday Riot in Edinburgh, June 1792', *Scottish Historical Review*, 7 (1910), 21-28.

government counter-offensive, which drew little distinction between the activities of liberty-tree-planting mobs and the cautious reformism expressed by most of the societies.

The response of the reform movement in Scotland, on the motion of Thomas Muir, a Glaswegian lawyer and radical, was to call a national convention of reformers to be held in Edinburgh in December 1792. The convention, while not geographically representative (some half of the 179 delegates were from Edinburgh societies) advanced cautious claims to represent the opinion of the political nation. It sought to project itself as loyal and moderate and resolved to pursue reform and simultaneously 'maintain the constitution of Great Britain on its genuinely acknowledged principles, consisting of King, Lords and Commons'. Its language was studiously constitutional, and its strategy, to circulate petitions to be signed in favour of a reform bill in parliament, was similarly unobjectionable.[28] Debates among reformers as to the correct basis on which to claim political rights, however, highlighted the diversity of the movement, and a minority of radicals would not allow the resolution legitimating Britain's constitution to be represented as having been unanimously passed.[29] The division of opinion was again apparent in debates over what reception ought to be given to a nationalistic address to the convention from the United Irishmen. While conjuring up the emotive national symbols of Buchanan, Fletcher and Wallace, the address urged Scotland, in dangerously revolutionary language, to pursue parliamentary reform with 'the Unity and energy of an embodied Nation'.[30] Sponsored by Muir, the address received little support, and was denounced, particularly by the Whigs; Robert Forsyth anxiously claiming that it 'borders on an attack on the British Constitution'.[31]

The circumspection of the more moderate reformers was even more apparent at the second national convention held in April and May of 1793. Crucially, the international context had changed when France declared war on Britain in February. When the convention met, the war was at the top of its agenda, and Thomas Fyshe Palmer, a Cambridge-educated Unitarian minister preaching in Dundee, successfully moved that the convention condemn it. He was opposed by John Morthland

---

28 Brims, 'The Scottish Democratic Movement', pp. 296-307.

29 Meikle, *Scotland and the French Revolution*, p. 249.

30 McFarland, *Ireland and Scotland in the Age of Revolution*, p. 248.

31 National Archives of Scotland [hereafter: NAS], Home Office Correspondence (Scotland), RH2/4/66, f. 352.

and Richard Fowler, both moderate Foxite Whigs who argued that the issue of reform ought to be kept separate from all other concerns. Their defeat reflected the level of popular opposition to the war at the convention, and it was a critical factor in the Foxite secession from the reform movement.[32]

The Whig abandonment of reform was symptomatic of a more general falling off of support. The second convention was attended by fewer delegates than the first and if some of this decline was certainly attributable to the course of events in France, the strength of the vigorous loyalist reaction also had its influence. This was advanced not only through printed propaganda, but also by the Church, local magistrates and loyalist associations. These associations emerged over the winter of 1792-93 and Brims has suggested that they were less numerous and popular than their English counterparts. This loyalist reaction issued anti-radical propaganda and pursued a ruthless campaign of intimidation and boycotting of radicals and their sympathizers; intimidation from which reformers and radicals from a higher social status were not exempt.[33]

Part of the state's response was the prosecution of a number of radicals for sedition. Even before the first convention, the government had used spies to maintain a close surveillance on the movement's leaders. In August and September 1793, before the third convention could meet, two of these, Thomas Muir and Thomas Fyshe Palmer, stood trial for sedition. As John Barrell has argued, this was part of a strategy that saw the legal officers attempting to move towards a definition of modern treason.[34] Muir, having been arrested in January and, having inadvisedly gone to France while on bail, was tried in August. The proceedings which led to his conviction were widely seen by radicals and reformers as the epitome of Scottish judicial repression. The jury was packed with members of the Goldsmith Hall Association, and the prosecution's case, advanced by the Lord Advocate, Robert Dundas, nephew of Henry, was flimsy in the extreme. Muir, however, embraced the role of political martyr and, defending himself, failed to deliver a legally effective defence. When the jury returned a 'guilty' verdict, even its members were shocked by the severity of the sentence – fourteen years' transportation to a penal colony in Botany

32 Brims, 'The Scottish Democratic Movement', pp. 405-12.

33 *Ibid.*, 348-65.

34 John Barrell, *Imagining the King's Death: Figurative Treason, Fantasies of Regicide 1793-1796* (Oxford, 2000).

Bay – and would have complained had numbers of them not received death threats from radicals. Palmer, who was tried the following month, also received a sentence of transportation.[35]

When the third convention met in October 1793, radicalism in Scotland was in retreat. The rejection of Scottish petitions in May had been an unequivocal rebuff by parliament, and a demoralizing demonstration that petitioning was not an effectual means of obtaining reform. Similarly, the trials of Muir and Palmer had forced a questioning of the constitutionality of reform itself, although they had provided the movement with political martyrs. More worrying still for Scottish radicals was the British situation. In December 1793 the Irish parliament in Dublin had given Catholics the right to vote, but it had subsequently made conventions illegal. British radicals feared that the government would attempt a similar piece of legislation. The third convention lost little time in declaring itself against the war and in favour of universal suffrage and annual parliaments. In what was virtually its last act it resolved unanimously 'to express its desire to cultivate a more close union with England' and this aim was achieved when, after a brief interlude, the delegates reassembled as the British Convention on 19 November.[36]

The third and subsequently British Convention has been seen as a desperate response to the loyalist reaction and an attempt to bolster a movement suffering from numerical weakness. Correspondence between Scottish and English radicals attests to a sense of weakness and, in May 1793, Thomas Hardy, secretary of the London Corresponding Society (LCS), had written to William Skirving and effectively offered the Scottish movement the lead.[37] This optimistic reading of the Scottish situation was echoed in the correspondence of one of the few English delegates who attended the British Convention, Maurice Margarot, who confidently informed the Norwich Societies of which he was the delegate

35 Henry Cockburn, *An Examination of the Trials for Sedition which have Hitherto Occurred in Scotland* (2 vols., Edinburgh, 1888), i, chs. 7-8; Brims, 'The Scottish Democratic Movement', pp. 427-57.

36 T. J. Howell, *A Complete Collection of State Trials and Proceedings for High Treason and Other Crimes and Misdemeanors, from the Earliest Period to the Year 1783* [hereafter: *State Trials*] (32 vols., London, 1817-19), xxiii, 413.

37 *The Reports of the Committee of Secrecy of the House of Commons on the Papers Belonging to the Society for Constitutional Information and the London Corresponding Society Seized by Order of Government and Presented to the House by Mr. Secretary Dundas* (Edinburgh, 1794), p. 105.

that 'our greatest hopes are on the country where I now am'.[38] On the face of it, the confidence was deserved, and the British Convention boasted 169 delegates when it began its proceedings. It is clear that government and financial pressures were taking their toll, however, and by 25 November only 98 delegates remained, a number which fell to 75 by 2 December. Brims has also shown that demographically there was a reduction in the number of 'country' delegates at the third and British conventions, around 54 on 29 October compared with some 80 at the first convention.[39]

The third and British conventions were entirely plebeian radical affairs and the government was perhaps shocked by what it viewed as a challenge to parliamentary sovereignty from a body which styled itself the 'British Convention of the Delegates of the People, Associated to Obtain Universal Suffrage and Annual Parliaments'. Although Brims has argued that the delegates regarded it as an assembly of representatives rather than a sovereign convention or 'anti-parliament' on the Paineite model, that was almost certainly how loyalists were apt to view it.[40] Perhaps the aspect of its proceedings that particularly alarmed the government and the loyalist press was its imitation of French forms and styles. Delegates addressed one another as 'citizen', divided themselves into 'sections' and dated their minutes the 'First Year of the British Convention'. In this idiom, the convention discussed not only parliamentary reform, but also the need for political education in the Highlands and elsewhere and the need to protect and maintain the radical newspaper the *Edinburgh Gazetteer*. When it came to discuss the Irish Convention bill, the convention appointed a secret committee of four that was to arrange for the meeting of a 'Convention of Emergency' whenever a similar bill should be introduced in Britain. The authorities were further startled by ambiguous references to the suspension of Habeas Corpus, an 'invasion' of the country and the admission of foreign troops as other valid reasons for summoning an emergency convention. The delegates, aware that the government intended to move against them, finally determined on 4 December that the moment of any 'illegal dispersion' of the convention would provide a similar summons. Several of the leading radicals were arrested and their papers seized the following morning and in the evening the Lord Provost and thirty consta-

---

38 Public Record Office [hereafter: PRO], Treasury Solicitor's Papers, TS11/953/3497. Maurice Margarot to Walsh and Wagstaff, 24 Nov. 1793.

39 Brims, 'The Scottish Democratic Movement', p. 497.

40 *Ibid.*, pp. 498-500.

bles dispersed the convention. It reassembled elsewhere, only to be closed down for good on the following evening. Alexander Scott, the editor of the *Edinburgh Gazetteer*, Charles Sinclair, Joseph Gerrald and Maurice Margarot, three of the English delegates, and William Skirving were subsequently indicted on a charge of sedition. Three of them, Gerrald, Margarot and Skirving were actually tried and, in another controversial series of political trials, followed Muir and Palmer in being sentenced to transportation to Botany Bay.[41] Events in Scotland, just as in Ireland, informed ideologies and actions and led to English radical calls for a convention, which formed the pretext for the infamous English treason trials of 1794. English radical justifications for a convention were saturated in the idea that Irish and Scottish repression was the product of English corruption and a precursor to similar measures in England. This was made plain in the LCS's *Address to the People of Great Britain and Ireland*: 'Can you believe that the those who send virtuous Irishmen and Scotchmen, fettered with felons to Botany Bay, do not meditate, and will not attempt to seize the first moment to send us after them?[42]

If it was a signal for action on the part of English radicals, few of the Scottish societies continued to operate openly in the atmosphere that followed the suppression of the British Convention. In May 1794 parliament suspended Habeas Corpus and its Scottish equivalent the Act Anent Wrongous Imprisonment and by the end of the following year the closing down of political space had been rendered complete by the Treasonable Practices and Seditious Meetings Acts, which placed draconian restrictions on public meetings and the freedom to associate.

With constitutional opportunities for the expression of radical politics utterly closed, Scottish radicals, if they acted at all, now did so furtively. In August and September1794 arrests were made in connection with an apparent insurrectionary armed conspiracy, after pikes had been discovered in the house of a former government spy, Robert Watt, who had played a prominent part in the British Convention. The parliamentary Committee of Secrecy that reported on this conspiracy painted it as one which had originated in the LCS, and represented it as part of a pan-British revolutionary conspiracy. In reality, it seems that the remnant of the British Convention, which had continued to meet into 1794, had stayed in close contact with the LCS and had undertaken to send dele-

41 Meikle, *Scotland and the French Revolution*, pp. 140-6.

42 *Trial of David Downie, for High Treason, before the Court, under the special Commission of Oyer and Terminer held at Edinburgh* (Edinburgh, 1795), p. 63.

gates to the mooted convention. The plan for insurrection had come from Watt himself and had been propagated through the convention's small Committee of Ways and Means. Watt and another radical, David Downie, were tried by a special commission of Oyer et Terminer for high treason and found guilty, though only Watt was executed.[43]

The loyalist reaction continued unabated and the subsequent course of events in France and the threat of invasion, which inspired new loyalist bodies of Volunteers, helped to toll the death knell of Scottish radicalism. Radicals still operated in Scotland and, although we know little about them, a body committed to Paineite republicanism and rational religion, the United Scotsmen, maintained a shadowy and oath-bound presence until 1798. Their presence was detected in the spate of disturbances in Scotland that followed the unpopular Militia Act of July 1797, and one of the movement's leaders and a previous associate of Palmer, George Mealmaker, was tried for sedition and the administering of unlawful oaths.[44] He too was sent to Botany Bay. In his address to the court, he displayed the kind of resignation to a martyr's fate that had characterized the response of those Scottish radicals who had been convicted before him: 'he saw that he was to be another victim to the pursuit of parliamentary reform; but he could easily submit and go to that distant country where others had gone before him. He did not fear it.'[45]

II.

It is thus apparent that Scottish radicals operated in a number of different contexts. They confronted, and expounded a peculiar critique of, the Scottish establishment, but they were also consciously part of a pan-British movement for political reform; one that operated in the galvanizing context of an international situation where all eyes were on France. If we were to take Scottish radicals at face value, on the strength of their official resolutions and addresses, we might characterize them as firmly rooted in a constitutional tradition which sought the restoration of political rights conferred by the British constitution but imperfectly enjoyed. Certainly, a considerable debate among Scottish radicals did focus on determining the 'real' meaning of the constitution and the rights it conveyed, and historians have highlighted the fact that within this constitutional discourse the-

43 Meikle, *Scotland and the French Revolution*, pp. 149-53.

44 McFarland, *Ireland and Scotland in the Age of Revolution*, ch. 5.

45 *State Trials*, xxvi, 1164.

there was broad interpretational scope.[46] Such an approach demanded that the argument for political rights be made from precedent and thus radicals had to determine the basis of Scotland's constitutional liberty.

This could be done by appealing to a politically 'usable' English past, which provided Scottish radicals with a coherent narrative of 'British' liberties. As such, reform could be pursued as the restoration of liberties conferred by an ancient constitution and suspended by the long tyranny of the 'Norman yoke'.[47] This approach was adopted at the first convention by a young Edinburgh medical student, Alexander Aitchison:

> But in faith we had nothing more to ask, than to be restored to our original rights – That he was certain that by the English Constitution so long ago as the days of King Alfred every free man has a vote in chusing his representative and that in those days Parliaments were annual.[48]

If many Scottish radicals were entirely at ease in appealing to an essentially English narrative of liberty, they could also combine it with elements of a Scottish narrative to create what Colin Kidd has termed an 'Anglo-British' patriotism.[49] This was particularly applied to the events of 1688-89, which remained absolutely central to Scottish radicals' conception of where their liberties were enshrined. There was clearly a practical element to this focus on precedent, and invoking the Glorious Revolution was a securely constitutional mode of appeal. It could be used in particular to refute claims that reformers were levellers and Jacobins. The settlement may not have gone far enough, but, by claiming it as their guide, Scottish reformers might refute, as did John Clark, the implications that reformers were 'entertaining notions of Liberty and Equality inimical to property'.[50] But it was also a powerful discourse which was flexible and thus admitted numerous interpretations. Hume's notion that the Glorious Revolution had established liberty in Britain for the first time was approved by many Scottish radicals, who often chose to emphasize Scotland's distinctive set-

---

46 J. A. Epstein, 'The Constitutional Idiom', 558-74; Kathleen Wilson, 'Inventing Revolution: 1688 and Eighteenth-Century Popular Politics', *Journal of British Studies*, 28 (1989), 349-86.

47 Christopher Hill, 'The Norman Yoke' in *Democracy in the Labour Movement: Essays in Honour of Dona Torr*, ed. John Saville (London, 1954), pp. 11-66; Thompson, *The Making of the English Working Class*, pp. 91-6.

48 NAS, RH2/4/66, ff. 356-7.

49 Colin Kidd, 'North Britishness and the Nature of Eighteenth-Century British Patriotisms', *Historical Journal*, 39 (1996), 361-82.

50 NAS, RH2/4/66, f. 355.

tlement of 1689. While still appealing to Magna Carta, Habeas Corpus and other totemic symbols of English liberty, Scottish radicals constantly coupled this with appeals to the Claim of Right, thus incorporating Scottish understandings of what was achieved at the Revolution into an essentially English narrative.[51]

The same was true, to an extent, of the powerful narrative of Scottish religious liberty, which was in some sense compatible with a predominantly secular constitutional approach. At the second series of sedition trials the English radicals tended to appeal to England's judicial martyrs of the seventeenth century, as, we should note, had Muir at his trial. Skirving referred instead to Scotland's experience of religious oppression in the seventeenth century, comparing the High Court of Justiciary in Edinburgh to the Star Chamber and characterizing proceedings against him as 'a revival of the conventicle prosecutions with a vengeance'.[52]

This alternative Scottish idiom was, however, more controversial as a basis for reform sentiments. Covenanting found a new relevance for a movement which increasingly sought to project itself as British. Indeed, in advertising for English delegates to attend the British Convention, Skirving had explicitly asserted that the Convention 'must establish that nobly intended union, termed, *the Solemn League and Covenant for ever*'.[53] There was a functional political element to this appeal that sought to commit British reformers to the cause of reform. It was used, not as a nationalistic symbol, but as a means of appealing to a clearly British tradition, albeit one focused on Scotland and its unique contribution to British liberty. Covenanting, however, remained unsafe ground on which to base a justification for political rights and, at Skirving's trial, the prosecution highlighted a Covenanting motion made at the third convention and unambiguously condemned it as 'most illegal and most seditious'.[54] It was a popular and indigenous appeal, however, and at his trial Skirving also highlighted his readiness to base calls for reform on the political tradition bequeathed by Scottish presbyterianism. He approvingly cited the earl of Buchan's nationalistic eulogy on the political theory of George Buchanan: 'it is to Scotland and a Scotchman that the world is indebted for the establishment of the

---

51 For example a delegate at the British Convention moved 'that it would be proper to publish the Magna Charta Bill and Claim of Rights and Habeas Corpus Act'. NAS, RH2/4/72, f. 169.

52 *State Trials*, xxiii, 497.

53 *Edinburgh Gazetteer*, 5 Nov. 1793.

54 *State Trials*, xxiii, 488.

philosophical and logical principles of a free constitution, both in theory and practice'.[55] This attachment to Buchananite notions of politics was apparent in Scottish radicalism and, in response to the French Revolution, the radical periodical *The Bee* had run a series of articles that hailed him as a 'herald of civil and religious liberty'.[56]

Such eulogies may have been uncontroversial, but Scottish presbyterianism and its theory of justified resistance were less amenable to the constitutional approach that characterized the resolutions of Scottish radicals. They were, nevertheless, evident. When the third convention was lamenting the fate of Muir and Palmer, Skirving offered a pointedly Buchananite reading of what tyranny might lie ahead. He expressed 'a hope that that period would not arrive when *resistance* becomes *duty* – when the will of the *ruler* is made *the law of the people*'.[57] Seldom was this alternative idiom espoused explicitly, however; more often the historian must posit its influence on the evidence of allusions and symbols. For example, it is probable that the chosen designation of the 'United Societies' of Strathaven was a conscious reference to those late-seventeenth-century radical presbyterian Dissenters, who maintained such a powerful cultural presence in the west of Scotland in particular.[58]

Hence, we might suggest that this indigenous radical reading of Scotland's past, which comprehended both Covenanting and the political theories of Scottish presbyterianism, was most likely to be expressed once constitutional options had been exhausted. Muir had intriguingly argued that Scottish liberty was as ancient as English liberty at the first convention, but defended himself in much the same secular manner as the English radicals when he came to trial. After his escape from Botany Bay, however, when he was in exile in France and seeking to persuade the Directory to invade Scotland, he appealed explicitly to this tradition. Brims discovered a brief history penned by Muir for the benefit of the French government that lamented the suppression of thousands of presbyterian 'republicans' in seventeenth-century Scotland, and was scathing of the attempts of English court-paid historians to dismiss Covenanting as blind fanaticism.[59]

---

55 *Ibid.*, 573.

56 McIlvanney, *Burns the Radical*, p. 17.

57 NAS, RH2/4/73, f. 56.

58 *State Trials*, xxiii, 1372.

59 Brims, 'The Covenanting Tradition', pp. 57-9.

If Scottish radicals tended to avoid openly espousing this partisan reading of Scottish history, because of its potentially unconstitutional implications, they may also have done so from the realisation that it represented only one possible religious response to the French Revolution. Rational Dissenters such as Palmer would not espouse religio-political sentiments based on the 'fanaticism' of Covenanting. Most Scottish radicals sought to avoid contentious religious discussions, but more ecumenical religious sentiments were apparent. The response to the French Revolution that viewed it in providential terms, as a sign of God's judgment, was apparent among radicals of different religious persuasions. Emma Vincent has convincingly demonstrated that most Scottish ministers responded by imputing all national evils to sin and exhorting the necessity of national repentance.[60] Radicals could clearly interpret events in France and Britain within this providential framework and Skirving, perhaps inadvisedly, warned the High Court of Justiciary at his trial that the French Revolution was the herald of the last judgment:

> It may be the day, the awful 'day that shall burn as an oven; and all the proud and they that do wickedly shall be stubble.' – Have they not been stubble in a neighbouring country? And should you not be instructed by the striking lesson before your eyes?[61]

Neil Douglas, a relief minister from Dundee, could also interpret the revolution in terms of God's judgment. His lengthy poem, *A Monitory Address to Great Britain*, highlighted the elite vices of duelling, lay patronage and slavery, and advocated the reform of morals as a national imperative. Political reform was to form part of this general moral reformation, and Douglas suggested that the lessons of this could be drawn from French experience which 'may pave the way for the spread of religious and civil liberty over the face of the earth'. For Douglas the 'tragical disasters' which had attended the revolution did not form a convincing argument against it and he asserted:

> They are, however, worse than blind who see not the hand of Providence therein; and that same Providence, which hath so visibly effected it, will, it is hoped, continue to watch over and defend it, in spite of all opposition; which must form the ardent wish of every lover of humanity – of every citizen of the world.[62]

---

60 Emma Vincent, 'The Responses of Scottish Churchmen to the French Revolution, 1789-1802', *Scottish Historical Review*, 73 (1994), 191-215.

61 *State Trials*, xxiii, 501.

62 Neil Douglas, *A Monitory Address to Great Britain: A Poem in Six Parts; To which is added Britain's Remembrancer, &c.* (Edinburgh, 1792), p. 14.

Although Scottish radicals tended to avoid involved discussions over the religious bases of their claims, religion still provided ample scope for controversy between radicals and there was still frequent acknowledgement that the cause of reform was a godly one. The conventions, for example, continued to open and close their meetings with prayers and almost unanimously passed the very latitudinarian motion:

> That the Convention shall recommend to the members of this Convention and to the Friends of Reform in Britain and Ireland to invoke the blessing of Almighty God, our Common Father in the Cause in which we are engaged.[63]

Scottish radicals thus appealed to various British and more explicitly Scottish traditions, both secular and religious, in their demands for parliamentary reform. Nevertheless, they were condemned in loyalist propaganda and declarations as 'Levellers and Republican incendiaries who, under the mask of Reform are doing their utmost to reduce this country to the situation of now barbarous France'.[64] One of the principal strategies of loyalist propaganda was to represent radicals as ignorant malcontents of low social standing, who were usually either Dissenters in religion or outright atheists. The 'typical' radical was comprehended in the character of Gibby Grunt, a seceding weaver who appears in dialogue with John Dunt, a presbyterian blacksmith questioning his own support of reform, in *Modern Politics, or, the Cat let out of the Pock*. Grunt is an ignorant drunkard, who threatens a loyalist schoolmaster with the spectre of the guillotine, and even defends the sanguinary excesses of the Jacobins. He is exactly the kind of ignorant fool, bewitched by, but with an imperfect understanding of, events in France, whom the self-interested radical leaders sought to use as 'the tools with which they intend to work out their scheme of plunging the Country into blood and ruin, in the hopes of catching something for themselves in the Shipwreck of the Nation'.[65]

Of all of the accusations levelled by loyalists at radicals, those of being essentially foreign and of supporting the more horrifying stages of the revolution in France, were the most damaging, especially when made consistently after Britain had gone to war. The *Caledonian Mercury*, which had not initially been hostile to the reform movement, was finally and de-

---

63 NAS, RH2/4/73, f. 224.

64 'Declaration of the Heritors and Inhabitants of the Parish of Culross' in *Letters &c. from Friends of the People: or, the Last Words and Dying Advice of a Weaver to his Children* (Edinburgh, 1792), p. 12.

65 *Modern Politics, or, the Cat let out of the Pock: A Dialogue* (Edinburgh, 1793), p. 4.

cisively turned against it by the British Convention's adoption of French forms and phrases. It reported that the delegates, finding that French phraseology empowered their harangues more effectively than 'the simplicity of the Caledonian accent' or 'the refinement of the English tongue' had begun acting like Jacobins and so 'before the *guillotine* was *decreed permanent*, it was judged proper to dissolve the assembly'.[66]

Just how influenced Scottish radicals were by the events and ideology of the French Revolution is difficult to discern. The French Revolution and Thomas Paine both urged reformers to claim no less than the universal rights of man, without reference to sacrosanct, particularist and historic traditions such as the rights of Englishmen or the rights of Britons. Paine abandoned the idea of reform based on precedent and was more explicit about converting natural rights into civil liberties than John Locke had been. His real innovation was a radical interpretation of the contract theory. According to Paine, the important contract was that which established political society and was an agreement made by every individual with every other individual. As such, the only legitimate government was that which represented the sovereign will of the people, which converted natural rights into civil liberties, and whose executive and legislative power was held in trust and could be revoked at any time by the people.[67]

Some aspects of this ideology certainly found ready support in Scotland, but Brims has convincingly argued that Scottish radicals did not simply adopt Paine's creed but responded to his work in a complex manner. Scottish radicals were generally opposed to the heterodox religious views of Paine and there was little popular support for the republicanism recommended by him and practised in France.[68] Some Scottish radicals were comfortable in 'disregarding all authorities and standing up for our rights as men', but it is difficult to find explicit avowals of reform based entirely on a rejection of historical precedents as Paine had encouraged.[69] We view these fleetingly, for example, in the two medals for the possession of which a Leith merchant, William Stewart, was tried for sedition in January 1793. He came to trial along with a bookseller, James Elder, who had reprinted the *Declaration of the Rights of Man and of Citizens* by the National Assembly of France. The medals themselves bore inscriptions of

66 *Caledonian Mercury*, 7 Dec. 1793.

67 H. T. Dickinson, *Liberty and Property: Political Ideology in Eighteenth-Century Britain* (London, 1977), pp. 240-4.

68 Brims, 'The Scottish Democratic Movement', pp. 223-33.

69 NAS, RH2/4/72, f. 180.

the dicta of the revolution, proclaiming 'The Nation is essentially the Source of all Sovereignty' and 'For a Nation to be free it is sufficient that it wills it'.[70] The two were acquitted, unlike the publishers of a more robust and lengthy defence of French revolutionary principles, who were also tried at the beginning of 1793. The latter had published James Thomson Callender's nationalistic and internationalist *Political Progress of Britain*, a text which utterly rejected the notion that Scottish liberty could be based on a precedent set in 1689. His model for reform was certainly 'the concise and philosophical decrees' of the French, rather than 'the feudal jargon of subjecting a people and their posterity forever to the assignees of a Dutchman who was universally detested'. His was a very Paineite interpretation and nowhere more so than in this lauding of the unadorned and rational language of the French Assembly in preference to the mystifying language used by writers such as Burke to defend their concept of the British constitution. In rejecting this Whig culture, however, even Callender could not help referring the reader to Bannockburn, as a symbol of the defeat of tyranny, and praising the writings of Buchanan.[71]

Paineite opinions were more likely to be put into print anonymously than to be espoused openly. As such George Mealmaker's *The Moral and Political Catechism of Man*, published in 1797 and a key text in studying the ideology of the United Scotsmen, suggests how far the doctrines of the French Revolution could be taken. The work took the form of a dialogue between 'a Citizen of the World' and 'an inhabitant of Britain' and as such clearly espoused the universalism that was so prominent in revolutionary ideology, and was popular among Scottish radicals. It presented the case for reform in terms of Paine's *Rights of Man* and even approached the outright deism of Paine's *Age of Reason* in its argument for disestablishment. Even so, as Brims has pointed out, Mealmaker could not go so far as to support Paine's views on state welfare, which would have clashed with his free trade principles. And McFarland has suggested that his notion of lawful resistance was rooted in Scottish presbyterian rather than rational and universalist ideas.[72]

---

70 Cockburn, *Examination of the Trials for Sedition*, i, 109.

71 J. T. Callender, *The Political Progress of Britain: or, an Impartial Account of the Principal Abuses in the Government of this Country, from the Revolution in 1688* (Edinburgh, 1792), p. 34.

72 McFarland, *Ireland and Scotland in the Age of Revolution*, pp. 154-7; Brims, 'The Scottish Democratic Movement, p. 232.

More often than not, however, notions of the universal rights of man and of the right of nations to form and reform their political arrangements, appear only as part of justifications which appeal to other precedents and ideas. The address *To the People and their Friends*, for having written which the editor of the *Historical Register*, James Tytler, was charged with sedition and fled the country, is an illustration of this idiosyncratic reading of Paine. Tytler reprobated the House of Commons as 'a vile junto of aristocrats' and his description of a parliament of usurpers was heavily redolent of Paine. He, like Paine, pointed to the illegitimacy of the Septennial Act and the absurdity of the House of Commons being able to extend the duration of its sitting.[73] As such, the national convention ought not to 'sanctify' it by recognizing it in petitions. His solution, however, dispenses with Paine's republicanism, and advocates petitioning the king. His justification for genuine civil disobedience through the non-payment of taxes was based on a combination of Magna Carta and the American appeal for 'no taxation without representation'.[74] Finally, we might perhaps suggest that a presbyterian conception of liberty is also apparent in Tytler. Certainly his support for the rights of man did not extend to full freedom of conscience, and in the *Historical Register* he argued against proposed relief to Unitarians as 'a striking instance of the impiety of the age'.[75] In his *Address* he played on popular notions of the links between catholicism and slavery, ignorance and superstition, by portraying the House of Commons as akin to the Catholic priesthood:

> As the Popish priests absorbed the worship due to the deity by stocks and stones and rascally saints, so have the House of Commons artfully drawn away the attention of the people of Britain from the king to themselves.[76]

Finally, we cannot ignore the various visual and symbolic demonstrations of support for French principles. Skirving claimed in court that the French aspects of the proceedings of the British Convention were mere 'bugbears' to frighten the government; and Brims seems to have largely followed this line and dismisses them as 'empty posturing'.[77] The work of some histori-

73 Thomas Paine, '*Rights of Man*. Part I' in *Paine: Political Writings*, ed. Bruce Kuklick (Cambridge, 1989), p. 91.

74 *State Trials*, xxiii, 3-4

75 *The Historical Register*, May 1792, p. 481.

76 *State Trials*, xxiii, 2-3.

77 J. D. Brims, 'From Reformers to "Jacobins": The Scottish Association of the Friends of the People' in *Conflict and Stability in Scottish Society, 1700-1850*, ed. T. M. Devine (East Linton, 1990), pp. 46-7.

ans, however, encourages us not to dismiss such activities in any cursory manner. According to Epstein, in a case study of the early-nineteenth-century radical use of the cap of liberty, the use of symbols and the manner in which they were used 'constituted a careful, complex and deliberate construction of meaning on the part of radicals'.[78] The widespread planting of trees of liberty or Margarot's sober and Frenchified dress at his trial can be interpreted as conscious affirmations of support for the revolution, rather than spontaneous but ultimately meaningless effusions of popular feeling.

III.

Scottish radicals demonstrated a variety of approaches to reform in the 1790s and appealed to a broad range of ideologies, precedents and authorities that reflected the Scottish, British and international contexts in which they operated. A pan-British discourse of popular constitutionalism coloured most of their proceedings, and was appealed to because it legitimated a whole range of actions as well as words that allowed Scottish radicals to confront the British establishment on its own terms. Its flexibility allowed it to become radicalized and to incorporate elements of more distinctly Scottish approaches to reform, thus making a powerful appeal to an alternative 'British' patriotism. The dynamic nature of British and European events meant that the pronouncements of radicals were never likely to be coherent or consistent.[79] In the face of a strong loyalist reaction, which sought to label all radicals as essentially foreign, the ability to exploit an alternative patriotism was of clear utility. When the constitutional modes of political expression had been closed down after the suppression of the British Convention, however, radicals might appeal to alternative idioms, such as those offered by the writings of Paine or the culture of Covenanting, which might more adequately justify resistance.

Above all, this dynamism prompted responses from Scottish radicals that were highly idiosyncratic. Skirving's radicalism, like that of many other Scots, owed much to the ideologies and traditions of a distinctly Scottish presbyterian political culture. But he also read to the convention from Johnson's *History of Magna Charta* and appealed to Anglo-Saxon precedent as a basis for political reform.[80] When he came to trial, he simi-

---

78 J. A. Epstein, *Radical Expression: Political Language, Ritual, and Symbol in England, 1790-1850* (Oxford, 1994), p. 98.

79 Philp, 'The Fragmented Ideology of Reform', pp. 53-5.

80 NAS, RH2/4/72, f. 172.

larly coupled a trenchantly presbyterian defence of reform and a millennial interpretation of the French Revolution with appeals to the pristine origins of British liberty in 1688-89.[81]

Thus, Scottish 'Jacobins' may not have been numerous, but Scotland had, for the first time, spawned a popular radical movement that was shaped by indigenous Scottish traditions and ideologies as much as by dynamic British and French contexts. Certainly, these radicals still represented a small minority of the Scottish population, and the success of a sustained loyalist reaction meant that the period of actual agitation was relatively short. What the radicals of the 1790s bequeathed, however, was a powerful legacy of confrontation with the state, and the beginnings of a distinctly Scottish tradition of radical politics that would be exploited and appropriated by subsequent generations of reformers.

81 *State Trials*, xxiii, 579.

Atle L. Wold

Loyalism in Scotland in the 1790s

In the early 1790s Britain experienced an upsurge of political radicalism and popular agitation for a reform of the British political system. Inspired by the events in France, old and new reformers demanded political change in Britain, and they soon gained significant popular support. This increase in radical activity also sparked a reaction from the more conservative sections of society, which gradually rallied in defence of the British constitution. This emerging loyalism also attracted considerable popular support. Loyalism was a British phenomenon, but the purpose of this essay is to investigate the development of loyalism in Scotland, with the aim of determining the nature and extent of Scottish support for the British state during the French Revolutionary War.

The loyalist response in Scotland began to gather momentum only in 1792, when in the summer and autumn of that year, a number of people came forward to offer their support for the government against the perceived threat of popular radicalism. They proposed to form loyalist associations aimed at creating a counterweight to the emerging radical societies. For the government, however, this created a dilemma. The 'Royal Proclamation against seditious and wicked writings' had been issued on 21 May 1792,[1] to urge local government representatives 'to be watchful of seditious literature and its authors'. It sought 'to stamp out riot and agitation',[2] *not* to encourage support from the general public. Both William Pitt and Henry Dundas were sceptical about the whole concept of encouraging popular organizations of this sort. Pitt even contemplated introducing legislation to prevent all kinds of political meetings. In the end, however, both Pitt and Dundas favoured supporting *one* loyalist association at the cost of all the others, in order to keep popular loyalism under control. The loyalist organization which received the support of the gov-

---

1 *London Gazette* (1792).

2 Frank O'Gorman, 'Pitt and the "Tory" Reaction to the French Revolution 1789-1815', in *Britain and the French Revolution 1789 – 1815*, ed. H. T. Dickinson (London, 1989), pp. 30-31. See also Donald E. Ginter, 'The Loyalist Associations Movement of 1792-93 and British Public Opinion', *The Historical Journal* [hereafter *HJ*], 9 (1966), 188.

ernment was John Reeves's 'Association for the Preservation of Liberty and Property against Republicans and Levellers', founded on 20 November 1792.[3]

While there is clear evidence of growing support for the government in Scotland in the second half of 1792,[4] the Association for the Preservation of Liberty and Property does not seem to have gained such a strong foothold in Scotland, as it did in England. Reeves' societies were never as numerous on the ground as they were south of the border, and the amount of Scottish correspondence that has survived in the organization's own records is not very extensive.[5] There is relatively little evidence on the forming of societies in Scotland. A correspondent in Edinburgh, for example, wrote to the secretary of the association in London in January 1793 expressing his dismay at the lack of enthusiasm for the movement which seemed to prevail there:

> I . . . regret that I have not heard of any Proposition having been made here for establishing associations on a smaller Scale; – such as these recommended by your Committee to be erected in different Parts of London & its Environs – the Expediency of which applies, in a certain Degree, to Edinburgh, & every large Town.[6]

The association's programme for distributing loyalist propaganda also seems to have received a mixed response. The sheriff of Fife wrote to John Reeves reporting that 'above 2000 Pamphlets have already been distributed in this County and I am happy to acquaint you that the ferment and irritation of mind that persuaded many of the lower order of People in this Country is greatly subsided at least for the time'.[7] Others, however, were

---

3 H. T. Dickinson, *The Politics of the People in Eighteenth-Century Britain* (Basingstoke, 1994), p. 281; H. T. Dickinson, 'Popular Conservatism and Militant Loyalism 1789-1815', in *Britain and the French Revolution 1789-1815*, p. 114; and Duffy, 'William Pitt and the Origins of the Loyalist Association Movement of 1792', *HJ*, 39 (1996), 944.

4 George Home of Wedderburn, for example, wrote in a letter to his cousin Patrick Home in London in late November that 'the Reform societies about Glasgow are daily diminishing in numbers, and do now consist only of the very refuse of the People'. National Archives of Scotland [hereafter NAS], GD 267/1/16 [Home of Wedderburn MSS], George Home to Patrick Home Esq. of Wedderburn M.P., Gower Street London, Edinburgh, 25 Nov. 1792.

5 Material relating to Scotland can be found in BL [British Library], Add. MSS, 16919, 16920, 16924, 16928, 16930 and 16931.

6 BL, Add. MSS, 16928, ff. 1-2, J. Marjoriebanks to J. Moore, Canongate Edinburgh, 1 Jan. 1793.

7 BL, Add. MSS, 16924, f. 43. Cland Boswell, Sheriff of Fife to John Reeves Esq., Cupar County of Fife, 6 Jan. 1793.

not as convinced of the necessity of circulating loyalist material in Scotland. Matthew Campbell, the sheriff-substitute of Wigton, for example, also wrote to John Reeves, informing him 'that this County is in the most perfect Tranquility and that distribution of Loyal & Constitutional Publications in this Country is only administrating Good medicine to a Healthy Body'.[8] While John Reeves's organization may not have made as strong a breakthrough in Scotland as it did in England, it will be argued here that the Scots demonstrated their loyalty just as forcefully in other ways.

Some of these demonstrations came in response to government encouragement, but many were also spurred on either by specific events during the decade or by the more general development of the war against Revolutionary France. A second Royal Proclamation against sedition was issued in December 1792, but, apart from this, no further attempts were made to rally support for the suppression of radicalism in general, and subsequent encouragement was aimed at more specific issues. The first of these was the Royal Proclamation issued after the first attack on the king at the state opening of parliament on 29 October 1795. Published within two days of the attack, the proclamation condemned the attempted assault on the monarch's person, and enjoined 'all Magistrates, and all other [of] our loving subjects, to use their utmost endeavours to discover and cause to be apprehended the authors, actors and abettors concerned in such outrages'.[9] Other loyalist demonstrations involved the recruitment of men for armed service and the public's financial contributions to the war effort. A 'Plan for an Augmentation of the Forces for Internal Defence' presented in March 1794,[10] and the 'Defence of the Realm Act' of 1798,[11] both included clauses which encouraged subjects to offer their personal service to the state on a voluntary basis, while the 'Voluntary Contribution for the Defence of the Country' was primarily an appeal from the government to the wealthy classes of Britain, and an attempt to secure their financial support of the state by a voluntary levy, rather than through a new set of taxes.[12]

---

8 *Ibid.*, f. 27, Matt Campbell, She. Sub., to John Reeves Esq., Wigton, 5 Jan. 1793.

9 *Caledonian Mercury*, 5 Nov. 1795, 'BY THE KING, A PROCLAMATION', Court of St. James's, 31 Oct. 1795.

10 NAS, GD 385/20/23 [Rattray of Craighall Muniments], 'Plan for an Augmentation of the Forces for Internal Defence'.

11 The relevant aspects of the act can be found in: NAS, GD 224/628/3/20 [Duke of Buccleuch papers], 'PROPOSALS, For rendering the Body of the People Instrumental to the General Defence, in case of Invasion'.

12 *Caledonian Mercury*, 8 Feb. 1798.

Many Scots also responded to important events without any encouragement from the government. The three most crucial British naval victories of the 1790s – Lord Howe's victory over the French on the 'Glorious First of June' 1794, Admiral Duncan's defeat of the Dutch fleet at Camperdown on 11 October 1797, and Nelson's decisive victory over the French fleet at the Battle of the Nile on 1 August 1798 – all drew loyalist responses of one kind or another, as did the less successful campaigns fought by the British army in Flanders. Obvious domestic causes for demonstrations of loyalty were the two attempts on the life of George III, in 1795 and 1800 respectively. Within Scotland, the King's Birthday riots in Edinburgh in 1792 and the activities of the British Convention in 1793 both sparked loyalist reactions. Not all demonstrations of loyalty were direct responses to either specific events or to government initiatives. Any discussion of loyalism must examine the extent to which the people took their own independent initiatives. This essay will not provide an exhaustive discussion of all possible kinds of loyalist demonstrations, but it will focus on those which were particularly prominent, which involved a substantial number of people, and which were of significance for the war effort.

I. Loyalist Addresses and Resolutions

By far the most extensive source of evidence on demonstrations of loyalty to the government and support for the war effort in the 1790s is that of loyalist addresses, resolutions and declarations. More than 400 of them were sent from Scotland alone during the Revolutionary War, and they remain one of the chief sources of loyalist sentiment and ideology in this period. A loyalist address would normally be sent directly to the king, but resolutions expressing loyalty and support were sometimes also sent to the representatives of local government. As demonstrations of loyalty, resolutions were almost invariably written and sent in response to specific events. There was no steady output of addresses year by year. Instead, loyalist resolutions came in waves, responding to some of the more crucial events of the decade. Sending loyal resolutions or addresses to the king and his ministers followed a long-standing British tradition of demonstrating support for the monarch and the government at times of national emergency, crisis, or celebration.[13] None the less, the mass-issuing of addresses had not been as common in Scotland as it had been in England before the 1790s

[13] Mitchell, 'The Association Movement of 1792-3', *HJ*, 4 (1961), 61.

and, in this sense, the waves of resolutions emanating from Scotland in 1792 and afterwards *were* unprecedented, and represented a new Scottish willingness to display support for the British monarch and government in London.

There were three large nation-wide waves of addresses between 1792 and 1802. The first came in response to the Royal Proclamation of May 1792, and persisted until well after a second Royal Proclamation had been issued in December of the same year. The second and third waves were both concerned with the two attacks on George III's person. The country's response to these events was a veritable flood of addresses to the king, streaming in from all corners of the kingdom. In the case of the Royal Proclamations, this indicated that the government's initiative had struck a cord with a significant number of people who had so far remained in quiet disapproval of the activities of the political radicals. The first Scottish resolutions to be published came from 'the Lord Provost, Magistrates and Council of the City of Edinburgh' and of Stirling, and were printed in the 2-5 June issue of the government's own publication, the *London Gazette*. Addressing the king directly, the Edinburgh officials opened their resolution by emphasizing 'their Zeal and Attachment to the Constitution of their Country' as well as 'their Loyalty to their Sovereign, and their Gratitude for that warm Manifestation of his fatherly Affection to his People, which is displayed in his late Royal Proclamation'. They then proceeded to express their abhorrence at the 'alarming Attempts of those Enemies to their Country, who seek to poison the Minds of the people of these Realms . . . by raising up the Shadows of Grievances which were never felt but in Imagination'. The Edinburgh address set a standard for the resolutions which were to follow. Typically, an address would open by expressing its signatories' thanks to the king for issuing the proclamation, then go on to praise the blessings which subjects enjoyed under the British constitution and present government of Britain, as well as their support for that government and attachment to that constitution. It then expressed disgust at the activities of political radicals, and pledged to suppress all sedition and attempts by 'evil-minded and designing Men, to disturb the Public Tranquillity', as an address from Argyllshire phrased it.[14] A number of addresses also wished the monarch a long and happy reign. A few stressed that if the British constitution had any 'imperfections' which were in need of being re-

---

14 *London Gazette*, 21-23 June 1792, 'the Freeholders, Heretors and Justices of the Peace of Argyleshire'.

dressed, then the 'wise and temperate Means which the Constitution itself has provided for its own Preservation' would be more than sufficient to achieve this end.[15] From February 1793 most addresses were also discussing the recent outbreak of war with France, and urging all Britons to rally to the defence of the state against French aggression.[16] By the time the second Royal Proclamation had been issued on 1 December 1792, a total of 80 Scottish loyalist resolutions had been printed in the *London Gazette*, nearly all of them from the local elite, and the majority by the beginning of August. The second proclamation did not lead to such an outpouring of addresses from local officials, but it did see a substantial increase in resolutions initiated by the public.[17] Of the more than 120 addresses printed in the *Caledonian Mercury* from June 1792 until the beginning of May 1793, only a handful came from public officials, while the majority originated from ordinary subjects. Only six had been printed by 1 December 1792, and forty by the end of the year. By and large, it was therefore mainly local government officials who replied to the first royal proclamation, whereas the Scottish public in general responded to the second proclamation. It can be safely concluded that the number of loyalist addresses sent from Scotland in response to the two proclamations must have reached at least 200.[18]

Most addresses, sent after the attacks on George III in 1795 and 1800, opened by either expressing abhorrence and astonishment at the recent attempt on the king's life, or by congratulating the monarch on his fortunate escape. All the addresses included both points. Thereafter these addresses went on to cover themes such as a belief that divine providence had shielded the king's life, and hopefully would continue to do so in the future. Some even held the king's escape to be proof that the

---

15 *Ibid.*, 7-10 July 1792, 'the Magistrates and Town Council of Forfar, in North Britain'.

16 See for example a second address sent by 'the Lord Provost, Magistrates and Council of the City of Edinburgh' in January 1793. *London Gazette*, 23-29 Jan. 1793. For similar addresses, see: *ibid.*, 2-5, 26-30 Mar. and 7-11 May 1793.

17 Of the 102 Scottish resolutions printed in the *London Gazette* in 1792 and 1793, a total of 79 were sent by public officials, 16 by presbyteries and 4 by universities. There was only one resolution sent by the 'inhabitants' of a burgh, and the remaining two came from 'the General Convention of the Royal Boroughs of Scotland', and 'the Bishop and Clergy of the Scotch Episcopal Church'.

18 Over the same period, another Edinburgh newspaper – the *Edinburgh Evening Courant* – printed nearly 60 Scottish resolutions, most, but not all, of which were also published in the *Caledonian Mercury*. See *Edinburgh Evening Courant*, 30 June 1792 – 7 Feb. 1793.

British system of government was not 'meant' to be altered. It was stressed that only a few deluded men would support such an attack, whereas the majority of the population would be appalled. Many addresses also expressed a declared willingness to risk life and fortune in defence of the king's person, and reassurances that the addressees would do everything in their power to combat sedition and tumult and to support the government's planned legislation against seditious activities. They also hoped that those who were behind the attack would be apprehended and punished. The number of addresses sent from Scotland after the first attempt on George III's life was in excess of 170, while the total after the second attack on the king amounted to at least 107. Roughly half of the addresses sent in 1795 originated with public officials,[19] while nearly three-fourths of the resolutions drafted after the second attempt came from this group. A significant proportion of non-elite, or popular, addresses were sent in 1795, which seems to indicate growing popular involvement in public debates.

In 1795 a number of addresses saw a connection between the attack on the king and the activities of the radicals. About 25 addresses suggested that there was such a link, although not all of them held the radicals directly responsible for the attack. A handful of addresses, however, *did* claim that the deed had been organized and committed by radicals.[20] In 1800, by contrast, not a single address mentioned the words reform, radical or sedition explicitly, nor was any form of *indirect* reference made to the political opposition in connection with this second attack on the king. To some extent, the reason for this may have been that the perpetrator had now been seized immediately after the attack, leaving little doubt as to who had committed the deed. It is none the less striking that no one was interested in exploiting this opportunity to smear the radicals. Instead, they chose to focus even more strongly on the *person* of the king, and on how anyone could even imagine harming such a virtuous and admirable monarch. In 1795 many addresses held it to be as much an attack on the British constitution and form of government as on the king as a man of flesh and blood. By 1800, however, no address appeared to see the assassination attempt as an attack on the government. Emphasis

---

19 There were 80 addresses sent by either provosts, magistrates and councils, or freeholders, heritors, gentlemen, noblemen, justices of the peace and commissioners of supply. Of the remaining addresses, 37 were sent by presbyteries, 24 by Volunteer corps and six from the Scottish universities.

20 See for example the resolution by the Paisley Volunteers. *London Gazette*, 5-8 Dec. 1795.

was placed instead on the dreadful fact that someone had tried to *murder* the king, or, in the words of the bishops and clergy of the Scottish Episcopal Church: 'to take away a Life so justly dear as that of the beloved Monarch of the British Empire'.[21] Moreover, it was not just *any* king whose life had been put in jeopardy. Indeed, George III was portrayed as the 'best of Kings', the 'Patriot King', as the 'Father of his People', and as the veritable pillar upon which the happiness of the whole British empire depended. This change from a focus on the assassination attempt as an attack by political radicals upon the British form of government, in 1795, to an attack upon the sacred person of the king, in 1800, was the result of two developments. First, domestic radicalism no longer posed a significant threat to the state in1800, and, second, the government's policy of presenting the George III as the benevolent Father of his People had been accepted by the general public.

Although the responses to the royal proclamations and to the two assassination attempts represented the most significant waves of loyalist addresses in this period, addresses were also sent to London on several other occasions, albeit in considerably smaller numbers. In 1797 at least six Scottish addresses were sent to the king following the second naval mutiny, condemning the mutineers,[22] and a further three resolutions appeared in the press, without there being any clear indications of whether they were also sent to the government in London.[23] A very few addresses were also sent to London following the two failed rounds of peace negotiations with the French in October 1796 and July 1797. On both occasions, they showed a deep-seated indignation at the approach

---

21 *London Gazette*, 21-24 June 1800.

22 NAS, RH2/4/80, f. 105, 'the Corps of Banffshire Volunteers', 15 June 1797; and *London Gazette*, 20-24 June 1797, 'the Ministers and Elders of the Presbytery of Irvine', 'the Merchants, Ship Owners, and others, concerned in the Trade of the Port of Ayr' and 'the Merchants, Ship Owners and Ship Masters of the Town and Port of Irvine'; *ibid.*, 24-27 June 1797, 'the Magistrates, Common-Council and Inhabitants of the Royal Burgh of Banff'; and *ibid.*, 27 June-1 July 1797, 'the Noblemen, Gentlemen, Justices of the Peace, and Commissioners of Supply of the County of Stirling'.

23 They were not addressed to the king specifically, as was the norm for loyalist addresses, but rather stated a set of resolutions, which had been reached at a 'General Meeting'. See *Caledonian Mercury*, 12 June 1797, 'a General Meeting of the Merchants, Ship-owners, Ship-masters, and other Inhabitants of the PORT of LEITH', 'Meeting of the Merchants, Ship-owners, Ship-masters, and other Inhabitants of the Port of KIRKALDY'.

adopted by the French.[24] More joyous occasions for sending loyal addresses to the king were the vital and spectacular naval victories of 1797 and 1798. At least eleven Scottish addresses were published in the *London Gazette* from early December 1797 until the end of 1798 concerning naval victories, and another three have survived in the correspondence of the Home Office.[25] Most of these addresses expressed a sense of relief, because these victories seemed to preserve the country from the danger of invasion, but some also found it difficult to disguise their satisfaction at the defeat of the French so soon after the Directory had declined Britain's peace proposals. First and foremost, however, they were occasions to rejoice at the 'irresistible Bravery and Skill' of the 'Admirals and Officers and Seamen' of the Royal Navy, who had saved the nation from disaster.[26]

All these addresses came in response to events which affected every inhabitant of Great Britain. In a few cases, however, loyalist resolutions were sent to local government officials, and addressed events or issues of a more local concern. Shortly after the King's Birthday riots in Edinburgh in 1792, for example, the company of merchants in the city presented an address, in which its members pledged to 'give every aid in their power' in support of the local authorities. They also expressed their thanks to the lord provost, magistrates and sheriff for their handling of the crisis and offered a reward of 50 guineas 'for the discovery of the leaders and instigators of the late disturbances, or of the writers of any of the incendiary letters or seditious advertisements which have lately appeared'.[27] Others quickly followed the initiative taken by these merchants. When the Edinburgh authorities decided to put an end to the radical activities of the British Convention on 6 December 1793, the two men in charge of breaking up the assembly –

---

24 See for example NAS, RH2/4/80, f. 13, address from 'the Noblemen The Freeholders and Heritors of the County of Haddington', Haddington, 17 Jan. 1797; *London Gazette*, 12-16, 26-30 Dec. 1797; and NLS [National Library of Scotland], 5.792(23), the Rev. James Roger, 'Essays on Government' (Edinburgh, 1797), p. 59.

25 See *London Gazette*, 26-30 Dec. 1797; *ibid*., 6-10 Mar., 27-30 Oct., 30 Oct.-3 Nov., 20-24 Nov., 24-27 Nov., 27 Nov.-1 Dec., and 4-8 December 1798; NAS, RH2/4/82, f. 223, address from Inverness, 27 Oct. 1797; *ibid*., f. 225, address by the Magistrates and Council of Aberdeen, Council Chamber Aberdeen, 23 Oct. 1797; *ibid*., f. 262, 'the Presbytery of Tain in the County of Ross', Tain, 29 Nov. 1797; and NAS, RH2/4/84, ff. 238-39, 'the Ministers and Elders of the Church of Scotland, met in the Commission of the General Assembly', Edinburgh, 21 Nov. 1798.

26 *Ibid*.

27 *Glasgow Courier*, 9 June 1792, 'Meeting of the *COMPANY of MERCHANTS* of the City of Edinburgh, MERCHANTS-HALL, JUNE 7 1792'.

Thomas Elder, the lord provost of Edinburgh and John Pringle, the sheriff-depute – published a proclamation the next day explaining why they had found it necessary to take this dramatic step.[28] This immediately met with a favourable response from many of the inhabitants in the city. They published addresses of thanks to the authorities for the resolute action they had taken,[29] and, in the following two months, further addresses were sent from different parts of the country,[30] including one from as far away as Inverness.[31] So impressed were the Edinburgh authorities with the response from the citizenry, that they published an official statement, thanking the inhabitants of the city for their support and assistance.[32]

II. Information and Initiatives

Drafting and sending loyal addresses probably involved more people than any other loyalist activity in the 1790s, yet other ways of demonstrating loyalty to the state, in which very few people took part, may have been of equal or even greater importance for the government's campaign against radicalism and in support of the war effort. One such activity in which Scots took part was that of providing the government with information about radical activities, or potential threats to the state, while another was to present ideas and initiatives for government policies of their own making, without any incentive or remuneration from the authorities. These amateur spies and would-be policy-makers often acted out of concern for themselves, their own personal interests, or the welfare of their localities. But just as often they seem to have thought that the information they brought forward, or the suggestions they presented, could be of crucial importance for the authorities and the well-being of British society in general.

---

28 See *Caledonian Mercury*, or *Edinburgh Evening Courant*, 7 Dec. 1793; or *Edinburgh Advertiser*, 6-10 Dec. 1793, 'PROCLAMATION, by the Right Hon. Thomas Elder, Lord Provost of the City of Edinburgh and John Pringle, Sheriff-Deputy of the County of Edinburgh'.

29 In the following issue of the *Caledonian Mercury*, no fewer than 16 incorporations and other professions in Edinburgh published addresses.

30 There were about twenty addresses in all. See *Caledonian Mercury*, 19, 26, 28 and 30 Dec. 1793, and 16 Jan. 1794; *Edinburgh Advertiser*, 10-13, 13-17, 17-20 and 27-31 Dec. 1793; *Edinburgh Evening Courant*, 12, 14 Dec. 1793, 2, 4, 6, 16 23 Jan., 10, 13 Feb.1794; and NAS, RH2/4/74, ff. 154-55, Resolution by the 'Magistrates and other Principal Inhabitants of Paisley', 17 Dec. 1793 [who condemned the British Convention for advocating universal suffrage].

31 *Caledonian Mercury*, 13 Feb. 1794, 'the Presbytery of Inverness'.

32 *Ibid.*, 18 Jan. 1794.

In early 1793, for example, a former soldier who had recently been in France wrote to the authorities to warn them of a French plot to assassinate George III, which he had heard about while in Paris. Denoting himself 'a True Born Briton', the ex-soldier stated: 'I assure you that there are 37 Frenchmen in London who were sworn before a party of the National Convention at Paris to assassinate his Majesty on the first Opportunity even though in open day'.[33] More typical of the kind of information some Scots would send to the authorities was the case presented to Henry Dundas in an anonymous letter from Dundee in late December 1792. The author of the letter – who may have chosen to remain anonymous for security reasons – enclosed a radical pamphlet entitled: *On the folly and wickedness of WAR*, which he claimed had been 'distributed very industriously about this town'. A similar case occurred in Perth about a month later, when the circulation of a resolution issued by the Friends of the People in Perth entitled *Solemn Protestation Against the War* prompted one of the town's inhabitants to write a fiercely worded letter to Henry Dundas. 'Would it not be proper to look after the rascals who signed the inclosed?' he asked, before pointing out that 'these papers are circulated with much industry thro this part of the Country'.[34]

The first – and probably most influential – policy proposal to have emanated from Scotland in the 1790s was the suggestion of instituting a national day of fasting. It was ostensibly the French Revolutionaries' attitude to religion that had prompted the idea, and one of the earliest suggestions came in a very brief anonymous letter to Henry Dundas in February 1793. 'The *Atheism* of the French is much declaimed against' the letter stated, and it continued: 'What say you to a *day* of *Fasting* in this Country, on the event of the War? Accompanied with a proper Proclamation it would do much good in Scotland'.[35] The central authorities in London approved of the idea, and several national fasts were consequently held in the following years, the first in April 1793.[36]

---

33 NAS, RH2/4/69, f. 280, 'A True Born Briton' to 'Sir' [Henry Dundas?], Edinburgh, 5 Feb. 1793.

34 NAS, RH2/4/69, f. 359, Anonymous letter to Henry Dundas, Feb. 1793; and *ibid*., f. 361, Resolution on the War issued by 'a meeting of the Delegates of the Societies of the Friends of the People in Perth', 29 Jan. 1793.

35 NAS, RH2/4/69, f. 321, Anonymous letter to Henry Dundas, 13 Feb. 1793 [original italics].

36 *Caledonian Mercury*, 30 Mar. 1793, '*DECLARATION*, OF THE BISHOP AND SCOTCH EPISCOPAL CLERGY WITHIN THE DIOCESE OF ABERDEEN'.

Many people were concerned about how the influence of the radicals could be thwarted. It was suggested that local authorities could threaten employers with sanctions such as revoking licences if they continued to employ workers with radical sympathies,[37] or employers could give public notice that they would refuse to employ anyone supporting radicalism or radical societies.[38] One anonymous writer suggested that parochial 'Friendly Societies' ought to be instituted for the purpose of organizing ordinary workers and keeping them at arms length from the influence of radical associations.[39] A few Scots also warned about the danger of radical infiltration of the educational system. One anonymous article printed in December 1792 questioned whether any 'Seminaries of Education' had so far given serious thought to 'the very important object of guarding against the corruption of the minds of the rising generation'.[40] In the wake of the naval mutinies of 1797 a number of Scots involved in merchant shipping asked that a distinction be drawn 'between Seamen who have done their duty to their King and Country, and those who have conducted themselves as enemies to both'. They wanted to be able to identify mutineers from their own localities and prevent them from receiving employment in the merchant marine in the future.[41] The repeated harvest failures of the 1790s prompted some Scots to suggest various means of preventing any wastage of flour. In July 1795 an editorial in the *Caledonian Mercury* warned that, 'any unnecessary consumption of grain, at such an alarming period as the present, one cannot help considering as highly reprehensible'. The 'unnecessary consumption' alluded to was the use of flour as 'hair-powder' and the editorial suggested that this practice should be placed under a temporary ban.[42] Five years later, by contrast – during another shortage of oatmeal – the Scots needed similar encouragement in order to be persuaded to exchange their traditional oats for wheat and barley.[43] Later the same year, a

---

37 NAS, RH2/4/65, ff. 19-20, James Mathison, Accountant in Edinburgh to Henry Dundas, 16 Nov. 1792.

38 The merchants of St. Andrews stepped forward and issued such a notice in Dec. 1792. NAS, RH2/4/67, f. 508, Loyalist address by the inhabitants of St. Andrews, 28 Dec. 1792.

39 *Caledonian Mercury*, 25 Sept. 1794, Article by 'A FRIEND OF ORDER'.

40 *Ibid.*, 27 Dec. 1792, Article 'TO THE *PRINTER OF THE CALEDONIAN MERCURY*', by 'A FRIEND *To the Rising Generation*'.

41 *Ibid.*, 12 June 1795, 'General Meeting of the Merchants, Ship-owner, Ship-masters, and other Inhabitants of the PORT of LEITH', 8 June 1797.

42 *Caledonian Mercury*, 27 July 1795.

43 *Caledonian Mercury*, 26 April 1800 [original italics].

meeting held by the local authorities in Midlothian even recommended 'the general use of *rice* and Indian corn', in order to reduce the consumption of oat meal.[44]

III. State Service

Personal service to the state did not necessarily mean military service, but most often it did, as was the case for the best-known, and most widely publicized form of such service in this period – that of joining a Volunteer corps. These paramilitary units arose in direct response to the government's 'Plan for an Augmentation of the Forces for Internal Defence' in March 1794, which to some extent constituted an attempt at channelling the resources of the loyalist association movement into a format more directly useful for the government. The Volunteer corps were intended to serve the dual purpose of a local police force, aimed at suppressing radicalism and popular disturbances, and as a means of defence against a possible French invasion. In terms of converting the loyal societies into armed units, however, the government's initiative was only moderately successful. J. E. Cookson has estimated that, whereas nearly 2000 loyalist associations had been set up in the whole of Britain in the two-year period from 1792 to 1794, there were only about 160 Volunteer corps formed in England and Wales over the course of 1794-96.[45] In Scotland, by contrast – where the Reeves societies were relatively few – volunteering proved immensely popular. By 1796, over one hundred Volunteer companies had been formed in Scotland,[46] and there was no absence of men willing to join such units. Indeed, as J. E. Cookson has remarked, 'the other outstanding feature of Scottish volunteering was the numbers that came forward'.[47] A steady stream of volunteers meant that the Scottish volunteer establishment remained proportionately much larger than that in England. No fewer than one in three infantry volunteers in Britain belonged to a Scottish corps in 1796[48] and, by the end of 1797, the Scottish volunteer infantry made up 44 per cent of the British total.[49]

---

44 *The Times*, 29 Dec. 1800.

45 J. E. Cookson, *The British Armed Nation, 1793-1815* (Oxford, 1997), pp. 24-7.

46 *Ibid.*, p. 140.

47 *Ibid.*, pp. 140-41.

48 *Ibid.*, p. 28.

49 Cookson's estimates were 18,124 volunteer infantry in Scotland, out of a total of 41,465 for the whole of Britain, *ibid.*, p. 69.

Voluntary personal service to the state, however, also played a significant role in the augmentation of the already existing military forces in Britain. The traditional Scottish defence force, the 'Fencibles',[50] also enjoyed a significant increase in numbers based on voluntary offers to raise and man new companies from 1792 onwards. Although a few of the leading Scottish noblemen had raised fencible forces in 1793, and a couple of private offers to do the same had been made the year before,[51] the significant increase in the size of the force came only after the government had issued its plan in 1794. Now the expansion was based on offers from a number of towns and counties across Scotland, the majority of which offered to raise one, two or sometimes three 'troops of fencible cavalry'.[52] Over the period 1793-95, Scotland enlisted no fewer than 15,000 men in fencible regiments, and another nine fencible corps, each consisting of about 600 men, were raised in 1798-99.[53] Those who offered to raise fencible troops or light cavalry did not, however, necessarily intend to serve themselves and, in most cases, the decision to present an offer was primarily one of subscribing funds, whereby bounties – or 'levy-money' – might be given to those who wished to volunteer for service. In this sense, the many offers of this kind that were made in 1794 were, perhaps, as much a matter of demonstrating loyalty to the state by giving *financial* support to the government, as of offering *personal service*. There were, however, other ways in which the Scots offered to serve the state in person.

Over the course of the 1790s many members of the local elites, and others, offered to serve as part-time constables in their local town or village. The initiative to volunteer for this kind of service probably originated in Edinburgh, where a 'Society of Constables' was already in existence by the beginning of 1794.[54] Aimed chiefly at policing the streets of the city, these constables came close to resembling a police force, and were mustered on occasions when unrest was expected. The popularity of

---

50 The fencibles were a uniquely Scottish force, based on the old Scottish pre-union militia.

51 In Dec. 1792, for example, Andrew McDowall had offered to raise 'a Corps of Fencibles' in Galloway, to consist of between 'two to five hundred men ... from amongst that Class of people I know to be true to the constitution, and attached to me'. NAS, RH2/4/67, f. 432, Andrew McDowall to Henry Dundas, 19 Dec. 1792.

52 A meeting of the local elite in Dumbarton offered to raise one troop, as did their peers in Linlithgow, whereas an offer of three troops was made in Perthshire, and a promise was made to raise a regiment of 1000 men in Orkney. See *Edinburgh Evening Courant*, 10, 12 May and 22 Nov. 1794, and *Caledonian Mercury*, 14 Aug. 1794.

53 Cookson, *Armed Nation*, p. 127, and note 7.

54 *Caledonian Mercury*, 13 Jan. 1794.

this service was demonstrated in late May 1794, when the existing force was augmented by upwards of 500 'of the most respectable inhabitants' of the city, who voluntarily enrolled themselves to serve as extraordinary constables,[55] possibly in response to the recently discovered 'Pike Plot'. Following the Edinburgh initiative, similar units of constables were subsequently formed elsewhere; in Kinross, Leith, Midlothian, Glasgow, Paisley, Aberdeen and Lanarkshire.[56]

Of potentially greater significance for the war effort were the many offers made by farmers and tenants in early 1797, who volunteered to place their 'carts and horses' at the disposal of the government in the event of an invasion. Precisely where, and with whom, the idea behind this initiative originated is not entirely clear, but it probably preceded the Defence of the Realm Act of 1798. One of the very first offers to be made came from 'a number of farmers in the vicinity of Edinburgh'. On 6 January they had 'come forward with their horses and carts to assist Government without any expence, to convey troops, baggage, &c. to where their services may be wanted . . . in case of Invasion'.[57] The idea was clearly to employ civilian resources in the defence of the country by offering logistical support for the military – much as it would later be set out in the provisions for 'driving the country' in the Defence of the Realm Act of 1798. The idea caught on elsewhere in Scotland and offers had soon been made across much of the country.[58]

The earl of Kinnoull revealed in a letter to the Home Secretary that he had had no hand in the offer from his tenants, although he admitted to 'feeling a Pride & Satisfaction that it comes from those so nearly commited with me'. His tenants, he wrote, had held a 'Voluntary Meeting' without his knowledge, at which they had decided to offer 'their Services of Carriages & Horses free from expence to Government'.[59] Presenting the authorities with an offer of carts and horses did not, however, necessarily imply personal service on the part of those who offered to supply these means of transportation. In quite a few cases, however, the offer was

---

55 *Edinburgh Evening Courant*, 31 May 1794. See also *Caledonian Mercury*, 5, 7 June 1794.

56 *Caledonian Mercury*, 7 Aug., 18 Sept., 20 Oct., 8, 10, 27 Nov. 1794, 4, 7 Sept. 1797, 8 Dec. 1800; and *Edinburgh Evening Courant*, 7 Aug., and 8 Nov. 1794.

57 *Glasgow Courier*, 7 January 1797.

58 See for example *Caledonian Mercury*, 12, 14 Jan., 16, 23, 25 Feb., 2 Mar. and 13 April 1797; and *Glasgow Courier*, 26 Jan., 9, 18 Mar. 1797.

59 NAS, RH2/4/80, ff. 17-18, Drummond Hay Kinnoull to the Duke of Portland, 26 Jan. 1797.

not just of carts and horses, but also included servants.[60] As a demonstration of loyalty, offering carts and horses to the government was more often a material contribution to the war effort, than one of personal service.

IV. Financial Support

The most widely adopted method of making a voluntary financial contribution in the 1790s was that of opening a subscription. These could be initiated for a variety of reasons, but most often they came in response to a specific event in the war and responded to a specific problem. As far as the initiating of new campaigns was concerned Edinburgh seems to have taken a leading role in Scotland. One of the very first subscriptions to be opened in Scotland in the 1790s was begun there in early October 1793, and was inspired by the state of the British army in Flanders.

It had come to public attention that the British soldiers fighting in the Low Countries had insufficient clothing for the coming winter in a 'cold and damp country', and a subscription was consequently initiated to procure 'flannel waistcoats' for the soldiers, so that 'the lives of many brave men' might be saved.[61] The campaign went on for four months, until the end of February 1794, by which time over £1600 had been raised from between 600 and 700 people in the city.[62] The lists of new subscribers – which the organizers of the campaign published in the press on a regular basis – included not only the amounts given by each and every individual donor, but also their professions. A close examination of these lists reveals that the subscribers came from a cross-section of society, although with a certain degree of bias towards wealthier people. Typically, there would be larger sums – in the area of £5 to £30 – subscribed by noblemen, merchants, magistrates, and advocates, whereas smaller sums, often less than a pound, would be contributed by various kinds of craftsmen and artisans, and sometimes even by labourers. The variety of professions and occupations represented can be seen from a list published in the middle of November 1793. This showed that subscriptions had come from a clerk in the Post-Office, a writer to the signet, a family in Fifeshire, an advocate, an accountant, a coppersmith, a farmer, a baker and 'a week's earnings

60 The tenants, and sub-tenants on the Estates of Charles Gordon of Wardhouse, for example, offered 'what horses, carts, and servants we have, for the purpose of carrying troops and military stores'. *Caledonian Mercury*, 20 Mar. 1797.

61 *Edinburgh Evening Courant*, 24 Oct. 1793.

62 *Ibid.*, 24 Feb. 1794.

from a Poor Woman, the Mother of a Soldier serving in Flanders'.[63] The Edinburgh initiative was soon imitated elsewhere in Scotland, and a subscription was also opened in London, modelled on 'the Contribution set on foot by a Committee at Edinburgh for the purchase of Flannel Waistcoats'.[64] To an extent, the 'flannel waistcoats' subscription of 1793-94 set a standard for the campaigns that were to follow. The majority of subsequent subscriptions were also highly publicized affairs, where a running total of the funds that had been collected at any given time – together with lists of new subscribers – were published in the press on a regular basis. Most of these subscriptions were also opened in response to a specific event in the war, and the social composition of those who contributed funds was largely similar to that of the first Edinburgh campaign. Nevertheless, most of them differed in one crucial respect. Rather than being aimed at supporting British forces abroad, they were concerned with the consequences of war, and with helping people at home in Britain. In most cases this meant collecting money to provide relief for seamen who had been injured in naval battles, or for the families of those sailors who had died. The first of these campaigns was begun a few weeks after Lord Howe's famous victory in 1794. It was intended to raise funds for the 'relief of the Sailors, Mariners, or others on board Lord Howe's fleet, disabled during the late gallant action, and for relief of the Widows and Children of Sufferers on that occasion'.[65] One week later, sufficient funds had already been collected to enable the organizers to print notices, giving instructions on how those who were eligible for support could lodge their claims,[66] and the subscription soon attracted contributions from outside Edinburgh.[67] Similar subscriptions were also initiated after the two subsequent naval victories at Camperdown in 1797 and the Nile in 1798.[68]

Subscriptions were, however, also opened for other reasons than to provide support for those who suffered as a consequence of naval battles, and they were in some instances of a more local orientation and conducted on a significantly smaller scale. In mid-November 1793, for exam-

---

63 *Ibid.*, 14 Nov. 1793.

64 *The Times*, 13 Nov. 1793, 'CROWN and ANCHOR TAVERN, STRAND', 11 November 1793.

65 *Ibid.*, 16 June 1794.

66 *Edinburgh Evening Courant*, 23 June 1794.

67 *Ibid.*, 28, 30 June, 3 July 1794; and *Caledonian Mercury*, 14 July 1794.

68 *Ibid.*, 28 Oct. 1797, 13 Jan., 13 Oct., 10 Dec. 1798; and *Glasgow Courier*, 4, 14 and 18 Nov. 1797.

ple, it was reported that a number of the inhabitants of Edinburgh – 'sensible of the great utility of the EDINBURGH VOLUNTEERS, and wishing to assist this Corps in defraying a part of their necessary expences' – had come together and subscribed over £300 for this purpose. [69] A subscription was opened in Edinburgh in March 1796 to provide for the widow and children of a sailor who had been killed onboard a merchant vessel in an engagement with a French privateer.[70] The magistrates and council of the burgh of Irvine were reported to have given 100 guineas to a fund which had been set up for the purpose of 'carrying on the war'.[71] A campaign aimed at providing relief for the 'Wives and Families' of British soldiers serving with the army in Holland was begun in November 1799.[72] A meeting held by the local elite in Lanarkshire in December 1800 had subscribed £9000 'for the purpose of purchasing from the merchants, such quantities of grain as may be necessary for the regular supply of the inhabitants of this county' during the prevailing scarcity of food.[73] Although these subscriptions were varied and imaginative, and in some cases they also raised significant amounts of money, they were none the less completely dwarfed by the 'Voluntary Contributions', a campaign which the government initiated in early 1798.

The voluntary contributions were as successful in Scotland, as in the whole of Great Britain. Lists of new subscribers – together with the amounts they had contributed – were again published regularly in the Scottish press for the whole duration of the subscription, which lasted from early February 1798 until it was officially closed on 1 December.[74] The number of contributors must have ran into many thousands. Although no running total appears to have been kept for the whole of Scotland, the majority of those who gave seem to have contributed in accordance to their means, and this – together with the sheer number of contributions – indicates that the sums collected must have been very significant indeed. Furthermore, a running total *was* kept for Edinburgh, at least for a while, and

---

69 *Edinburgh Evening Courant*, 15 Nov., 13 Dec. 1793.

70 *Ibid.*, 3 Mar. 1796.

71 NAS, RH2/4/83, f. 120, Eglinton Provost to the Duke of Portland, 8 Feb. 1798.

72 This time the initiative for the subscription was taken in London, and then copied in Edinburgh. *Caledonian Mercury*, 7 Nov. 1799.

73 *Ibid.*, 8 December 1800, 'Meeting of the Noblemen, Gentlemen, Freeholders, Justices of the Peace, Commissioners of Supply, Clergy and Heritors of the County of Lanark', Town Hall of Hamilton, 2 Dec. 1800.

74 *Caledonian Mercury*, 29 Nov. 1798.

by the end of April 1798, a total of £69,743 had been collected in the city.[75] In the early months of the campaign the subscribers were largely those at whom the government had set its primary aim – the wealthier section of society – but, gradually, more ordinary people also contributed. Larger contributions were again principally given by the local elite of a town or county, such as the gentlemen of Dumfries who gave in excess of £3000,[76] while smaller amounts were contributed by less wealthy and even by quite poor people. In the parish of Wemyss, for example, a total of £57 was given by 84 of the local inhabitants, of whom 24 were denoted as labourers, 14 as weavers and the remaining 46 as different kinds of artisans, mostly shoemakers and tailors.[77] Lady Arniston, Henry Dundas's mother, initiated a separate 'Ladies Subscription' in Edinburgh,[78] which had raised well over £400 by the middle of June.[79] A number of Catholics residing in Edinburgh decided to step forward as a group and offer their contributions in March, regretting only that 'the smallness of their numbers, and, the narrowness of their circumstances, do not permit them to assist their Country in the manner they would wish'.[80]

Besides subscription campaigns, the main way of giving financial support to the government in the 1790s was to offer rewards or bounties to volunteers for service in the armed forces. Most of these bounties were used to enlist men in the Royal Navy, but there were also a number issued for fencible units, and a few for Volunteer corps.[81] As with the subscriptions campaigns, the offer of bounties was largely a newspaper-based activity, and local government officials again gave a lead. Thomas Elder, the lord provost of Edinburgh, took the initiative, when, on 20 December 1792, he placed an advertisement in the Edinburgh press under the heading of 'BOUNTY TO SEAMEN', by which he offered a reward of:

> TWO GUINEAS over and above his Majesty's Bounty, to every Able Seaman, and ONE GUINEA to ever Ordinary Seaman, not under Twenty nor above Fifty Years of Age, who shall, during the continuance of his Majesty's Bounty, appear in the Council Chamber, and voluntarily enter himself to serve in the Royal Navy.

---

75 *Caledonian Mercury*, 26 April 1798.

76 *Ibid.*, 17 Mar. 1798.

77 *Ibid.*, 2 June 1798.

78 *Caledonian Mercury*, 26 Feb. 1798.

79 *Edinburgh Advertiser*, 18-21 June 1793.

80 *Caledonian Mercury*, 22 Mar. 1798.

81 There were few, if any bounties for regular line regiments published in the Scottish press.

Elder's offer was made on behalf of the magistrates and city council in Edinburgh and it concluded with the patriotic words 'GOD SAVE THE KING!', followed by his own name.[82] For the next two years, Thomas Elder's advertisement was printed in the press on a regular basis – undergoing only minor alterations during that time. It offered a template upon which most subsequent bounty-offers would be based.

Although it was the local authorities in Edinburgh who had first taken the initiative, subsequent navy bounties were remarkably varied in terms of who offered them. In order to present a bounty, it was obviously necessary to raise or have access to funds, and the different ways in which navy-bounties were financed give an indication of who stood behind them. Many offers were sustained by subscriptions, usually initiated by the elite of a county, town or parish, but to which all ranks of society were normally allowed to contribute. Other bounties were issued by local government officials such as magistrates and town councils, while a third category were bounties given by different kinds of societies, institutions or businesses, and a fourth by individuals who were setting up their own self-funded offers. Bounties to volunteers for naval service were issued by the local authorities in Perth, Stirling, Montrose, St. Andrews, Aberdeen, Linlithgow, Dumfries, Dundee, Greenock, Banff, Mussleburgh, Inverness, Forfar, Pittenweem, Thurso, Paisley and Kirkcudbright, as well as by the authorities in the burghs of Wigton, Culross, Dysart and Newburgh.[83] Bounties based on subscriptions were issued in Edinburgh, Glasgow and Haddington, as well as in the counties of Berwick, Fife, Perth, Aberdeen, Kincardine, Wigton, Stirling, Lanark and Ayr. They were also offered by the Inverkeithing Sailor Society, which set up its own bounty of three guineas to able seamen in early February 1793,[84] and by individual Scots. Those who offered their own individual bounties had to rely exclusively on their own personal funds to support the scheme. Two Linlithgow merchants, George and Andrew Bartholomew, resolved to 'offer a Bounty, over and above all other bounties, of One Guinea to all Seamen and Landmen belonging to this burgh and parish . . . and to continue this Bounty till the French are made to march back into their own country'.

[82] *Caledonian Mercury* and *Edinburgh Evening Courant*, 20 Dec. 1792, 'BOUNTY TO SEAMEN, By the Right Hon. The Lord Provost, Magistrates, and Council of the City of Edinburgh'.

[83] *Caledonian Mercury*, 5, 7, 11, 18, 21, 25, 28 Feb., 4, 16, 23 Mar., 1, 4 April 1793; and *Edinburgh Advertiser*, 26 Feb.-1 Mar., 1-5 Mar. 1793.

[84] *Caledonian Mercury*, 7 Feb. 1793.

No specific restriction was placed on the number of bounties that could be issued, only that to receive one, the claimant would have to be from 'their own town and parish'.[85]

An editorial in the *Caledonian Mercury* pointed out as early as mid-January 1793, that 'a greater number of seamen' had entered into his Majesty's service as a consequence of the Edinburgh-bounty 'than was ever known in such a short space of time', and this, it was hoped, 'will preclude the necessity of resorting to press warrants'.[86] An anonymous article in July 1794 even suggested that any surplus funds from the Lord Howe subscription should be set aside so that there would be 'no occasion for a press warrant' in future.[87] In late March 1793 the Inverkeithing Sailor Society published a notice, in which they stated that since 'a house of rendezvous has been erected, and a press-gang established within this town, which has of late committed several illegal and oppressive acts of violence, unprecedented in all other places, upon the inhabitants and neighbourhood', they could see no other possible outcome than to 'UNANIMOUSLY recall their former advertisement offering a bounty'.[88]

By late summer 1793 the issuing of bounties largely came to an end and it was only with the passing of the three Navy Acts in March 1795 that a number of new bounty-offers were again published in the press.[89] Because of the high number of recruits early in the war, the shortage of available manpower in Scotland was now beginning to make itself felt. This – together with the specific quota requirement set by the Navy Acts – was reflected in the much higher reward that were offered in these newly issued bounties. The commissioners who had been appointed to raise volunteers at Leith offered bounties of twenty guineas to seamen and fifteen to landsmen, and promised to cover not only 'travelling charges' and 'every other reasonable expence' for the recipients, but also to 'REWARD HANDSOMELY those who take trouble in their service, by recommending Volunteers or otherwise'. Similar bounties were offered in the ports of Anstruther and Borrowstounness,[90] as well as by the commissioners at

85 *Edinburgh Advertiser*, 22-26 Mar. 1793.

86 *Caledonian Mercury*, 17 Jan. 1793.

87 *Edinburgh Evening Courant*, 4 July 1794, article by 'A FRIEND TO KING AND COUNTRY'.

88 *Caledonian Mercury*, 30 Mar. 1793.

89 *Statutes at Large* (London, 1798), 28 George III, Cap. V, XI, and XXIX.

90 *Caledonian Mercury*, 6 April 1795.

Dunbar,[91] and the merchants and ship owners at Stornoway.[92] After 1795 there were hardly any bounties offered to volunteers for naval service, and the same was largely the case for fencible units.[93]

Although the subscriptions for fencible forces began only in 1794, bounties were already being offered in 1793 for the few regiments which were raised that year. The town of Dunfermline, for example, presented a bounty of two guineas to volunteers for the Breadalbane Regiment in late March,[94] as did the magistrates and town council of St. Andrews.[95] Further advertisements were printed in 1794 and in early 1795 offering rewards which were largely similar to those given to fencible and navy recruits in 1793. The magistrates and town council of Auchtermuchty, a burgh in Fifeshire offered a bounty of 'one guinea over and above his Majesty's Bounty, to any person enlisting the new regiment under the command of Colonel Graham' in February 1794.[96]

V. How loyal were the Scots?

The question which naturally arises is the extent to which the Scots were prepared to defend the Union of Great Britain, its current government and existing political system, at a time of crisis. How loyal were the Scots? It is the suggested here that the Scots demonstrated a higher degree of loyalty than has often been supposed. In some respects they may have been even greater supporters of the British state, than many of the inhabitants in England.

The range of different types of demonstrations of loyalty in Scotland is striking. Many demonstrations were initiated by the government and, in quite a few cases, local officials needed to provide a lead before the general public took up the idea. But the Scots did respond to the encouragement they were given by the authorities, and often in overwhelming numbers. More crucially, a significant number of Scots also showed a willingness to initiate ways of demonstrating loyalty, entirely of their own making and without any initiative or remuneration from the authorities. The extent of such activities serves to justify the conclusion that many Scots were pre-

91 *Ibid.*, 20 April 1795.

92 *Ibid.*, 23 April 1795.

93 Bounties for volunteer corps remained an exception throughout the war.

94 *Edinburgh Advertiser*, 29 Mar.-2 April 1793; and *Caledonian Mercury*, 30 Mar. 1793.

95 *Ibid.*, 26-29 Mar. 1793.

96 *Edinburgh Evening Courant*, 27 Feb. 1794.

pared to make efforts in defence of the British state. So many people, from all social categories, were prepared not only to make an effort, but also to make concrete sacrifices – either by offering financial support, or personal service – in order to achieve this end. A question-mark may legitimately be placed on the significance of the loyalist addresses, on the grounds that it required little effort or sacrifice on anyone's part to draft and send a resolution. For the elite of Scottish society the cost of not demonstrating support for the state in such a manner may have been greater than that of doing so. It was, after all, they – as the main property-owners and the enfranchised classes of Scotland – who had most to lose from a wholesale reform or change of the British political system along the lines proposed by the radicals. Seen in this light, however, it is perhaps equally significant that many ordinary people – who had little or no direct stake in the state and the political system – also made efforts to attend meetings and sign loyal addresses.

VI. Loyalist Ideology

A conservative ideology aimed at defending the British constitution and government had been developed in Britain in the second half of the eighteenth century, largely in response to the challenge posed by the American revolution and the agenda of British reformers.[97] When the French Revolution led to a renewal of radical activities in Britain, many of those who wished to retain the political *status quo* repeated the arguments advanced by earlier conservative thinkers and pamphleteers, and developed them further in the context of the new radical challenge. To some extent, British conservatism had always adopted a defensive stance, but the defensive nature of the conservative argument was perhaps even more marked after 1792 than it had been in earlier decades. This was due partly to the new progressive principles put forward by the French revolutionaries, and partly to the revival of the radical argument at home, which had received a powerful boost with Thomas Paine's *Rights of Man*. Gradually, however, the loyalist defence of the British constitution and its benefits also became imperative because of the radical development of the French Revolution and the outbreak of war. The principal objective of loyalist ideology was to outline and to explain the 'blessings' of the British constitution, as well as to refute the criticisms advanced by the radicals.

---

97 See H. T. Dickinson, *Liberty and Property: Political Ideology in Eighteenth-Century Britain* (London, 1977), Chapter 8.

Scottish propagandists took a significant part in this defensive campaign, which was waged throughout the whole decade. Many of the arguments which were presented in defence of the British constitution in pamphlets and newspaper articles had much in common with the central points raised in the loyalist addresses of 1792-93. Stress was placed on the fortunate situation in which Britons found themselves. They were blessed with the best constitution in the world, which was not only 'the envy of surrounding nations',[98] but also represented 'the grandest effort of political wisdom ever exhibited on the earth, the pride of Britain, the glory of the isles', as the Reverend Thomas Macknight phrased it.[99] Indeed, the British form of government was held to have reached a level of 'maturity and perfection unequalled on the face of the Globe',[100] and the unsurpassed benefits accruing from this uniquely successful political system were outlined at great length. The peculiar advantages associated with a mixed government and balanced constitution was emphasized by many. The Reverend James Roger, for example, held that 'all the beauties of the three simple forms' of government – those of monarchy, aristocracy and democracy – had been successfully combined in the British constitution.[101] An anonymous pamphlet stressed that' the defects of these *simple* forms of Government, are rectified or counteracted when they are *all united in one complicated, and yet harmonizing system*'.[102] Liberty and property were two central concepts in British eighteenth-century conservative ideology, and the effective protection which loyalist writers claimed the British constitution secured for these rights – for all Britons, regardless of their wealth or social status – was underlined in many pamphlets and essays. Similar points were made about the rule of law, a principle loyalist pamphleteers held to be perfectly safeguarded by the British constitution, and equality before the law, on which

98 *The Times*, 31 Jan. 1793, General Meeting of County Delegates in Scotland, Edinburgh, 10 Dec. 1792.

99 NLS, 3.2547, The Rev. Thomas Macknight, 'The Means of National Security, Considered as a Ground for Thankfulness to Divine Providence. A DISCOURSE, Addressed to the Volunteers of Leith, on the 23d Nov. 1794, and published at their request' (London, 1795), p. 16.

100 NLS, L.36.h.5, Laurence Moyes, 'Gratitude to God: a SERMON on Jeremiah vi. 17. preached in the church of Larbert, upon a Day of Thanksgiving, appointed by the SYNOD of PERTH and STIRLING' (Falkirk, 1794), p. 14.

101 NLS, 5.792(23), Roger, 'ESSAY on GOVERNMENT', p. 28.

102 NLS, L.C.2266, 'a New Year's Gift to the people of Great Britain: containing the resolutions of a society, formed for the purpose of undeceiving and enlightening its Own Members, and now humbly offered to the consideration of the people of GREAT BRITAIN' (Edinburgh, 1793), p. 15.

many Scottish seem to have placed particular emphasis.[103] Some also pointed to the prevailing prosperity of Britain, and held that it was to a large extent the result of Britain's liberal and stable regime.[104] Others, however, were less interested in mounting a defence of the British constitution. Instead, they tried to divert attention elsewhere by emphasizing the importance of a reform of 'manners and morals' before, or even instead of, political reform. It was held that no successful reform of the political system could be achieved until the moral character of the British population had been rejuvenated and improved. It was fool-hardy and irresponsible of the radicals to campaign for political changes as long as the people's manners and morals in general remained in an unreformed state. Rather than complain about alleged abuses in the British constitution, or the supposedly corrupted nature of Britain's governing class, the radicals – as well as the people in general – ought to focus on themselves and on their own moral improvement.[105]

Once they had established that the British constitution was the best that could be achieved, and they had refuted the principles and ideas put forward by Thomas Paine and other radical thinkers, the loyalist pamphleteers went on to attack the radicals and the French revolutionaries more directly. Questions were raised with respect to the motives which the radicals had for promoting reform, and whether their true intentions were other than those they professed in public. The Rev. Andrew Hunter commented that:

> Frequently the cry about abuses in government and the need for reformation in the state, is raised by worthless and seditious persons, who have either squandered away their own fortunes in vice and folly, or who have been disappointed in schemes of ambition, and are eager by such means to raise themselves to situations of honour and affluence.[106]

---

[103] See for example NLS, L.36.h.5(4), Robert Walker, 'A SERMON, Preached in the Church of Canongate, on occasion of the General National Fast, February 27. 1794' (Edinburgh, 1794).

[104] NLS, 3.584(4), Thomas Somerville, 'OBSERVATIONS ON THE CONSTITUTION AND PRESENT STATE OF BRITAIN' (Edinburgh, 1793), pp. 4-6, 10-11.

[105] See for example *Edinburgh Evening Courant*, 27 Dec. 1792, 'To the PRINTER', by 'BOB SHORT', Edinburgh, 24 Dec. 1792; NLS, 5.2484(12), William Dunn, 'An ADDRESS by a *SCOTSMAN* to his Countrymen and Fellow Citizens, respecting the Situation of Public Affairs, THE REFORM, and the War Impending from France' (Glasgow, 1793); and NLS, L.36.h.5(8), James Steuart, 'A plan for REFORM, Proposed to the Christian People, a Sermon, Preached at Anderston the First Day of the New Year' (Glasgow, 1793).

[106] NLS, L.36.h.5(6), The Rev. Andrew Hunter, 'The Duties of Subjects: a Sermon preached in the Tron Church, Edinburgh, December 16th 1792' (Edinburgh, 1793), p. 7.

The radicals were attacked as dishonest and evil-designing men who were not to be trusted, and nowhere was this more evident than in the corresponding societies which had 'solicited the aid, and courted the friendship of France'. This was at least partly responsible for the outbreak of war.[107] The state of revolutionary France was contrasted to the favourable state of Britain. The chaos, anarchy and bloodshed prevailing in France was described in exaggerated detail, and comparisons were drawn between the rule of law in Britain and the injustices prevalent in France. The true liberty enjoyed by Britons was compared to the licentiousness of the French. Much of this literature must come under the category of 'black propaganda', aimed more at smearing the French Revolutionaries than at accurately describing events in France.

Although Scottish propagandists took part in a British debate, and addressed issues of a British nature, this did not stop them from adapting their arguments to Scottish readers. Hannah More's *Cheap Repository Tracts* were adapted to a Scottish setting and translated into Scots dialect only shortly after they had been published in England,[108] and efforts were made to place the events in France in a Scottish context, or to explain them, so that they would be more easily understood by ordinary Scots. An anonymous pamphlet from 1793, for example, addressed the French republican government's brutal defeat of the city of Lyon – a royalist stronghold – and the subsequent execution of many of its inhabitants after it had fallen, with the comment:

> It is to be remarked, that Lyons was one of the most wealthy and industrious towns in the kingdom, – the largest city after Paris, and contained upwards of two hundred thousand inhabitants, – that is more than three times as many as the city of Edinburgh.[109]

Another anonymous pamphlet compared the imprisonment and execution of the French queen, Marie Antoinette, with the fate of the Scottish queen Mary Stewart,[110] while the *Edinburgh Evening Courant* claimed in

---

[107] NLS, L.119.b, William Porteous, 'The GOOD OLD WAY recommended: Two Discourses, delivered on Thursday, 18. April, 1793, the day appointed by the King to be observed as a National Fast.' (Glasgow, 1793), p. 12.

[108] NLS, 3.2730, Tam Thrum, an auld weaver, 'Look before ye Loup; or A HEALIN' SA' for the Crack it Crowns of *COUNTRY POLITICIANS*' (Edinburgh, 1793).

[109] NLS, Nha.V22, 'The *FIRST FRUITS* of the FRENCH REVOLUTION' (Edinburgh, 1793), p. 11.

[110] NLS, Yule.61, 'A Short view of the POLITICS of FRANCE with remarks on its Internal Situation' (Edinburgh, 1794), p. 27.

April 1794 that 'the French Constitution is rapidly approaching to the *Cromwellian* system'.[111] It commented on the death of Robespierre that he had 'had a design of making himself the Cromwell of this country'.[112]

Other commentators focused on the benefits the Scots had obtained from the Union with England in 1707. An anonymous article printed in the *Glasgow Courier*, for example, asked readers to 'review the history of Scotland – When were her natives happy?' Was it in the seventeenth century, when she was ruled by 'indigent and wretched Princes', and when 'all was gloom, desolation, and despair', or was it in the present when Scotland enjoyed the 'security of person, property, and reputation' under the British constitution? Clearly, the answer had to be that Scotland was currently in a better situation than ever before in her history and, since this was the case: 'are we to hazard the change of a system so manifestly productive of the greatest happiness that this or any other people ever enjoyed?'[113] A related point was made by John Young. He argued that a reform of the representation in parliament was unlikely to be to the benefit of Scotland, since 'we could not enjoy an equal share of it'. Scotland's representation in the Westminster parliament and some of her influence over British politics would not be improved by an increase in the number of Scottish MPs, or a redistribution of seats when Scottish representation could never equal that of England.[114] The message behind these statements was stark and clear. A reform of the political system in Britain was not in Scotland's interest. Indeed, the Scots might have even more to lose than the English by a wholesale change of the British constitution and they therefore ought to stand up in its defence.

111 *Edinburgh Evening Courant*, 17 April 1794 [original italics].

112 *Ibid.*, 30 Aug. 1794.

113 NAS, RH2/4/66, f. 321. 'To the PEOPLE OF SCOTLAND', by a 'FELLOW SUBJECT' [excerpt from the *Glasgow Courier*, 13 Dec. 1792].

114 NLS, BCL.D5770, John Young, 'ESSAYS on the following INTERESTING SUBJECTS' [Edinburgh, 1794].

Eckhart Hellmuth

After Fox's Libel Act

Or, How to Talk about the Liberty of the Press in the 1790s[*]

In the spring of 1792 Parliament passed Fox's Libel Act. This meant that attempts to limit the role of the jury in libel cases were overturned. Fox's Libel Act stated 'that on every trial for the making or publishing of any libel, the jury may give a general verdict of Guilty or Not Guilty, upon the whole matter put in issue; and shall not be required or directed, by the court or judge, to find the defendant or defendants Guilty, merely on the proof of the publication of the paper charged to be a libel, and the sense ascribed to the same in the Indictment or Information.'[1] The passing of Fox's Libel Act put an end to a long-running dispute – one which had been going on for more than fifty years – about the role of juries in libel trials.[2] In this dispute, critics had objected to the fact that judges, not juries, were empowered to decide whether the act had been committed with criminal intent, and whether the writing was seditious or defamatory. Added to this was the fact that the law did not recognize truth as a defence. Consequently, libel trials which followed this traditional procedure were seen as instruments for the suppression of voices critical of the government and the domestication of public opinion. The libel trials of John Wilkes (1763/64), John Almon, Henry Woodfall, John Miller (1770), and William Shipley, Dean of St Asaph (1783), in particular, had given rise to criticism of this sort. And contemporaries from the Enlightened milieu pleaded decisively for juries to be given the right to return a true general verdict in cases of seditious libel. On the assumption that juries were a bulwark against arbitrariness on the part of the authorities, such a step was seen as an important stage on the way to greater press freedom. Fox's Libel Act undoubtedly fulfilled one of the demands which

---

* I would like to thank Angela Davies for the translation.

1 32 Geo. 3, c. 60 (1792).

2 On this see the detailed account by Thomas A. Green, *Verdict According to Conscience: The English Criminal Trial Jury, 1200–1800* (Chicago, 1985), pp. 318–355; see also R. H. Helmholz and Thomas A. Green, *Juries, Libel, & Justice: The Role of English Juries in Seventeenth- and Eighteenth-Century Trials for Libel and Slander* (Los Angeles, 1984); H. M. Lubasz, 'Public Opinion Comes of Age: Reform of the Libel Law in the Eighteenth Century', *History Today*, 8 (1958), 453-461.

the reform movement had made during the 1760s, 1770s, and 1780s. It would, however, be wrong to assume that, with the passing of Fox's Libel Act, the discourse on the freedom of the press came to an end – on the contrary.

While Fox's Libel Bill was still being debated in the House of Lords, a royal proclamation was issued ordering all magistrates 'to discover and prosecute the authors of divers wicked and seditious writings which had been printed, published and industriously dispersed, tending to excite tumult and disorder'.[3] Alarmed by the politicization of the lower orders encouraged by, among others, the London Corresponding Society, Pitt and his government declared war on the radical press. But this was not all. In November 1792 the Association for the Preservation of Liberty and Property was formed under the leadership of John Reeves.[4] This was the start of a wave of foundations of Loyalist societies which very quickly spread all over the country. The Loyalists saw one of their main tasks as restraining seditious writing. In order to do this, they employed various means. First, they called for the detection and prosecution, through *ex officio* information, of 'subversive' authors, as well as their publishers, and the booksellers who distributed their works. Beyond this, they initiated a boycott. Thus, for example, a declaration by the committee of the Association for the Preservation of Liberty and Property stated: 'That this committee, being persuaded that great mischief has been for some time past effected in this country by the circulation of Newspapers filled with

---

3 *Annual Register*, 34 (1792), 158–160.

4 On John Reeves and the Loyalist movement see, among others, Harry T. Dickinson, 'Popular Loyalism in Britain in the 1790s', in *The Transformation of Polical Culture: England and Germany in the Late Eighteenth Century*, ed. Eckhart Hellmuth (Oxford, 1990), pp. 503–533; idem, 'Popular Conservatism and Militant Loyalism, 1789-1815' in *Britain and the French Revolution, 1789-1815*, ed. Harry T. Dickinson (London, 1988), pp. 103-125; Robert R. Dozier, *For King, Country, and Constitution: The English Loyalists and the French Revolution* (Lexington KY, 1983); David Eastwood, 'Patriotism and the English State in the 1790s', in *The French Revolutuion and British Popular Politics*, ed. Mark Philp (Cambridge, 1991), pp. 146-68; Mark Philp, 'Vulgar Conservatism, 1792-3', *English Historical Review*, 110 (1995), 42-69; D. E. Ginter, 'The Loyalist Association Movement of 1792-3 and British Public Opinion', *Historical Journal*, 9 (1966), 179-90; Austin Mitchell, 'The Association Movement of 1792-3', *Historical Journal*, 4 (1961), 56-77; Michael Duffy, 'William Pitt and the Origins of the Loyalist Association Movement of 1792', *Historical Journal*, 39 (1996), 943-62; Thomas P. Schofield, 'Conservative Political Thought in Britain in Response to the French Revolution', *Historical Journal*, 29 (1986), 601-22; Michael Weinzierl, *Freiheit, Eigentum und keine Gleichheit: Die Transformation der englischen politischen Kultur und die Anfänge des modernen Konservativismus* (Munich, 1993).

disloyalty and sedition, the writers of which manifestly appear by their language to be in the pay of French emissaries, who wish to destroy our excellent Constitution, do earnestly recommend it to all good Englishmen, whether Masters of Private Families, or Keepers of Inns, Taverns, or Coffee-Houses, to discontinue and discourage the use and circulation of all such disloyal and seditious Newspapers.'[5] From the start, the political strategies adopted by the Association for the Preservation of Liberty and Property included the threatening gesture. Their announcements – as a declaration of December 1792, for example, makes clear – aimed to intimidate and spread uncertainty:

> That a Caution be hereby given to all sellers of Newspapers, Newscarriers, Persons delivering Hand-bills for Club-meetings and the like, that if such Papers are seditious and treasonable, they are also guilty, equally with the original Publisher, Printer, or Author; and that it becomes them seriously to consider what are the Newspapers, Papers of Invitation to Clubs and Meetings, which they sell, carry, or distribute, and whether they are of a Nature to bring upon them the Penalties of the Law.[6]

The Loyalists obviously aimed to pursue a sort of vigilante politics which they hoped would silence radical voices.

In order to counteract tendencies of this sort, the society known as Friends of the Liberty of the Press was established in December 1793.[7] It drew its members mainly from the rather élitist Friends of the People and the socially more open Society for Constitutional Information. It clearly also extended to the 'Jacobin' camp. The Friends of the Liberty of the Press to some extent represented a coalition between a parliamentary and an extra-parliamentary opposition. More than twenty MPs joined it, among them Richard Brinsley Sheridan, Charles Grey, Thomas Erskine, Philip Francis, George Tierney and Samuel Whitbread, as did prominent representatives of the extra-parliamentary reform movement. The latter included such prominent figures as John Horne Tooke, John Thelwall, Major John Cartwright and Joseph Towers. The Friends of the Liberty of the Press engaged in all the activities that are so familiar from the late eighteenth century. They held meetings, passed resolutions, published

---

5 Pamphlet of the Association for Preserving Liberty and Property, 4 Dec. 1792 (BL Lo s.sh. 648.c.26(12)).

6 Pamphlet of the Association for Preserving Liberty and Property, 6 Dec. 1792 (BL Lo s.sh. 648.c.26(12)).

7 On this see Robert R. Rea, 'The Liberty of the Press as an Issue in English Politics, 1792–1793', *The Historian*, 24 (1961), 26–43. The society was variously called Friends *of* and Friends *to* the Liberty of the Press.

pamphlets, and cultivated all the usual forms of political sociability. At times, they could mobilize between 700 and 900 supporters. And, it seems, similar societies were set up in Sheffield, Durham, Manchester, and Derby.

This prepared the ground for a new round in the public discourse on the liberty of the press. Within a very short time, the Association for the Preservation of Liberty and Property and the Friends of the Liberty of the Press, together with their respective sympathizers, were engaged in a vehement dispute which lasted until 1795 and 1796. This was the context in which, for example, Robert Hall's *Apology for the Freedom of the Press* and Archibald Bruce's *Reflections on the Freedom of Writing* were written. The discourse on the problem of the freedom of the press that ensued after Fox's Libel Act can be read from two different perspectives. First, it can be seen as an important stage in the development of a 'modern' understanding of the freedom of the press.[8] Second, it can be seen as an example of the general nature of the political discourse in Britain at the end of the eighteenth century.[9]

I.

The discourse on the freedom of the press that developed after 1792 took place in a situation that had not existed in the same way before because the Association for the Preservation of Liberty and Property represented a new phenomenon. This association, for the first time, placed the principle of social self-organization into the service of persecuting 'subversive' opinions and tried to control the press on a non-governmental basis. The Friends of the Liberty of the Press immediately perceived the critical core of the activities of the Association for the Preservation of Liberty and Property. To them it was clear that the principle of social self-

8 On this see my general remarks in Eckhart Hellmuth, '"The palladium of all other English liberties": Reflections on the Liberty of the Press in England during the 1760s and 1770s', in *The Transformation of Political Culture. England and Germany in the Late Eighteenth Century*, ed. Eckhart Hellmuth (Oxford, 1990), pp. 467-501.

9 On the political discourse in Britain at the end of the 18th century see, among others, Gregory Claeys, 'The French Revolution Debate and British Political Thought', *History of Political Thought*, 11 (1990), 59-80; Olivia Smith, *The Politics of Language, 1791-1818* (Oxford, 1984); Steven Blakemore, *Burke and the Fall of Language: The French Revolution as Linguistic Event* (Hanover NH, 1988), James T. Boulton, *The Language of Politics in the Age of Wilkes and Burke* (London, 1963); *The Impact of the French Revolution*, ed. Iain Hampsher-Monk (Cambridge, 2005); *Burke, Paine, Godwin, and the Revolution Controversy*, ed. Marilyn Butler (Cambridge, 1984).

organization was being stretched too far here. They accused the Loyalists of undermining the state's monopoly of power, and thus social peace, by intervening, in an unauthorized manner, in the course of the law. Thus, a declaration, of which they distributed 10 000 copies, stated: 'To maintain the fearless tranquility of human life, the prime blessing of Social Union, the power of accusation was not given to *uninjured* individuals, much less to *voluntary, undefined, unauthorised* Associations of Men, acting without responsibility, and open to irregular and private motives of action, but was conferred upon the Supreme Executive Magistrate, as more likely to look down upon the Mass of the community with an unimpassioned eye.'[10] And the Friends of the Liberty of the Press argued further that if it was highly problematical for a party which was not involved in initiating a prosecution, then this applied especially in the case of libel offences, for by their nature, such offences could not be precisely defined. As a result, there was always the danger of arbitrariness. As far as the Friends of the Liberty of the Press were concerned, the activity of the Loyalists was 'doubtfull as to its legality, unconstitutional in its principle, oppressive in its operation, and destructive of the Liberty of the Press'.[11]

But how did the activists in the Association for the Preservation of Liberty and Property justify their intention to exercise control of the press and of opinion on a non-governmental basis? How did these self-appointed protectors of the existing political and social order convince the public that it was legitimate to place the principle of social self-organization in the service of prosecuting 'subversive' opinions? They did this, as the example of Thomas Barnard shows,[12] with a mixture of populist demagoguery and pseudo-legal arguments. Thus, Barnard[13] first tried to convey the impression that in taking these steps, the Association

---

10 *Declaration of the Friends of the Liberty of the Press; Assembled at the Crown and Anchor Tavern, Saturday, January 19, 1793, written by the Hon. Thomas Erskine* (London, 1793), p. 2.

11 *Ibid.*, p. 7.

12 Thomas Barnard, *Observations on the Proceeding of the Friends of the Liberty of the Press, etc., December 22, 1792: And an Answer to Mr. Erskine's Speech, of January 19, 1793* (London, 1793). Similarly, Anon., *The Legal and Constitutional Principles of the Declaration of the Friends of the Liberty of the Press, written by the Hon. Thomas Erskine, Examined; and the Associations Vindicated* (London, 1793).

13 For Barnard's biography, see Thompson Cooper, 'Barnard, Thomas (bap. 1727, d. 1806)', rev. J. Falvey, in *Oxford Dictionary of National Biography*. Online URL (side dated 2004; accessed 18.01.2006):
< http://www.oxforddnb.com/view/article/1457 >

for the Preservation of Liberty and Property was, as it were, executing the will of the people. This society had been spontaneously established, according to Barnard: 'the people' had called it into life.[14] Barnard here displayed a clear awareness of speaking for a movement that could draw on broad support. In addition, Barnard was concerned to provide legal proof of the legitimacy of the activities of the Association for the Preservation of Liberty and Property. To the objection, raised by the Friends of the Liberty of the Press, that a party that was not involved was not entitled to initiate a prosecution, Barnard replied: 'That I as positively contradict, and assert, that by the common law, even from the earliest ages, every individual was not only allowed to prefer an accusation, but that it was bounden duty as far as in him lay to bring every offender to justice.'[15] As his prime witnesses, Barnard cited William Blackstone, among others. In addition, he mentioned serious crimes, such as treason and felony, in order to demonstrate that the English legal system had always called upon the individual to contribute to the clearing up and prosecution of crimes.[16] And what applied to the individual, Barnard argued by analogy, must also apply to a group of individuals. Consequently, societies such as the Association for the Preservation of Liberty and Property were legitimate. In this context, Barnard referred, among other things, to the tradition of the Prosecution Societies. And he added further historical precedents, which seemed to him to prove the legitimacy of the activities of the Association for the Preservation of Liberty and Property. These included an example from the late seventeenth century: 'A plot had been discovered to assassinate the King [William III], and to restore James, who was to have been assisted by a considerable French Army; and his adherents, with great signs of exultation, threatened an almost immediate insurrection. – What was done in this dilemma? An Association was instantly formed by the well-wishers of the Revolution.'[17] The purpose of this reference to the Assassination Plot of 1696 was obvious. One hundred years previously, in the face of the grav-

---

14 The full quotation is as follows: 'The people at large felt the force, truth and necessity of this, and acted accordingly. They felt it becoming their character as good citizens, as lovers of order and true liberty, no longer to remain torpid or inactive spectators of the impending danger. They did come forward, and the salvation of this country, I believe, was the consequence of their laudable and timely exertion.' Barnard, *Observations*, p. 6.

15 *Ibid.*

16 Cf. *ibid.*, pp. 10ff.

17 *Ibid.*, p. 19.

est danger to the community, loyal citizens had come together to form an association for the protection of the constitution; Reeves and his supporters were acting in the same way in the early 1790s. The squabbles of the 1790s were compared with a situation of crisis in which the monarch had been threatened by a murder plot.[18]

Thus, Loyalists hotly defended their vigilante-style politics. This, however, did not mean that they had abandoned the principle of press freedom, for there was a general consensus among contemporaries, even the 'conservatives' among them, that print culture had enhanced the progress of civilization.[19] Consequently, they presented themselves as advocates of 'true' press freedom.[20] That is, a distinction was drawn between two forms of freedom of the press. 'The term, Freedom of the Press', wrote John Bowles,[21] for example, one of the most productive writers on the Loyalist side, 'may be used either to signify *that* salutary freedom which is characteristic of a free people, or *that* licentious freedom which knows no bounds, which defies all law, order, and decorum, and which is the most destructive engine both to the Press, and to every other barrier of the Constitution.'[22] And Thomas Barnard wrote in a similar vein:

> The true, genuine Liberty of the press ..., the manly discussion of every political measure, or form of government, the freedom of thought, and the open communication of it, is neither menaced nor attacked. ... All that is aimed at, is only to restrain the extravagant licentiousness, into which, this freedom of the Press has so wantonly

---

18 This argument fitted in well with the Loyalist campaign of stirring up fear of regicide. On this see John Barrell, *Imagining the King's Death. Figurative Treason, Fantasies of Regicide 1793-1796* (Oxford, 2000), esp. ch. 2, pp. 87-89.

19 On this see, among others, Paul Keen, *The Crisis of Literature in the 1790s: Print Culture and the Public Sphere* (Cambridge, 1999), p. 27.

20 'I am', wrote a member of the Association for Preserving Liberty and Property, using an expression that was both informative and revealing, 'a real friend to fair and candid discussion, which instead of being hostile, must always be favourable to the British Constitution'. Anon., 'A Protest against T. Paine's Rights of Man: Addressed to the Members of a Book Society, in Consequence of the Vote of their Committee for Including the above Work in a List of New Publications Resolved to be Purchased for the Use of the Society (Publications Printed by Order of the Society for Preserving Liberty and Property against Republicans and Levellers Number III)', in *Association Papers Part I: Publications printed by Special Order of the Society for Preserving Liberty and Property against Republicans and Levellers* (London, 1793), p. 8.

21 Even before Fox's Libel Act, Bowles had already energetically opposed any reform of the libel law. On Bowles see Emma Vincent MacLeod, 'John Bowles and the French Revolutionary Wars, 1792-1802', *History*, 78 (1993), 394-420.

22 John Bowles, *A Short Answer to the Declaration of the Persons Calling Themselves the Friends of the Liberty of the Press* (London, 1793), p. 14.

> degenerated: – That Press, which daily teemed with productions, not only hostile to this Constitution, but which inculcated principles, utterly subversive of social order, directly tending to introduce the horrors of anarchy and confusion, and to dissolve every tye which unites man to his fellow creatures.[23]

Thus, the traditional formula of 'liberty' versus 'licentiousness' was reactivated. Throughout the entire eighteenth century, it had been among the standard repertoire of those who objected to any opening and expansion of the public sphere.[24] Like others before them, Bowles and Barnard tried to use it to remove the stigma of reaction from themselves, while at the same time retaining a programme of repression.

'Licentiousness' became a term of abuse used to disqualify the reformist and radical press, which was accused of aiming at the overthrow of the political and social order. These resentments were articulated in particular in the attacks on Paine's *Rights of Man*. For Loyalists, Paine's work was an exemplary embodiment of the 'revolutionary' potential of the printed word. Although attempts were made to play down his publishing success, and to attach to him the odium of being a curiosity,[25] the irritation he caused was only too obvious. The *Rights of Man* was considered a 'work which endeavours to convert the invaluable privilege of a free Press into an instrument of destruction to the state'.[26] And further:

> Under the mask of discussion, they [the disquisitions of Mr. Paine] really point to action, and that of the most pernicious and criminal nature – they lead not to any practicable good, but to turbulence and general commotion. If they were to have their desired effect, the constitution would be annihilated; our lives, our liberties, and our property would be deprived of legal protection; Government would be overturned;

---

23 Thomas Barnard, *Observations on the Proceedings of the Friends of the Liberty of the Press*, pp. 22-23.

24 On this, see the examples in Eckhart Hellmuth, ' "The palladium of all other English liberties" ', at pp. 478-479.

25 See, e.g., Anon., 'Protest against T. Paine's Rights of Man', p. 2: 'In the Advertisement to the Second Part of the "Rights of Man", the vain Author makes his boast of the extensive and numerous distribution of the copies of the First Part, and he seems to infer from thence that the sense of the Public is in favour. How erroneous is such an inference! A book so remarkably distinguished for wild extravagance, consumate audacity, and daring insolence, as "The Rights of Man", could not fail to engage a certain degree of public attention, upon the same principle that the exhibition of a monstrous animal production will excite notice and attract gazers in proportion to the hideous deformity of the spectacle. But those who judge of the merit of a book of its progress into notoriety, will frequently find themselves mistaken.'

26 *Ibid.*, p. 2.

> and in vain might we look into the darksome void of futurity to catch even a faint and dubious glimpse of security against unbridled licentiousness and unrestained violence.[27]

The verdict on the *Rights of Man* was so passionate not least because of the imputation that Paine's work was addressed to the lower classes, that is, to a readership which, it was thought, would be overtaxed by a text of this sort.[28] The judgement resonated with fear of the politicization of – as Loyalist jargon put it – the 'minds of those who occupy the lower stations of society'.[29] 'Thus upon the whole', it was claimed, 'are the modern "Rights of Man" intended to take advantage of all that is weak and all that is wicked in Society'.[30] And the dangers that reading radical political writings posed for the common man were urgently evoked. In agreement with the conservative understanding of society circulating among Loyalists,[31] the social costs of political literature *à la* Paine were described: 'Instead of displaying virtue as the only source of real felicity, it is the objects of the modern "Rights of Man" to create restlessness and dissatisfaction, and to persuade mankind, that they suffer injuries which they do not perceive, they sustain hardships which they do not feel, that their comforts are visionary and their happiness mere delusion.'[32] In some respects these arguments, which cast doubt on the capacity of particular social groups for rational political behaviour, were reminiscent of the propaganda attempts which had been made to combat the radicalism of the 1760s. In similar vein, the apologists of the political establishment had accused the Wilkes movement of using its press campaigns to rally social groups which were not actually capable of political behaviour.[33] Now, however, the tone

---

27 *Ibid.*, p. 8.

28 *Ibid.*, pp. 8–9: 'Such doctrines although falacious and sophisticated in the extreme, nay, although in a great measure they carry their own refutation along with them, may, nevertheless, among persons of particular descriptions, and on whom they are chiefley designed to operate, produce the most mischievous impressions. They are not, indeed, calculated to produce this effect upon strong, experienced and well-informed minds; they are framed for the meridian of those understandings which are not accustomed to weigh and to discriminate: which are ever ready, from indolence, weakness, or inexperience, to receive such impressions.'

29 *Ibid.*, p. 9.

30 *Ibid.*, p. 11.

31 On the views of society held by Loyalists, see esp. Dickinson, 'Popular Loyalism in Britain in the 1790s'.

32 See Anon., 'Protest against T. Paine's Rights of Man', p. 9.

33 Hellmuth, '"The palladium of all other English liberties"', pp. 482-3.

seemed to be harsher. Paine's potential readers were described, among other things, as the 'common pest of Society'.[34]

Loyalists, however, did not accuse only radical authors such as Paine of working to overthrow the political and social order. They directed the same imputations at those, like the Friends of the Liberty of the Press, who strongly advocated the principle of freedom of the press. Thus, in 1793 the Association for the Preservation of Liberty and Property published satires on the activities of the Friends of the Liberty of the Press in which they were defamed as advocates of disorder and violence and destroyers of the constitution.[35] The Friends of the Liberty of the Press became the Friends of the Abuse of the Liberty of the Press. The fictitious membership list of the Friends of the Abuse of the Liberty of the Press resembled a pantheon of past and present revolutionaries, and included the following names: 'Mr. Oliver Cromwell', 'John Lilbourne', 'William Prynne', 'Damned Barebones', 'Citizen Marat', 'Citizen Robespierre', and 'Citizen Paine'.[36] Other, made-up, names ('Alexander the Coppersmith', 'Thomas Drawwater, Esq. of the Pump at Aldgate'[37]) were intended to signal that these advocates of free public discussion included dubious figures from a plebeian milieu. And the Friends of the Liberty of the Press were accused of not caring at all about preserving the freedom of the press. Their real goal, it was suggested, was to pervert and abuse this right. This, in any case, was the sense of a parody of the declaration on the freedom of the press which the Friends of the Liberty of the Press printed regularly in their pamphlets. Among other things, this parody read:

> Unanimously Resolved 1. That as the Liberty of the Press is a right inseparable from the principles of a Free Government, and essential to the security of the British Constitution, so the Abuse of that Liberty, carried to a certain point, is the surest method we can take for overturning both. 2. That as the freedom of Discussion is allowable, Freedom of Calumniating may very easily be substituted for it: that as the principles of Civil Government may be examined, so the practices of it may be misrepresented; and that as the discussion of Public Opinions is allowable, so the

---

34 Anon., 'Protest against T. Paine's Rights of Man', p. 10.

35 See, e.g., Anon., *The Speech of Alexander the Coppersmith, L.L.D., Spoken at the Meeting of the Friends the Abuse of the Freedom of the Press, January 19, 1793* (London, 1793); Anon., *Proceedings of the Friends of the Liberty of the Press: on December, the 22d, 1792, and January 17th, and March 9th, 1793* (London, 1793).

36 *Ibid.*, p. 14.

37 *Ibid.*, pp. 5, 15.

> introduction of discontent into all Private Opinions is, for our purposes, highly desirable.[38]

The whole pamphlet was designed to impart to the Friends of the Liberty of the Press the odium of conspiracy and treachery. To a certain extent the ideology of conspiracy, which developed (in conservative circles) throughout Europe at the end of the eighteenth century, resonated here.[39]

II.

Radicals and reformers were not slow in replying to this Loyalist campaign. There were songs and toasts to the liberty of the press and its advocates ('The Liberty of the Press – Together with its most shining Advocate Mr. Erskine'; 'Mr. Fox – The Rights of the People'; 'The Press – with Fox and Liberty').[40] Clumsy rhymes evoked the loss of press freedom and conjured up the dawning of a dark age.[41] And Joseph Towers, Dissenting minister, active in numerous reform organizations and a leading member of the Friends of the Liberty of the Press,[42] presented extracts from pamphlets produced by Loyalist societies in the English provinces, which to him provided evidence that Loyalists were setting themselves up, with the enthusiasm of zealots, as censors of the political discourse.[43] It ended in a highly bizarre comparison between British and Prussian conditions that

---

38 *Ibid.*, pp. 3–5. The Friends of the Liberty of the Press were so annoyed by this parody of their declaration that they immediately had a pamphlet printed with both texts – their original declaration and the distorted version put out by the Association for the Preservation of Liberty and Property: *Friends of the People, Friends to themselves!!! Resolution of a Society formed for bringing to Perfection the Art of Political Canting* (London 1793).

39 On this see, among others, Gordon S. Wood, 'Conspiracy and the Paranoid Style: Causality and Deceit in the Eighteenth Century', *William and Mary Quarterly*, 3rd ser., 39 (1982), 401-441.

40 Cf. *Declaration of the Friends of the Liberty of the Press; assembled at the Crown and Anchor Tavern, Saturday, January 19, 1793, Written by the Hon. Thomas Erskine; to which is Added the other Proceedings of the Day* (London, 1793), pp. 13, 14, 17.

41 Anon., *Whitehall Alarmed! and a Council Called!* (London, 1793).

42 On Towers see esp. Thomas W. Davis, entry on Joseph Towers in *Biographical Dictionary of Modern British Radicals*, vol 1: *1770-1830*, ed. Joseph O. Baylen and Norbert J. Gossman (Hassocks, Sussex, 1979), pp. 493-496; F. K. Donnelly, 'Joseph Towers and the Collapse of Rational Dissent', *Enlightenment and Dissent*, 6 (1987), 31-40.

43 Joseph Towers, *A Dialogue between an Associator and a well-informed Englishman, on the Grounds of the Late Associations* (London, 1793), pp. 28-32.

was intended to signal that Loyalism was on the way to destroying one of the fundamental rights in the motherland of liberty. 'At all events', he wrote, 'a man who loved liberty, would change much for the better, by going from London to Berlin; where, though an highly military and despotic government is established, the people are not deprived of the freedom of conversation. ... The associators, and those who have acted in concert with them, have endeavoured to suppress all freedom of political discussion.'[44]

In addition to alarm calls such as these, an attempt was made to rebut the accusation made by the Loyalist side that the radical press was undermining the foundations of the political and social order. Daniel Isaac Eaton did this with wit and irony. In his brilliant satire, *The Pernicious Effect of the Art of Printing upon Society, Exposed,* he held up the Loyalist hysteria to public ridicule. Eaton, with Thomas Spence probably the most subversive satirist of radicalism in the French Revolutionary age,[45] here assumed the role of an opponent of free public debate, and by taking the arguments of the Loyalists to absurd extremes, made them collapse. Mocking Burke and his nostalgia for the 'chivalrous past', Eaton first conjured up the past, a 'Golden Age' when 'the feudal system [had] prevailed'.[46] During this 'Golden Age', the common man had willingly submitted to his fate in peace and war, and had accepted the existing social order without grumbling. 'The lower orders', he claimed, 'though in other respects immersed in the most profound ignorance, knew full well ... that the existence of society depended upon distinctions of rank, fortune &c.'[47] This intact world had been exposed to the forces of disintegration by the invention of the 'diabolical art' of printing. Thus, the lower orders had begun to develop confused ideas, including that 'one man is as good as another', 'society is at present founded upon false principles', 'no regard should be paid to rank and titles', 'every man has a right to share in the government', and that 'laws should be the same to all'. And, Eaton continued: 'This, with a great deal more such stuff, is called the rights of man – blessed fruits of the Art of Printing – the scum

---

44 *Ibid.*, pp. 32-33.

45 On Eaton as a satirist, see esp. Marcus Wood, *Radical Satire and Print Culture 1790–1822* (Oxford, 1994), pp. 57–95; Olivia Smith, *The Politics of Language 1791-1819* (Oxford, 1984), ch. 3, pp. 68-109.

46 Daniel Isaac Eaton, *The Pernicious Effects of the Art of Printing upon Society, Exposed: A Short Essay, Addressed to the Friends of Social Order* (London, 1793), p .6.

47 *Ibid.*, p. 3.

of the earth, the swinish multitude, talking of their rights! And insolently claiming, nay, almost demanding, that political liberty shall be the same to all – to the high and the low – to the rich and the poor – what audacity! what unparalleled effrontery!'[48] This complaint about the rebelliousness of the lower orders led into a surreal catalogue of repressive demands: 'Let all Printing-presses be committed to the flames – all letter foundries be destroyed – schools and seminaries of learning be abolished ... all discourse upon government and religion prohibited ... and lastly issue a proclamation against reading, and burn all private libraries.'[49] Using this sort of absurd humour, Eaton obviously wanted to expose – in his eyes – the irrational character of Loyalist politics and propaganda. The stigma of irrationality, which Loyalist authors as a rule projected on to the emergent plebeian public sphere, was here reflected back on to Loyalism itself. Thus, Eaton was also implying that the Loyalist programme of suppressing the radical press was contrary to the laws of reason; that ultimately, all attempts to control public opinion were doomed to failure.

What Eaton merely implied through the satirical character of his work was expressed much more directly by other writers, such as the Presbyterian clergyman, Archibald Bruce.[50] In his 1794 work *Reflections on the Freedom of Writing*,[51] one of the longest texts written on the problem of press freedom in the eighteenth century, he attempted to demonstrate, by drawing on numerous historical examples, the pointlessness and lack of success of official intervention and repression in the context of the printed word. He drew upon European and English history in order to show that new ideas on politics and religion, even if they were initially repressed, had ultimately asserted themselves. 'One might', wrote Bruce among other things, 'as well attempt to repress the ocean, when it rises

---

48 *Ibid.*, pp. 8–9.

49 *Ibid.*, p. 15.

50 Bruce was a minister of the Secession church in Scotland and from 1786 a professor of divinity. He published numerous texts, with a particular focus on relations between civil government and religion. On Bruce see Derek Hall, 'Bruce, Archibald (1748-1816)', in *Oxford Dictionary of National Biography*. Online URL (side dated 2004; accessed 23.09.2004):< http://www.oxforddnb.com/view/article/3725 >

51 Archibald Bruce, *Reflections on Freedom of Writing; and the Impropriety of Attempting to Suppress it by Penal Laws. Occasioned by the Proclamation against Seditious Publications, and the Measures Consequent upon it; Viewed chiefly in the Aspect they Bear to Religious Liberty, and Ecclesiastical Reform* (Edinburgh, 1794). Bruce was obviously in contact with the Friends of the Liberty of the Press, because he printed one of their poems in an appendix to his work.

and rages, with a mound of sand, as to oppose the tide of public opinion.'[52] His study of the past, however, seemed to Bruce to contain another lesson as well, namely, that the persecution of 'deviant' writing as a rule brought other repressive measures with it. 'The persecution of books', he wrote, 'has seldom been unaccompanied with that of men.'[53] For Bruce, free public discussion was part of the essence of a free political order: 'In a free government, a free circulation of opinions, and the fullest discussion of public matters should be permitted.'[54] This meant, at the same time, that freedom of the press was an indispensable prerequisite for general liberty.

For the Enlightened camp, this insight was among the central ideas disseminated by their propaganda. Thus, a declaration which the Friends of the Liberty of the Press regularly reprinted in their pamphlets claimed: 'The Liberty of the Press is a right inseparable from the Principles of a free government.'[55] And Joseph Towers put it in a similar way: 'It is absurd to suppose, that public liberty can subsist, where there is not freedom of the press.'[56] The principle that 'public liberty' was connected with 'freedom of the press' was consistently advocated by Towers, who had supported a reform of the libel laws as early as the 1780s,[57] with serious implications. He did not, for example, hesitate to turn it against revolutionary France. He attributed the French Revolution's slide into *terreur* to the fact that the revolutionaries had not declared press freedom sacrosanct: 'During the succession of the different factions in France, since the first revolution, it has ... been a great evil, that the freedom of the press has not been more inviolably maintained. If this had been preserved, without interruption, the party of Robespierre could not have acquired the ascendancy they did, nor would they have been able to have

52 *Ibid.*, p. 40.

53 *Ibid.*, p. 20.

54 *Ibid.*, p. 10.

55 See, e.g., *Proceedings of the Friends of the Liberty of the Press*, p. 1.

56 Joseph Towers, *Remarks on the Conduct, Principles, and Publications, of the Association at the Crown and Anchor, in the Strand, for Preserving Liberty and Property against Republicans and Levellers* (1793), reprinted in idem, *Tracts on Political Subjects* (3 vols., London, 1796), iii, 248–298, at p. 260.

57 Towers, *Observations on the Rights and Duties of Juries in Trials for Libels together with Remarks on the Origins and Nature of the Law of Libels* (London, 1784); idem, *An Enquiry whether Juries are or are not Judges of Law as well as of Fact* (London, 1785).

brought some of the best Republicans in France to the scaffold.'[58] Freedom of the press, Towers claimed, immunized society against the loss of general freedom. 'In every country', Towers therefore demanded, 'whether contending for its liberties, or in actual possession of them, it may be laid down as an universal and invariable rule, that the enemies of the freedom of the press are the enemies of general liberty and of general felicity.'[59] Towers's statement was directed not only against the revolutionary actors whom he held responsible for the debasement of the new political system across the Channel. At the same time, it could be read as a critical commentary on conditions in his own country.

In order to give their campaign for freedom of the press a greater degree of legitimacy, reformers and radicals referred to prominent writers of the past, sometimes displaying a remarkable flexibility and evoking intellectual traditions of highly diverse origins. This was the case with Thomas Erskine, for example. As a leading member of the Society of the Friends of the Liberty of the Press, a Foxite Whig in Parliament, and an eloquent defence lawyer in a series of libel cases and treason trials, he had become a cult figure for radicals and reformers.[60] In December 1792 he defended Thomas Paine, who had been arraigned for 'seditious libel' on the publication of the second part of his *Rights of Man*.[61] As Paine had fled to France, he was tried in his absence. At the trial, Erskine's plea was several hours long, and was interspersed with references to the main names in the political theory of the seventeenth and eighteenth centuries (including Locke, Harrington, Montesquieu, and Burke).[62] Among the authors quoted by Erskine were three whom he called 'classics in our language',[63]

---

58 Towers, *Thoughts of the Commencement of a New Parliament: With an Appendix, Containing Remarks on the Letter of the Right Hon. Edmund Burke, on the Revolution in France*, reprinted idem, *Tracts on Political Subjects*, iii, 5–180, at p. 94. This quotation, like the following one, are not in the first edition of 1791. Rather, both come from an annotation which Towers made in a reprint of this text in his *Tracts on Political Subjects* (1796).

59 *Ibid.*

60 On Erskine see, most recently, Annabel Patterson, *Nobody's Perfect. A New Whig Interpretation of History* (New Haven CT, 2002), pp. 201-237.

61 On this see, among others, John Keane, *Tom Paine. A Political Life* (London, 1995), pp. 345ff.

62 'Mr. Erskine's Speech for the Defendant', in *The Speeches of the Hon. Thomas Erskine (now Lord Erskine), when at the Bar on Subjects Connected with the Liberty of the Press, and against Constructive Treasons; Collected by James Ridgway* (4 vols., London, 1810-13), ii, 87-182.

63 *Ibid.*, p. 142.

each of whom had, in his own way, looked closely at the problem of press freedom. These were the man of the Scottish enlightenment David Hume, the republican John Milton and, astonishingly, the arch-Tory Dr Samuel Johnson. Dr Johnson served as the chief witness for the view that the distinction between 'liberty' and 'licentiousness', upon which Loyalist propaganda placed such great value, was ultimately indefinable.[64] Hume's essay *Of the Liberty of the Press* was used to demonstrate the press's function as a controlling power.[65] Above all, however, there was an intense debate with Milton and his *Areopagitica*,[66] published in 1644. Thus, we find quoted here Milton's vivid image which shows that by its very nature, intellectual exchange cannot be regulated and controlled: 'To prevent men thinking and acting for themselves, by restraints on the press, is like to the exploits of that gallant man, who thought to pound up the crows by shutting his park gate.'[67] And Erskine commented in detail on the passages in which Milton called on the Long Parliament to distance itself from all repressive measures against the press:

> It is the liberty, Lords and Commons, which your own valorous and happy counsels have purchased us; liberty, which is the nurse of all great wits; this is that which hath rarefied and enlightened our spirits like the influence of heaven; this is that which hath enfranchised, enlarged, and lifted up our apprehension, degrees above themselves. Ye cannot make us now less capable, less knowing, less eagerly pursuing the truth, unless ye first make yourselves, that made us so, less the lovers, less the founders of our true liberty. We can grow ignorant again, brutish, formal, and slavish, as you found us; but you then must first become that which you cannot be, oppressive, arbitrary, and tyrannous, as they were from whom ye have freed us. That our hearts

64 *Ibid.*, pp. 149-50.

65 Among other things, Erskine quoted the following passage by Hume: 'The spirit of the people must frequently be roused, in order to curb the ambition of the Court; and the dread of rousing this spirit must be employed to prevent that ambition. Nothing is so effectual to this purpose as the liberty of THE PRESS, by which all the learning, wit and genius of the nation, may be employed on the side of freedom; and every one be animated to its defence. As long, therefore, as the republican part of our government can maintain itself against the monarchical, it will naturally be careful to keep the press open, as of importance to its own preservation.' *Ibid.*, pp. 147-148.

66 *Ibid.*, pp. 142-144, pp. 178-180.

67 *Ibid.*, p. 145. As a rule, Erskine quoted Milton verbatim, but in this case he quoted relatively freely. The relevant passage in Milton reads: 'And he who were pleasantly dispos'd, could not well avoid to lik'n it to the exploit of that gallant man who thought to pound up the crows by shutting his Parkgate.' John Milton, *Areopagitica*, in *Complete Prose Works of John Milton*, vol. 2 (1643-1648), ed. Ernest Sirluck (New Haven CT, 1959), pp. 480-570, at p. 520.

> are now more capacious, our thoughts now more erected to the search and expectation of greatest and exactest things, is the issue of your own virtue propagated in us. Give me the liberty to know, to utter and to argue freely according to conscience, above all liberties.[68]

The use of this particular quotation from the *Areopagitica* did more than bring Milton's pathos to life; it cleverly enlisted a 150-year-old text in the battle of words during the age of the French Revolution. In the language of the seventeenth century, Pitt and his parliamentary followers were reproached with the fact that all the sanctions against the radical press which had been initiated or were planned were inappropriate to an Enlightened age, and, ultimately, were contrary to their own principles.

Erskine's rhetorical *tour de force* was, quite clearly, designed from the start to have an impact beyond the actual trial proceedings. Thus, reports of the trial against Paine, including Erskine's plea, were soon published by the contemporary press.[69] Among others, Thomas Spence published almost the entire text of Erskine's speech in a number of instalments in his ultra-radical journal, *Pig's Meat,* which aimed at a wider readership beyond polite society.[70] For Spence it was clear that those passages which went beyond Paine's trial and addressed press freedom as a fundamental problem had special weight, as the journal's index had separate entries for the extracts from the works of Milton, Hume, and Dr Johnson.[71] Moreover, in his 'creative anthology of texts concerning liberty, oppression,

---

68 *Ibid.*, pp. 146-147.

69 In the period 1792-1793 almost 20 reports of the trial appeared in Britain and the USA.

70 Thomas Spence, *Pig's Meat, or Lessons for the Swinish Multitude* (3 vols., London, 1793-95), i, 168-175, 189-193, and 223-228; ii, 117-124, 152-157, 178-182, and 242-274. On Spence and *Pig's Meat* see, among others, Marcus Wood, *Radical Satire and Print Culture, 1790-1832* (Oxford, 1994), ch. 2, pp. 57-95; idem, 'Thomas Spence and Modes of Subversion', *Enlightenment and Dissent*, 10 (1991), 51-77; Olivia Smith, *The Politics of Language* (Oxford, 1984), ch. 3, pp. 68-109. On Spence's role in the discourse of the 1790s see, most recently, Jack Fruchtman, 'Two Doubting Thomases: The British Progressive Enlightenment and the French Revolution', in *Radicalism and Revolution in Britain, 1775-1848: Essays in Honour of Malcolm I. Thomis*, ed. Michael T. Davis (Basingstoke, 2000), pp. 30-40 (with a bibliography of further reading).

71 In addition, the table of contents separately lists two further contributions on the freedom of the press, to which Erskine referred in his plea. These were texts by Alexander Wedderburn, 1st Baron Loughborough and Charles Stanhope, 3rd Earl of Stanhope.

taxation, revolution, reform, and the luxury of rulers',[72] Spence included another 'classic' on the freedom of the press. He reprinted Thomas Gordon's article *On the Freedom of Speech*,[73] which had first been published in 1720 in *Cato's Letters*, the chief manifesto of the radical whig ideology of the early eighteenth century.[74] In this article, Gordon celebrated 'freedom of speech' which, as far as he was concerned, was synonymous with the 'liberty of the press', as 'the great bulwark of liberty'.[75] He had also established a connection between protecting property and free public debate: 'The security of property, and the freedom of speech always go together; and in those wretched countries, where a man cannot call his tongue his own, he can scarce call any thing else his own.'[76] This sentence which, significantly, was quoted not only by Spence but also by other opponents of the Loyalists,[77] gained a new meaning in the context of the conflicts of the 1790s. It became a means of undermining the credibility of the Society for the Preservation of Liberty and Property. This passage from *Cato's Letters* was referred to in order to expose the motto of 'liberty and property', which the Loyalists used for their political work, as empty rhetoric.

The texts on freedom of the press collected in Spence's *Pig's Meat* and Erskine's plea in Paine's trial provide an almost text-book example of the diverse origins of the intellectual stock of the radicals and reformers.[78]

---

72 Marcus Wood, *Radical Satire and Print Culture, 1790-1822* (Oxford, 1994), p. 88.

73 Spence, *Pig's Meat*, i, 2-6.

74 On this see, among others, Ronald Hamowy, 'Cato's Letters, John Locke, and the Republican Paradigm', *History of Political Thought*, 11 (1990), 273-294.

75 Spence, *Pig's Meat*, i, 3.

76 *Ibid.*, i, 2.

77 Towers, *Remarks on the Conduct, Principles, and Publications, of the Association at the Crown and Anchor*, pp. 248-298, at p. 260.

78 On this see esp. Mark Philp, 'The Fragmented Ideology of Reform', in *The French Revolution and British Popular Politics*, ed. idem (Cambridge, 1991), pp. 50-77, at p. 72. On the intellectual stock of radicals and reformers in general at the end of the eighteenth century, see, among others, Harry T. Dickinson, *Liberty and Property: Political Ideology in Eighteenth-Century Britain* (London, 1977), pp. 237-269; Albert Goodwin, *The Friends of Liberty: The English Democratic Movement in the Age of the French Revolution* (London, 1979); John Dinwiddy, 'Conceptions of Revolution in the English Radicalism of the 1790s', in *The Transformation of Political Culture: England and Germany in the Late Eighteenth Century*, ed. Eckhart Hellmuth (Oxford, 1990), pp. 535-560; Christopher Jones, *Radical Sensibility: Literature and Ideas in the 1790s* (London, 1993); Günter Lottes, *Politische Aufklärung und plebejisches Publikum: Zur Theorie und Praxis des englischen Radikalismus im späten 18. Jahrhundert* (Munich, 1979).

Spence's *Pig's Meat* and Erskine's plea in the trial against Paine, however, also demonstrate that Milton's *Areopagitica* still enjoyed continuing prestige at the end of the eighteenth century. It may be true that 'the eighteenth century ... on the whole liked Milton's poetry and disliked his politics',[79] but his *Areopagitica* evoked a remarkable response. It was constantly reprinted throughout the entire eighteenth century, including in 1792.[80] It achieved something like iconic status in the intellectual stock of the Enlightened camp, becoming a key text in the defence of free, public debate.[81] It was considered an 'admirable defence of the best of human Rights'.[82] Reformers and radicals hardly seem to have given a thought to the polyvalence of Milton's 'Speech for the Liberty of Unlicensed Printing'. As the examples of Erskine and Spence show, what they were interested in is what has been called the 'liberal' *Areopagitica*.[83]

The fact that the *Areopagitica* still evoked a response a century and a half after its first publication can hardly be regarded as a coincidence. Milton's text obviously captured the *Zeitgeist*, not least because it started from a concept of 'truth' which demanded a permanent discourse in the medium of the printed word. For Milton, 'truth' was not static, but, as he called it, 'a streaming fountain'.[84] In other words, 'truth' was constantly being re-created in an unending process. The prerequisite for this process was that a wealth of opinions could be articulated, even incorrect ones.

79 Blair Worden, *Roundhead Reputations: The English Civil Wars and the Passions of Posterity* (London, 2001), p. 237.

80 Further reprints appeared in 1738, 1753, 1772, 1780 and 1791.

81 It is revealing in this context that in 1791 a pamphlet was published with the title: *Areopagitica: An Essay on the Liberty of the Press. Dedicated to the Rt. Hon. Charles James Fox, The Friend of Truth and Liberty* (London, 1792). Contrary to what the title seems to suggest, this was not a reprint of the *Areopagitica*. Rather, it was a plea for the reform of libel trials. The fact that the anonymous author of this pamphlet simply adapted the title of this classic work on the freedom of the press was an expression of deep respect for Milton and his work.

82 This praise for Milton and his *Areopagitica* originally came from James Thomson, and can be found in the foreword which he wrote for his 1738 edition of the *Areopagitica*. The Society for Constitutional Information reprinted this foreword in 1780. On this see *Substance of the speech of the Rev. Mr. Walker at the General Meeting of the County of Nottingham, held at Mansfield, on Monday the 28th of February 1780: to which is Added, Mr. Thomson's preface to a Speech of Mr. John Milton, for the Liberty of Unlicensed Printing, to the Parliament of England; Printed and Distributed gratis by the Society for Constitutional Information* (London, 1780). The quotation is at p. 9.

83 On this see William Kolbrener, *Milton's Warring Angels: A Study of Critical Engagements* (Cambridge, 1997), pp. 11-27.

84 Milton, *Areopagitica*, p. 543.

Characteristically, the sentence in which Milton expressed this was among the passages from the *Areopagitica* which Erskine quoted in Thomas Paine's trial. With Milton he argued that 'All Opinions, YEA ERRORS, known, read and collated, are of main service & assistence toward the speedy attainment of what is truest'.[85]

What Erskine expressed here, with reference to Milton, can be regarded as a sort of commonplace of the intellectual stock of reform-orientated and radical writers. The Baptist minister Robert Hall,[86] for example, used the same argument in his *Apology for the Freedom of the Press*, published in 1793. For Hall there could be no doubt that 'truth' could be found only in an absolutely open discourse, which included erroneous opinions. Consequently, Hall rejected any form of state intervention directed against the process of freely seeking the truth: 'To render the magistrate a judge of truth, and engage his authority in the suppression of opinions, shews an inattention to the nature and design of political society.'[87] This dictum was based on a fundamental consideration of the origins of political society and the rights of the magistrate which flowed from it. 'When a nation forms a government', argued Hall, 'it is not *wisdom* but *power* which they place in the hands of the magistrate.'[88] From this he concluded that the magistrate was legitimately responsible only for those 'objects' 'which power can operate upon.'[89] For Hall, these were 'the administration of justice, the protection of property, and the defence of every member of the community of violance and outrage.'[90] Conversely, this means that it was not the magistrate's job 'to distinguish truth from error, and to countenance one set of opinions to the prejudice of another',[91] for this would mean applying 'power in a manner mischievous and absurd'.[92] In principle, Hall assumed that free public debate promoted

---

85 'Mr. Erskine's Speech for the Defendant', in *The Speeches of the Hon. Thomas Erskine*, ii, 87-182, at p. 144.

86 For Hall's biography see Rosemary Chadwick, 'Hall, Robert (1764-1831)', in *Oxford Dictionary of National Biography*. Online URL (side dated 2004; accessed 23.09.2004): < http://www.oxforddnb.com/view/article/11982 >

87 Robert Hall, *An Apology for the Freedom of the Press and for General Liberty: To which are Prefixed Remarks on Bishop Horsley's Sermon, Preached on the Thirtieth of January Last* (London, 1793), p. 2.

88 *Ibid.*

89 *Ibid.*

90 *Ibid.*

91 *Ibid.*

92 *Ibid.*

human progress. He tried to justify this view by reference to examples from the past, including Luther. Moreover, he presented free public debate as the essence of an Enlightened existence. 'The most capital advantage an enlightened people can enjoy', he wrote, 'is the liberty of discussing every subject which can fall within the compass of the human mind.'[93]

Hall shared this Enlightened enthusiasm with Archibald Bruce, another Nonconformist writer. In his work already mentioned above, *Reflections on the Freedom of Writing*, he argued explicitly and eloquently for a public debate with many voices, free of all repression, and subject only to the laws of reason. What he had in mind was a sort of competition of ideas in which, he wrote, 'weapons of the same kind should alone be employed'.[94] By this, he meant that 'writing should be opposed to writings; arguments should be played against arguments; reason should be combated with reason, and wit with wit'.[95] Bruce assigned the central role in this competition of ideas to independent intelligence, that is, to 'men of a free spirit'. According to Bruce, 'men of a free spirit' were distinguished by, among other things, the fact that their lives were shaped by critical reflection, that they kept their distance from party politics, and that they did not allow themselves to be tied down by the constricting routine of public office.[96] They were the ones whose analytical understanding gave the public debate crucial impulses, especially in respect of the political issues of the day. Thus, Bruce writes:

> It is theirs to invent, and to improve, to prompt and direct: it is theirs to rouze up latent powers, and to concenter attention on common interests: to point out new rights and privileges, or watch over those already acquired: to form the new model of a state, or secure one already settled from corruption and gradual decay: to suggest ideas of higher perfection, than any human constitution can ever boast; in fine, to be impartial censors of the great, and of men in public trust, and a sort of literary tribunes on the side of the people.[97]

93 *Ibid*. This process of discussion was also intended to include the field of politics. Thus we read in Hall, among other things: 'This being an institution (government) purely human, one would imagine it were the proper province for freedom of discussion in its utmost extent. It is surely just that every one should have a right to examine those measures by which the happiness of all may be affected. The control of the public mind over the conduct of ministers exerted through the medium of the press, has been regarded by the best writers both in our country and on the continent, as the main support of our liberties. While this remains we cannot be enslaved, when it is empaired or diminished, we shall soon cease to be free.' *Ibid*., p. 7.

94 Bruce, *Reflections on Freedom of Writing*, p. 40.

95 *Ibid*., pp. 40–41.

96 *Ibid*., p. 41.

97 *Ibid*., pp. 41–42.

The ideal which led Bruce was that of a 'republic of letters', whose discursive practice extended to the political field. In this sense, we read in Bruce: 'The liberty claimed and allowed in the republic of Letters, in matters of criticism, ... , may be safely allowed also in political subjects.'[98] Bruce did not write this sentence himself, but quoted it from Raynal's *Histoire philosophique et politique.*[99] And Bruce quoted another passage from the work of the great French *philosophe* because it obviously coincided with his own ideas about the function of the writer in political associations: 'Every writer of genius is born a magistrate of his country, and he ought to enlighten it as much as it is in his power. ... His tribunal is the whole nation, his judge is the public.'[100]

From Bruce's text speaks the self-confidence of a man who was at home in the communication networks of the late eighteenth century and believed that he could change the world by means of the printed word.[101] This attitude was typically found among large sections of the reforming and radical-minded milieu of the 1790s, which believed that political writers represented an antidote to the corrupt, oligarchically structured political system, and that the time was ripe for a debate on fundamental political principles. This, again, had consequences for the contemporary debate on the problem of press freedom, because reformers and radicals attempted to shift the co-ordinates of what could be said in the public discussion in such a way that a fundamental debate of this sort became possible. This became clear in the debate conducted on the legitimacy of criticizing the constitution.

III.

The 1790s were a decade when the traditional political vocabulary was eroded. This also applied to the term 'constitution'.[102] Radicals, above all, spread the message that nobody knew exactly what this term meant. For

---

98 *Ibid.*, p. 12.

99 Guillaume Thomas, François Raynal, *Histoire philosophique et politique des établissements et du commerce des Européens dans les deux Indes* (Paris, 1770). Three English language editions of this work were published (Edinburgh 1776 and 1779, Aberdeen 1779).

100 Bruce, *Reflections on Freedom of Writing*, p. 11.

101 On this see Keen, *Crisis of Literature*, esp. pp. 28-30.

102 On this see esp. James A. Epstein, '"Our real constitution": Trial Defence and Radical Memory in the Age of Revolution', in *Re-reading the Constitution: New Narratives in the Political History of England's Long Nineteenth Century*, ed. James Vernon (Cambridge, 1996), pp. 22-51; James Vernon, *Radical Expression: Political Language, Ritual and Symbol in England, 1790-1850* (Oxford, 1994), pp. 3-5.

them 'the constitution represented a kind of haunted house, full of mystery and ruled by figments of the imagination'.[103] Moreover, some contemporaries were unclear about whether Britain had a constitution at all. Those who took revolutionary France as a model, and recognized only a written constitution which was based on natural law and guaranteed wide-ranging individual freedoms, simply denied the existence of a British constitution. 'Can then Mr. Burke', Paine, for example, wrote in his *Rights of Man*, 'produce the English Constitution? If he cannot, we may fairly conclude, that though it has been much talked about, no such thing as a constitution exists, or ever did exist, and consequently that the people have yet a constitution to form.'[104] This view was diametrically opposed to the position taken by Loyalists. Thus, the Scottish clergyman John Young wrote: 'But, in spite of Mr. Paine, and all his new colleagues, the world knows that Britain has a constitution. ... It consists of a system of laws, by which the people of Great Britain have agreed to be governed. It comprehends the common law, which though it has never been written, is as well known, and much better established, than any printed Constitution, either in France or in America. It is explained and extended in various acts of Parliament. It is summed up in Magna Charta, and in the Bill of Rights.'[105] Young's words were the expression of a rigid constitutional conservatism widespread among Loyalists.[106] These Loyalist authors constantly praised their own constitution, or what they considered it to be, and declared it sacrosanct. This constitutional conservatism was expressed not only in contemporary journalism, but also had a place in English and Scottish courts of law, for in the 1790s a number of leading radicals faced charges of sedition, seditious libel, and high treason.[107] They faced the accusation that they were no longer concerned to

---

103 Epstein, ' "Our real constitution"', p. 23.

104 Thomas Paine, *The Rights of Man, Part I* (1791), in *Thomas Paine: Political Writings*, ed. Bruce Kuklick (Cambridge, 1989), pp. 49-143, at pp. 81-82.

105 John Young, *Essays on the Following Interesting Subjects: I. Government, II. Revolutions, III. The British Constitution etc.* (Glasgow, 1794), pp. 41-42.

106 On this see, among others, Dickinson, 'Popular Loyalism in Britain in the 1790s', pp. 503-533.

107 On this see, among others, Epstein, '"Our real constitution"'; Lisa Steffen, *Defining a British State: Treason and National Identity, 1608-1820* (Basingstoke, 2001), pp. 99-139; F. K. Prochaska, 'English State Trials in the 1790s: A Case Study', *Journal of British Studies*, 13 (1973), 63-82; Clive Emsley, 'An Aspect of Pitt's "Terror": Prosecution for Sedition during the 1790s', *Social History*, 6 (1981), 155-184; Philip Harling, 'The Law of Libel and the Limits of Repression, 1790-1832', *Historical Journal*, 44 (2001), 107-134.

reform the existing political system, but that they were working, in word and deed, to undermine and ultimately overthrow the constitution.

One of the most prominent trials of this kind was that of Thomas Paine who, as has already been mentioned, was accused of 'seditious libel' for the second part of his *Rights of Man* and tried in his absence. Paine had, indeed, fundamentally attacked the largely customary English constitutional order which had evolved historically. This became very clear in Paine's criticism of the Bill of Rights, a constitutional document that, like Magna Carta, was one of the sacred cows of the eighteenth-century constitutional debate.[108] Paine believed that the Bill of Rights was no more than a myth of the English constitution. He regarded it as promoted by selfish interests, and saw it as the result of a compromise between the Crown and the Convention Parliament, whose legitimacy he denied.[109] 'What is it', he wrote, 'but a bargain, which the parts of the government made with each other to divide powers, profits and privileges? You shall have so much, and I will have the rest: and with respect to the nation, it said, for *your share*, you *shall have the right of petitioning*. This being the case, the bill of rights is more properly a bill of wrongs, and of insult.'[110] Paine's interpretation of the Glorious Revolution and the Bill of Rights was central to the charges levelled against him.[111] Similarly, the Attorney General drew upon other passages from the *Rights of Man*. These included Paine's fundamental doubts about the legitimacy of hereditary monarchy,[112] and his description of Parliament as an obsequious and obedient instrument of government.[113] He was accused of 'a wilful, deliberate intention to vilify and degrade, and thereby to bring into abhorrence and contempt the whole constitution of the government of

[108] On this see Eckhart Hellmuth, 'Die Debatte um die "Bill of Rights" im 18. Jahrhundert', in *Grund- und Freiheitsrechte von der ständischen zur spätbürgerlichen Gesellschaft*, ed. Günther Birtsch (Göttingen, 1987), pp. 117-134.

[109] Thomas Paine, *Rights of Man, Part II* (1792), in *Thomas Paine: Political Writings*, ed. Kuklick, pp. 145-203, at p. 181: 'As to what is called the convention parliament, it was a thing that made itself, and then made the authority by which it acted. A few persons got together, and called themselves by that name. Several of them had never been elected, and none of them for the purpose.'

[110] *Ibid.*

[111] 'The Attorney General's Speech in Support of the Prosecution', in *Speeches of the Hon. Thomas Erskine*, ii, 46-86, at pp. 60-62.

[112] *Ibid.*, pp. 55-56.

[113] *Ibid.*, pp. 66-67.

this country'.[114] The jury agreed with this assessment of Paine and his *Rights of Man*, and found him guilty without even consulting. This judgement was clearly condoned by those who agitated for 'King' and 'Country'.

These attempts to declare such a crucial area of public interest and political debate out of bounds met determined resistance from the radical and reformist camp. Although there was only limited sympathy for Paine and his republicanism, the principle that this sort of criticism of the constitution should not be subjected to criminal sanctions was undisputed. Thus, the declaration on the freedom of the press which the Friends of the Liberty of the Press regularly reproduced in their pamphlets was clearly designed to clear the ground for a debate on political fundamentals.[115] They wanted only writings that deliberately called for disobedience to the authorities or the law to be criminalized. They argued: 'That no writing ought to be considered as a public Libel, and made the subject of criminal prosecution, unless such writing shall appear to be published with a design, to exite the People to resist the Civil Magistrate, or obstruct the execution of the existing laws.'[116] In determining what, in fact, was a libel, the crucial thing was to prove malicious intent, as Thomas Erskine explained during Thomas Paine's trial. What needed to be proved was that the author had deliberately set out to undermine social and political peace.[117] And Robert Hall summed this up in his *Apology for the Freedom of the Press*: 'An enquiry respecting the comparative excel-

---

114 *Ibid.*, p. 49.

115 On this see *ibid.*, p. xxx.

116 *Proceedings of the Friends of the Liberty of the Press*, pp. 1-2.

117 'Mr. Erskine's Speech for the Defendant', pp. 96-97: 'If, indeed, he writes what he does not think; – if, contemplating the misery of others, he wickedly condems what his own understanding approves;–or, even admitting his real disgust against the government or its corruptions, if he calumniates living magistrates, – or holds out to individuals, that they have a right to run before the public mind in their conduct, – that they may oppose by contumacy or force what private reason only disapproves; – that they may disobey the law, because their judgment condemns it; – or resist the public will, because they honestly wish to change it – he is then a criminal upon every principle of rational policy, as well as upon the immemorial precedents of English justice; because such a person seeks to disunite individuals from their duty to the whole, and excites to overt acts of misconduct in a part of the community, instead of endeavouring to change, by the impulse of reason, that universal assent which, in this and in every country, constitutes the law for all.'

lence of civil constitutions can be forbidden on no other pretence, than of its tendency to sedition and anarchy.'[118]

But this indirect legitimation of fundamental criticism of the constitution was not the end of the story. Against the background of Paine's trial, it was also explicitly stated that republicanism was perfectly legitimate. Joseph Towers, for example, wrote in one of his tracts: 'But there may certainly be speculative men in the kingdom, who conceive, that a republic would be better than a limited monarchy. It is no crime for any man to entertain that opinion, if he be guilty of no illegal act in order to support it. There have always been such speculative men in this country, and there ever will be such men in it, till we are become a nation of slaves.'[119] And Robert Hall spoke out with equal vigour against all repressive measures directed against contemporary republican writing:

> Under pretence of its being seditious to express any disapprobation of the *form* of our government, the most alarming attempts are made to wrest the liberty of the press out of our hands. It is far from being my intention to step up a defence of republican principles, as I am persuaded whatever imperfections may attend the British constitution, it is competent to all the ends of government, and the best adapted of any to the *actual* situation of this kingdom. Yet I am convinced there is no crime in being a republican, and that while he obeys the laws, every man has a right to entertain what sentiments he pleases on our form of government, and to discuss this with the same freedom as any other topic.[120]

Such declarations were based on far-reaching considerations. These included the assumption that nobody was able precisely to define the British constitution. Whereas the United States and France had written constitutions which were based on natural law and guaranteed wide-ranging indi-

---

[118] Hall, *Apology for the Freedom of the Press*, pp. 13-14. Hall was aware that the definition of a 'tendency' was anything but clear-cut. He therefore warned against all too easily imputing a 'tendency to sedition and anarchy': 'The doctrine of tendencies is extremely subtle and complicated. Whatever would diminish our veneration for the christian religion, or shake our belief in the being of God, will be allowed to be of very evil tendency; yet few, I imagine, who are acquainted with history, would wish to see the writings of sceptists or deists suppressed by law; being persuaded it would be lodging a very dangerous power in the hands of the magistrate, and the truth is best supported by its own evidence. This dread of certain opinions on account of their tendency, has been the copious spring of all those religious wars and persecutions, which are the disgrace and calamity of modern times.'

[119] Joseph Towers, *A Dialogue between an Associator and a well-informed Englishman, on the Grounds of the Late Associations and the Commencement of a War with France* (London, 1793), p. 12.

[120] Hall, *Apology for the Freedom of the Press*, pp. 8-9.

vidual freedoms, the British equivalent was more a sort of myth.[121] Thus, in his *Reflection on the Freedom of Writing*, Bruce argued that the concept of the 'constitution' was highly equivocal and therefore vulnerable to exploitation in support of naked political ambition: 'There are few words more equivocally employed or capable of a more abusive use than the Constitution. ... It has served equally the purpose of all parties; and scarce any two writers or speakers will be found to entertain exactly the same view of it. It is often used apparently with scarce meaning at all.'[122] The consequences to be drawn from this sceptical position are obvious: if there was no consensus about what the term 'constitution' actually meant, any attempt to control the public discourse on the subject by legal means was senseless.

More important in this context, however, was the thought that the British constitution in force at the end of the eighteenth century had evolved historically, over time, and was therefore something that could change in future. It was assumed that the British constitution was being gradually perfected in a process which had largely been initiated by free public discussion. In the context of this sort of reasoning George Rous put the following rhetorical question to a meeting of the Friends of the Liberty of the Press: 'If the right of discussion had not been used by those who lived in the old times, what would the government of England have been in the present moment?'[123] It was Thomas Erskine, however, who most fully developed the idea that the historical nature of the constitution implied the right to criticize it. He started by looking at ideas on the permanence of constitutions, referring to, among others, Filmer, Burke, and Locke. He rejected Filmer's theory of the divine origins and sacrosanct nature of the authorities, as well as Burke's ideology of the *status quo*.[124] Instead, Erskine turned to Locke. He quoted the passage from the *Two Treatises on Government* which stated that contracts entered into with

---

121 On this see, above all, Epstein, '"Our real constitution"', pp. 23-25.

122 Archibald Bruce, *Reflections on the Freedom of Writing* (Edinburgh, 1794), p. 68. The problem that Bruce was addressing here was additionally complicated by the fact that contemporaries did not distinguish clearly between the terms 'constitution' and 'government'. The term 'government', as a number of passages which follow also demonstrate, could be used in the sense of 'constitution'; thus it did not, in every case, refer to the government.

123 *The Speech of the Hon. Thomas Erskine, At a Meeting of the Friends to the Liberty of the Press, at the Free–Mason's Tavern, Dec. 22, 1792. With the Resolutions, etc. of that Truly Patriotic Society* (London, 1792), p. 4.

124 'Mr. Erskine's Speech for the Defendant', pp. 126-128.

governments, especially where they curtailed freedoms, could not be binding on later generations.[125] Erskine also spoke of the 'great unalienable right of the people, to reform or to change their governments'.[126] This theory of the legitimacy of constitutional change fed through to the problem of the freedom of the press. As far as Erskine was concerned, the freedom of the press was an indispensable instrument for effecting those revisions of the constitution which became necessary from time to time. In his view, the constitution owed its present state to this freedom:

> [F]or had it not been for this unalienable right ..., how should we have had this constitution which we so loudly boast of – If, in the march of the human mind, no man could have gone before the establishments of the time he lived in, how could our establishment, by reiterated changes, have become what it is – If no man could have awakened the public mind to errors and abuses in our government, how could it have passed on from stage to stage, through reformation and revolution?[127]

It was this process of critically commenting upon and gradually perfecting the constitution that reformers and radicals wanted to see continuing in the present. Among the principles they appealed to were those of popular sovereignty and 'government by consent', which were expressed most clearly in Robert Hall's *Apology for the Freedom of the Press*. Hall derived the right to modify the constitution by means of public criticism from the maxim that the constitution should be based on the free consent of the people: 'Government is the creature of the people and that which they have a right to examine. The great Author of Nature having placed the right of dominion in no particular hands, hath left every point relating to it to be settled by the consent and approbation of mankind.'[128] And elsewhere, he wrote: 'But if we allow the people are the true origin of political power, it is absurd to require them to resign the right of discussing any question that can arise either upon its form or its measures, as this would put it for ever out of their power to revoke the trust which they have placed in the hands of the rulers.'[129]

---

125 *Ibid.*, p. 134: 'It is true, that whatever engagements or promises any one has made for himself, he is under the obligation of them, but cannot, by any compact whatsoever, bind his children or posterity: for his son, when a man, being altogether as free as the father, any act of the father can no more give away the liberty of the son, than it can of any body else.'

126 *Ibid.*, p. 139.

127 *Ibid.*, p. 99.

128 Hall, *Apology for the Freedom of the Press*, pp. 9-10.

129 *Ibid.*, pp. 10-11.

A very different and rather unexpected note, however, could be struck in this discourse on the freedom of the press and criticizing the constitution. This becomes evident in the case of *Reflections on the Freedom of Writing* by the Presbyterian clergyman Archibald Bruce.[130] Not only was it written largely in Biblically-saturated language, it also had a clearly millenarian dimension.[131] For example, we read: 'Many striking symptoms are at present appearing, that indicate some very memorable and general revolution in the system of governments, and in the constitution and public character of nations, to be fast approaching. The stupendous operations of that providence which rules in the kingdoms of men, and in the church, that has so often poured contempt on princes, and debased those who walked in pride, seem evidently to point that way.'[132] Further, Bruce wrote of the 'last ages, as unfolded in the last book of inspiration' and the 'restoration of truth, justice and universal peace'.[133] The new Jerusalem dominated by the spirit of Enlightened reason which Bruce envisaged seemed to him attainable in two different ways: either via the collapse of the existing political and social order; or – and this was the way he favoured – by a comprehensive dialogue between the authorities and their subjects on the reform of the constitution. Bruce passionately advocated free public discussion of this issue:

> There must still be reserved a power of discussing, of judging, objecting to, and of changing, by the laws of permanent reason and justice, not only the particular laws, but the discriminating form of its settled government, its very constitution upon sufficient grounds, as when any of them are radically bad, or are become grievous and oppressive; seeing they are ordinances or constitutions merely human, and have no claim to support when they either are incompatible with a higher and more sacred law, or with the immediate end for which they were appointed, [the] general good.[134]

Where, as in Bruce's case, the chord of divine right was also touched, any fears about possible negative consequences disappeared. Given the immi-

---

130 On Bruce, see the brief account by John D. Brims, 'The Scottish "Jacobins": Scottish Nationalism and the British Union', in *Scotland and England, 1286–1815*, ed. Roger A. Mason (Edinburgh, 1987), pp. 247-265, at pp. 254-255.

131 On millenarianism at the end of the 18th century see, among others, John Mee, 'Millenarian Visions and Utopian Speculations', in *The Enlightenment World*, ed. Martin Fitzpatrick, Peter Jones, Christa Knellwolf, Iain McCalman (London, 2004), pp. 536-550 (with a bibliography of further reading).

132 Bruce, *Reflections on Freedom of Writing*, p. 85.

133 *Ibid.*, p. 85.

134 *Ibid.*, p. 73.

nence of the Millennium, remodelling the constitution took absolute priority: 'Neither the plea of long prescription, the venerable solemnity or sacredness supposed to belong to them, the engagements or oaths wherewith governors or subjects have in time past been bound to them, nor the fear of accidental dangers or convulsions that may attend the change, nor yet the negative of a part of the constituted legislature, or of the ordinary executive powers of the state, can be sufficient reason for postponing for ever the needful alteration.'[135]

Ultimately, radicals and reformers were demanding the right to put the British constitution to a comprehensive and public test. They did not accept the argument, which Loyalist propaganda so long insisted upon, of the superiority of the British constitution. They did not attack this view head-on, however; instead, they tried to undermine it. If, they argued, the British constitution really was as superior as the Loyalists claimed, then it had no need to fear the test of publicity. 'Every thing', wrote Robert Hall, 'that is really excellent will bear examination, it will even invite it. ... Is our constitution a good one, it will gain in our esteem by the severest inquiry.'[136] For radicals and reformers, the free press was the tribunal before which the existing constitution, and especially its shortcomings and weaknesses, could be brought. And this was the sense in which Thomas Erskine defined press freedom:

> The proposition which I mean to maintain as the basis of the liberty of the press, and without which it is an empty sound, is this – that every man ... may address himself to the universal reason of a whole nation, ... – that he may analyze the principles of its

[135] *Ibid.*, pp. 73-74.

[136] Hall, *Apology for the Freedom of the Press*, p. 9. And he goes on: 'Is it bad, then its imperfection should be laid open and exposed. Is it, as is generally confessed, of a mixed nature, excellent in theory, but defective in its practice; freedom of discussion will be still requisite to point out the nature and source of its corruptions and apply suitable remedies.' Similarly Towers, *Dialogue*, pp. 11-12, who levelled the following accusation at the Loyalist side: 'And as to the apprehension of the dangers that may arise from what is called libelling the constitution, these appear to me the idle terrors of men, who are ignorant even of the first principles of civil government. If the constitution be good, it will bear the fullest and the freest investigation. Indeed, the greatest libellers of the constitution are many of the associaters; they who suppose, that it will not stand the test of examination, and that it cannot be supported, but by suppressing the freedom of speaking and writing. We are sometimes told, that our constitution of government is the best in the world. ... If this be the case, is it possible, that either the constitution, or the government, can be in any real danger from the publication of a few pamphlets?'.

> constitution, – point out its errors and defects, – examine and publish its corruptions, – warn his fellow citizens against their ruinous consequences, and exert his whole faculties in pointing out the most advantageous changes in establishments which he considers to be radically defective, or sliding from their object by abuse.[137]

This right to criticize the constitution was to apply even to those who wanted to revise the constitution in a conservative direction. At least, this is what Charles Earl Stanhope argued. Even if such 'right-wing' criticism of the constitution was diametrically opposed to his own political views, he believed that it had a legitimate place in public discourse.[138]

IV.

This was by no means the end of the discourse on the liberty of the press and the criticism of the constitution. Discussion of this subject revived under somewhat unexpected circumstances a few years later, when Loyalist writers became interested in the subject. This happened in 1795–96, when John Reeves, the leading Loyalist, was charged with 'seditious libel' and put on trial.[139] The cause was his book, *Thoughts on the English Government* (1795),[140] largely a polemic against the Foxite Whigs, whom he accused of making common cause with the extra-parliamentary radical movement. Further, Reeves's text was permeated with reflections on the

137 'Mr. Erskine's Speech for the Defendant', pp. 95-96.

138 See Charles Earl Stanhope, *The Rights of Juries Defended: With Authorities of Law in Support of Those Rights on the Objection to Mr. Fox's Libel Bill Refuted* (London, 1792), pp. 142-143: 'Mere speculative Writings on the Constitution are not Libels, however absurd they may be. Suppose for Instance, that a Man were to write a speculative work, to prove that a Trial by a single Judge would be far preferable to the Trial by Jury; or that a Parliament, composed only of a King and a House of Peers, would be beyond Comparison better than a Legislature of King, Lords and Commons. No man could possibly reprobate such a work more than I should; but if the work did not exite the People to Sedition, such speculative Publications could certainly never be deemed a Libel; for, Absurdity is no Part of the Definition of a Libel.'

139 For details of this episode see David Eastwood, 'John Reeves and the Contested Idea of the Constitution', *British Journal of Eighteenth-Century Studies*, 16 (1993), 197-212; A. V. Beedell, 'John Reeves's Prosecution for a Seditious Libel, 1795-6: A Study in Political Cynicism', *Historical Journal*, 36 (1993), 799-824; Michael Weinzierl, 'John Reeves and the Controversy over the Constitutional Role of Parliament in England during the French Revolution', *Parliaments, Estates and Representation*, 5 (1985), 71-77.

140 John Reeves, *Thoughts on the English Government* (London, 1795).

constitution, including a passage in which he most bizarrely defined the monarchy as the centre of the English constitution, while regarding Lords and Commons as merely derivative powers.[141] Despite the metaphorical style in which he clothed his arguments, it was quite clear that Reeves opposed the traditional idea of a balance of power within the framework of a mixed constitution. In doing so, Reeves certainly offended large sections of the political élite. Given the prominence of its author, it was almost inevitable that *Thoughts on the English Government* would give offence. In the past Reeves had unscrupulously accused radical authors of working to overthrow the established constitution; now he himself stood accused of disloyalty to the constitution. Fox and his followers did not hesitate to bring the case before Parliament. With almost no opposition, indeed, with the approval of all parliamentary groups including the Pittites, Parliament passed a motion on 14 December 1795 initiating criminal proceedings against Reeves for 'seditious libel'. Reeves was subsequently acquitted, but this is not of great interest to us here. More important is the Loyalist propaganda that preceded the trial.

Loyalist authors such as George Chalmers and Joseph Cawthorne, of course, tried to prove that Reeves's ideas were in line with the constitution and emphasized his work in the struggle against radicalism. But they also went beyond this rather pragmatic level of argument and addressed the fundamental problems of a free press and freedom of expression. And here we witness a certain convergence between radical and Loyalist

---

[141] On this see *ibid.*, pp. 12-13: 'With the exception therefore, of the advice and consent of the Two Houses of Parliament and the interposition of juries, the Government and the administration of it in all its parts, may be said to rest wholly and solely with the King and those appointed by him. Those two adjuncts of Parliaments and Juries are subsidiary and occasional; but the King's Power is a substantive one, always visible and active... In fine the Government of England is a Monarchy. The Monarch is the ancient stock from which have sprung those goodly branches of the Legislature, the Lords and Commons, that at the same time give ornament to the tree, and afford shelter to those who seek protection under it. But these are still only branches, and derive their origin and their nutrient from their common parent; they may be lopped off and the Tree is Tree still; shorn indeed of its honour, but not, like them, cast into the fire. The Kingly Government may go on, in all its functions without Lords or Commons; it has heretofore done so for years and in our times it does so during every recess of Parliament; but without the King his Parliament is no more.'

ideology. Thus, it was possible for a writer such as George Chalmers[142] to elevate the freedom of the press into a fundamental right in a way which would have done credit to any Foxite Whig or Radical. Chalmers, the chief clerk of the Committee of Trade and an intimate of John Reeves,[143] did not see the non-renewal of the Licensing Act at the end of the seventeenth century as a simple modification of the English legal system; rather, he regarded the events of 1694 as the dawn of a new era: 'Then it was, that the *common law* right, the *Magna Charta* right of free thinking, of free writing, and of free publishing, was again engrafted on the *ancient stock*; whereon, being planted in a congenial soil, and cultivated by free hands, the *tree of Liberty* has since flourished luxuriantly, putting forth every season, goodley branches, which, I trust, will never be *lopped off*.'[144] And elsewhere he wrote, with similar enthusiasm: 'If it be a genuine maxim of English law, that every free hand may act freely, unless they be restrained by positive statute, it must be incontrovertible law, that since the epoch of 1694, every man, every woman, and every child, has an indubitable right to think, write, and print freely.'[145] This position on fundamental rights gave rise to critical ideas which it is, indeed, astonishing to find voiced by a Loyalist author. Blackstone, the political and social Establishment's pet interpreter of the constitution, was condemned, quite correctly, for the fact that his 'classic' definition of the freedom of the press[146] merely described this right in legalistic terms.[147] Even the Bill of Rights was not spared. Chalmers, for example, complained that the freedom of the press was not enshrined in this document

[142] George Chalmers, *A Vindication of the Privilege of the People, in Respect to the Constitutional Right of Free Discussion* (London, 1796).

[143] For a biography of Chalmers see Alexander Du Toit, 'Chalmers, George (bap. 1742, d.1825)', in *Oxford Dictionary of National Biography.* Online URL (side dated 2004; accessed 30.11.2005):
< http://www.oxforddnb.com/view/article/5028 >

[144] Chalmers, *Vindication of the Privilege of the People*, pp. 21-22.

[145] *Ibid.*, p. 22.

[146] His definition of the freedom of the press can be found in William Blackstone, *Commentaries on the Law of England* (4 vols., London, 1765-69), iv, 153.

[147] Cf. Chalmers, *Vindication of the Privilege of the People*, p. 21: 'It is remarkable, that Blackstone, when treating formally on the Rights of Englishmen, says not a word about that sacred privilege of the mind, the privilege of thinking, writing and printing; he does, indeed, take incidental notice of this essential right, when he treats of libel among the crimes; but, he here considers this constitutional privilege, as a mere exemption from punishment, rather than an absolute right.'

which was so central to England's constitutional development.[148] This, incidentally, was a position he shared with the Nonconformist clergyman Joseph Towers, one of the most determined opponents of Reeves and the Loyalist movement.[149]

We can find even more surprising points of contact between radicalism and Loyalism. Loyalist authors pointed to prominent libel cases that counted as milestones in the establishment of the principle of freedom of the press, and which formed part of the ideological heritage of reformist and radical circles. Loyalists used these cases as precedents in order to demonstrate the obsolescence of the case brought against Reeves. They included the 1789 trial of John Stockdale, a London bookseller, who had been defended by Thomas Erskine. George Chalmers described this case in detail in his *Vindications*. Among other things, he quoted Erskine's defence of Stockdale, but changed the emphasis so that it appeared to be a plea in favour of Reeves.[150] Thus, Thomas Erskine, one of the cult figures of the 'liberal' camp, was cast in the role of defending the arch-conservative John Reeves.[151] And Joseph Cawthorne, a

---

148 See *ibid.*, p. 21: 'It is still more remarkable, that the Declaration of Rights is studiously silent on this important liberty, without which all other liberties are insecure. The fact is, the Revolution left us without the liberty of the press.'

149 Cf. Joseph Towers, *An Oration Delivered at the London Tavern, on the Fourth of November, 1788, on Occasion of the Commemoration of the Revolution* (London, 1788), pp. 19-21 and 24-25.

150 See Chalmers, *Vindication of the Privilege of the People*, pp. 47-48: 'It is obviously the language of a warm man, engaged in the honest defence of the constitution, and who is brought to what he thinks a just conclusion in argument, which, perhaps, becomes offensive in proportion to its truth. Truth is, undoubtedly, no warrant for writing what is reproachful of any private man; but, as to writing on general subjects, which are not charged as an infringement on the of individuals, but as of a seditious tendency, it is far otherwise....When, in the progress of legislation, or of high national justice in Parliament, they who are amenable to no law, are supposed to have adopted through mistake, or error, a principle which, if drawn into precedent, might be dangerous to the public; I shall not admit it to be a libel, in the course of a legal and bona fide publication, to stake that such a principle had in fact been adopted; for, the people of England are not to be kept in dark, touching the proceedings of their representatives. Let us, therefore, coolly examine this supposed offence, and see what it amounts to.' On the original case see the trial report in *Speeches of the Hon. Thomas Erskine*, ii, 205-288.

151 Of course, this was a two-edged sword. In referring to Erskine, Chalmers hoped to be able to expose the radical and reforming milieu. He wanted to show that while radicals and refomers claimed far-reaching freedom of the press and of opinion for themselves, in case of doubt they refused their political opponents the same rights.

'pensioned Government pamphleteer of unusually independent views',[152] who provided the best-founded contribution to Reeves's defence, did not hesitate to place a positive gloss on the General Warrants Affair – that is, the episode from which John Wilkes, the most prominent radical of the 1760s, had eventually emerged as the victor in the struggle against the authorities' attempts to limit public discourse.[153]

It is no coincidence that Loyalist authors picked on the Stockdale trial and the General Warrants Affair, for in both cases Parliament had initiated criminal proceedings for 'seditious libel', and the parallel with Reeves's case was obvious. But there was more to it than that. Just as repeated attempts by Parliament to prohibit public debate on certain issues in the 1760s and 1770s had given rise to fundamental doubts about the extent of its powers, the events surrounding Reeves also provoked a rethinking on fundamental issues. The difference was that it now came from the loyalist rather than the radical side. Cawthorne described Parliament as follows: 'This legislative bugbear, which is often held out *in terrorem*, to the people, under the hideous form of privileges undefined and incomprehensible [the description of discretionary and omnipotent power] puts me in mind of the Catholic carpenter, who was required to worship the wooden image he had made, as the people know what they have created.'[154] He went on to compare the behaviour of Parliament with that of the 'Catholic Inquisition' and the 'Court of Star Chamber', comparisons which had generally been drawn by the Enlightened camp in their struggle against the restrictions on freedom of the press and freedom of expression.[155] Cawthorne accused Parliament in such strong language because he believed that, in the action it was taking against Reeves's anti-parliamentary tract, *Thoughts on the English Government*, it had set itself up 'in the manner of an arbitrary Tribunal', to play the role of 'Judges and Jury in their own case'.[156] Finally, he charged Parliament

---

152 Barrell, *Imagining the King's Death*, p. 245.

153 See Joseph Cawthorne, *A Letter to the King, in Justification of a Pamphlet, Entitled, 'Thoughts on the English Government': With an Appendix in Answer to Mr. Fox's Declaration of the Whig-Club* (London, 1796), pp. 75-77.

154 *Ibid.*, p. 18.

155 Cf. e.g., *ibid.*, p. 11 and p. 79.

156 *Ibid.*, p. 110. Similarly also p. 39: 'The unauthorised conduct of the House of Commons in this Case is truly alarming. It erects itself into an Inquisition and pronounces judgements in its own cause, contrary to the principles and practice of every Court of Justice.'

with undermining the division of power by its behaviour.[157] It had arrogated to itself powers which the sovereign people had never granted it:

> When the people delegate their constitutional or legislative rights, they do not invest their Representatives with any judicial authority whatsoever. And since they possess no jurisdiction but what they receive from their constituents, for the general purposes of the people, from what source do they derive an inquisitorial capacity? ... It is an arbitrary assumption of power, and such an usurpation of power as plunges dagger in the bowels of the constitution.[158]

In order to prevent misunderstandings, it should be pointed out that Cawthorne's aim was not a programme of 'liberal' reform. Although his support for the freedom of the press led into criticism of Parliament's privileged position and the extent of its power, this does not mean that he advocated a more open parliamentary system or wider political participation. On the contrary, his constitutional ideal was a strong and efficient monarchy with extended powers.[159] And although it may seem paradoxical, this desire for a 'conservative' revision of the constitution was linked with the origins of a comparatively 'modern' theory of the freedom of the press.

Cawthorne, however, did not hesitate to make use of the repertoire of arguments that had been developed around the above-mentioned case against Paine. Specifically, this means that the idea, cultivated by Paine's supporters, of the historical character of the constitution and its reform by public criticism entered the intellectual stock of the Loyalists with Cawthorne's help. For Cawthorne, it was axiomatic that constitutions were not static, fixed entities, but that they changed over time. He regarded them as creations of the fallible human spirit. And he did not doubt that even the British constitution, although superior to other con-

---

157 Cf. *ibid.*, pp. 4-5: 'The parliament assumes an inquisitorial capacity, in this, as it has improperly done in other cases, which the House of Commons, as purely legislative, does not possess. It would be absurd in the extreme, to suppose that the power of representation, delegated by the people for legislative purposes, should constitute an inquisitorial authority over them for judicial purposes. It is perhaps the greatest beauty of our Constitution, that neither of the three Estates of the Kingdom possess an inquisitorial capacity, the second branch excepted, and that is a court of Appeal from the judicial authority. It would be congenial with the system of an absolute Government were either the legislative or executive power to possess an inquisitorial jurisdiction. The idea is a monstrum horrendum in a free state. It is a gross perversion of the Legislature, commonly called the constitution, and as gross a Libel on the judicial authority, or the Laws of the Land: It is Treason against a Government that wisely keeps the authorities of the State asunder.'

158 *Ibid.*, pp. 5-6.

159 On this cf. e.g., *ibid.* pp. 25-26, p. 34.

stitutions, had its defects.[160] 'It is therefore', he concluded, 'the most preposterous in the English to account it Treason to dispute the eternity and immutability of their Constitution.'[161] In his view, it was not in the nature of constitutions to be permanent; rather, they were in need of gradual perfection.[162] And further: 'As Nations grow enlightened by experience and reflection they will adapt their Constitutions and their Laws to the wisdom of the age in which they live.'[163] Ultimately, the question of which particular constitution was appropriate to the specific historical situation could only be clarified via public discussion: 'the proof of utility and expediency is left to the conviction and the judgement of the public'.[164] Fully aware of the plurality of views that existed upon the subject, Cawthorne nevertheless advocated this sort of general public discourse: 'Upon this subject [reforming the constitution], so important to a free Nation, the sentiments of a Free and enlightened people will be as different as their complexions.'[165] These considerations led him to make a fervent plea for a free debate on political and constitutional issues:

---

160 *Ibid.*, p. 17: 'Time has indeed shewn the superiority of our constitution over the other Governments of Europe, but it has also discovered great defects, for where is perfection to be found? And as these defects are of great magnitude, can it be wondered that ingenious men should give an opinion how they may be removed, and the system of government made more perfect, and, by consequence, more conducive to the dignity of the State and the happiness of the people?'.

161 *Ibid.*, pp. 18*-19*.

162 On this cf. e.g., *ibid.* pp. 45-46: 'I, as an Englishman, sincerely wish that its principles may have immensity for their space, and eternity for their duration. But, notwithstanding the sincerity of my devotion, and my ardent wish that the Constitution may be immortal, I do not think that human wisdom is infallible, or human institutions immutable. It would be an indignity to the human mind, nay, it would be an impiety to think so. The constitution is no more immutable, than the Laws of the Land are infallible, and the same reasons that are assigned for the improvement of the one, may be adduced for the greater perfection of the other. When the wisdom of ancient and modern nations fixed on a system of Government, they did not engage for its immutability. Every period has been sensible of the uncertainty even of the wisest human establishments. Hence the alterations and revolutions in Government!' See also *ibid.*, pp. 14-15: 'If Nations have made the selection, it does not preclude speculative opinions founded on the effects which their various systems have produced for the purpose of reconsideration and comparison. Human wisdom, which is often called public virtue, arises from that reflection which experience occasions. Human nature is ever, by the improvement of civilization, in search of wisdom for its happiness and security.'

163 *Ibid.*, p. 46.

164 *Ibid.*, p. 13.

165 *Ibid.*, p. 84.

> *Englishmen* have an inherent and constitutional right (that is, a natural right secured to them by the nature of their government) to speak of the principles and effects of a Government entirely monarchical, or an absolute monarchy of the nature and tendency of Aristocracy; and of the principles and effects of Democracy; either separately, or as they are connected with a monarchical system, commonly called a mixed government, or a limited monarchy. In treating of these subjects, which so intimately concern all civilized human nature, the contemplation would be useless to civilization were they not to give an opinion, and leave mankind to consider which system is best adopted to the genius and policy of their representatives states; namely a government entirely monarchical; a limited monarchy; or a republican government.[166]

Positions such as those taken by George Chalmers and Joseph Cawthorne undoubtedly had an affinity with ideas that a few years earlier had been put forward by the radicals and reformers. It seems that Loyalism's potential for reflection went beyond demagogical reactions to the free public discussion of 1792-93. Clearly, Loyalism spoke with many voices.[167] Moreover, the dynamic of the discourse forced Loyalist authors constantly to reposition themselves and to respond alertly to what the other side said. As the examples of Chalmers and Cawthorne show, this could go as far as adopting positions of one's political opponents. Thus, the borders between the political camps became fluid, and respective political identities lost their unequivocal nature. This is by no means as astonishing as it may seem at first sight. For some time, historians looking at the landscape of discourse in the late eighteenth century have been voicing scepticism about the idea of firmly established and ideologically clearly defined political camps. And we have been warned against operating with dichotomies such as 'left' and 'right', 'progressive' and 'traditional'. Thus, according to Mark Philp: 'The greater complexity we recognize in the ideological terrain of the period, and the more sophisticated our account of the motives behind people's expressions of commitment, the more porous and problematic become the ideological categories of radical and conservative'.[168]

***

[166] *Ibid.*, pp. 13-14.

[167] On this see, most recently, Amanda Goodrich, *Debating England's Aristocracy in the 1790s: Pamphlets, Polemics and Political Ideas* (Woodbridge, 2005), Among other things, she writes: 'Loyalism was a multi-faceted movement which shifted and changed in the flexible and fluid channels of the French Revolution debate.' *Ibid.*, p. 167.

[168] Mark Philp, 'Vulgar Conservatism', at p. 68.

The discourse which reformers, radicals, and Loyalists conducted about freedom of the press in the 1790s is ambiguous and it is sometimes also irritating. Those seeking clearly defined positions, stringent arguments, and dominant idioms in this textual landscape soon find themselves in difficulty. Naturally, individual attempts were made to address the problem of freedom of the press in broadly based and to some extent coherent treatises. Names such as Robert Hall and Archibald Bruce come to mind in this context. But for long periods, this discourse was conducted by means of spontaneous speech acts, rhetorical flourishes, and sometimes also the erratic. What has been said about the discourse of the late eighteenth century in general also applies to this case: 'The historical evidence shows that most late eighteenth century writers drew freely on a wide range of intellectual traditions and mobilised rhetoric from a variety of political languages.'[169] This eclecticism could go so far that, as the examples of Chalmers and Cawthorne demonstrate, a sort of intellectual cross-dressing came about. One could, as it were, slip into the clothes of the other side.

In this diffuse discourse, one new set of ideas was developed. This was the notion that the right to free public discussion included the right to criticize the constitution. Whereas in the 1760s and 1770s intellectual efforts in the discourse on freedom of the press had concentrated mainly on defining the role of the press in relation to government and Parliament as a power critical of the government and of Parliament, the concept of press freedom now gained other connotations. Thus, a feature specific to English 'freedom of the press' was defined as the right 'to publish speculative Works upon the Constitution, whether they contain Praise or Censure'.[170] Freedom of the press without the opportunity to pass critical comment on the constitution was rejected as 'Russian Freedom of the Press'.[171] These sentences, originally written by the Foxite Whig, Charles Earl Stanhope, in the debate about Fox's Libel Act, were integrated by Thomas Erskine in his plea in Thomas Paine's trial.[172] But they could just as well have been quoted by the Loyalist authors who stood up for John Reeves in 1795. For both sides, however paradoxical it might seem, worked to produce this 'modern' interpretation of freedom of the press.

---

169 Mark Philp, 'English Republicanism in the 1790s', *Journal of Political Philosophy*, 6 (1998), 235-262, at p. 249.

170 Stanhope, *The Rights of Juries Defended*, p. 144.

171 *Ibid.*

172 'Mr. Erskine's Speech for the Defendant', pp. 151-152.

Anton Kirchhofer

Revolutionizing the Review?

British Periodical Genres of the 1790s and the *Edinburgh Review*

I. Periodical Genres and the Voices in Public Debate

The immediate focus of this essay is on periodical genres. Its goal is to explore, define and contextualize the emergence of a new format of the Review[1]: a format first employed by the *Edinburgh Review* in 1802 and destined to set the dominant pattern of the Review genre beyond the middle of the nineteenth century.[2]

The generic identity chosen by a journal, as I will understand it here, is not simply a matter of abstract formal characteristics. It is a major factor shaping the public position of the journal. It contributes to defining a journal's status and it has a bearing on the weight, the character and the scope of the material it contains. Genre is a basic choice predetermining the relation in which the journal and all its contributions will stand to the public debate as a whole. A focus on periodical genres is therefore, in fact, a focus on the nexus between choices of generic identity and modes of participation in public debate.

Now the continual attention both to events and developments in France and to their potential or actual impact on Britain undoubtedly forms a major concern in the British public debate throughout the 1790s. It is to be expected, therefore, that the particular philosophical, political and literary anxieties characteristic of this continual attention will play a significant role for the positioning of any periodical in that debate. But

1 I follow the established practice 'by which "Review" with an initial capital refers to a review journal and is thus clearly distinguishable from the individual "review" items', Antonia Forster, 'Introduction', *Index to Book Reviews in England, 1749-1774* (Carbondale and Edwardsville, 1990), p. 14, n5.

2 It should be stressed that of course this is not the *only* generic variety. Several monthly Reviews continued to appear well into the nineteenth century, some switching to a quarterly interval of publication much later. A distinct variety is the weekly Review, represented by journals such as the *Literary Gazette* (1817-1862) and the *Athenæum* (1828-1921). In the 1860s, the *Fortnightly Review* (1865-1954) and the *Contemporary Review* (1866–) established a new format of the monthly Review that made the *Edinburgh Review* and its generic companions appear antiquated. All of these developments are, however, beyond the scope of this essay.

they will operate alongside the specific factors that govern the existence of the medium. In other words, they will act in conjunction with the pressures that those aiming to maintain their journal as a public voice are facing: the struggle for a share in the market, the competition among rival publications, the task of living up convincingly to the requirements of their chosen format, of maintaining their claim to relevance and their appeal for a specific or general readership.

Keeping in view the nexus between market position, generic identity and modes of participation in public debate, I propose to revisit a problem which Zeynep Tenger and Paul Trolander have placed in the context of the British 'Reaction to the French Revolution': the 'Transformation of the English Literary Periodical'.[3] That such a transformation took place had long been a critical commonplace and, traditionally, the foundation of the *Edinburgh Review* in 1802 had been taken as the mark for a new departure in periodical literature. The precise quality of the change had proved more difficult to determine. In many cases, critics and scholars identified a particular characteristic of the *Edinburgh Review* as its new and distinctive feature, only to be told by subsequent critics that the same feature was already to be found in the Reviews that had previously existed. Research in the 1990s has tended to emphasize the continuities between the journalism of the 1790s and the *Edinburgh Review*, aligning it with the new partisan journals such as the *Anti-Jacobin; or, Weekly Examiner* and the *Anti-Jacobin Review and Magazine*. The transformation of the literary periodical, as it is described by Tenger and Trolander, consists in the explicit rejection of the traditional Enlightenment ideal of critical impartiality in favour of the explicit adoption of a party-political bias. This change is not initiated by the *Edinburgh Review*; it occurs during the decade preceding the foundation of this journal and originates in the conservative reaction to the French Revolution. What distinguishes the *Edinburgh* from the older Reviews is simply the fact that it goes along with the change and practises the new openly biased variety of criticism.

This account is unsatisfactory in two respects. First, it offers a reductive view of the relation in which the *Edinburgh Review* stands to the journals of the 1790s. As I will try to show, we are dealing with several distinct types of journals, embodying each a specific form of critical sub-

3 Zeynep Tenger and Paul Trolander, 'The Politics of Literary Production: The Reaction to the French Revolution and the Transformation of the English Literary Periodical', *Studies in Eighteenth-Century Culture*, 24 (1995), 279–95.

jectivity and labouring each under its own characteristic pressures in forging and maintaining a particular generic identity. The material does not reveal a single change, but a series of modifications that occur at the intersections of generic identity, market position and modes of participation in public debate. Second, the question why the *Edinburgh Review* would come to be seen as such an inaugural moment is not addressed at all. But among the individual and disparate modifications that we will be able to trace in some detail across the several journals, there is one that will only be found in the *Edinburgh Review*. It consists in a partial redefinition of the critical task, in an addition to the catalogue of critical problems of a task which has become so familiar to us since that its point of emergence is easily overlooked. What the *Edinburgh Review* shares with much subsequent criticism rather than with any of its periodical predecessors, is that it recognizes as a major object of critical concern the plurality of tendencies and influences that manifest themselves in given situations or developments, as well as the complexity that marks the connections between publications, tendencies and events.

To insist on the difference between the *Anti-Jacobin Review and Magazine* and the *Edinburgh Review* is therefore not exclusively a matter of historical justice: this difference is significant because it throws into relief and allows us to situate more clearly a characteristic constellation which offers a framework for critical practice to this day. I will return to this proposition once the background against which this move is set has been established more fully.

II. Generic Reorientation: From a 'Complete View of Modern Literature' to 'Tendencies of Public Opinion'

The outward features distinguishing the *Edinburgh Review* from the Reviews of the 1790s can be briefly summarized. The Reviews in the second half of the eighteenth century followed the format set by the *Monthly Review* and the *Critical Review*, established in 1749 and 1756 respectively. The half-yearly volume contained six monthly numbers. On an average of 80 pages per number, sold at one shilling, the Review contained a mixture of longer reviews and shorter notices of new books (typically around 40 in total). The articles were individually numbered and headed by the publication details of the works that were being reviewed. They were anonymous, and the whole periodical was supposed to be the collective work of a group of gentlemen. The *English Review* and *Analytical Review*, founded in 1782 and 1788 respectively, followed the same pattern. Under the pressure of the growing mass of publications claiming critical attention, the *Monthly* increased its size to 120 pages and its price to one shilling and sixpence in 1790 and the *Critical* followed suit in 1791. The most recent addition, the *British Critic* (founded in 1793), modelled itself along the same lines.

The *Edinburgh Review* retained the character of an anonymous work produced by a collective of gentlemen. But it extended its interval of publication to quarterly, so that two numbers now made up a half-yearly volume. It reduced the number of articles and increased their average length (offering initially between 20 and 30 articles[4] on around 280 pages) and, at 6 shillings per number, its price per printed page was nearly twice that of the older Reviews.

It will be useful to begin with a brief review of the qualitative change that critics have associated with these quantitative modifications. For Walter Bagehot, who looked back at the 'First Edinburgh Reviewers' in 1855, the *Edinburgh Review* was the prototype of the nineteenth-century Quarterlies like his own *National Review*, since it 'may be said to be, in this country, the commencement on large topics of suitable views for sensible persons'.[5] There was a new target audience, the review no longer exclusively addressed scholars, '[p]rofessed students'; 'the appeal now is to the mass of sensible persons'.[6] Now it is certainly true that the *Edinburgh Review* addressed a general educated audience, but more recent research has shown that this was already the audience of the old Reviews. Derek Roper has pointed out that along with scholars and the Universities, 'subscribers [to the old Reviews] include landowners great and small; clergymen . . . and scholars; professional men and commercial men'.[7] Leslie Stephen, writing a year after Bagehot's death, saw the *Edinburgh*'s 'great merit' in the fact 'that it was no mere publisher's

---

4 The number of articles was gradually further reduced to around a dozen. Cf. Marilyn Butler, 'Culture's Medium: The Role of the Review', in *The Cambridge Companion to British Romanticism*, ed. Stuart Curran (Cambridge, 1993), p. 131.

5 Walter Bagehot, 'The First Edinburgh Reviewers', [1855] in *Literary Studies* (2 vols., Hartford, 1891), i, 7.

6 Bagehot, 'First Edinburgh Reviewers', 6.

7 Derek Roper, *Reviewing before the Edinburgh 1788–1802* (Newark, 1978), p. 24. On reading audiences during this period, see Jon Klancher, *The Making of English Reading Audiences: 1790-1832* (Madison, 1987).

organ, like its rivals',[8] and his view is echoed in the first book-length study of the early years of the journal.[9] Again, more recent research has shown the assumption that reviewing prior to the *Edinburgh* was largely subservient to booksellers to be unjustifiable.[10] What this free attribution of supposed deficits documents above all, is the extent to which, in a retrospective point of view, the *Edinburgh Review* did in fact, in Joanne Shattock's phrase, 'eclipse' the cultural presence of the earlier Reviews.[11]

The study which pioneered the 'rehabilitation' of the older Reviews is Derek Roper's *Reviewing before the Edinburgh*. Roper himself sees the *Edinburgh*'s 'selective approach to the works chosen for review' as the chief contrast to the earlier reviews.[12] More recently, however, Tenger and Trolander have stressed that the ever growing number of publications was a problem that had already given the monthly Reviews a great deal of trouble. They also demonstrate that there had, in fact, always been a principle of selection in operation even while Reviews carried a greater number of articles in a smaller space.[13]

The difference stressed by Tenger and Trolander themselves is a shift from the impartiality of the earlier Reviews towards the open Whig partisanship of the *Edinburgh*, a professed ideal of ideological commitment rather than of critical objectivity. This shift is mediated by the conservative reaction to the French Revolution. Burke's new positive evaluation of 'prejudice' was echoed by numerous conservative periodicals of the 1790s, and the *Edinburgh Review* chose to play the game with the weapons of its political opponents rather than uphold the Enlightenment values to which the Reviews had previously paid allegiance.[14]

---

8 Leslie Stephen, 'The First Edinburgh Reviewers', *Hours in a Library* (2 vols., London, 1909), ii, 248–9.

9 See John Clive, *Scotch Reviewers: The Edinburgh Review 1802-1815* (London, 1957), pp. 32–3.

10 Cf. Roper, *Reviewing before the Edinburgh*, pp. 30–2, as well as Tenger and Trolander, 'Politics of Literary Production', 294, n30. Antonia Forster has pointed out that even the practice of sending out review copies to journals had not been widely established yet (Forster, 'Introduction', p. 10).

11 Cf. Joanne Shattock, *Politics and Reviewers: The 'Edinburgh' and the 'Quarterly' in the Early Victorian Age* (London, 1989), p. 4.

12 Roper, *Reviewing before the Edinburgh*, p. 40.

13 Tenger and Trolander, 'Politics of Literary Production', 279.

14 Tenger and Trolander, 'Politics of Literary Production', 282-5, 287.

It is true that, as Tenger and Trolander point out, some journals in the 1790s had begun to commit themselves politically. The *Anti-Jacobin Review and Magazine*, to which we will return in greater detail, had proclaimed: 'we are deeply prejudiced in favour of our country; and are highly partial to her constitution and laws, to her religion and government'.[15] Other periodicals of the 1790s had announced their principles in a similar, if generally less aggressive manner. The *Monthly Magazine* had pledged its support to 'those liberal principles . . . which have been either deserted or virulently opposed by other Periodical Miscellanies'.[16] Among the Reviews, the *British Critic* had announced its commitment to the Church of England and 'the constitution'.

But for all that the criterion of open political partisanship is inadequate in order to characterize the change. On the one hand, in spite of the ideal of impartiality, even the older journals were perceived to be more or less explicitly committed to parties and interest groups. 'Is it not . . . natural for a republican to call for the Monthly Review, a dissenter for the Analytical, and a high-churchman for the British Critic?',[17] the *English Review* asks in an address to its readers.[18] On the other hand, although its 'buff and blue cover, the colors of the Whig liberal Foxite party', may have 'tacitly proclaimed the editors' attachment to "party" principles',[19] the *Edinburgh Review* of 1802 does not foreground any such attachment. As Leslie Stephen already noted in 1878, the 'great political importance of the *Edinburgh Review* belongs to a later period'.[20] For its first six years, 'the *Review* had not been conducted in such a way as to pledge itself beyond all redemption in the eyes of staunch Tories'.[21] It was a political article published in October 1808 that 'first made the [Edinburgh] Reviewers conspicuous as Liberals'.[22] Susan Manning's recent analysis of Walter Scott's contributions to the early volumes of the *Edinburgh* would seem to corroborate this view, as well as the assumption that it was this 'coming out' as a Liberal organ that cata-

15 'Prospectus', *Anti-Jacobin Review and Magazine*, 1 (1798), 5. This is one of the key passages quoted by Tenger and Trolander (cf. 287).

16 'Preface', *Monthly Magazine*, 1 (1796), iii.

17 'Prospectus', *English Review*, 23 (1794), 5.

18 Roper elaborates this point more fully in his section on 'Politics and the Reviews', pp. 172-83.

19 Tenger and Trolander, 'Politics of Literary Production', 287.

20 Stephen, 'First Edinburgh Reviewers', 220.

21 *Ibid.*

22 *Ibid.*, 221.

lysed the foundation in the following year of the *Quarterly Review* as a Tory counterpart of the *Edinburgh*.[23]

The shift effected in 1802 is of a different quality. It should not be sought in the journal's own affiliation with a party or a tendency, but rather in the fact that the *Edinburgh Review* will select the plurality of perceived or existing tendencies as an object of critical discussion. I will attempt to define and locate this shift more precisely, first through a contrast between the generic rationales of the *Edinburgh Review* and its generic predecessors, and subsequently in a more extensive analysis of the early numbers of the *Anti-Jacobin Review and Magazine*.

The generic definition to which the Reviews of the second half of the eighteenth century had answered was this: they were *histories of literature*, according to the contemporary sense of the term. Their subtitles in fact invariably said as much. The *Critical Review* described itself as *Annals of Literature*, the *English Review* as *an Abstract of English and Foreign Literature*, and the *Analytical Review* claimed to be a *History of Literature, Domestic and Foreign*. However well or ill they performed their task, they aimed to provide a comprehensive account of all recent publications.

That this generic rationale was still operative in the 1790s can be seen, for instance, in the preface to the first volume of the *British Critic*. The journal claims to be 'a sort of History of British Literature', a 'literary register' giving 'a concise view of the progress of British Literature' for the period of May to August 1793.[24] The headings under which it arranges a survey of its articles gives a sense of what the reviewers of the late eighteenth century mean when they say 'literature': Divinity, History, Biography, Antiquities, Travels, Topography, Politics, Law, Poetry, English Classics Republished, Translations of Classic Authors, Mathematics, Medicine, Chemistry, Natural History, Botany (and, finally, Miscellaneous).

The *Edinburgh Review* would go on to review a similar topical range of publications.[25] But it no longer claimed, like its predecessors, the character of a 'history of literature'. It does not call itself a 'Literary Journal', as the

23 Cf. Susan Manning, 'Walter Scott, Antiquarianism and the Political Discourse of the *Edinburgh Review*, 1802-11', in *British Romanticism and the 'Edinburgh Review': Bicentenary Essays*, ed. Massimiliano Demata and Duncan Wu (Basingstoke, 2002), pp. 102–23.

24 *British Critic*, 1 (1793), xii and iii.

25 In addition, the new field of political economy will be given prominent attention in the journal, cf. Biancamaria Fontana, *Rethinking the Politics of Commercial Society: The 'Edinburgh Review' 1802-1832* (Cambridge, 1985).

Monthly Review did, but a 'Critical Journal'. It marks therefore, first of all, the point when 'literature' (in the contemporary sense of the term) ceases to be the object with which a Review definitionally deals. The 'Advertisement' prefixed to the first volume says this explicitly:

> [T]he conductors of the EDINBURGH REVIEW propose . . . to decline any attempt at exhibiting a complete view of modern literature; and to confine their notice, in a great degree, to works that either have attained, or deserve, a certain portion of celebrity.[26]

The goal of 'exhibiting a complete view of modern literature' that had hitherto alone entitled a periodical to describe itself as a Review was abandoned in favour of a different criterion. Instead of the mass of new publications the Review now monitored the public debate. It would review books either because they had already become the object of public debate, or because they ought to, and it reserved the option of using its review articles as a vehicle for intervening in this debate.

Like the reduction in the number of articles, the lengthened interval of publication is a consequence of this new orientation of the Review. The publishers 'have been induced to prefer a quarterly, to a monthly period of publication, that they may always have before them a greater variety for selection, and be occasionally guided in their choice by the tendencies of public opinion'.[27] The adoption of a longer interval of publication allows them better to monitor the public debate and to take into account, 'occasionally', the 'tendencies of public opinion'.[28]

Both modifications then imply another fundamental shift. As Antonia Forster has noted, the old Reviews worked on the basis of the claim that they covered the whole market and that 'they alone were enough' as an account of new publications.[29] In introducing both the criterion of 'celebrity' and the quarterly publication, the *Edinburgh Review* situates

---

26 'Advertisement', *Edinburgh Review*, 1 (1802–3), A3^{r}.

27 'Advertisement', *Edinburgh Review*, 1 (1802–3), A3^{v}.

28 Tenger and Trolander have proposed what appears to me an inaccurate reading of this passage. To them, it indicates an abdication of the Review's function to 'judge' and 'direct' the public taste, a new subservience to public opinion (287). The reproach that they were 'in fact mere echoes of commonplace opinion' had already been levelled against the early volumes of the *Edinburgh Review* by Leslie Stephen ('First Edinburgh Reviewers', p. 240), but the passage in question here merely states that it is in their choice of books for review, not in their critical judgments of them, that the reviewers will 'be guided' by public opinion.

29 Cf. Forster, 'Introduction', 8.

itself at one remove from political and publishing events. It presupposes and recognizes the existence of a public debate about these events, and it reacts to this debate rather than to the events themselves.[30]

To devise this new rationale for the Review genre is to remove, if not to solve the difficulties which the existing Reviews had faced in living up to the old rationale. In order to conform to the character of a history of literature, they had responded to the growing number of publications by the fifty per cent increase in size (and price) to which I have already referred. On the other hand, in response to a more pressing sense of the need to attend to current developments, all Reviews (with the exception of the *Monthly*) began to include five- to ten-page summaries variously entitled 'Public Affairs' or 'National Affairs' in the course of the 1790s. But the very existence of such a separate section shows that a concern with issues of current relevance, however pressing, remained an alien element while the Review was definitionally bound to the task of assessing the achievements produced by the literature of the country. Both of these problems disappear once the Review is redefined as a periodical genre that practises the critique of current publications in order to monitor and analyse current relevance itself. The journal that brought about this redefinition was the *Edinburgh Review*, rather than the *Anti-Jacobin Review and Magazine*.

III. Reviews and Tendencies (I)

The *Anti-Jacobin Review and Magazine* is nevertheless worth a closer look in this context for several reasons. The most obvious is that it has recently

30 This ties in with Roper's observation that the *Edinburgh Review* was very rarely the first to notice important new writers, although Roper makes very little of this circumstance: 'selectivity . . . threw upon editors a . . . heavy burden: that of deciding which few books out of so many should be noticed. Under the earlier system as many books as possible had been seen by the editor and then read more closely by the reviewer, giving some chance at least that important new writing would be identified. What method of screening new books was practised by Jeffrey and Gifford I do not know; but it is remarkable that of the important new writers who appeared between 1802 and 1820 – Jane Austen, Byron, Hazlitt, Hunt, Keats, Scott, Shelley – none was first recognized in the *Edinburgh* or the *Quarterly*. Similarly, all but a handful of new works by known writers were reviewed in the smaller periodicals before the big quarterlies noticed them' (pp. 40–1). Roper's puzzlement is the best proof of the fact that it is not 'selectivity' alone, but 'celebrity', i.e., the public status already achieved, which marks the new principle.

been placed in the company of the *Edinburgh Review* more than once.[31] Moreover, it is a periodical that evidently juggles various generic identities (is it a Review, is it a magazine, can it be both at the same time?). It can therefore serve as a window on the surrounding periodical market as well as on alternative generic identities, and can provide context for locating more precisely the market position of the Review. Most important, however, the *Anti-Jacobin* and the *Edinburgh* viewed side by side will reveal the way in which the *Edinburgh*'s reorientation of the Review is not exclusively a response to generic pressures, but also a reaction – not to the French Revolution, but to the reaction to the French Revolution.

1. Gillray's 'New Morality' and (Anti-)Jacobin Tendencies

I will begin with an item from the first number of the journal which bears relevance to tendencies and periodical genres, although it does not itself qualify for appearance in a Review. James Gillray's graphic print – its full title is 'New Morality; or, The Promis'd Installment of the High Priest of the Theophilanthropes, with the Homage of Leviathan and his Suite' – may be read as a perception of and an engagement with a particular tendency of public opinion.[32] It offers a visual representation of those who contribute to this tendency and envisages its likely results. These are twofold. On the one hand, the replacement of the Christian religion by Theophilanthropy, an 'enlightened' version of religion invented by the English Deist, David Williams, and propagated by the French politician Louis Marie De La Révellière-Lépeaux, at that time president of the Directory. On the other hand, the loss of British sovereignty: '*Ere long, perhaps*', says the poem underneath the print, alluding to the fact that 'Lepaux' (as his name is misspelled) had proposed a decree by which France offered 'protection' to revolutionary movements in other European countries, '*to this astonish'd Isle/Fresh from the Shores of subjugated*

---

31 In addition to Tenger and Trolander, see Kim Wheatley, 'Paranoid Politics: The *Quarterly* and *Edinburgh* Reviews', *Prose Studies*, 15 (1992), 319-43. I will discuss Wheatley's claim that both the *Anti-Jacobin* and the *Edinburgh Reviews*' handling of tendencies is 'paranoid' in the final section of this paper.

32 The print is reproduced by permission of the British Library from the *Anti-Jacobin Review and Magazine*, 1 (July–December 1798), foldout between pp. 114 and 115, shelfmark 261.I.1. For a full description see Mary Dorothy George, *Catalogue of Political and Personal Satires Preserved in the Department of Prints and Drawings in the British Museum*, vii, *1793–1800* (London, 1942), 468–472. I will offer a partial reading which singles out the points I hold to be relevant for my argument.

Nile,/*Shall BUONAPARTE'S victor Fleet protect/The genuine* Theophilanthropic *Sect*'.

The 'true character' of theophilanthropy is represented as follows: 'Lepaux' officiates in front of an altar on which female allegories of Justice, Philanthropy and Sensibility are placed. Philanthropy, treading on 'Ties of Nature' and 'Amor Patriae', grasps the globe which she is about to devour. Justice, a 'frenzied hag' trampling 'on the sword and scales of Justice',[33] has taken up a dagger in each hand and looks around for victims. Sensibility, holding a book inscribed 'Rousseau' and weeping over the dead bird in her hand, stands on a severed head. On the right, in front of the altar, are a sack labelled 'Philanthropic Requisition' and filled with treasures looted from Christian Churches, and a bundle of books: tied up and designated for use as toilet paper ('pour les Commodités') are the Holy Bible and the Book of Common Prayer. Philanthropy – one is invited to infer from the way in which Philanthropy is grasping and devouring the globe, from Justice's daggers and the severed head on which Sensibility has placed her right foot – is false religion and false sentimentality masking French expansionism and a reign of terror.

Not everybody shared this view of France and Theophilanthropy – '[*r*]*ejoiced our CLUBS shall greet him*', the poem predicts. The fact that there are numerous public voices in Britain, which would welcome the abolition of Christianity and the subjection of Britain to France, is reflected in the array of figures who come to pay homage to the new religion and its high-priest. Most of these are wearing the cap and tricolor cockade characteristic of the French revolutionaries. The publications that constitute their offerings are those that would seem to promote the very development whose dire consequences the print envisages. We may pick out [Godwin's] *Enquirer*, [Wollstonecraft's] *Wrongs of Women*, [Horne] *Tookes Speeches*, or the *Monthly Magazine* from the pile that has been heaped up at Lépaux's feet already. More are added from all directions. *Priestleys Political Sermons*, [Godwin's] *Political Justice* and *Thelwalls Lectures* are among them, and two donkeys, Southey and Coleridge, reverently present their *Sapphics* and *Dactylics*.

Among this mass of Jacobin prints, there are also several periodicals, characterized and 'unmasked' by distorted allegories. Immediately surrounding Lépaux are four monkey-like news-boys. Two of these are blowing trumpets – the traditional attributes of *Fama* – and holding the two 'Jacobin' morning papers: the *Morning Post* and the *Morning Chroni-*

---

[33] *Ibid.*, 469.

cle. The other two are bearing a torch and a star and are respectively labelled *Star* and *Courier* – the 'Jacobin Evening Papers'. This quartet of papers is already invoked in the satirical poem on which the print is based: 'Couriers *and* Stars, *Sedition's Evening Host, / Thou* Morning Chronicle *and* Morning Post' are among those who are urged to 'praise Lepaux'. In the first rank of the train of Jacobins, together with Southey and Coleridge, we discover another set of journals, not mentioned in the poem: the 'Cornucopia of Ignorance', formed by the three classical monthly Reviews then in existence, the *Monthly*, the *Critical* and the *Analytical*.

We can read this print, first of all, as an extreme instance of attention to 'the tendencies of public opinion'. And we may notice that periodicals of different genres are identified, along with a range of public figures and of other publications, as contributing to this tendency. On these facts, we may base a preliminary observation: the operation of specific tendencies of public opinion is a major concern in the public debate, and the Reviews are drawn into the controversial construction of such tendencies, even before the Review genre first defines these tendencies as a major focus of its attention.

But apart from this generalization, we may put the print to further use by taking into account its having been commissioned for the first number of the *Anti-Jacobin Review and Magazine*. The composite title of that periodical evokes simultaneously the struggle between conservative and radical tendencies, in which this print inscribes itself, the basic competition among journals for a share in the market, and the role of generic choices in positioning the voices in public debate.

2. 'The Anti-Jacobin' and the Significance of Success in the Market

'This is the last number of the WATCHMAN', S. T. Coleridge states in his last 'Address to the Readers of the Watchman' at the close of its tenth number: 'The reason is short and satisfactory – the Work does not pay its expences'.[34] To occupy and to be able to sustain a position in the market is the basic prerequisite of periodicity. In order to qualify for the designation of periodical at all, a publication must appear and reappear at specified intervals, and a material basis must exist in order to allow it to do so.

---

34 Samuel Taylor Coleridge, *Collected Works*, ii, *The Watchman*, ed. Lewis Patton (London, 1970), 374.

Success in the market, at the same time, is more than a financial matter. It becomes a forceful argument in favour of the political stance taken by a journal, because it proves that the journal exists in response to a public demand. '[O]ur success affords a much nobler theme for exultation than would arise from considerations of a private nature', the *Anti-Jacobin Review and Magazine* claims in the preface to its first volume, after boasting of its circulation of 3,250 for each number: 'It clearly demonstrates . . . the existence of an innate rooted attachment to sound principles, religious and political, which only requires to be called forth, in order to shine with transcendent lustre'.[35] Correspondingly, the insinuation that a journal can only be published with funding by interested parties aims to destroy precisely such a claim to representativeness.[36]

When Coleridge makes his final announcement, he is therefore careful to obviate the impression that the journal's lack of financial profitability is due to a corresponding lack of public support for its political stance. If the *Watchman* does not sell in sufficient quantities, this is because there are other new journals that perform its chosen role more effectively:

> Those who took it [i.e. *The Watchman*] as a mere journal of weekly events, must have been unacquainted with FLOWER'S Cambridge Intelligencer . . . Those on the other hand, who expected from it much and varied original composition, have naturally relinquished it in favour of the New MONTHLY MAGAZINE . . . [37]

These farewell remarks thus take on the additional function of an advertisement. The *Cambridge Intelligencer* is a newspaper 'fearlessly fighting the good fight against Tyranny'. As for the *Monthly Magazine*, Coleridge wishes that it may long 'continue to deserve the support of the Patriot and Philanthropist'.[38] *The Watchman* has been forced out of the market not by a public aversion to the principles for which it stood, but because of the presence of organs which serve these principles better.

Gillray's 'New Morality' has evidently been commissioned by the conductors of the *Anti-Jacobin Review and Magazine* in order to supplement similar assistance that might help establish the journal on the market. This is already implied in the fact that the journal has appropriated part of the title of its 'predecessor'. The closing reference given for the lines under-

---

35 'Prefatory Address to the Reader', *Anti-Jacobin Review and Magazine*, 1 (1798), ii.

36 Accusations of being in the pay of the Treasury or in the pay of France respectively are traded freely throughout the 1790s. The designation 'French paper' on the *Courier* in Gillray's print is one instance of this.

37 Coleridge, *Watchman*, 374.

38 *Ibid.*

neath Gillray's print ('Vide *Anti-Jacobin*') is not to the present publication, but to the *Anti-Jacobin; or, Weekly Examiner*, which had just been discontinued amid claims of remarkable success, though without any indication that a successor was about to appear. 'New Morality' is the title of a long satirical poem which appeared in its last number.[39] The fact that Gillray's graphic print 'illustrates' a section of this poem is clearly intended to substantiate a claim to succeed to a journal 'whose principles we adopt, and whose paths we mean to pursue',[40] as the Prospectus assures prospective readers.

The parallels that become visible in this claim for continuity help to throw into relief the differences between the two *Anti-Jacobin* projects: the first *Anti-Jacobin* is a 'Weekly Examiner', whereas the second *Anti-Jacobin* is a 'Review and Magazine'. This generic difference is very likely the reason why Gillray's graphic print includes more periodical genres than the poem underneath it. The morning and evening papers, which *are* mentioned in the poem, form part of the daily and weekly press whose attitudes and reports were the primary target of the first *Anti-Jacobin*'s anxiety and attention. The journals *not* referred to in the poem – the *Monthly Magazine* and the three Reviews forming the 'Cornucopia of Ignorance' – are the dominant 'Jacobin' organs among the monthlies. And this is the section of the market where the second *Anti-Jacobin* wishes to make an impact and where, as a 'Review and Magazine', it belongs itself.

3. The 'Review and Magazine' and the Problem of Generic Identity

The generic identity of the magazine is fundamentally different from that of the Review. The monthly magazine, according to the pattern set by the *Gentleman's Magazine* (founded in 1731), was a miscellany that combined a wide range of material, often 'recycled' from previous publications (some, but not all, periodical). Reviews of selected books, either original or reprinted from a Review, were an optional element in the miscellany, achieving something of a regular status in the wake of the establishment of the *Monthly* and *Critical Reviews*.[41] But they were never sufficiently numerous to enable a magazine seriously to rival the Review's claim to be

39 'New Morality', in *The Anti-Jacobin; or, Weekly Examiner* (No. 36, 9 July 1798; repr. London, 1799), ii, 623-40.

40 'Prospectus', in *Anti-Jacobin Review and Magazine*, 1 (1798), 1.

41 Cf. Forster, 'Introduction', 12-13.

a history of literature. Instead, its rationale was derived from the Horatian motto *prodesse et delectare*. Some, like the *Gentleman's Magazine*, displayed this motto on their title-page. Others, like the *Universal Magazine of Knowledge and Pleasure* incorporated it into their titles. But in any case, the Miscellany was predicated on a promise to provide to its readers *entertainment and instruction*.

The mix of materials brought together on this principle may be indicated by the categories that can be found in a typical miscellany:

Extracts from other publications.	Foreign and Domestic Intelligence.
Illustrations.	Parliamentary Reports.
Poetry.	Meteorological Observations.
Contributions by correspondents on a variety of topics.	Current Prices (e.g. of grain).
	Stocks.
Anecdotes.	Promotions, Marriages, Obituaries.
Biographical Accounts.	Reviews of selected books (optional).

In contrast to the comprehensive claim to which the eighteenth-century Review was definitionally committed, the Miscellany thus had the characteristic of selectivity built into its generic definition.

The flexibility in choosing materials that might afford entertainment or instruction (or both) also made it much easier for the Miscellany than for the Review to devote itself to the advocacy of particular political or philosophical positions. The *British Critic* had spent much energy on combining an affirmation of critical impartiality with its commitment to High-Church and Tory principles. The *Monthly Magazine*, by contrast, did not run the risk of compromising its generic identity when it professed its political and philosophical advocacy. The two points appear simply side by side in the preface to the first volume:

> WHEN the *Monthly Magazine* was first planned, two leading ideas occupied the minds of those who undertook to conduct it. The first was, that of laying before the Public . . . various objects of information and discussion, both amusing and instructive, which have not usually made a part of the contents of similar Publications . . . The second (which we are equally ready to avow) was that of lending aid to the propagation of those liberal principles respecting some of the most important concerns of mankind, which have been either deserted or virulently opposed by other Periodical Miscellanies; and upon the manly and rational support of which the Fame and Fate of the age must ultimately depend.[42]

42 'Preface', *Monthly Magazine*, 1 (1796), iii.

Even while the conductors stress the greater emphasis on useful knowledge than a typical magazine might contain,[43] they are able to subsume this under the generic rationale of presenting what will be 'amusing and instructive'. And the addition of a decided commitment to the 'liberal principles' opposed by other 'Periodical Miscellanies' shows no signs of incompatibility with the generic identity of the journal.

The Miscellanies paid for their superiority in flexibility and popular appeal with an inferiority in prestige. They might aim to add the dignity conferred by the generic status of the Review to their attractions by emphasizing the importance of the Review elements in their mix of materials. Full titles like the *Literary Magazine and Universal Review* (vols. i-iii, 1756-58), the *General Magazine and Impartial Review* (vols. i-vi, 1787-92), the *Literary Magazine and British Review* (vols i-xii, 1788-94), or – the longest established among such journals – the *European Magazine and London Review* (vols. i-lxxxvii, 1782-1825) bear witness that such attempts were repeatedly made and held their own on the market at least for a period. But these journals still remained magazines, committed to offering a variety of useful and entertaining items. None of them fell into the category by which Coleridge, in a laconic entry in his notebooks, described the Reviews, when he spoke of them as 'a kind of Establishment'.[44]

Against this background of existing generic options, the *Anti-Jacobin Review and Magazine* does not in fact establish a new pattern. Its make-up in the six numbers that form the first volume is neither that of the Magazine nor that of the Review, although in accordance with the expectations raised by its title, it incorporates elements of both. As announced in the Prospectus, where the conductors declared that 'it, also, forms a part of [their] plan, to give Original Criticisms, chiefly on political works', each number contains a section of book reviews discussing between six and sixteen new publications. Both the thematic limitation and the comparatively small number of articles, never taking up more than half of any issue, deviate from the review pattern as it was still current. Another section of the periodical contains miscellaneous items of the sort that would be typical for a magazine (Gillray's print is one of these). Here, the promises of the Prospectus are closer to the received pattern of the monthly miscellany.

---

43 This refers to statistical material, and to progress in practical knowledge as for example in agricultural techniques.

44 Samuel Taylor Coleridge, *The Notebooks*, i. *1794-1804*, ed. Kathleen Coburn (London, 1957), entry 131 (1795-6).

The conductors will render 'the MISCELLANEOUS parts of [their] Magazine, prosaic and poetical . . . as interesting as may be to [their] readers'. They will 'shall strive to make [their] undertaking of general use'. And the 'usual supplements to publications of this nature, such as Lists of Births, Marriages, Deaths, &c. &c. will not be omitted'.[45] While this is a set of features whose selectivity might seem more consistent with the traditional magazine pattern than with that of the Review, what must be insisted on is the co-presence of conflicting signals.[46]

To this ambiguous assembly of generic features, the subtitle of the journal adds a third generic designation, according to which censuring – monitoring and blaming – is its characteristic mode of participation in public discourse. The *Anti-Jacobin Review and Magazine* is a *Monthly Political and Literary Censor.* In its capacity of censor, the journal revives a genre that occasionally recurs in public debate, and institutionalizes it. Each number contains, sandwiched between the sections 'Original Criticism' and 'Miscellaneous', a department headed 'The Reviewers Reviewed', and devoted to a critique of the criticism found in other monthly journals. 'We shall frequently *review* the *Monthly*, *criticise* the *Critical*, and analyse the *Analytical Reviews*, on the principle already adopted by the WEEKLY EXAMINER, in its comments on the daily prints',[47] the Prospectus announces. The magazines, especially the *Monthly*, come in for their share, too.[48] At least for the early numbers, it might be contended that the composite main title of the journal identifies primarily the journal's targets of attack – 'Jacobin Reviews' and 'Jacobin magazines' – even if this attack involves a certain measure of mimicry of the generic features typical of its targets.

The cohesion of the journal, its aggregate identity, is not in fact due to a distinctive generic identity. The triple character of a Review, a magazine and a 'monthly censor' is rather the source of a noticeable tension, which makes itself felt especially, where the conductors have to negotiate readers' controversial responses to the diverse generic expectations

---

45 All preceding quotations from 'Prospectus', *Anti-Jacobin Review and Magazine,* 1 (1798), 3.

46 And there are many more of these: The title-page, for example, carries the classical magazine motto 'prodesse et delectare', while the layout, which dispenses with the characteristic double columns of the magazine, is typical of the Review.

47 *Ibid.*

48 Cf., e.g., the 'Detection of the Monthly Magazine', *Anti-Jacobin Review and Magazine,* 1 (1798), 198–201.

raised by the journal.[49] Thus, the December issue no longer carries one of those 'satyrical prints which have hitherto accompanied our publication'. These had met with mixed responses from readers, '[s]ome regarding them as exquisite embellishments, and others considering them as derogatory from the dignity of the Work'. A journal that not only sets out to defend the religious and political establishment, but numbers among its aspirations that of a being itself (in Coleridge's phrase) a 'kind of Establishment', is liable to puzzle readers by the inclusion of materials 'foreign' to this generic identity. The 'dignity' of the Review and the presence of 'satyrical', if 'exquisite', embellishments, go together uneasily.[50]

The burden of giving unity to the journal rests on its exclusive and antagonistic concentration on the manifestations of Jacobinism. The only element that informs all its contributions, critical, miscellaneous or censuring, is the attack on 'Jacobinism', whose basis is the journalists' intimate, comprehensive and unproblematic knowledge of this tendency. It is this knowledge on which the conductors of the journal insist on over and over again. 'We know the spirit of Jacobinism too well to be deceived by any appearances which it may assume that are foreign from its nature', they state for example in the preface to the first volume, congratulating themselves for their success in attacking the 'Jacobin' monthlies:

> we know its purpose to be fixed and determined; though vanquished in one shape, it will rise up in another; and nothing short of its annihilation can justify confidence, or produce security. We shall, therefore, continue to watch its motions, with anxious solicitude, and incessant attention: we are not unacquainted with its secret recesses; we have traced it from the root, through all its various ramifications, to the very summit; and our efforts will not cease until we have not only lopped off every noxious branch, but felled the hideous trunk itself to the ground.[51]

The latency of Jacobinism ('its secret recesses') and its polymorphous quality ('vanquished in one shape, it will rise up in another') pose no ob-

---

49 This instability may be seen, too, in the relative weight of the several sections, which is far from constant even in the first six numbers. While 'Miscellanies vary in length from 25 to 40 out of an average of just over 120 pages, 'The Reviewers Reviewed' grows almost constantly smaller. From 47 pages in the first number (for July), it shrinks to 15 pages in the December number. 'Original Criticism' (47 pages in July and 61 in December) expands correspondingly, though not quite in the same ratio. (It will come to occupy an even greater proportion in subsequent volumes.)

50 All quotations in this paragraph: 'To Our Readers', *Anti-Jacobin Review and Magazine*, 1 (1798), 739.

51 'Prefatory Address to the Reader', *Anti-Jacobin Review and Magazine,* 1 (1798), v.

stacles to their interpretive power. Their expertise merely needs to be put into practice (through 'anxious solicitude and incessant attention').

The *Anti-Jacobin Review and Magazine*'s concern with a particular 'tendency of public opinion' does not rest on a generically defined basis that would serve for its framework. The journal's character is exclusively predicated on an expert knowledge of 'the spirit of Jacobinism'.

IV. Reviews and Tendencies (II)

1. The 'Edinburgh Review' and the French Revolution

While its generic identity remains precarious, and while it certainly did not redefine the Review, the second *Anti-Jacobin* clearly may be credited with another effect. It contributed to habituating journals to being called to account and taken to task for the tendencies that other critics might detect in them as well as in other media of public debate. Any debt that the *Edinburgh* might owe in this quarter, would seem to concern the link between the Review genre and the attention to tendencies.

But the *Edinburgh's* handling of this connection is significantly different. It both detached the attention to tendencies from the sole concentration on Jacobinism and changed the premises on which this attention is based. I would like to bring out the quality of this difference in a re-reading of the first article of the first number of the *Edinburgh Review*, on which recent critics have drawn as evidence of the similarity between the *Anti-Jacobin Review and Magazine* and the *Edinburgh Review*.[52]

This article deals with an account of the causes and the course of the French Revolution. The author under review, J.J. Mounier, the president of the first National Assembly, aims to disprove claims advanced by earlier writers, that the revolutionary events in France were the result of the writings and actions of French philosophers, or of conspiracies either of

52 To Tenger and Trolander, the *Edinburgh* reviewers here seize the first opportunity that offers for 'quietly placing the periodical on the conservative side of the debate and [for] tacitly aligning it against the old principles of philosophical reform', by 'suggesting that reform was the root of that French political evil, the Revolution' (Tenger and Trolander, 'Politics of Literary Production', 287). According to Kim Wheatley, the early nineteenth-century Reviews have inherited from publications like the *Anti-Jacobin Review and Magazine* a 'paranoid' rhetoric that gives substance and credence to 'conspiracy theories directed not against an individual but against a whole way of life'. She reads the Mounier article as evidence that 'the *Edinburgh* reviewers share the assumptions underlying the paranoid style' with their conservative counterparts (Wheatley, 'Paranoid Politics', 321 and 333).

Freemasons or Illuminaties. Mounier undertakes to demonstrate instead that the revolution 'was brought about . . . by the ordinary causes of political change', and that its successive turns were 'the result of contending interests, and the consequences of a political conjuncture'.[53]

The *Edinburgh Review* disagrees with both Mounier and those whom he contradicts. It dismisses any conspiracy theories outright, as inadequately reductive: 'Events are always produced by the co-operation of complicated causes.'[54] But, unlike Mounier, it is positive that the French Revolution could not have happened had there not been 'a previous tendency to a revolution'.[55] In disposing 'public opinion' in favour of 'the idea of liberty',[56] 'the writings of those popular philosophers who have contended for political freedom had some share in bringing about the Revolution in France'.[57]

In conjunction with this conviction, however, two considerable reservations are introduced, that will constitute significant critical problems. For one thing, the existence of an influence does not imply the existence of a previous intention to bring about precisely these consequences. The writers who contributed to the emergence of the 'previous tendency' 'may have produced effects very different from what they intended, and very different even from what their works might seem calculated to produce'.[58]

Next, intentionality apart, the precise nature of the link between the 'previous tendency' and the actual events is very difficult (and maybe impossible) to determine:

> There are no *data* from which we can estimate the relative force of such an influence; nor does language afford us any terms that are fitted to express its proportions. We must be satisfied with holding that it existed, and that those who deny its operation altogether, are almost as much mistaken as those who make it account for everything.[59]

The conviction that an influence existed must be held in spite of a twofold deficiency. On the one hand, a lack of evidence: the absence of 'hard facts': there are 'no *data*'. On the other hand, a deficit in critical vocabulary: there are no 'terms that are fitted to express its proportions'.

---

53 'Mounier, *De L'Influence des Philosophes, &c.*', *Edinburgh Review*, 1 (1802-3), 2 and 5.

54 *Ibid.*, 13.

55 *Ibid.*, 7.

56 *Ibid.*, 8.

57 *Ibid.*, 9.

58 *Ibid.*

59 *Ibid.* [italics in the original].

It is necessary to look closely at the effect of these problems. At first sight, they appear to result in a paradox. One may wonder indeed how it is possible at all to assert confidently the existence of an influence, since there is neither any way of knowing or of describing its exact nature, nor any direct link between the effective influence and the wish to exert an influence. But in the statement of these problems lies, first of all, the vast difference that exists between the attention to tendencies of public opinion characteristic of the *Edinburgh Review* and the *Anti-Jacobin Review and Magazine* respectively.

In the latter journal's review of Mounier's book, published in two instalments in December 1801 and April 1802, no such difficulties had presented themselves. Defending in particular John Robison's *Proofs of a Conspiracy against all the Religions and Governments of Europe*,[60] the reviewer confidently reasserts the 'evidence' for the conspiracy theories which Mounier tries to disprove. As in Gillray's print, the identification of a whole set of publications and public figures acting towards the common goal of overthrowing Christianity and civil government is not subject to doubts and checks. Mounier's book itself is interpreted as new proof of the continuing force of Jacobinism. It is 'nothing more than an apology for the pernicious philosophism of France and its professors',[61] written at the instigation of the Jacobin 'German literati' assembled at the court of Saxe-Weimar, where Mounier himself was living in exile.[62] In the fourth year of its publication, the *Anti-Jacobin Review and Magazine* still enjoyed the powerful and unproblematic interpretive expertise that allowed it invariably to detect and expose the operations of the polymorphous and latent spirit of Jacobinism.

Where the *Anti-Jacobin Review and Magazine* arrives at a foregone conclusion, the *Edinburgh Review* raises difficulties that preclude any such short-cuts between publications and events without, however, denying the possibility of a connection, whatever its precise form. The determined critical caution and moderation which the *Edinburgh Review* displays in dealing with the tendencies that operated in the French Revolution implies an attack on the arrogation of critical expertise in journals like the second *Anti-Jacobin*. The most immediate effect of this is that the inti-

---

60 Robison was professor of Natural Philosophy at Edinburgh, and is one of the writers attacked by Mounier.

61 *Anti-Jacobin Review and Magazine*, 'Mounier *on the Influence attributed to Philosophers*', 11 (1802), 337.

62 *Anti-Jacobin Review and Magazine*, 'Mounier', 10 (1801), 495.

mate knowledge on which the *Anti-Jacobin Review and Magazine* is predicated appears illusory in the light of the *Edinburgh Review*'s entire lack of such knowledge.

We may read, therefore, the specific handling of tendencies by the *Edinburgh Review* as a reaction to the earlier reaction to the French Revolution found in journals such as the *Anti-Jacobin Review and Magazine*.

2. The 'Edinburgh Review' and the Genealogy of Critical Discourse

But there is a wider implication to this difference. For the *Edinburgh Review* recognized and discussed many other tendencies.[63] It identifies a new concern eminently suitable for sustaining the 'dignity', the superior prestige of the Review when it focuses critical attention on the operation of influential, yet elusive tendencies, whose influence as well as potential latency and polymorphousness requires a procedure that is fully aware of the difficulties with which its subject is fraught. In doing so, it defines, in fact, a discursive space that the 'higher criticism', which becomes the hallmark of the nineteenth-century Review, will come to occupy.

An extensive field of critical speculation will arise in response to the difficulties stated by the *Edinburgh Review*. If the interconnections between books, tendencies and events are far from straightforward, then the critical analysis of any single book, tendency or event may be called to take this fact into account. The awareness of the discrepancies between intentions and effects constitutes an appeal to critics to inquire not only what effects writers may intend, and what effects 'their works might seem calculated to produce', but also what their unintentional effects might be and under what circumstances these might conceivably arise. The critical vocabulary, too, will evolve new terms for discussing complexes of individuals, writings and tendencies. The polemically fraught label of the

---

63 The same number, for example, contains an article in which the 'creed' of 'a sect of poets, that has established itself in this country within these ten or twelve years' and whose members are 'dissenters from the established systems in poetry and criticism' ('Southey's *Thalaba*', *Edinburgh Review*, 1 (1802-3), 63) is elaborately described and subjected to adverse criticism. Following Derek Roper, Marilyn Butler has pointed out that the author of this review, Francis Jeffrey, had previously reviewed *Thalaba* for the *Monthly Review* without discussing it as the representative of a tendency of which he disapproves (cf. Butler, 'Culture's Medium', p. 133). This may be motivated by a wish to seek publicity through controversy, as Butler proposes, but it is evidence, too, of the point that I have insisted on repeatedly: the characteristic addition made by the *Edinburgh Review* to the set of critical concerns is the focus of attention on 'tendencies'.

'sect'[64] will be joined by the more elastic and flexible concepts: the 'movements', the '(under)currents', the 'tendencies' and all the '-isms' that will abound in nineteenth-century criticism. What makes all this possible is the combination of certainty about the existence of 'influences' (which publications, tendencies, ideas and events each may have on one another) and an awareness of the considerable difficulties of knowing and speaking about them.

The difficulty of the task is essential. It is essential to its status as a serious critical concern, establishing and maintaining its suitability as a problem to be dealt with in the highly prestigious discourse of the Review. What needs to be ruled out (i.e., denied discursive validity) are the two alternatives that would simplify the task. These are the indiscriminate attribution of any phenomenon to the tendency or influence under discussion on the one hand, and the straightforward denial of the existence of any such influence or tendency on the other. The complex treatment of a given tendency or influence is inseparably based on the conviction, formulated in a passage that I have already quoted above, 'that those who deny its operation altogether, are almost as much mistaken as those who make it account for everything'.

What we find defined here are the conditions for the scholarly discussion of tendencies to this date. Once the importance and the difficulty of discussing adequately the complex interrelation of publications, tendencies and events have been thoroughly established as the concern of serious criticism, it will be possible allot critical blame both to those who fail to recognize tendencies and to those who identify them indiscriminately. In fact, anyone who has responded to the task – and that includes the *Edinburgh Review* itself – may be faulted for their inadequate performance of it. But only those who rely on a superior critical insight into the complex interplay of publications, tendencies and ideas in the early nineteenth century will be able to fault the *Edinburgh* reviewers in retrospect, as Leslie Stephen did, for being 'quite indifferent or openly hostile to most of the new forces which stirred men's minds' and for 'studiously shut[ting] their eyes to any newer intellectual and social movements'.[65] When Kim Wheatley describes the criticism of both the *Anti-Jacobin Review and Magazine* and the *Edinburgh Review* as 'paranoid,' giving in too frequently to

---

64 Cf. the reference to the '*genuine* Theo-philanthropic *Sect*' in the poem underneath Gillray's print; the term is avoided in the article on Mounier, but used, for example, in the review of *Thalaba* quoted in the preceding footnote.

65 Stephen, 'First Edinburgh Reviewers', ii, 247 and 248.

to the 'impulse to seek single-cause explanations',[66] she is still relying on the definition of the problematic that the *Edinburgh Review* itself had raised as the task of periodical criticism.

What emerges then from our description, if we resume its large traits, is a succession of significant events in what we should call with Michel Foucault the *genealogy* of critical discourse. The criticism of the traditional eighteenth-century Reviews was practised to meet their generic rationale of being 'histories of literature'. They gave individual attention to as many publications as possible. Journals like the *Anti-Jacobin Review and Magazine* confronted a criticism hitherto largely unaccustomed to pay any concerted attention to influences and tendencies with an obsession by a single pervasive and threatening tendency. Its analytic activity strode boldly and unhampered by interpretive difficulties. At the same time it was practised, as we have also seen, under the conditions of what might be called an institutional handicap: it was set within an eclectic framework appropriating features of various periodical genres without combining them into a new type of periodical. The *Edinburgh Review* instituted the 'problematic tendency', giving the entire problematic the shape in which we still recognize it. This shift was accompanied by a matching change in the definition of the generic basis that was to sustain the critical attention to problematic tendencies. But the career of the difficult and important task implied here – perceiving and describing tendencies that may be latent and polymorphous, grasping the influence of writings and ideas that may be subtle or manifest – has continued far beyond the nineteenth-century Quarterlies which became its chief institutional framework in the wake of the foundation of the *Edinburgh Review*.

This concern has remained paramount long after the decline of the Quarterlies. If the sketch that I have offered of an important episode in the genealogy of critical discourse were to supply more than a clearer view of the relation in which the *Edinburgh Review* stands to the journals of the 1790s, it might supply us with a question that we do not often pose. Why is it and what does it mean that we are still so ready to accept the critical task of a complex treatment of tendencies and influences while 'those who make [them] account for everything' and 'those who deny [their] operation altogether' appear to us to be equally 'mistaken'?

66 Wheatley, 'Paranoid Politics', 338.

James Gillray, *New Morality, or The Promis'd Installment of the High-Priest of the Theophilanthropes, with the Homage of Leviathan and his Suite*, Etching, 1798. (British Library, London)

Benjamin Pauley

'Far from a Consummate Lawyer'

William Godwin and the Treason Trials of the 1790s

In April 1795 *The British Critic* published a letter from an anonymous correspondent taking William Godwin to task for misunderstanding matters of English law in *Things as They Are; or, The Adventures of Caleb Williams*, his novel of the previous year. The writer offers a catalogue of Godwin's legal inaccuracies and argues that, taken together, these mistakes form a pattern of error, misrepresentation, and ignorance so thorough and so damning as to vitiate the novelist's entire project: 'in all the instances in which [the author] has affected to state the law of the land, and to reason from it, [he] has stated it falsely; and . . . in so doing, he has outraged Philosophy, Reason, and Morality, the foundation, object, and end of which is Truth'.[1] In July the same magazine printed Godwin's reply to his critic. In this letter, Godwin takes issue with the critic's insinuation that the aim of the novel is 'to throw an odium on the laws of his country', and insists:

> The object is of a much greater magnitude. It is to expose the evils which arise out of the present system of civilized society; and having exposed them, to lead the enquiring reader to examine whether they are, or are not . . . irremediable; in a word, to disengage the minds of men from prepossession, and launch them upon the sea of moral and philosophical enquiry.[2]

Godwin concedes that he may have misstated certain points of English jurisprudence: 'I acknowledge that I am far from a consummate lawyer. I acknowledge that I do not bear that affection for the laws of my country which should lead me to study them farther than the pressure of immediate occasion may seem to demand'. He maintains, however, that his novel is a faithful representation of 'the administration of justice and equity, with its consequences, as it exists in the world at large, and in Great Britain in particular'.[3] Godwin closes his response by affirming his benevolent intentions in writing the novel: 'I trust no person tolerably impartial can

---

1 Anonymous, 'Correspondence', *The British Critic*, 5 (April 1795), 446-47.

2 William Godwin, 'Correspondence: To the Editor of the British Critic', *The British Critic*, 6 (July 1795), 94.

3 *Ibid.*, 95, 94.

peruse my writings, without perceiving, what I myself intimately feel, that I have no sentiment nearer my heart than a liberal and disinterested concern for the true welfare of my species'.[4]

This exchange offers an exquisitely condensed view of the terms in which Godwin came to frame his critique of legal institutions in the mid-1790s. Godwin's insistence that his legal-minded critic's remarks are mere quibbles that miss the novel's true object is central to this posture, but, curiously, so is his explicit disavowal of legal expertise. Godwin had little use for formal systems of law. In his ambitious work of political theory, the *Enquiry Concerning Political Justice*, Godwin argues that as reasoned debate moves political opinion closer and closer towards perfection the need for central government and its institutions – such as law courts – will disappear altogether. Godwin maintains that the present system of law actually impedes political progress rather than facilitating it. On the one hand, Godwin argues, the law discourages open and ingenuous debate, relying on the threat of force to inhibit bad behaviour, rather than employing reason, persuasion, and remonstrance to elicit good behaviour.[5] Moreover, the law's reliance on general categories (like 'burglary' or 'homicide') violently distorts all the nuances of motive and intention behind people's infinitely varied actions in order to fit particular cases to the Procrustean bed of statute and precedent. 'It should seem to be the business of justice to distinguish the qualities of men', Godwin insists, 'and not, which has hitherto been the practice, to confound them'.[6] Godwin's arguments against law involve more than simply negative critique, however. In fact, his vision of gradual political enlightenment and freedom from formal law turns on a highly self-conscious cultivation of an idea of lay status that contrasts sharply with the institutional and professional worlds of English law. According to Godwin, formal law perplexes rather than clarifies our ideas of justice. 'A lawyer', Godwin contends, 'can scarcely fail to be a dishonest man. . . . He that is perpetually conversant in quibbles, false colours and sophistry cannot equally cultivate the generous emotions of the soul, and the nice distinctions of rectitude'.[7] In place of the byzantine apparatus of the English legal system, Godwin envisions members of the community at large deliberating upon individual cases as they arise and

4 *Ibid.*, 95.

5 William Godwin, *Enquiry Concerning Political Justice and its Influence on Modern Morals and Happiness*, ed. Isaac Kramnick (London, 1985), pp. 640ff.

6 *Ibid.*, p. 686.

7 *Ibid.*, p. 689.

reaching determinations according to their 'plain unperverted sense . . . founded in the ideas they [entertain] of general justice'.[8] True justice, then, is not to be found in any body of formal jurisprudence, but rather in open discussion among ordinary people of 'unperverted' sense.

This highly charged notion of lay status appears repeatedly in Godwin's writings of this period. The trope that Godwin employs in his reply to his critic – that of an honest man responding to sophistical legal charges with all the conviction of conscious sincerity – is a dramatization of principles he espoused in *Political Justice*. Godwin also contemplated variations on this imaginary scenario in *Caleb Williams*, however, and, what is still more intriguing, assayed its possibilities as a rhetorical posture for concrete political action. *Caleb Williams* was published on 26 May 1794, almost exactly midway between the first and second editions of *Political Justice*.[9] Indeed, Godwin began composing his novel in the same month that *Political Justice* was first published. He intended the book to be an illustration in fictional form of many of the tenets developed in his philosophical work.[10] In this period, apart from the composition of his novel, Godwin was largely exercised with a series of legal dramas arising from the Pitt government's aggressive campaign against political dissent and radicalism.[11] In these cases, Godwin saw plain indications not only of the alarming state of Britain's political climate, but also of the moral and theoretical bankruptcy of English law. Far from dispensing justice, the law seemed to be reduced to an instrument for suppressing critical discussion and maintaining the *status quo*. For a time, the hysterical prosecution of political radicals made Scottish and English

---

8 *Ibid.*, p. 687.

9 The first edition of *Political Justice* appeared on 14 February 1793. The second edition, though dated 1796, was published 26 November 1795. See Don Locke, *A Fantasy of Reason: The Life and Thought of William Godwin* (London, 1980), p. 91.

10 Caleb's inventory of the oppressive technologies of incarceration employed during his imprisonment in a country gaol, for example, represents an overtly polemical critique of the law's reliance on force rather than reason. During the course of his incarceration Caleb is subjected to increasingly extravagant bonds, and he comes to see 'the doors, the locks, the bolts, the chains, the massy walls and grated windows' which confine him as fit emblems not only of the punitive force of the criminal justice system, but of the 'whole machine of society'. William Godwin, *Caleb Williams*, ed. David McCracken (New York, 1977), pp. 181, 183.

11 In one form or another, Godwin commented on the cases of Daniel Crichton, Thomas Muir and Thomas Fyshe Palmer, and of Joseph Gerrald (all convicted of sedition), and on the indictment for high treason of Thomas Hardy, John Horne Tooke, John Thelwall, Thomas Holcroft, and eight others.

courtrooms a principal arena of political debate and action in Great Britain.[12] Though Godwin was deeply concerned by these political developments, he was not a jurist either by temperament or by training, and so had to seek other grounds on which to engage the issues of the day. Both in response to the immediate crises of the treason trials of the 1790s and as a component of his larger philosophical project, Godwin sought a foundation for his critique of English law in the rhetorically fertile persona of the lay person unlearned in law, and, for that very reason, unperverted in his sense of general justice.

The trial of Daniel Crichton provided Godwin with his first opportunity to imaginatively project onto an actual case the claims made in *Political Justice* for the power of sincere expostulation.[13] Godwin had mentioned Crichton's case in the preface to the first edition of *Political Justice*, citing it as an illustration of the extremes to which government intolerance of dissent had advanced,[14] but he revisited the case in a letter 'To such persons as may be appointed to serve upon juries for the trial of seditious and treasonable words', written on 18 January 1793 and published (under the name 'Mucius') in the *Morning Chronicle* of 30 March. In this letter, Godwin exhorts potential jurors to see past whatever prejudice might attach to the charge of 'sedition' and to grasp the heart of the matter. Their countrymen were being charged with crimes that carried the death penalty simply for being honestly convinced that there was a better path for their country to take. Godwin asks the jurors only to consider that those accused may be honest men, though in error, and

[12] John Barrell offers a superb account of the ways that these prosecutions became sites in which the nature of treason was hotly debated. See John Barrell, *Imagining the King's Death: Figurative Treason, Fantasies of Regicide, 1793-1796* (Oxford, 2000).

[13] Crichton was a Scots journeyman tallow chandler who, after having gotten drunk, visited the Tower of London as a tourist. When shown the royal regalia by a Tower attendant, Crichton was alleged to have exclaimed, 'Damn the King! We have no king in Scotland, and we will soon have no king in England!' For his outburst, Crichton was arrested and tried for sedition; he was imprisoned for three months.

[14] It had been suggested, Godwin noted, that the government would prosecute all unconstitutional papers and pamphlets. The case of Crichton, he submitted, argues that the government's prosecutions would extend as well to stray exclamations by drunken workmen. If *Political Justice* were to be prosecuted – a book explicitly urging study and reflection, and not violent action – then, Godwin concluded, the government would make plain its enmity to any exercise of the rational faculty whatsoever (Godwin, *Political Justice*, p. 70).

asks whether it is not better to tolerate honest and civil disagreement than to enforce uniformity of opinion through prosecution. As he imagines the course such a trial might take, Godwin sketches for his readers the career of an honest juror, who, armed only with 'plain good sense and determined honesty', persuades his fellow jurors to reach a just verdict, despite the threats of a biased judge and the 'practised wiles of a hoary headed lawyer'. Such a juror, Godwin suggests, would be able to show 'with a frank and simple tale, that he is the true friend of order and peace'.[15] Godwin then inserts himself into the transaction:

> Would to Heaven it were practicable for [Crichton's] cause to be tried over again, and that the laws of my country would permit me, who am no lawyer, to plead it. It would be impossible for any jury to resist the clear justice and the strong reason with which it might be pleaded.[16]

Throughout this hypothetical drama, Godwin consistently places the capacity for effecting justice in the hands of laymen. Godwin does more than appeal to native English pride in the jury system, he goes so far as to demonize the legal professionals in his imaginary drama (the judge and the 'hoary headed lawyer') as murderous ogres bent on the destruction of innocent men. The curious emphasis that 'Mucius' lays on his own lay status underscores the ethical appeal that Godwin hopes his scene will carry. Godwin's formulation almost seems to imply that it is *because* he is not a lawyer that he would be able to plead Crichton's case so forcefully; the English laws that disqualify him from pleading in court thus seem to have deprived Crichton of an effective advocate to the extent that they consigned the defence to the hands of professionals.

If Crichton's case allowed Godwin to project a fantasy of lay sincerity triumphant over the cynical abuse of the legal system for political purposes, the case of Joseph Gerrald seemed to present an opportunity to realize that fantasy in practice. Gerrald, who spent much of his earlier life in the West Indies and America, was a member of the London Corresponding Society. In that capacity he attended the British Convention of supporters of parliamentary reform, held in Edinburgh in November 1793. This convention was organized largely as a response to the conviction on charges of sedition of Thomas Muir, who had attended the second Edinburgh Convention of the previous year. The British Conven-

15 William Godwin, *Uncollected Writings (1785-1822)*, ed. Jack W. Marken and Burton R. Pollin (Gainesville, Fla., 1968), p. 124.

16 *Ibid.*, p. 126.

tion was more strident in its rhetoric – much of it borrowed from French revolutionary practice – than the earlier conventions had been. The authorities in Edinburgh moved to disperse the convention in early December, arresting several prominent delegates, including Gerrald. Gerrald secured his bail and returned to London for a time, but willingly returned to Edinburgh to stand trial in March 1794, much against the advice of his friends.[17] Godwin visited Gerrald on several occasions to consult with him on his defence, and recorded his advice in a letter dated 23 January 1794.[18] Godwin saw Gerrald's trial as a potential watershed in the advance of reasoned political debate against reactionary suppression of dissent. Gerrald's arrest seemed to Godwin to have been so plainly motivated by political malice that the public could not fail to be convinced of the authorities' injustice upon hearing the bare facts of the case. In his letter to Gerrald, Godwin suggests that his acquittal 'may be the means of converting thousands, and, progressively, millions, to the cause of freedom and public justice'.[19] Solely by the impressiveness of forceful reasoning, supported by his undeniable sincerity, Godwin avers, Gerrald might hope to overcome even the prejudices of an unsympathetic jury instructed by hostile judges. Godwin encourages Gerrald to cultivate a proper ethical tone and insists that his principal concern must be to convince the jury that the meeting of the Edinburgh convention was in fact lawful. Gerrald must accomplish his ends not by reference to particular statutes or legal precedents, however, but by elevating the question to a more comprehensively political sphere.

---

17 A nineteenth-century historian of the Scottish sedition trials, Lord Cockburn, notes the importunity with which Gerrald's friend and teacher, Samuel Parr, urged Gerrald not to return to Edinburgh. Parr assured Gerrald that he personally would find means to indemnify the men who had stood Gerrald's bail. Gerrald refused on principle. See Lord [Henry Thomas] Cockburn, *An Examination of the Trials for Sedition which have hitherto Occurred in Scotland* (2 vols., Edinburgh, 1888; reprinted New York, 1970), ii, 42-43.

18 The story of Godwin's involvement with Gerrald's case has been told by many of his biographers, though not in great detail. See, for example, Peter H. Marshall, *William Godwin* (New Haven, 1984), pp. 134-35; George Woodcock, *William Godwin: A Biographical Study* (London, 1946), pp. 106-107; and C. Kegan Paul, *William Godwin: His Friends and Contemporaries* (2 vols., London, 1876), i, 123-25, which presents the comments of Godwin's daughter, Mary Shelley, on Gerrald's case. Godwin's letter to Gerrald is reproduced in Paul, *William Godwin: His Friends and Contemporaries*, i, 125-28.

19 Paul, *William Godwin: His Friends and Contemporaries*, i, 126.

> Do not fritter away your defence by anxiety about little things; do not perplex the jury by dividing their attention. Depend upon it, that if you can establish to their full conviction the one great point – the lawfulness of your meeting – you will obtain a verdict.
> That point is fully contained in the Bill of Rights, is the fundamental article of that constitution which Englishmen have been taught to admire. Appeal (for so upon your principles you can) to an authority paramount to the English constitution, to all written law and parchment constitutions; the Law of universal Reason, authorising men to consult [with one another on the means by which they are to be governed].[20]

In a similar vein, Godwin encourages Gerrald to recast the question of his arrest in such a way as to show that he and the other members of the convention were the true friends of the constitution, and that the members of the government who connived at their arrest were the ones who were truly dangerous to British liberty. Repeatedly, Godwin exhorts Gerrald to raise the level of discourse to touch on general truths, in the light of which the sordid particularities of arbitrary despotism evident in his arrest could not fail to become evident.

The record of the proceedings, however, shows just how grounded in 'little things' Gerrald's case really was. Gerrald had some difficulty finding counsel to represent him, as many lawyers in Edinburgh were reluctant to be associated with the defence of such a notorious figure.[21] Although he was extraordinarily late in submitting his petition for assigned counsel, the court ensured that two lawyers, the prominent Whig advocates Adam Gillies and Malcolm Laing, were available to assist with the defence. Gillies and Laing were very active in the indictment phase of Gerrald's trial, and approached the case with lawyerly efficiency, as is apparent from a published record of the trial.[22] Gerrald's counsel pursued semantic nuances aggressively in an effort to establish precisely what the prosecution had – and had not – said in its indictment. Although they hoped to avoid the indictment altogether, Gillies and Laing

---

20 *Ibid.*, i, 127.

21 Although Gerrald had served as an advocate in Pennsylvania, his case was to be tried under Scottish law, with which he was unfamiliar. The record of Gerrald's trial repeatedly shows the defendant's ignorance of and confusion about the technical details of pleading and proceeding under Scottish law.

22 *The Trial of Joseph Gerrald, Delegate from the London Corresponding Society, to the British Convention. Before the High Court of Justiciary, at Edinburgh, on the 3d, 10th, 13th, and 14th of March, 1794, for Sedition: Taken in short-hand by Mr. Ramsey* (2nd edn., Edinburgh, [1794]).

also offered a close reading of the applicable statutes in an effort pre-emptively to limit the type of crime (and, consequently, the kind of punishment) to be contemplated. They emphasized the distinction in Scottish law between two species of sedition, 'verbal' and 'real'. Because Gerrald was charged simply with 'sedition', they argued, he could, at most, be indicted for the lesser offence of verbal sedition, since the general term could not in law be construed to extend to the more specific, more serious offence. If Gerrald were to be indicted, they insisted, it must be for the lesser crime, with a lesser penalty at stake. The relevant ancient statute, they noted, gave the punishment for this species of sedition as 'banishment', which, by recourse to Johnson's *Dictionary* and the examples of usage it cited, they argued meant no more than banishment *from* the realm – in this case Scotland – and could not extend to transportation beyond seas, but only to Gerrald's enforced return to England.

The court acknowledged that the defence's arguments were quite learned and ingenious, but ultimately accepted none of them. Gerrald was duly indicted and moved on to trial.[23] Gillies and Laing continued to be active in the examination and cross-examination of witnesses, but Gerrald presented his own defence. Gerrald's defence constituted a tableau of just the sort that Godwin had fantasized about in his letter regarding Crichton's case. Seizing upon the Solicitor General's explanation that, in the present case, it was the intention that constituted the criminality or innocence of the action, Gerrald insisted that the purity of his intentions would exonerate him: 'If the criminality of the intention alone can constitute the offence, either in a legal or a moral point of view, I trust I shall be able to make out a clear case'.[24] Eschewing 'legal chicanery' and 'legal quibbles' of the sort that Gillies and Laing had pursued so energetically on his behalf during the indictment phase, Gerrald launched into what proved to be a three-and-a-half hour speech, the bulk of which consisted of a discursus on no less than 'the fundamental principles of society itself', intended to prove that the ends at which the Edinburgh convention aimed (annual parliaments and universal suffrage) were 'not

---

23 Curiously, it is Gillies' appeal to Johnson's *Dictionary* that is singled out for particular attention. Counsel from both sides, as well as the judges, are at great pains either to establish or deny the authority of a work of general philology over the specialized usage of Scottish law and the Scottish courts.

24 *Trial of Joseph Gerrald*, p. 153.

only conformable to every maxim of good government, but congenial to the spirit of the British Constitution'.[25]

Gerrald's speech impressed at least some of the auditors present in court, and it has been widely admired by modern commentators sympathetic both to Gerrald's cause and to Godwin's politics.[26] Whatever its affective power, however, Gerrald's speech was not legally efficacious.[27] After deliberating for twenty minutes, the jury returned a verdict of guilty. Gerrald's counsel attempted to object to the verdict, though they confessed that it did not appear to be procedurally flawed. Gillies protested that the jury could not possibly have considered in twenty minutes the several hundred pages of written evidence that the prosecution had submitted – which the Solicitor General himself had suggested might contain exculpatory evidence. The peculiar circumstances of Gerrald's defence, Gillies argued, placed a particular obligation on the jury to give the evidence due consideration.

> It was the more necessary for the jury to have considered this body of evidence, because the pannel did not take advantage of a counsel to state his defence; and, however great his talents be, he is not, he cannot be possessed of that legal knowledge and of those professional habits necessary to enable any man to comment upon evidence.[28]

---

25 *Ibid.*, 183. In this speech, Gerrald supports the call for universal suffrage by elaborating a contractarian view of society that places a strong emphasis on the importance of the consent of the governed. Rather than giving up any portion of their rights upon the formation of a government, Gerrald insists, individuals 'only adopt a different mode of enjoying them'. In the course of his speech, Gerrald cites Locke, Hooker, Blackstone, Sir William Jones, and, having first noted Montesquieu's assertion that the roots of British liberty are to be found in the forests of Germany, Tacitus' *Germania.*

26 Cockburn, who knew people who had been at the trial, says that he had always heard Gerrald's speaking style characterized as a 'graceful impressiveness', and cites the impressions of a young Thomas Campbell. Cockburn, *Trials for Sedition*, ii, 83. Modern commentators uniformly praise the ingenuousness of Gerrald's oration. See, for example, George Woodcock, *William Godwin*, p. 107. Gary Kelly notes the approval of at least two of the auditors in the courtroom and suggests that the speech is a perfect type of the sincere expostulation in which Godwin so fervently wished to place his faith. Gary Kelly, *The English Jacobin Novel, 1780-1805* (Oxford, 1976), p. 197.

27 Peter Marshall finely captures the essential quixotic audacity of Gerrald's line of defence in his perhaps unintentionally droll formulation: 'Needless to say, Gerrald was found guilty'. Marshall, *William Godwin*, p. 135.

28 *Trial of Joseph Gerrald*, p. 244.

As the justices reminded him, however, the written evidence was submitted by the prosecution. Gerrald had himself entered no evidence whatsoever, and had also never indicated that any of his arguments were founded on material in the exhibits that the prosecution had introduced. Thus, the jury was not obliged to consider any more of the evidence than that comparatively small segment on which the prosecution had founded one of its claims. While there might indeed be exculpatory matter in the papers, the jury had not been asked to take cognizance of it, and so could not be blamed for not having done so.

Gillies next insisted that the jury ought to have stated in its verdict that it had considered Gerrald's speech, the great learning, intricacy, and length of which demanded attention. The Lord Justice Clerk (Lord Braxfield) responded that the jury was not required to stipulate that it had considered the oral arguments, but only that it had weighed the evidence. Moreover, Braxfield continued, the jury was not only *not* obliged to state that it had considered the oral argument but was, in this case, obliged in fact to disregard that argument entirely:

> My lords, the jury did their duty in not considering that defence: it was a defence against the relevancy of the indictment, and the first two hours of his speech went to show that all he had done was innocent. But, my lords, was it not offered to the Court in a very long pleading and found relevant? [29]

In short, much the greatest part of Gerrald's speech, quite apart from its admitted eloquence, was, forensically speaking, simply not germane. There was no use arguing against the grounds of the indictment after the indictment had already been returned and the case had moved on to the trial phase. In effect, then, Gerrald had not presented any defence at all, for nothing he had advanced went to points actually at issue in the trial.

In the case of Joseph Gerrald, perspicuous reasoning, ethical sincerity, and the appeal to universal reason failed to carry all before them as Godwin – and, no doubt, as Gerrald – would have wished. Certainly, it is doubtful whether even immense 'legal knowledge' and well-honed 'professional habits' could have saved Gerrald from the very real political malice with which his trial was conducted. But Godwin's advice to ignore the technicalities of proceedings at law, and to disregard the norms and standards of forensic argument, was clearly of no help to Gerrald's

29 *Ibid.*, p. 247. In his history of the sedition trials, Cockburn makes no secret of his low opinion of Braxfield's conduct on the bench, and raises significant questions about the legal arguments Braxfield advanced in support of Gerrald's sentence.

cause.[30] Gerrald was eventually offered a pardon by the Home Secretary, but on terms that he refused to accept. He was transported to Australia in May 1795 and, due to his poor health, died within five months.

Godwin appears to have been genuinely affected by Gerrald's fate: there are several melancholy references to 'poor Gerrald' in Godwin's diary, and he is often credited with the elegiac inscription on a monument raised to Gerrald's memory in New South Wales. But Gerrald's fate seems also to have influenced the composition of *Caleb Williams*. In his account of the composition of the novel, Godwin notes that, having gotten 'as far as the early pages of [the] third volume', he had developed a case of writer's block that lasted from 2 January to 1 April 1794 – precisely the period he was most engaged with Gerrald's case – at which point he took up the novel again and completed it on 30 April.[31] While the end of Godwin's novel is in no simple way determined by the outcome of Gerrald's case (he had, after all, been working on the book for just over a year by the time Gerrald was convicted), the defeat of sincere expostulation by the engines of law casts a long shadow over Godwin's

30 Gerrald's decision to present his own defence is crucial to locating his trial in the context of the political prosecutions of the mid-1790s. Thomas Muir, tried in August 1793, was himself trained as an advocate but had approached Henry Erskine (brother of the eminent barrister Thomas Erskine) for his defence. Erskine agreed to defend Muir, but only on the condition that the conduct of the case should be wholly under his own direction; Erskine would not have Muir address the court. Muir balked at Erskine's conditions and presented his own (unsuccessful) defence. Cockburn, *Trials for Sedition*, i, 149. Cockburn draws a convincing picture of the relentlessness with which Braxfield, the Lord Justice Clerk of Edinburgh's High Court of Justiciary, sought to ensure that all the reformers brought to trial in his court were convicted. Given Braxfield's well-known hostility, James Epstein argues, Gerrald's decision to present his own defence was quite possibly motivated not by any sense that he could gain a favourable verdict, but rather by the desire to stage a sort of political theatrical piece. By Epstein's account, Gerrald may have hoped that the drama of his martyrdom might advance the popular cause of reform. Epstein's interpretation renders equivocal the question of whether Gerrald was specifically following Godwin's advice on legal strategy at all, and problematizes any notion that Gerrald was merely naïve in his approach to the trial. James Epstein, '"Our real constitution": Trial Defence and Radical Memory in the Age of Revolution', in *Re-reading the Constitution: New Narratives in the Political History of England's Long Nineteenth Century*, ed. James Vernon (Cambridge, 1996), pp. 34-37.

31 See Godwin's preface for the 1832 Bentley's Standard Novels edition, reprinted in Godwin, *Caleb Williams*, p. 341.

text.[32] *Caleb Williams* tells the story of a servant persecuted by his master after discovering that his master had committed a murder many years before. By tracing Caleb's path from a country gaol where he is confined after being prosecuted on fictitious charges, through his life as a fugitive from his master's campaign of surveillance and character assassination, the novel offers a picture of a society in which the powerful oppress the weak with impunity, in large part because the weak are not able to make themselves heard. In this novel, which adapts elements of gothic fiction to address political questions, Godwin explores the confrontation between untutored sincerity and the forms of law with greater ambivalence than his confident advice to Gerrald might lead us to expect.

Caleb Williams is a text whose didactic claims are structured by a logic of echo and homology. Godwin's assertion of the political seriousness of his novel turns on the resemblance between the character of the nation's public and private lives. In Godwin's preface to the novel, he frames his project as an intervention in the debate over political reform, which is to say, the debate that had produced Joseph Gerrald as its most recent casualty.[33] Godwin presents his novel as a kind of thought experiment designed to illustrate the 'practical effects' of 'the existing constitution of society'. Perhaps anticipating scepticism at the author of *Political Justice* turning his hand to novel writing, Godwin offers a rationale for his fictional project that bears repeating at length:

---

32 Readers of Godwin's novel have noted the resemblances between Caleb and Gerrald, and have been particularly interested in reading the altered ending of Godwin's text in light of the outcome of Gerrald's case. See, for example, Kelly, *English Jacobin Novel*, pp. 196-97; and Nicholas M. Williams, '"The Subject of Detection": Legal Rhetoric and Subjectivity in *Caleb Williams*', *Eighteenth-Century Fiction*, 9 (1997), 479-82. Ian Ousby sets the novel's condemnation of Caleb as a 'spy' on his master's secrets in the context of widespread disgust at the government's use of paid informants in the prosecution of Hardy in 1794. Noting that the trials of Hardy, Tooke, *et. al.* occurred after *Caleb Williams* was published, Ousby suggests that, though these trials could not have directly affected its composition, '[Godwin's] novel grew out of the political milieu of which the trials are the clearest historical expression'. Ousby does not address Gerrald's case, however, which would seem to have a demonstrably more direct bearing on Godwin's novel. Ian Ousby, '"My servant Caleb": Godwin's *Caleb Williams* and the Political Trials of the 1790s', *University of Toronto Quarterly*, 44 (1974), 49.

33 Godwin's publisher suppressed this preface in the first edition as too provocative and inflammatory. Godwin dated his preface 12 May 1794, which was the day Thomas Hardy was arrested for treason. The preface was restored in the second edition.

> What is now presented to the public is no refined and abstract speculation; it is a study and delineation of things passing in the moral world. It is . . . now known to philosophers that the spirit and character of the government intrudes itself into every rank of society. But this is a truth highly worthy to be communicated to persons whom books of philosophy and science are never likely to reach. Accordingly it was proposed in the invention of the following work, to comprehend, as far as the progressive nature of a single story would allow, a general review of the modes of domestic and unrecorded despotism, by which man becomes the destroyer of man. If the author shall have taught a valuable lesson, without subtracting from the interest and passion by which a performance of this sort ought to be characterised, he will have reason to congratulate himself upon the vehicle he has chosen.[34]

Because society derives its spirit and character from the government that is placed over it, Godwin reasons, a careful observation and representation of domestic ills and abuses could be taken to ramify upward, implicating by induction the political order whose influence allows those abuses to flourish.

The significance of Godwin's turn to narrative is twofold. On the one hand, as he suggests, a carefully studied narrative might provide a clear view in miniature of ills that could be described only with great difficulty in an 'abstract speculation'. He felt that his choice of narrative form had more than heuristic convenience to recommend it, however, for a narrative not wanting in 'interest and passion' might be more likely to reach the broad generality of readers who most need to understand the true tendencies of 'the existing constitution of society', but who are least likely to read works of philosophy. Godwin's particular choice of narrative form – a gothic tale of flight and pursuit – seems particularly felicitous for both of these reasons.[35] The gothic plot, with its uncanny repetitions, reflects at the level of the narrative itself the same logic of resemblance and homology that Godwin had adduced as the political and didactic rationale for his turn to fiction. As readers of *Caleb Williams* begin to detect the essential

---

34 Godwin, *Caleb Williams*, p. 1.

35 Harvey Gross suggests that the 'fictional autobiography told as a narrative of flight and pursuit' was 'the most dramatic form [Godwin] knew'. Harvey Gross, 'The Pursuer and the Pursued: A Study of *Caleb Williams*', *Texas Studies in Literature and Language*, 1 (1959), 406. Pamela Clemit notes that, upon setting out to write *Caleb Williams*, Godwin steadily worked through the novels of Smollett, Fielding, and Defoe to concentrate on works by Richardson and Radcliffe. Clemit suggests that 'What appealed to Godwin most [about Radcliffe's gothic fictions] in the 1790s was . . . her psychological exploration of domestic power relations, which could be exploited for a systematized analysis of political oppression'. Pamela Clemit, *The Godwinian Novel: The Rational Fictions of Godwin, Brockden Brown, Mary Shelley* (Oxford, 1993), pp. 46, 54.

resemblances between different episodes in the narrative, they are invited to see as well the resemblance between events in the novel and events unfolding under the present spirit of government. Moreover, Godwin seems to have had some hopes that the gothic novel might be particularly congenial to a mass readership. After reading the manuscript of *Caleb Williams*, Elizabeth Inchbald anticipated the novel's effects on its readers in an enthusiastic letter to Godwin: 'It is my opinion that fine ladies, milliners, mantua makers, and boarding-school girls will love to tremble over it, and that men of taste and judgment will admire the superior talents, the *incessant* energy of mind you have evinced'.[36] The readership Inchbald imagines in this passage, though it does not exclude 'men of taste and judgment', is markedly female and, in part at least, working class. By embracing the gothic form familiar to this imagined readership, Godwin was able to borrow a powerful set of figures with which to explain the political state of Great Britain in the 1790s. 'The existing constitution of society', in short, is a gothic nightmare.

The novel's first volume provides the pre-history of Caleb's adventures. Caleb transcribes the history of his master's early life as it was told to him by another servant, Collins. After completing a tour of the continent (the details of which illustrate both his fine sense and his deep attachment to notions of chivalric honour), Ferdinando Falkland returns to England to take up residence on his ancestral estate. Almost immediately, the genteel Falkland falls into conflict with his neighbour, Barnabas Tyrrel. In the character of Tyrrel, Godwin meant to offer 'a true model of the English squire'.[37] Tyrrel is as callous, narrow, and irascible as Falkland is cultivated, generous, and sensible. Accustomed to pre-eminence despite his loutish manner, he is an arbitrary despot to his inferiors (a benign enough landlord, so long as his tenants do precisely as he would have them) and a bully to his equals. Angered by the progress that the refined Falkland has quickly made in the good opinion of the local gentry, Tyrrel comes to see his new neighbour as a hated rival. In two key episodes – his persecution of his young cousin, Emily Melvile, and his efforts to destroy a tenant who had crossed him – Tyrrel's barbarity is exacerbated by Falkland's efforts to set aside their differences long enough to expostulate with him on his actions. Ultimately, when his programmes of harassment have brought about Emily's death and the

[36] Quoted in Paul, *William Godwin: His Friends and Contemporaries*, i, 139.

[37] Godwin, *Caleb Williams*, p. 16.

utter ruin of the Hawkinses, Tyrrel is shunned by his neighbours. Though he attempts to reassert his social dominance at a local assembly, Falkland rebukes him eloquently and publicly, driving him from the gathering with the sheer energy of his censure. Tyrrel returns to the assembly a few hours later and, in a drunken fit, thrashes Falkland before the entire company. Falkland's keen sense of honour is mortified by this beating, but he is robbed of the opportunity for satisfaction when Tyrrel is found stabbed to death near the assembly hall. Suspicion inevitably falls on Falkland, and, though his peers in the squirearchy are reluctant to accuse him of murder, a large but informal public hearing – something that is *like* a trial but, pointedly, is not *actually* a trial – is convened. Falkland gives a moving speech protesting his own innocence and is exonerated by unanimous voice. Though Tyrrel's tenants, the Hawkinses, are eventually condemned for the murder, Falkland never overcomes the wound that the entire transaction dealt to his sense of honour, and lives as a recluse on his estate ever after.

Elizabeth Inchbald told Godwin flatly that she found the first volume of his novel 'far inferior to the two last'.[38] While the story of the ultimately fatal conflict between two diametrically opposed country squires told in the first volume may not be so 'sublimely horrible' or 'captivatingly frightful' as Caleb's own harrowing tale in the second and third volumes, it is in fact central to Godwin's design. Of course, the most important function of the story told in the first volume is that it conceals the forbidden knowledge that arouses Caleb's fatal curiosity and precipitates the contest between him and Falkland that is the heart of the novel: Falkland was indeed the true murderer of Tyrrel, and so was complicit in the deaths of both the Hawkinses as well. The episodes in the first volume also have thematic importance in their own right, however, illustrating some of the targets of Godwin's social and political critique. To take only one instance, Tyrrel's campaign against the Hawkinses – whom he destroys out of pique at Mr. Hawkins' reluctance to have his promising son made a servant in Tyrrel's household – allows Godwin to sketch the casual despotism that traditional patterns of rural hierarchy facilitate. (The fact that this episode does *not* offer any of the frisson of gothic terror that Inchbald savoured in the later volumes, but reads instead as a depressingly plausible account of malicious prosecution bolsters Godwin's claims that his polemic indictment is merely a faithful repre-

38 Paul, *William Godwin: His Friends and Contemporaries*, i, 139.

sentation of 'things as they are'.)[39] Furthermore, the episodes of the first volume present narrative patterns that Godwin repeats in the later volumes to reinforce the essential congruity between private and public despotisms. Godwin creates echoes of Tyrrel's excesses in the programme of surveillance and persecution that Falkland's pathologically jealous regard for his reputation induces him to pursue against Caleb, for example. That the otherwise estimable Falkland becomes scarcely distinguishable from the brutish Tyrrel indicates for Godwin, as Mark Philp suggests, that 'even the pearls of patrician culture become corrupted through the insidious influence of its values and become capable of performing all sorts of iniquitous acts to preserve these'.[40] The overtly gothic tale of Emily Melvile fulfils both these functions in Godwin's narrative. On the one hand, Emily's story provides Godwin with an occasion to explore the political subtext of women's enforced dependence and subordination. At the same time, Emily's story sets a gothic precedent for Caleb's adventures; the nightmarish distortions of domesticity that Emily experiences at Tyrrel's hands serve as an analogue for Caleb's experiences in what Andrew McCann has called the 'pathological public sphere'.[41]

Incensed by his young cousin's unmeaning infatuation with his rival, Tyrrel resolves to force the girl to marry an uncouth farmer, Grimes. When Emily refuses to accept her cousin's arbitrary will, he makes her his prisoner, confining her to her rooms under lock and key and the watchful eye of an unsympathetic housemaid. Emily's plight, subject to the caprices of an unassailably powerful male captor, and fraught with sexual menace, evokes commonplaces of gothic terror, but Godwin makes thoroughly explicit the gendered political valences of that terror. Emily's expostula-

---

39 In response to criticism in *The British Critic* that English courts would not facilitate half the tyrannies attributed to Tyrell in the novel, Godwin insisted 'It was not the business of such a work to enquire whether the law authorised a rich man to spoilt the crop of a poor one, to poison his cattle, or to commit him to jail upon an absurd and sophistical charge of burglary. It was enough that oppressions of a similar nature, and of equal magnitude, are known to be perpetually practised with impunity . . . I ask any man, in the least degree informed as to the history of squires and their tenants in Great Britain, whether he can read this episode, and not recognise its counterpart in what he has himself heard and seen'. Godwin, 'To The Editor of the British Critic', 94-95.

40 Mark Philp, *Godwin's Political Justice* (Ithaca, N.Y., 1986), p. 108.

41 Andrew McCann, 'William Godwin and the Pathological Public Sphere: Theorizing Communicative Action in the 1790s', *Prose Studies*, 18 (1995), 199-222.

tions with her cousin employ a curious tincture of the language of political rights as she conflates her right to choose her own husband with a more comprehensive notion of autonomy, 'the privilege of a reasonable being, to live unmolested in poverty and innocence'.[42] When Emily persists in her refusal, Tyrrel seeks to effect her ruin by other means. He directs Grimes to help Emily flee from the house in order then to lead her to an isolated spot in the forest, where the farmer is to rape her. Fortunately, Emily is able to escape from Grimes' clutches and find shelter under the protection of Falkland, who happens to be passing by the remote part of the wood where Grimes has taken her. Falkland entrusts Emily to the care of a 'good lady', and seems confident that he has placed her out of danger. Emily's troubles are not at an end, however, for Tyrrel modulates his torment into a different register. Having exhausted the resources of gothic persecution, Tyrrel turns instead to legal prosecution, and obtains a warrant for Emily's arrest as a runaway debtor who has defrauded him of £1,100 he spent on her maintenance during the fourteen years she lived under his roof. When even his hardened steward, Barnes, demurs at this exercise in reinterpretation, Tyrrel thunders, 'Do not tell me of It cannot, and It can. It has been done before, and it shall be done again. Let him dispute it that dares. I will do it now, and stand to it afterwards'.[43] The warrant is duly executed, and Emily is arrested, despite the dangerous state of her health; she dies in gaol within days, before her case can come to trial, where Tyrrel's construction would have been put to the test.

What is at stake here, for Godwin, is not whether English law would really have authorized an arrest warrant, or whether Emily could really have been found liable if the case had come to trial.[44] What the law 'really' says is immaterial, Godwin maintains, since Tyrrel's access to law is guaranteed not by the merits of his cause, but by his ability to overawe his inferiors and dependants. Tyrrel's change in tactic is underwritten by what amounts to an effort of narrative imagination. Whereas Emily had earlier found the filial and domestic categories of cousin, dependant, and benefactor distorted by Tyrrel's malice into the gothic classes of prisoner and tormentor, Tyrrel recasts their roles yet again, reconstruing the facts

---

42 Godwin, *Caleb Williams*, p. 57.

43 *Ibid*., p. 82.

44 As in his critique of the episode of the Hawkinses (see n. 39, above), the legal-minded correspondent to *The British Critic* branded Emily's arrest implausible: no squire in the commission of the peace would really attempt such a thing for fear of becoming liable to a prosecution for murder. Anonymous, 'Correspondence', 446.

of their relationship into terms more readily apprehended by the law, namely debtor and creditor. The issue is that Tyrrel is able to appropriate the terms of the law as a specious cover for his malice, and to subcontract the agents and processes of law to carry out his private ends.[45] His legal strategy is therefore essentially continuous with his earlier efforts to terrify Emily into submission. Indeed, Godwin's narrator speculates that the scheme of prosecution first occurred to Tyrrel only because his habits of mind 'had long been accustomed to contemplate every possible medium of tyranny and revenge', of which litigation, equally with gothic imprisonment or rape, is merely one.[46] Where Tyrrel is concerned, Godwin suggests, recourse to law is simply persecution by other means. The real object of Godwin's critique here is that the law seems perfectly amenable to such misappropriation. However preposterous the claim that Emily had contracted a debt to her cousin for her maintenance might seem to any impartial observer, however patently dangerous it might be to execute the arrest warrant given her precarious health, Tyrrel's social privilege enables him to enforce his version of events. The various efforts that Emily's defenders make to point out the falsity or inhumanity of Tyrrel's claims fail to influence the officers of the law charged with the task of bringing the girl to justice. The bailiffs' refusal to listen to a story told with desperate sincerity and supported even by the ocular proof of Emily's sick form becomes a sign of an impercipience in the law that borders on the diabolical.

The power of Godwin's critique of the 'existing constitution of society' in *Caleb Williams* is above all a function, as Inchbald recognized, of the 'captivatingly frightful' quality he is able to lend Caleb's life as a fugitive in the second and third volumes of the novel. This effect derives largely from Godwin's liberal borrowings from gothic fiction: the mysterious distortions of the laws of cause and effect (as when Falkland's effects turn up in the locked trunk that Caleb had secreted before fleeing his master's house), the weird eruptions of violence and stress (as with Caleb's narrow escape from the crone who lives in the robbers' retreat), and the apparent menacing omniscience of Caleb's tormentor, Falkland,

45 Consistently, the text highlights the ways in which Tyrrel acts through intermediaries. Both Grimes and Barnes, for example, are described as Tyrrel's 'instruments'; Tyrrel 'employs . . . a respectable limb of the law' named, suggestively, Swineard, to set the process against Emily in motion; and the bailiff who actually carries out the arrest can best describe his action in a passive construction: 'We only do as we are directed'. Godwin, *Caleb Williams*, pp. 58, 81, 83, 84.

46 *Ibid.*, p. 81.

who seems always to have anticipated and pre-empted Caleb's every desperate strategy. The most important device that Godwin lifted from the conventions of the gothic, however, is a trope that we might call narrative claustration – the horrifying inability to tell a story. Godwin draws explicit attention to this narrative convention in the story of Emily Melvile. When Caleb (assuming the voice of Collins) relates Falkland's rescue of the girl from Grimes' attempted rape, Godwin points to the general nature of gothic terror in a phrase that appears to be an indirect rendering of Falkland's thoughts: 'Such conspiracies as that of which she was intended to have been the victim, depend for their success upon the person against whom they are formed being out of the reach of help, and the moment they are detected they are annihilated'.[47] For most gothic heroines, the difficulty lies in communicating their plight to some figure outside the nightmarishly closed system of their imprisonment; once the boundaries of that claustrophobic system have been breached, however, the heroine is as good as free. This is precisely what does not happen for Caleb. Having spent the first third of the second volume discovering the truth of his master's story, Caleb spends the rest of the novel trying to get anyone to believe him when he tells it.

The struggle between Caleb and Falkland is a struggle over the knowledge – and potential telling – of a story. When Caleb has all but certainly established that Falkland was the true murderer of Tyrrel, Falkland confesses his guilt, but extorts Caleb's oath that he will never disclose his master's secret to anyone.[48] Caleb readily agrees, but does not at first recognize, as he will soon come to understand, the degree to which his movement is circumscribed by Falkland's injunction. Falkland will not be content simply with a solemn pledge by Caleb never to turn informant. Indeed, nothing short of direct, personal, and perpetual supervision of Caleb's actions will satisfy the squire. It is when Falkland prohibits Caleb from developing a nearer acquaintance with Falkland's brother, Mr. Forester, in whom Caleb has found a congenial spirit, that Caleb begins to grasp the true enormity of his situation:

> Mr. Falkland was not an old man; . . . he might live as long as I should. . . . All my actions observed; all my gestures marked. I could move neither to the right nor the left, but the eye of my keeper was upon me. He watched me; and his vigilance was a sick-

[47] *Ibid.*, p. 66.

[48] *Ibid.*, pp. 135-36.

> ness to my heart. For me there was no more of freedom, no more of hilarity, of thoughtlessness, or of youth.[49]

Though not confined under lock and key, Caleb is every bit as effectually Falkland's prisoner as Emily had been Tyrrel's. Indeed, by the logic of gothic terror, Caleb's imprisonment is all the more complete for not being physical. Caleb's prison is his oath never to reveal Falkland's secret. But part and parcel of the prohibition on disclosing the substance of Falkland's secret is a concomitant prohibition on revealing that Falkland has a secret at all; and if Caleb cannot reveal that Falkland has a secret, he is prevented from naming the terms of his imprisonment. Thus, by its very nature, Caleb's oath interdicts precisely those activities – disclosure and narration – that ordinarily are the means of dissipating gothic terror. In this manipulation of the gothic trope of narrative claustration, *Caleb Williams* replays in fiction the same inability of truthfulness and sincerity to gain a fair hearing that had, for Godwin, been the signal characteristic of the trial of Joseph Gerrald.

Caleb, like Emily, soon experiences the comparative ease with which Falkland's persecution moves from the domestic to the public sphere. Unable to tolerate Falkland's vigilance, Caleb attempts to escape to London, only to be recalled by a letter from Forester urging him to return to face a charge that Falkland has alleged against him and, if possible, to clear his name. Falkland, like Tyrrel, appears to turn to the processes of law to achieve his own ends; aiming, at root, simply to retrieve Caleb into the sphere of his immediate supervision, Falkland lights on a criminal charge as the readiest expedient. Caleb willingly returns, confident both in his innocence and in the capacity of 'a plain, unvarnished tale' to convince his hearers that he is innocent.[50] Caleb's appearance before Falkland and Forester is the first of several tableaux evocative of Gerrald's trial. With his faith in the efficacy of sincere narration, Caleb cannot help but be confused by Forester's advice to 'Make the best story you can for yourself; true, if truth, as I hope, will serve your purpose; but, if not, the most plausible and ingenious you can invent'.[51] Caleb is persuaded that he can have no need of ingenuity where ingenuousness must be sufficient demonstration of the truth of his account. But he soon discovers that even his most impassioned speeches asserting his innocence, though they have some ef-

49 *Ibid.*, p. 143.

50 *Ibid.*, p. 160.

51 *Ibid.*, pp. 162-63.

fect on his audience, cannot counteract the mute testimony of the objects that Falkland appears mysteriously to have placed among the belongings that he had secreted before attempting his escape from Falkland's estate. Caleb's inability to disclose Falkland's secret plays a crucial role in this transaction. Called upon to account for some aspects of his behaviour, Caleb is able only to answer:

> There are certain parts of my story that I have not told. If they were told, they would not conduce to my disadvantage, and they would make the present accusation appear still more astonishing. But I cannot, as yet at least, prevail upon myself to tell them.[52]

Caleb is thus prevented from presenting the most material element of his defence, and is committed to gaol by Forester to await trial at the next assizes.[53]

Caleb's attempts to establish his innocence in the eyes of Forester are compromised by his inability or unwillingness to tell his full story, labouring as he is under his former solemn promise to Falkland. But Caleb remains convinced that it is in his power to vindicate himself at any time by breaking that injunction and revealing the entirety of his story. In his second important appearance before a magistrate, however, Caleb learns that his narrative resources are not wholly under his control or at his disposal. After months living as an outcast and a fugitive, Caleb is re-apprehended and taken before a magistrate to have his identity confirmed, so that he can be extradited back to the jurisdiction from which he had escaped. Caleb resolves 'once for all to turn the tables on [his] accuser'.[54] By revealing that Falkland was the murderer of Tyrrel, Caleb supposes that he can make his innocence clear to the magistrate by supplying a plausible

---

52 *Ibid.*, p. 170.

53 Interestingly, Falkland attempts to prevent Caleb's incarceration. Falkland had intended this episode simply as a piece of theatre to discredit Caleb, to prevent him from ever gaining credit, should he try to disclose the truth of Tyrrel's murder. Having seemingly accomplished what he wanted, Falkland attempts to pull back from the legal implications of Caleb's indictment, grounding his dissent on his own code of chivalric honour. Godwin, *Caleb Williams*, p. 175. Falkland's sentiments seem to be an imperfect version of certain arguments advanced in *Political Justice*. There, Godwin grounds his critique of the legal system on the contention that the administration of justice in its current form is underwritten by mere force – the courts exist to bring the full coercive power of the state to bear on an isolated individual. See n. 10, above.

54 Godwin, *Caleb Williams*, p. 275.

motive to explain why Falkland should have orchestrated an elaborate scheme that would tend towards Caleb's death:

> I always declared . . . that I was the perpetrator of no guilt, but that the guilt wholly belonged to my accuser. He privately conveyed these effects among my property, and then charged me with the robbery. I now declare more than that, that this man is a murderer, that I detected his criminality, and that for that reason he is determined to deprive me of life. I presume, gentlemen, that you do consider it as your business to take this declaration. I am persuaded you will by no means be disposed to contribute to the atrocious injustice under which I suffer, to the imprisonment and condemnation of an innocent man in order that a murderer may go free.[55]

Here, Caleb finally discloses the entire truth of his story, and has every confidence that his conviction of his own innocence will be communicated irresistibly to his auditors and will effect his immediate release.

But Caleb's speech does not have the intended effect. As was the case with Gerrald's defence, Caleb's sincerity and eloquence gain no forensic purchase. The magistrate informs Caleb that he can take no cognizance of the allegation, because Caleb was not an accessory to the murder in question:

> First I have to tell you as a magistrate, that I can have nothing to do with your declaration. If you had been concerned in the murder you talk of, that would alter the case. But it is out of all reasonable rule, for a magistrate to take an information from a felon, except against his accomplices. . . . A fine time of it indeed it would be, if, when gentlemen of six thousand a year take up their servants for robbing them, those servants could trump up such accusations as these, and could get any magistrate or court of justice to listen to them![56]

Whatever the truth of Caleb's assertion, it gains no hearing from the court. Certainly, there is an element of personal prejudice in the magistrate's scornful dismissal of Caleb's story, but Caleb's inability to make his story heard is also a structural function of the law's artificial modes of hearing and evaluating stories. Procedural considerations militate against the magistrate's hearkening to Caleb's story even if he were inclined to do so. Shortly after this exchange, Caleb learns the true degree to which his troubles up to this point have been produced by the impersonal mechanisms of law, rather than by any calculated malevolence on Falkland's part. After he is dismissed by the magistrate, Caleb awaits trial, but, when no one appears to prosecute him, he is released. That same night, he is seized by two men and carried before Falkland, who informs him that, far

---

55 *Ibid.*

56 *Ibid.*, p. 276.

from designing his incarceration, he had actually sought to prevent it. The hundred guinea reward that seemed designed to interest the whole of society in his apprehension had been offered not by Falkland, but by the upright Forester, whose inflexible notions of law and order have been the true source of Caleb's troubles with the law.[57] What Caleb concludes of the magistrate who has refused to hear his accusation of Falkland could just as well be taken to describe Forester: 'the law has neither eyes, nor ears, nor bowels of humanity; and it turns into marble the hearts of all those that are nursed in its principles'.[58]

Thus far, the adventures of Caleb Williams would seem only to confirm what the case of Joseph Gerrald had suggested: that the artificial system of English justice is fundamentally flawed, insofar as it is incapable of apprehending (or unwilling to apprehend) the truth of a plain tale sincerely told. Indeed, the character of the frame narrative – Caleb's memoirs to posterity – seems designed to cultivate a readership that will be better able to appreciate such truths. Near the end of the novel, when Caleb has brought his narration up to his own present, from which the foregoing narrative has been retrospected, he reiterates his reasons for composing his tale:

> I conceived that my story faithfully digested would carry in it an impression of truth that few men would be able to resist; or at worst that, by leaving it behind me when I should no longer continue to exist, posterity might be induced to do me justice, and, seeing in my example what sort of evils are entailed upon mankind as it is at present constituted, might be inclined to turn their attention upon the fountain from which such bitter waters have been accustomed to flow.[59]

Denied a hearing in the courts, Caleb's story must appeal to a different jurisdiction, the judgment of readers prepared to weigh the story as a whole and to take a reckoning of the ethical posture of the narrator. Godwin thus seems to claim for the novel a power of truth-telling supe-

---

57 *Ibid.*, p. 281. From this point on, though Caleb's troubles are not at an end, they no longer have anything to do with the English legal system. In his subsequent wanderings, Caleb is hounded not by bailiffs, but by a cheap criminal biography, 'The Wonderful and Surprising History of Caleb Williams', that Falkland's agent, Gines, has conceived and caused to be circulated throughout the kingdom. For a discussion of Godwin's attitudes towards popular print culture in *Caleb Williams*, see Garrett A. Sullivan, Jr., '"A Story To Be Hastily Gobbled Up": *Caleb Williams* and Print Culture', *Studies in Romanticism*, 32 (1993), 323-37; and McCann, 'William Godwin and the Pathological Public Sphere'.

58 Godwin, *Caleb Williams*, pp. 277-78.

59 *Ibid.*, p. 304.

rior to legal argument, and to claim for the novel's readers a power of discerning truth superior to the artificial system of English justice.

Plausible as this might sound, however, the startling ending of Godwin's novel makes such an account unsustainable. Having resolved to quit England forever, Caleb is stopped near the port by Falkland's agent, Gines, who informs Caleb that Falkland has decreed that, though he may go anywhere he pleases within the realm of England, Scotland, and Wales, he may not go overseas out of Falkland's supervision. Incensed, if possible, beyond anything he ever was before, Caleb resolves once again to charge Falkland with the murder of Tyrrel. Caleb is confident that this attempt will ultimately succeed. Not only will his indignation endue him with an almost supernatural persuasiveness, Caleb reasons, but he will also not be prevented by the technical disabilities that plagued him in the past:

> I will tell a tale! – The justice of the country shall hear me! . . . I will speak with a voice more fearful than thunder! . . . I am under no prosecution now! I shall not now appear to be endeavouring to remove a criminal indictment from myself, by throwing it back on its author![60]

Remarkably, Caleb's final attempt to impeach Falkland is ultimately successful, but Caleb is able to find no triumph in his success. Upon seeing Falkland in the courtroom, much declined in health, all of the indignation that had carried Caleb forward drains away from him, and is replaced by pity for his ruined master and abhorrence for the part he is about to play in Falkland's destruction. Once begun, however, Caleb cannot back out of the proceeding he has set in motion. Instead of a speech of fiery condemnation, Caleb speaks of his agony in having to bring the charge he advances. This speech, unlike all of Caleb's others, gains the assent of all hearers. Moved by Caleb's grief, Falkland confesses his crimes and submits to justice. Caleb ends his tale in self-recrimination, however, ruing his fatal decision to avail himself of the courts to bring about the destruction of a man with many qualities worthy of reverence.

In Godwin's original manuscript ending, Caleb's attempt to bring Falkland to justice fails. Caleb is committed once more to gaol, where he descends into madness; his narrative trails off into incoherence, and he may be the victim of poisoning. Some of Godwin's readers have found this original ending more congruent with the tendency of the novel up to that

---

60 *Ibid.*, p. 314.

point – Caleb's dissolution seems a much more likely outcome of 'things as they are', where the courts refuse to believe the sincere narration of a poor man over the hypocritical lies of a wealthy and powerful one.[61] Others, like Gary Kelly, have found the published version more satisfying, both as a matter of ideology and as a question of narrative art. Kelly argues that the published ending 'raises the novel above the doctrinaire', and sees the 'import' of the revised ending as 'optimistic: Truth can prevail, even against the combined forces of those who support "things as they are"; the chain of necessity can be broken by one determined individual'.[62] On this reading, we might see the end of the novel as a kind of wish fulfilment, Godwin's imaginative compensation for his very real disappointment at the outcome of Gerrald's trial.[63] This line of interpretation would not seem to be able to account for Caleb's remorse, however; if this is a triumph of 'Truth', it seems a very hollow one. In the moment of his apparent victory, Caleb is forced to confront the fact that he, too, like Tyrrel and Falkland before him, has availed himself of the instrumentality of law to bring about the ruin of a fellow creature, the full truth of whose story the law is an improper instrument to judge. Mark Philp suggests, perceptively, that

> What happens in the second ending is not that Caleb's innocence is vindicated and Falkland's guilt punished, since these events occur only within the legal realm. . . . Men of virtue, which, for all their flaws both Caleb and Falkland aspire to be, can only achieve progress and the resolution of conflict through reason and discussion and through the full exercise of their private judgment. Neither force nor the Procrustean bed of law can solve such conflicts.[64]

The problem that Gerrald's trial – and Caleb's – highlights for Godwin proves ultimately to be not simply that the powerless cannot obtain justice under the law, but that the law is not an arena that can yield true justice at all.

If Godwin had really expected Gerrald's courtroom oration to secure the triumphant outcome he had imagined for Crichton's hypothetical lay advocate in the letter of Mucius, he must have been disappointed. The fact that Caleb *does* secure such a result but finds it wholly unsatisfac-

---

61 D. Gilbert Dumas, for example, the original discoverer of Godwin's manuscript ending, found the rejected ending more ideologically consistent with the rest of the novel and with Godwin's other writings.

62 Kelly, *English Jacobin Novel*, pp. 197, 185. See also Ulrich Broich, 'British Radical Thought and the Radical Novel', *English Studies Today*, 1 (2002), 16-60.

63 Cf. Kelly, *English Jacobin Novel*, p. 196.

64 Philp, *Godwin's* Political Justice, pp. 114-15.

tory suggests, however, that Godwin's ideas about the possibilities for asserting native sincerity in a legal forum had grown more complex in the approximately six weeks between Gerrald's trial and the end of April, when he completed *Caleb Williams*. How then are we to account for the fact that, some four months after the novel was published, on 18 September 1794, Godwin offered advice to John Thelwall (who intended to defend himself against the charge of treason before a court in London) that sounds remarkably similar to what he had suggested to Gerrald? Godwin writes: 'To quote authorities is a vulgar business; every soulless hypocrite can do that . . . Appeal to that eternal law which the heart of every man of common sense immediately recognizes'.[65] Given Godwin's reputation for visionary politics and abstract speculation, it is tempting to suspect that he had simply not learned anything from Gerrald's dismal fate, and that the abruptly re-written ending of *Caleb Williams* represents only confusion, rather than any newfound clarity. Shortly after his letter to Thelwall, however, Godwin entered publicly (though anonymously) into the controversy surrounding the trial of Thomas Hardy. In his *Cursory Strictures* on the charge delivered by Chief Justice James Eyre to the jury in Hardy's case, Godwin attempted a new variation on his rhetorical use of lay status. In the *Cursory Strictures*, Godwin claims to detect the Chief Justice in the process of inventing a new kind of treason never recorded in any English law or pronounced upon by any previous English court; Eyre's version of the law of treason, according to Godwin, was a pieced-together fabric of insinuation and innuendo. To see Godwin disputing with Eyre over the interpretation and application of 25 Edward III, cap. 2, is, indeed, surprising. A prefatory note to the pamphlet suggests that the work's 'only crime is, perhaps, the containing more law than the Charge on which it animadverts'.[66] Such claims seem strange when applied to anything written by Godwin, who, as I have suggested, was no devoted scholar of English law.

John Barrell is sceptical of the efficacy of Godwin's activities surrounding the 1794 trials. Of Godwin's recommendation to Thelwall, Barrell says:

> This was foolish advice to give to a man about to go on trial for his life; but the Strictures itself might have been a more coherent text had it been written in the spirit of that advice. As an attempt to construct the terms of a defence for the prisoners, and

65 Quoted in *ibid.*, p. 118. Marshall supplies the date for this letter; see Marshall, *William Godwin*, p. 423 n. 128.

66 Godwin, *Uncollected Writings*, p. 146.

> to meet Eyre on his own ground, it was unlikely to instil doubts in the Crown lawyers or the judges on the commission.[67]

I would suggest, however, that what Godwin attempts in the *Cursory Strictures* is not precisely to meet Eyre on his own ground, but rather to shift subtly the ground that Eyre stands on. Godwin's principal critique of Eyre's *Charge* is that his method of building up a case for treason (by assembling a series of conjectures about what people may have thought and speculating about what remote outcomes may, nevertheless, be considered to be the foreseeable consequence of certain actions) seems to render indefinite precisely what actions are treasonable. The most forceful moments in Godwin's argument centre on a vision of ordinary subjects who have no idea from day to day what they are and are not permitted to do: 'Are we to understand that henceforth the man most deeply read in the laws of his country, and most assiduously conforming his actions to them, shall be liable to be arraigned and capitally punished for a crime, that no law describes, that no precedent or adjudged case ascertains?'[68] In Godwin's account, Eyre becomes another of the 'profligate judges' who have tried to encroach upon the plain dictates of 25 Edward III, cap. 2; but, Godwin insists, 'Englishmen have always found it necessary in the sequel to strip [the statute] of its mischievous appendages and artificial glosses, and restore it to its original simplicity and lustre'.[69] Much as in Mucius' letter on the trial of Crichton the previous year, Godwin appeals to an idea of lay people – the heroic 'Englishmen', who are always distinguished from 'judges' – combating the sophistries of legal professionals. It is true, as the author of an answer to the *Cursory Strictures* (probably Sir Francis Buller) pointed out, that Godwin's account of Eyre's legal argument is slightly off base – rather than inventing new classes of treason at every turn, Eyre had been discussing the variety of actions that might possibly amount to overt acts establishing a treasonable intention. Still, the *Cursory Strictures* may have contributed to the widespread sense that the crown's charges were malicious. At any rate, Hardy was acquitted, as were Tooke and Thelwall; the charges against several others, including Holcroft, were dropped. Barrell suggests that the rhetorical success of Godwin's *Cursory Strictures* may have come 'partly in spite or even because of the fact that his grasp of the technicalities of the law of treason

67 Barrell, *Imagining the King's Death*, p. 302.

68 Godwin, *Uncollected Writings*, p. 152.

69 *Ibid.*, p. 148.

was shaky at best'.[70] If this is so, however, and I think it is, it is not merely because Godwin was an incompetent jurist, but rather because he had finally found a way to appeal persuasively to the fact that he was 'far from a consummate lawyer'.

70 Barrell, *Imagining the King's Death*, p. 302.

Martin Schmidt

Dugald Stewart, 'Conjectural History', and the Decline of Enlightenment Historical Writing in the 1790s*

The differences between Enlightenment historical writing and its nineteenth-century counterpart have frequently been recognized as the result of a profound change that historiography in Europe underwent around 1800. Innovations were varied and at times conflicted with each other, but had a deep impact and long-lasting effect. For example, research on primary sources replaced the previously dominant study of memoirs.[1] The mechanistic explanatory models which had been predominant in the eighteenth century largely went out of fashion and were replaced by narrative accounts modelled on the plot structures of romance, comedy and tragedy.[2] As history was increasingly narrativized and fictionalized, genres such as the chronicle and the treatise gave way to the historical novel and biography.[3] Significant influences on the humanities came from, among other things, Romanticism and the nineteenth-century religious revival, which partly displaced the thinking of the Enlightenment: an awareness of tradition typical of the age of historicism was joined to an Enlightenment belief in progress; idealism provided competition for empiricism; and interest in civil society was replaced by a preference for the individual and 'great men'.[4]

---

* I should like to thank Angela Davies for translating this essay. I am also grateful to Nicholas Phillipson for his encouragement and criticism.

1 Eckhardt Fuchs gives a brief survey in 'Conceptions of Scientific History in the Nineteenth-Century West', in *Turning Points in Historiography: A Cross-Cultural Perspective*, ed. Q. Edward Wang and Georg G. Iggers (Rochester, NY, 2002), pp. 147-61.

2 Hayden White, *Metahistory: The Historical Imagination in Nineteenth-Century Europe* (Baltimore, MD, 1973), pp. 48-69. Numerous studies of the subject have appeared in the wake of White's pioneering work.

3 Mark Salber Phillips investigates the change in literary genres within historiography in *Society and Sentiment: Genres of Historical Writing in Britain, 1740-1820* (Princeton, NJ, 2000).

4 See, among others, Christopher Parker, *The English Idea of History from Coleridge to Collingwood* (Aldershot, 2000), esp. pp. 9 and 28; Silvia Sebastiani, 'Conjectural History vs. the Bible: Eighteenth-Century Scottish Historians and the Idea of History in the *Encyclopaedia Britannica*', *Storia della storiografia*, 39 (2001), 51-61; Duncan Forbes, *The Liberal Anglican Idea of History* (Cambridge, 1952); Peter Allan Dale, *The Victorian Critic and the Idea of History: Carlyle, Arnold, Pater* (London, 1977), esp. pp. 1-11, 45-58, 91-104.

What established itself in the upheavals of the revolutionary age was not always what we today would call 'modern'. The fate of philosophical history as practised in Scotland during the second half of the eighteenth century is a typical example. This form of history-writing, typical of the most advanced representatives of the Scottish Enlightenment, traced the history of civil society – its institutions, laws, beliefs and manners. Following the Newtonian principles of mechanistic causality, historians searched the past for anthropological, environmental, and socio-economic conditions and traced their influence on the shape of human society in the different ages. In many cases, they followed a stadial theory of social development, and divided history into different phases, from hunters and gatherers to modern commercial society.[5] On the basis of these insights into social history, scholars long considered philosophical history as a precursor of nineteenth-century social theories,[6] and their approach has often been seen as a milestone in the development of modern historiography and sociology.[7] It is, additionally, seen as an expression of Scotland's socio-economic modernization in the eighteenth century.[8]

Yet despite its modernity, the tradition of philosophical history largely died out in Scotland and in Britain as a whole after the 1790s. The epitomes of this school, Adam Ferguson's *Essay on the History of Civil Society* (1767) and John Millar's *Origin of the Distinction of Ranks* (1771), were only re-

---

5 Christopher J. Berry, *The Social Theory of the Scottish Enlightenment* (Edinburgh, 1997), pp. 61-73, gives a brief outline of this Scottish historiography.

6 Ronald Lindley Meek, 'Smith, Turgot, and the "Four Stages" Theory' (1970-71), in *idem*, *Smith, Marx, & After: Ten Essays in the Development of Economic Thought* (London, 1977), p. 18; among those who are sceptical is Harro M. Höpfl, 'From Savage to Scotsman: Conjectural History in the Scottish Enlightenment', *Journal of British Studies*, 17 (1978), 19 and 32.

7 Cf. Duncan Forbes, '"Scientific" Whiggism: Adam Smith and John Millar', *The Cambridge Journal*, 7 (1953/54), 669-70; William Christian Lehmann, *John Millar of Glasgow, 1735-1801: His Life and Thought and his Contributions to Sociological Analysis* (Cambridge, 1960), pp. 145-63; Alexander Broadie, *The Scottish Enlightenment: The Historical Age of the Historical Nation* (Edinburgh, 2001), pp. 64-77, esp. p. 71; Sebastiani, 'Conjectural History vs. the Bible', 52.

8 John D. Brewer, 'Conjectural History, Sociology, and Social Change in Eighteenth-Century Scotland: Adam Ferguson and the Division of Labour', in *The Making of Scotland: Nation, Culture, and Social Change*, ed. David McCrone, Stephen Kendrick and Pat Straw (Edinburgh, 1989), pp. 13-30; David Allan, *Virtue, Learning, and the Scottish Enlightenment: Ideas of Scholarship in Early-Modern History* (Edinburgh, 1993), p. 155.

published once each in Britain after 1793.[9] Younger authors, such as William Alexander, John Adams and John Logan, who did not publish their work until the 1780s, mostly disappeared from the scene as quickly as they had appeared on it. Later historians, such as James Mill, James Mackintosh, Thomas Macaulay and other writers associated with the *Edinburgh Review*, modelled themselves in part on their predecessors in Scotland.[10] But often they merely picked out particular aspects of philosophical history, such as the stadial theory, for example, and the arguments into which they integrated these fragments within their own work often differed greatly from those of their eighteenth-century models.[11] Marinell Ash has summed up this paradoxical situation as the 'strange death of Scottish history': one of the most advanced and modern disciplines of the Scottish Enlightenment apparently survived the turn of the century only as a mere torso.[12]

In order to trace the origins of this decline, we must examine the difficulties which the philosophical historians and the advocates of this tradition faced during the revolutionary era. Among the many authors who commented on philosophical history at this time, the philosopher Dugald Stewart had special weight. As Adam Ferguson's successor to the chair of moral philosophy at Edinburgh, Stewart was one of the last advocates of the circle which had cultivated philosophical history. Until the publication of his *Dissertation Exhibiting the Progress of Metaphysical, Ethical and Politi-*

---

9 The NSTC lists only one new edition of *Essays on Civil Society* (Edinburgh, 1814), and one commemorative edition of Millar's *Origin of Ranks* with a biography (Edinburgh, 1806). Kames's *Sketches of the History of Man* was only reissued twice (Glasgow, 1817; 1819).

10 John Wyon Burrow, *Evolution and Society: A Study in Victorian Social Theory* (Cambridge, 1966), esp. pp. 42-64; Burrow, *A Liberal Descent: Victorian Historians and the English Past* (Cambridge, 1981), pp. 41-7; Biancamaria Fontana, *Rethinking the Politics of Commericial Society: The 'Edinburgh Review' 1802-1832* (Cambridge, 1985), pp. 11-45. For the *Review*'s negative attitude towards Millar, however, see [Francis Jeffrey], 'Millar's *View of the English Government*', *Edinburgh Review*, 3 (1803-04), 154-81, esp. 156-9.

11 Burrow, *Evolution and Society*, pp. 43-5. James Mill, for example, did not use the stadial theory primarily to demonstrate universal developmental processes. Rather, it provided him with a scale of values on which to contrast Britain's optimum level of development with the condition of India, seen as inferior and primitive. See Jane Rendall, 'Scottish Orientalism: From Robertson to James Mill', *Historical Journal*, 25 (1982), 43-69, esp. 44 and 60.

12 Marinell Ash, *The Strange Death of Scottish History* (Edinburgh, 1980). Cf. also Stefan Collini, Donald Winch and John W. Burrow, *That Noble Science of Politics: A Study in Nineteenth-Century Intellectual History* (Cambridge, 1987), pp. 60-1. On the opposite position, see Fontana, *Rethinking Politics*, esp. p. 45.

cal Philosophy (1815-21), Stewart was not, strictly speaking, working as an historian. But in his first academic publications, which dated from the 1790s, he repeatedly expressed opinions on the evolution of human consciousness, the history of philosophy and the contemporary problems of historiography. This applied equally to the first volume of his *Elements of the Philosophy of the Human Mind* (1792), in which he expounded his psychology of perception, and to the classroom text, *Outlines of Moral Philosophy* (1793), and even more to his commemorative address for Adam Smith, given at the Royal Society of Edinburgh in 1793 and published in 1794 as an 'Account of Adam Smith'.

Stewart's writings, to be sure, present the reader with considerable difficulties, as different types of arguments frequently overlap in them. Paraphrases of other works, incidental comments and original reflections are not clearly separated, but are often intertwined with each other. This has resulted in confusion, especially in recent research. Thus, the phrase 'conjectural history', which Stewart coined, has often been seen as a synonym for philosophical history. Yet it has also been taken as an independent approach to history and, as such, has been distinguished from presumably more traditional philosophical history.[13] As a result researchers are divided over the issue of whether Stewart was merely reproducing what was normal usage for many historians in the eighteenth century, whether he wanted to be provocative by producing controversial theses, or whether he was an original thinker on the theory of history.[14]

---

13 Christopher Berry, for example, regarded the term as a synonym for 'philosophical history' (Berry, *Social Theory*, pp. 61-73), whereas 'narrative' and 'conjectural modes of history' were distinguished by, for example, Richard B. Sher, *Church and University in the Scottish Enlightenment: The Moderate Literati of Edinburgh* (Princeton, NJ, 1985), pp. 316-7; John Robertson, 'The Scottish Contribution to the Enlightenment', in *The Scottish Enlightenment: Essays in Reinterpretation*, ed. Paul B. Wood (Rochester, NY, 2000), pp. 49-51; and Neil K. Hargraves, 'National History and "Philosophical" History: Character and Narrative in William Robertson's *History of Scotland*', *History of European Ideas*, 26 (2000), esp. 19-20. Höpfl, 'From Savage to Scotsman', 19 and 23 is critical. In the present essay, 'conjectural history' is understood as a distinct version of 'philosophical history'.

14 In addition to the literature already cited, see also Allan, *Virtue, Learning, Enlightenment*, pp. 151-6, and Höpfl, 'From Savage to Scotsman', 22-40. Roger Emerson went so far as to argue that since Antiquity it had been usual to reconstruct the past 'by conjecture'; *ergo* the Scottish Enlightenment had not produced a new type of historiography. Roger L. Emerson, 'Conjectural History and Scottish Philosophers', *Historical Papers / Communications Historiques* [Canadian Historical Association], no vol. no. (1984), 63-90, esp. 65.

The present essay attempts to cast more light on the fate of philosophical history, and on Stewart's role within the transformation of historiography. Special attention will be paid to the circumstances in which Stewart was working. It can be argued, with good reason, that in the 1790s Stewart was pursuing highly controversial interests which forced him to adopt an especially circumspect and reticent method of arguing. Thus, John Burrow, for example, has suggested that Stewart may have been concerned 'to dissociate . . . the method of conjectural history – from political radicalism'.[15] And, recently, Jennifer Tannoch-Bland has argued that during the revolutionary period Stewart was unable to reveal openly what she regards as his radical convictions, but had to publish them in the guise of the respected genre of historical biography.[16] Looking beyond such general influences emanating from the political climate of the time, we will also ask whether Stewart in his works was addressing quite specific adversaries and opposing opinions.

I.

One clue which allows us to deduce the aim that Stewart had in mind in the 1790s can be found in a footnote to his 'Account of Smith'. In it, Stewart makes clear that in the 'Account' and in the *Elements of Philosophy* his intention had been 'to vindicate . . . some of Mr. Smith's political speculation against the charge of being founded rather on theory than on actual experience'.[17] The contrast drawn between 'theory' and 'actual experience' can be seen as a reference to the opposing voices which Stewart challenged. The devaluation of 'theory' as a delusion with no grounding in reality, and respect for 'actual experience' as pragmatic expertise were widely held attitudes, and, in the early 1790s, this

---

15 Burrow, *Evolution and Society*, p. 54.

16 Jennifer Maree Tannoch-Bland, 'The Primacy of Moral Philosophy: Dugald Stewart and the Scottish Enlightenment' (online-publ. PhD thesis, University of Brisbane, 2000), pp. 101-16. The thesis can be obtained at the URL (site dated 2003; last visit: 5.5.2003):
< http://www.gu.au/ins/lils/adt/public/adt-QGU2001.0006/ >.

17 Stewart, 'Account of the Life and Writings of Adam Smith, LL.D.' (1793, 1794/1810), in *The Collected Works of Dugald Stewart*, ed. William Hamilton (11 vols., Edinburgh, 1854-60), x, 93, note 2. This note was added to the 1810 edition.

approach was given added weight by the publication of Edmund Burke's *Reflections on the Revolution in France* (1790).[18]

For Burke, 'theory' epitomized the style of thinking of the French Enlightenment which, in his view, inevitably led to the destruction of the established social order. In his view, the integrity of society was based on religion, on the one hand, and on moral qualities such as politeness, sociability, and imagination, on the other.[19] In France, Burke believed, the ground had been pulled from beneath religion and morality by a fatal union of monied interests and men of letters. Burke blamed 'Sophisters, œconomists, and calculators', 'professor[s] of metaphysics', and 'political Men of Letters' indiscriminately for the revolution.[20] As their purely 'theoretical' concept of society took no account of the moral conditions and historical traditions of social existence, the thinkers and heralds of the Enlightenment, the 'careerists' of the eighteenth century, destroyed to some extent the foundations on which they had risen:[21]

> All the pleasing illusions, which made power gentle, and obedience liberal, which harmonized the different shades of life, and which, by a bland assimilation, incorporated into politics the sentiments which beautify and soften private society, are to be dissolved by this new conquering empire of light and reason. All the decent drapery of life is to be rudely torn off. All the superadded ideas, furnished from the wardrobe of a moral imagination, which the heart owns, and the understanding ratifies, . . . are to be exploded as a ridiculous, absurd, and antiquated fashion.[22]

---

18 As is well known to historians of early modern thought, this form of objection to 'theory' originated from the tradition of belief in an 'Ancient Constitution'. The classic exposition of this belief is John G.A. Pocock, *The Ancient Constitution and the Feudal Law: A Study of English Historical Thought in the Seventeenth Century* (1957) (Cambridge, 1987), pp. 30-55.

19 These principles show, of course, that Burke himself was an heir of the Enlightenment. On this see, among others, Richard Bourke, 'Edmund Burke and Enlightenment Sociability: Justice, Honour, and the Principles of Government', *History of Political Thought*, 21 (2000), 632-56.

20 Quotations from Edmund Burke, *Reflections on the Revolution in France* (1790), ed. Jonathan C. D. Clark (Stanford, CA, 2001), pp. 238, 220 and 275. Cf. Hadva Ben-Israel, *English Historians on the French Revolution* (Cambridge, 1968), p. 16; Seamus Deane, *The French Revolution and Enlightenment in England, 1789-1832* (Cambridge, Mass., 1988), pp. 4-20; Peter J. Stanlis, *Edmund Burke: The Enlightenment and Revolution* (New Brunswick, NJ, 1991), esp. pp. 115-58 and 195-215; Susan Dunn, 'Revolutionary Men of Letters and the Pursuit of Radical Change: The Views of Burke, Tocqueville, Adams, Madison, and Jefferson', *William and Mary Quarterly*, 3rd ser., 53 (1996), 730-3.

21 See esp. John G. A. Pocock, 'The Political Economy of Burke's Analysis of the French Revolution', *Historical Journal*, 25 (1982), 331-49.

22 Burke, *Reflections on the Revolution in France*, pp. 239-40.

One conclusion which Burke drew from the allegedly anti-social spirit of the *philosophes* and their opposition to the *ancien régime* was that it was necessary to reject 'abstract theory' in favour of 'actual experience'. In his view, statesmen, in the first instance, had to possess substantial 'experience' and a broad knowledge of all the details of any subject in order not to damage, by their actions, the prescriptive structures of the social organism:

> It requires a deep knowledge of human nature and human necessities, and of the things which facilitate or obstruct the various ends which are to be pursued by the mechanism of civil institutions. . . . The science of constructing a commonwealth, or renovating it, is, like every other experimental science, not to be taught *à priori*. . . . The science of government being therefore so practical in itself, and intended for such practical purposes, a matter which requires experience, and even more experience than any person can gain in his whole life, however sagacious and observing he may be, it is with infinite caution that any man ought to venture upon pulling down an edifice which has answered in any tolerable degree for ages the common purposes of society, or building it up again, without having models and patterns of approved utility before his eyes.[23]

Burke's resentment against the 'empire of light and reason' was not directed explicitly against Scottish philosophy. Indirectly, however, the men of the Scottish Enlightenment were also affected by Burke's diatribes. Stewart must have felt provoked, for example, by Burke's attacks on the physiocrats who were among the main pioneers of Political Economy and had paved the way for Stewart's own subject. Burke's criticism therefore affected Stewart's view of himself, and thus obliged him to respond. This was all the more urgent, as, after 1793, Burke's views gained increasing influence over the public. Public opinion, however, was not really capable of distinguishing between the Scottish and the French Enlightenments, and it tended to condemn both philosophy and modern social sciences in general.[24] As a result, criticism of the Enlightenment spread more and more widely, and was being expressed in an increasingly extreme manner.[25]

---

23 *Ibid.*, pp. 219-20.

24 From a wealth of writings I shall cite only one sermon whose title reflects this trend: Thomas Brooke Clarke, *The Benefits of Christianity Contrasted with the Pernicious Influence of Modern Philosophy upon Civil Society: A Sermon, on a Day of Thanksgiving for the Providential Escape of His Majesty from the Late Atrocious Outrage upon His Sacred Person, etc.* (London, 1796).

25 See, e.g., John Robison, *Proofs of a Conspiracy against All the Religions and Governments of Europe, Carried on in the Secret Meetings of Free Masons, Illuminati, and Reading Societies: Collected from Good Authorities* (3rd edn., London, 1798), p. 536. On the Edinburgh natural historian, Robison, see Jack B. Morrell, 'Professors Robison and Playfair, and the "*Theophobia Gallica*": Natural Philosophy, Religion, and Politics in Edinburgh, 1789-1815', *Notes and Records*, 26 (1971), 43-63.

In most cases, however, Stewart expressed direct criticism of Burke's views only in a covert way. Not without irony, for example, Stewart referred to a parliamentary speech made by Burke in 1774, in which Burke had demonstrated the 'insufficiency of mere experience to qualify a man for new and untried situations in the administration of government'.[26] Obviously it was the primacy of experience/tradition over theory/innovation in Burke's *Reflections* that had provoked Stewart's reaction. Without explicitly naming Burke, he clearly took up Burke's dichotomy and came to the defence of the 'theorists':

> But not to dispute about words: there are plainly two sets of political reasoners; one of which consider the actual institutions of mankind as the only safe foundation for our conclusions, and think every plan of legislation chimerical, which is not copied from one which has already been realized; while the other apprehend that, in many cases, we may reason safely *a priori* from the known principles of human nature combined with the particular circumstances of the times. The former are commonly understood as contending from experience in opposition to theory; the latter are accused of trusting to theory unsupported by experience; but it ought to be remembered, that the political theorist, if he proceeds cautiously and philosophically, founds his conclusions ultimately on experience, no less than the political empiric; . . .[27]

This passage alone shows that, as a 'theorist', Stewart felt on the defensive. By the end of 1792 at the latest, therefore, he was in the position of having to defend the Scottish social scientists against the charge of being too theoretical, and, moreover, claiming to be able to initiate political reform. A theory such as this was suspected of fostering revolution. Stewart therefore had to make clear that 'scientific Whiggism' had nothing in common with the subversive plans of revolutionary and social utopian circles. Stewart's response can be seen as a three-pronged approach to this task. First, he wrote a justification of the method of abstracting from empirical data that was practised in Scotland. Second, he mounted a defence of Political Economy in particular, which could be regarded as the politically most explosive discipline. And both parts of his argument were closely

---

26 Stewart was referring to Burke's unfavourable description of George Grenville in Burke's 'celebrated speech on American Taxation'. Stewart, *Elements of the Philosophy of the Human Mind*, vol. 1 (1792, rev. 1802-27), in *Collected Works*, ii, 216 and 216-7. Burke had stated that 'when a new and troubled scene is opened, and the file affords no precedent, then it is that a greater knowledge of mankind and a far more extensive comprehension of things, are requisite, than ever office gave, or than office ever can give'. Burke, 'Speech on American Taxation, 19 April 1774' (1775), in *The Writings and Speeches of Edmund Burke*, vol. 2: *Party, Parliament, and the American Crisis, 1766-1774*, ed. Paul Langford (Oxford, 1981), pp. 408-63, quote at p. 432.

27 Stewart, *Elements of Philosophy*, p. 220.

intertwined with his Whig view of history, which was therefore the third element of Scottish philosophy that Stewart had to justify against the critics.

II.

Stewart worked out a philosophical justification for the procedure of abstraction as early as in the first volume of his *Elements of Philosophy* (1792). In it, drawing strongly on the linguistic theories of Condillac, Smith and Reid, Stewart analysed the forms of human perception and cognition, and placed them on a scale ranging from incoherent sensations to more complex syntheses.[28] Stewart described both the learning process of individuals and the scientific progress of humankind over the centuries as a gradual development from simple to complex patterns of thought.[29] Like Condillac and Smith, Stewart also assumed that this process had been crucially determined by the historical development of language itself. In the course of its evolution, language had developed to the extent of making 'general terms' available as instruments of scientific knowledge. In this way language itself contributed to simplifying the popularization and practical application of knowledge. And the resulting scientific progress constantly set this process off anew, thus encouraging further abstractions:

> [I]t appears how much the progress of human reason, which necessarily accompanies the progress of society, is owing to the introduction of general terms . . . In consequence of the gradual improvements which take place in language as an instrument of thought, the classifications both of things and facts with which the infant faculties of each successive race are conversant, are more just and more comprehensive than those of their predecessors; the discoveries which, in one age, were confined to the studious and enlightened few, becoming in the next the established creed of the learned; and in the third, forming part of the elementary principles of education.[30]

---

28 Stewart explicitly (pp. 159-60) referred to Smith's *Considerations Concerning the First Formation of Languages* (1761) and Condillac's *Cours d'Étude pour l'Instruction du Prince de Parme* IV (1775), in which Condillac reiterates the positions taken in his *Essai sur l'Origine des Connaissances Humaines* (1746) and partly modifies them. On Condillac see Hans Aarsleff, *The Study of Language in England, 1780-1860* (1967) (Minneapolis, 1983), pp. 16-29. On Smith see Nicholas Phillipson, 'Language, Sociability, and History: Some Reflections on the Foundations of Adam Smith's Science of Man', in *Economy, Polity, and Society: British Intellectual History, 1750-1950*, ed. Stefan Collini, Richard Whatmore and Brian Young (Cambridge, 2000), pp. 70-84.

29 Stewart, *Elements of Philosophy*, pp. 209-12.

30 *Ibid.*, p. 210.

Stewart defended the method of abstraction against Burke's criticisms by referring to its significance for the continued development of humankind. Yet Steward did concede that abstract thought contained at least one potential source of error. He regarded the idea held by many theorists that general terms and abstract knowledge were identical with reality as a weak point. Stewart was convinced that this error had been inherent in the thinking of Antiquity, and that the same mistake was constantly being made by modern adherents of the Platonic and Aristotelian traditions. For Stewart, only the opposing position of nominalism seemed scientifically serious and appropriate to the times. Nominalists knew that 'general principles' were merely 'arbitrary creations' or 'approximations to the truth', 'the defects of which must be supplied by habits acquired by personal experience'.[31] Thus, Stewart demanded that abstract principles be formed only on the basis of the empirical observation of detailed data. And if abstract principles were to find an application in legislation, they had to be adapted to the specific circumstances of the particular situation: 'Without a proper attention to the circumstances by which their application to particular cases must be modified, they will be a perpetual source of mistake and of disappointment'.[32] Consequently, Stewart described his own attitude as a sort of *via media* between the extremes of 'theory' and 'experience': in his view, book learning with no relation to reality was as flawed as the mere agglomeration of facts and details.[33]

III.

In the *Elements*, Stewart also endorsed the claim made by social scientists and, in particular, by political economists, that their ideas should influence politics. He criticized legislation based only on experience and on an appeal to the past as an outdated and dangerous form of politics. In his view, the constantly changing 'passions and opinions of men' meant that 'experience' had much too short a half-life to be able to provide the foundation for serious politics. Rather, he suggested, the modern world forced politicians to make solid plans for the future that had to go beyond merely holding on to tradition. Solid planning for the future required reliable forecasts of the future needs and expectations of

---

31 *Ibid.*, pp. 207 and 213; for Stewart's nominalism see p. 173.

32 *Ibid.*, p. 206.

33 *Ibid.*, pp. 217-9. For an analysis of this section of the *Elements*, cf. Donald Winch's interpretation in Collini, Winch and Burrow, *That Noble Science*, pp. 32-38.

society, and, in Stewart's view, such forecasts could not be made without drawing on the theories of Political Economy. Thus, Stewart regarded the insights which economists gained through abstraction not merely as politically useful, but as the only sustainable basis for politics that was appropriate to the times. Unlike knowledge based solely on experience and tradition, the new social sciences could help to anticipate future developments and to set up general guidelines for political action.[34] And, in Stewart's opinion, it was imperative that the social sciences should stimulate reform:

> [T]he perfection of political wisdom does not consist in an indiscriminate zeal against reformers, but in a gradual and prudent accommodation of established institutions to the varying opinions, manners, and circumstances of mankind.[35]

Among the public, the image of Political Economy, as weighed down by theory and linked to political reform, had aroused the suspicion that it was no more than a cleverly disguised variation of revolutionary radicalism. Stewart also had to reply to this accusation. He argued that the planning of political economists was not confined to the drawing board.[36] Rather, Political Economy was shaped by the order of nature, and its aim was merely the 'gradual abolition of those arbitrary and unjust arrangements, by which the order of nature is disturbed'.[37] Moreover, Stewart argued, Political Economy was not based exclusively on theory, but, when properly analysed, could be seen to be founded on generally comprehensible, everyday processes that took place everywhere. The pragmatism of political economists was demonstrated, he went on, by the fact that they neither prescribed a fixed political order for the statesman, nor ever counted on their plans being completely realized. Stewart accused the radicals of incorrectly attributing all abuses to the failure of individual politicians and putting their hopes in illusory plans for the reform of humankind.[38] But Stewart clearly separated Political Economy from this. He regarded the political suggestions of political economists as a rough guideline which acted as a

---

34 Stewart, *Elements of Philosophy*, pp. 222-7; quotation at p. 223. To critics of theory Stewart also pointed out that while 'experience' needed to be confirmed by experiment, in legislation experiments were completely impractical and even dangerous (*ibid.*, pp. 223-4).

35 *Ibid.*, p. 229.

36 On the following, *ibid.*, pp. 232-40.

37 *Ibid.*, quotation at p. 234.

38 *Ibid.*, p. 232. This argument shows that Stewart's ideas of progress had little in common with the ideas of perfectibility held by many men of the French Enlightenment.

'*limit* to . . . progressive improvement' and had a 'tendency to discourage every plan of [violent] innovation'.[39]

Stewart's steadfast championing of the Scottish Enlightenment and of certain French philosophers has frequently been seen as indicating that a radical element, a 'Condorcet-like moral perfectibilism', was inherent in his political thinking.[40] All in all, however, Stewart placed more emphasis on the moderate-progressive, or 'reforming conservative' character of the Scottish Enlightenment. Against the critics of theory and innovation, Stewart argued that the Scottish social scientists were quite clearly devoted to empirical facts. Moreover, he strongly defended the methodology of Scottish philosophy and of Political Economy by referring to their conservative and socially integrative qualities. Stewart saw Political Economy in particular as having the potential to eliminate causes of friction and to improve the weak points in society.

IV.

In addition to the two points already discussed, Stewart had to defend himself against another major criticism, namely, that Enlightenment social science lacked an *historical* foundation. Anyone who, like the scientific Whigs, spoke about reform, innovation and progress in the 1790s attracted suspicion that they wanted to undermine historical tradition. Although Stewart had justified the Scottish philosophy as a 'reforming conservative' project, he held fast to a vision of history shaped by constant progress: 'All the foregoing reasonings proceed', wrote Stewart, on the 'supposition of . . . [mankind's] progressive improvement'.[41] Thus, in addition to the methodology and economic theory of the Scottish Enlightenment, Stewart also had to defend his view of history against widespread public misgivings.

In his *Elements of Philosophy*, Stewart mainly examined the view of history held by his critics. His main target was the cultural pessimism of his critics, who saw states, nations and everything created by human beings as

---

39 *Ibid.*, p. 236.

40 Tannoch-Bland, 'Primacy of Moral Philosophy', p. 96; cf. pp. 105-6, 181. Cf. also Collini, Winch and Burrow, *That Noble Science*, p. 39. It is well-known that Stewart, like the majority of his countrymen, initially sympathized with some of the aims of the Revolution. He seems to have continued to do so till early in 1793: cf. Gordon Macintyre, *Dugald Stewart: The Pride and Ornament of Scotland* (Brighton, 2003), pp. 71-4 and 84-90.

41 Stewart, *Elements of Philosophy*, p. 241.

destined to decline.[42] Stewart brought forward a number of arguments against these ideas of disintegration. He expressed his confidence that the invention of printing, but also progress in the technology of warfare, had created political conditions which would counter a reversion to 'barbarism'.[43] Stewart additionally referred to the idea of divine providence in support of his view that history was following a positive course.[44] Finally, he defended his belief in progress by underlining its positive moral effects:

> These views with respect to the probable improvement of the world, are so conducive to the comfort of those who entertain them, that even although they were founded in delusion, a wise man would be disposed to cherish them. . . . [W]hatever may be thought of their truth, their practical tendency is surely favourable to human happiness . . .[45]

It is hard to imagine that this strategy won critics of the idea of progress over to Stewart's side. Stewart's own admission that his view of history was perhaps 'founded in delusion' presumably increased the scepticism of his opponents. Yet, Stewart did not leave it there. As early as the following year he examined the view of history of the Scottish Enlightenment anew, and in greater detail, in his 'Account of Smith'. He no longer focused on the historical pessimism of his critics, but concentrated instead on making Adam Smith's philosophical history plausible to his readers. Stewart also took this as an opportunity to present a more consistent version of his own view of history than he had given in his *Elements of Philosophy*. He no longer justified the idea of progress by reference to its positive moral effects, but tried instead to impress on his readers the conviction that progress was a real phenomenon.

For this purpose, he took as his subject the discussion of the material improvement of the lower classes, which many conservatives saw as a threat. Stewart opposed this with the old Whig argument that the level of prosperity recently achieved should not, as in ancient societies, be regarded as a socially destructive phenomenon. Rather, he argued, it should be understood as a stabilizing factor encouraging self-improvement:

> [The] diffusion of wealth among the lower orders . . . is necessary to inspire men with the desire of knowledge, and to afford them the leisure which is requisite for acquiring it; and it is only by the rewards which such a state of society holds up to industry

42 *Ibid.*, pp. 241-51.
43 *Ibid.*, pp. 242-3.
44 *Ibid.*, pp. 248-9.
45 *Ibid.*, p. 247.

and ambition, that the selfish passions of the multitude can be interested in the intellectual improvement of their children.[46]

Stewart thus emphasized more strongly than before that he did not regard progress as a mere delusion, but as something real. To some extent, however, he was guilty of circular reasoning. He adduced the ideas of history held by philosophical historians and political economists in order to legitimize philosophical history and Political Economy. From the point of view of contemporaries, Stewart's argument at least raised the question of how progress or the 'experience of former times' could be recognized with certainty.

Probably not least for this reason Stewart decided to go back further in his enquiries and to provide a methodological legitimation of philosophical history. The central problem which he addressed in his 'Account of Smith' was the lack of documented facts over long periods of history. From Stewart's point of view, these periods were of great significance. Only in the long-term perspective, he argued, did the progress of humankind and the specific socio-political conditions of modernity stand out clearly:

> [L]ong before that state of society when men begin to think of recording their transactions, many of the most important steps of their progress have been made. A few insulated facts may perhaps be collected from the casual observations of travellers, who have viewed the arrangements of rude nations; but nothing, it is evident, can be obtained in this way, which approaches to a regular and connected detail of human improvement.[47]

Thus, Stewart had above all to explain how a history free of proven facts and details could be closer to reality than a compilation of mere facts. In doing so, Stewart once again returned to the objection, made by Burke and other writers, that modern philosophy was removed from reality.

Stewart's much discussed response to the problem was the concept of 'conjecture':

> In this want of direct evidence, we are under a necessity of supplying the place of fact by conjecture; and ... of considering in what manner ... [men] are likely to have proceeded, from the principles of their nature, and the circumstances of their external situation.[48]

Past phenomena could be reconstructed by means of theoretical speculation in cases where a lack of information meant that no image could

---

46 Stewart, 'Account of Smith', p. 58.

47 *Ibid.*, p. 33.

48 *Ibid.*, pp. 33-4.

otherwise be obtained: 'By investigating the general Laws of Nature, and by reasoning from them synthetically, . . . [one] can often trace an established order, where a mere observer of facts would perceive nothing but irregularity'.[49] To Stewart this procedure seemed necessary if his age were to gain any idea at all of the early history of human progress and the complexity of modern society. As long as historians adhered to firmly established principles of causality and described only the most elementary causal connections, 'conjectural histories' could, in Steward's opinion, claim a very high degree of plausibility.[50] When an historian had managed 'to render the theoretical chain complete',[51] he had, in Stewart's view, completed his task and had demonstrated that progress was more than 'merely founded in delusion'. From this, Stewart concluded that his Whig view of history was not simply an ideal to be aspired to, but was a solid, theoretically-founded and investigable fact.

V.

An important question is whether Stewart's reflections represent a break with the traditions of Scottish historiography or whether he was merely following normal practice among Scottish scholars. If Stewart was breaking with tradition, he must have had a reason to do so, and his method of argument should cast some light on the status of philosophical history in the discourse of the 1790s.

Stewart himself did not claim to have developed an original concept. He presented conjectural history as an established model of historical research that had been accepted by Smith, Kames, Millar, and others. In principle, Stewart's idea of 'conjecture' was really not new, but largely drawn from David Hume's deliberations on 'reasoning from conjecture' in his *Treatise of Human Nature* (1739-40).[52] Condillac's views on the need

---

49 Stewart, *Outlines of Moral Philosophy*, Introd. and Part 1 (1793, 1801, 1808), in *Collected Works*, ii, 7. Cf. 'Account of Smith', pp. 33-34.

50 Stewart, 'Account of Smith', pp. 34 and 37.

51 Stewart, *Dissertation Exhibiting the Progress of Metaphysical, Ethical and Political Philosophy, since the Revival of Letters in Europe* (1815-21), in *Collected Works*, i, 3.

52 David Hume, *A Treatise of Human Nature* (1739-40), ed. David Fate Norton and Mary J. Norton (Oxford, 2000), 1/3, esp. 1/3/11-1/3/15 (pp. 86-118; quotation at p. 86). Stewart's teacher Thomas Reid apparently rejected philosophical history: Thomas Reid to Henry Home, Lord Kames, 16 December 1780, in Alexander Fraser Tytler, *Memoirs of the Life and Writings of the Honourable Henry Home of Kames* (2 vols., Edinburgh, 1807), i, 58-68.

for 'educated guesses' in the study of history may also have influenced Stewart.[53] By comparison with his predecessors, however, Stewart made striking modifications and he placed his emphases differently. In effect, he even *distanced* himself from the views which historians in the eighteenth century had advanced. The difference is illustrated particularly by the concept of 'conjectural history', which held positive connotations for Stewart, but not for previous historians. For eighteenth-century writers the term 'conjecture' – despite, or rather, because of, Hume – was in general pejorative, mostly alluding to a lack of academic seriousness and empirical precision.[54] William Robertson, for example, accepted 'probable evidence', but strictly rejected 'conjecture':

> Those regions of conjecture and controversy belong not to the historian. His is a more limited province, confined to what is established by certain or highly probable evidence.[55]

Adam Ferguson also rejected the use of 'conjecture'. He therefore criticized historians in the past who had 'substitute[d] hypothesis instead of reality and confound[ed] the provinces of imagination and reason, of poetry and science'.[56] The methodology which he recommended as a model was what he saw as the scientifically precise practice of the natural historians: 'The natural historian thinks himself obliged to collect facts, not to offer conjectures'.[57] Historians reserved the term 'conjecture' for occa-

---

53 Étienne Bonnot de Condillac, *Introduction à l'Étude de l'Histoire Ancienne* I (1775), in *Oeuvres de Condillac: Revues, corrigées par l'Auteur...* (23 vols., Paris, AN VI/1798), ix, 20-5. On Condillac's 'educated guesses' see John Frederick Logan, *Condillac, Historian* (Ann Arbor, Mich., 1971), pp. 118-21. His contemporaries would certainly not have relished Stewart taking recourse to Hume and Condillac in the overheated atmosphere of the revolutionary years.

54 Many more could be added to the numerous authors cited by Allan, *Virtue, Learning*, pp. 152-4, e.g., John Millar, *The Origin of the Distinction of Ranks: Or, An Inquiry into the Circumstances which Give Rise to Influence and Authority in the Different Members of Society* (1771, 1779), ed. John Craig (Edinburgh, 1806), p. 10; William Robertson, *The History of America*, vol. 2 (1777, 1792), in *The Works of William Robertson* (12 vols., London, 1792), viii, 28-9 and 58; Robert Henry, *The History of Great Britain: From the First Invasion of it by the Romans under Julius Caesar; Written on a New Plan* (1771-93), suppl. Malcolm Laing, ed. Henry Moncreiff Wellwood, William Balderstone and William Finlay (12 vols., London, 1805-06), i, p. xxiv; [Jeffrey], 'Millar's *View of Government*', 157; Hugh Murray, *Enquiries Historical and Moral, Respecting the Character of Nations, and the Progress of Society* (Edinburgh, 1808), pp. 167-8.

55 Robertson, *History of America*, p. 29.

56 Ferguson, *Essay on Civil Society*, p. 4.

57 *Ibid.*, p. 3.

sional intellectual interpolations and passing comments;[58] the majority of eighteenth-century historians, however, were critical of the term when used more widely. They certainly did not find their views of correct historical practice adequately reflected in Stewart's concept of 'Theoretical or Conjectural History'.

The reason for the differences of opinion between Stewart and his predecessors was apparently their different understanding of the tasks and methods of the historian. The basic problem of having to fill gaps in knowledge occupied Stewart's predecessors as much as it did Stewart. Yet, Ferguson and Millar cherished the hope of being able to close these gaps by using sources drawn from other regions, and by observing contemporary 'primitive' peoples living close to nature. They therefore placed great importance on the use of travel reports, which seemed to them an established method for preventing 'mere speculation' about the natural state or the early history of mankind. By observing existing 'primitive' peoples, and transferring these observations to past ages, they believed that they could gain access to the early history of humankind, as it was 'within the reach of our own observation, and in the records of history'.[59] While it was well known that travel reports were often unreliable, historians were trusted to use their judgement to filter from this evidence secure and important data by means of comparison and careful consideration:

> [T]he reader has an opportunity of comparing [the different writers'] . . . several descriptions, and from their agreement or disagreement is enabled to ascertain the credit that is due to them. . . . The evidence becomes as complete as the nature of the thing will admit. We cannot refuse our assent to such evidence, without falling into a degree of scepticism by which the credibility of all historical testimony would be in a great measure destroyed.[60]

In this manner, the men of the Enlightenment believed, a relatively dense body of knowledge could be accumulated that would be enough to satisfy their demands for a reconstruction of the various societies of the past that would be as comprehensive as possible. By comparing societies at different stages, important developmental stages of social history could be reconstructed without losing sight of the 'whole'.

---

58 Robertson, *History of America*, p. 49. In France, by contrast, the term had much more positive connotations.

59 Ferguson, *Essay on Civil Society*, p. 3. Cf. John Logan, *Elements of the Philosophy of History*, Part 1 (Edinburgh, 1781), p. 19.

60 Millar, *Origin of Ranks*, p. 13.

Stewart, by contrast, took a completely different approach. He was not interested in the comprehensive reconstruction of whole societies and their stages of social development. The broad spectrum of anthropological, geographical, political, moral philosophical and sociological topics which had concerned the philosophical historians largely disappeared from Stewart's field of vision. Stewart abandoned the quest of previous historians for an encyclopaedic reconstruction of the 'whole', and suggested instead that individual strands of development should be picked out for analysis from out of the enormous number of known historical events. Thus, Stewart briefly defined his conception of history as: '[c]onjectural speculations concerning the natural advances of the Species, in any particular line of improvement'.[61] Fact-filled descriptions of individual peoples and societies no longer interested him, and he also turned away with disapproval from the travel reports which had provided the philosophical historians with one their main sources: 'A few insulated facts may perhaps be collected from the casual observations of travellers', Stewart commented on this genre, 'but nothing, it is evident, can be obtained in this way, which approaches to a regular and connected detail of human improvement'.[62]

It was in line with this more limited as well as focused approach that Stewart elevated the much despised term 'conjecture' (or 'theory') into the guiding principle of his history writing. He patently wanted this concept to set off a programmatic re-orientation. According to Stewart, the task of historians was 'to render the theoretical chain complete' and 'to form conjectures concerning the future, from the observation of the past'.[63] Historians should concentrate on extrapolating and plausibly reconstructing individual strands of development (in order to provide politicians with guidelines for their interventions in current processes). The soundness of the theoretical model which determined whether the reconstructed 'details of human improvement' were reliable was therefore more significant for Stewart than the reality of the past as a whole:

> [W]hen different theoretical histories are proposed by different writers, . . . these theories are not always to be understood as standing in opposition to each other. If the progress delineated in all of them be plausible, it is possible at least, that they may all have been realized . . . But whether they have been realized or no, is often a question of little consequence. In most cases, it is of more importance to ascertain the

61 Stewart, *Outlines of Moral Philosophy*, ii, 34.

62 Stewart, 'Account of Smith', p. 33.

63 Stewart, *Dissertation on the Progress of Philosophy*, p. 3; *Outlines of Moral Philosophy*, ii, 5.

> progress that is most simple, than the progress that is most agreeable to fact; for . . . the real progress is not always the most natural. It may have been determined by particular accidents, . . . which cannot be considered as forming any part of that general provision which nature has made for the improvement of the race.[64]

VI.

With this new style of historiography, Stewart was venturing onto terrain that the majority of his contemporaries regarded as extremely dangerous. From their point of view, his move threatened to replace secured knowledge with 'home made' theories, utopian plans and subjective prognoses. In their opinion, such procedures were in danger of getting out of control, and they could also result in the spread of subversive ideas. Beyond this, it is striking that in his writings on conjectural history Stewart no longer measured himself by the yardsticks which had previously characterized his portrayal of Scottish methodology and Political Economy. Stewart had defended Political Economy as empirically based, socially useful, moderately progressive, and historically appropriate. Given the dominant anti-revolutionary mood in the country, these arguments were more likely to find public approval than the strategy which Stewart used to present his conjectural history. He put the full spotlight on precisely those qualities – artificial construction, ambiguity and lack of facts – that had been anathematized by contemporary criticism.

Reactions to Stewart's theory of history were therefore dismissive, if not downright hostile. Even historians who still adhered to some of the principles of philosophical history, such as the geographer, Hugh Murray (1779-1846), decisively rejected Stewart's conjectural history:

> It has been supposed, that every conclusion which can be formed respecting the earliest stages in the progress of man, must be beyond the reach of authentic history, and can rest only upon uncertain conjecture. But . . . the operations of nature are not regulated by the standard of human wisdom. . . . [A]n attempt to delineate her processes, according to our own previous ideas, can hardly fail of leading into error. . . . [I]f the enquirer has recourse to conjecture, it will be less from the absolute want of facts, than for not duly availing himself of those which are within his reach.[65]

---

64 Stewart, 'Account of Smith', p. 37.

65 Murray, *Enquiries Historical and Moral, Respecting the Character of Nations, and the Progress of Society* (Edinburgh, 1808), pp. 167-8.

Leading Scottish historians, such as Alexander F. Tytler (1747-1813), also criticized conjectural history in the sharpest terms:

> The recording of authentic facts, the display of historic truth, is much less an object with such writers [i.e., conjectural historians], than ingenious argument, and plausible theory. Forgetting that it is only the most extensive knowledge of the actual history of man, in every age and country, that can enable us even to form a conjecture, where authentic history is silent; and dismissing entirely from their consideration those powerful springs of revolution, accident, and individual character, such philosophers are bold enough to determine not only what man ought to be, but to prove, by *à priori* reasoning, what in certain situations he has been, and in similar circumstances ever must be. It is to this sort of speculation that Mr. Stewart, in his *Life of Smith*, has given the name of *Theoretical* or *Conjectural History*, and assigned to it a higher praise than perhaps is strictly its due. . . .
>
> To readers of a metaphysical turn . . . such inquiries afford the highest pleasure; while by the more sober, cautious, yet penetrating intellect, they are received with jealousy, scrutinized with phlegm, and in the end coldly laid aside, as airy, vague, and unsubstantial speculations.[66]

Years after Stewart's death, conjectural history was still being criticized even when it was hardly practised in Britain any longer. The English historian William Smyth (1765-1849), for example, kept the anti-revolutionary criticism of conjectural history alive in his *Lectures on the French Revolution* of the 1820s and 1830s. By this time, this form of historiography had long been exiled, as it were, and was regarded by Smyth merely as a 'favourite sort of composition among foreign writers':

> [Foreign writers] delight in displaying the sweeping opinions of their daring minds, and in dazzling their audience by the wonders of their speculations and their brilliant discoveries of great principles; principles, that, however unknown to mankind themselves, have in fact, as they suppose, actuated their conduct and produced by a concatenated and irresistible necessity the events of history. . . . Their grand abstract positions are often very disputable, and are always objectionable as introducing into the mind those doctrines of necessity and irresistible concatenation of events in politics, so favourable to unfeeling revolutions, and so fatal to all counsels of moderation and preventive wisdom.[67]

---

66 Alexander Fraser Tytler, *Memoirs of the Life and Writings of the Honourable Henry Home of Kames* (2 vols., Edinburgh, 1807), i, 200n; ii, 112.

67 William Smyth, *Lectures on History*, 2nd ser.: *On the French Revolution* (3 vols., London, 1842), iii, 404-5 (from the 'General Summary' of 1837). Smyth, however, listed a few selected passages from Smith, Robertson and Mackintosh as recommended reading.

VII.

Critics seized on the irritating word 'conjecture', and expressed their fear that Stewart was opening the door wide to arbitrary theories, unbridled speculations and possibly politically dangerous tendencies. A detailed reading of Stewart's writings, however, does not justify these fears. There is much to suggest that Stewart's concept of conjectural history was associated with 'moderation and preventive wisdom', and that Stewart regarded his programme as a constructive contribution to the debate about Enlightenment sciences and their future. For although he pressed far ahead on individual points of controversy, he obviously made many concessions to his contemporaries who had been so alarmed by the French Revolution.

Thus, on political issues, Stewart made efforts to accommodate the position taken by his opponents. He clearly distinguished his commitment to social and economic reform from attempts to reform the franchise. In Stewart's eyes, the adoption of a 'liberal' reform policy as proposed by Political Economy had absolute priority over all other political and social change. In his view, political stability and harmony depended less on democratization than on politics being informed by the principles of Political Economy:

> [T]he happiness of mankind depends, not on the share which the people possesses, directly or indirectly, in the enactment of laws, but on the equity and expediency of the laws that are enacted. The share which the people possesses in the government is interesting chiefly to the small number of men whose object is the attainment of political importance; but the equity and expediency of the laws are interesting to every member of the community: and more especially to those whose personal insignificance leaves them no encouragement, but what they derive from the general spirit of the government under which they live.[68]

A second important element of Stewart's argument, his idea of progress, also proves, on closer inspection, not to be as radical as was generally assumed. Like the majority of historians who subscribed to Newtonian or Cartesian views, Stewart tried to predict the future by extrapolation from the past. The history of past social change, he suggested, showed where a need to act would become apparent in future and under what conditions this action would take place. Stewart thus linked the 'spirit of innovation' to conditions which history imposed on political action in the present and

---

[68] Stewart, 'Account of Smith', pp. 54-5.

the future. He therefore equated progress not with a fundamental upheaval in living conditions, but with the unbroken continuity of social processes. For Stewart did not postulate the 'fragmentation' of history, which Reinhart Koselleck, among others, regarded as typical of the most 'resolute' part of the Enlightenment.[69] Unlike many men of the French Enlightenment, who wanted to make a clean break with the past of which they disapproved, Stewart accepted the existing way of ordering social life as the indispensable basis for scientific forecasts and future-orientated policies:

> All the different kinds of philosophical inquiry, and all that practical knowledge which guides our conduct in life, presuppose such an established order in the succession of events, as enables us to form conjectures concerning the future, from the observation of the past.[70]

Stewart regarded this concern for the existing order as a '*limit* to . . . progressive improvement'. Thus, he advocated an idea of progress that can be called moderate, at least by comparison with the views of many French historians, and which in part also defied Burke's criticism that Enlightened social theory lacked an historical foundation.

Stewart's third big concession to the anti-revolutionary mood of the times concerned the fear that the social sciences might lead astray politically large parts of the nation. Stewart reacted to this accusation by setting narrow limits for the popularization of both Political Economy and conjectural history. One of his motives was certainly to protect them against misuse by radicals. Stewart wanted to reserve the expertise of political economists for the 'imagination of . . . the speculative few'.[71] He also intended to restrict the spread of conjectural history to an elite, and to regulate its teaching strictly. In his opinion, economic and social history were suitable subjects only for established scholars, whereas students who were being introduced to history required firmer ground to be placed under their feet:

> To a philosophical mind, no study certainly can be more delightful than this species of history [i.e., conjectural history]; but as an organ of instruction, I am not disposed to estimate its practical utility . . . highly . . . It does not seem to me at all adapted to

69 Reinhart Koselleck, '*Historia Magistra Vitae*: Über die Auflösung des Topos im Horizont neuzeitlich bewegter Geschichte' (1967), in *idem*, *Vergangene Zukunft: Zur Semantik geschichtlicher Zeiten* (Frankfurt, 1989), pp. 38-66, quotations at pp. 56 and 60.

70 Stewart, *Outlines of Moral Philosophy*, ii, 5.

71 Stewart, 'Account of Smith', p. 56.

> interest the curiosity of novices: nor is it so well calculated to engage the attention of those who wish to enlarge their scientific knowledge, as of persons accustomed to reflect on the phenomena and laws of the intellectual world.[72]

Stewart regarded the analysis of economy and society as potentially too explosive to be exposed to just anybody's speculations. For the broader public and for students, therefore, Stewart recommended the history of science as a more straightforward subject for conjectural history:

> The mathematical sciences, both pure and mixed, afford, in many of their branches, very favourable subjects for theoretical history; and a very competent judge, the late M. D'Alembert, has recommended this arrangement of their elementary principles, which is founded on the natural succession of inventions and discoveries, as the best adopted for interesting the curiosity and exercising the genius of students.[73]

Stewart advocated the history of science, which he himself chose as the subject of his essay in the *Encyclopaedia Britannica*, for other reasons as well. Not only were the required books and teaching materials widely available, but, more important, the scientific knowledge whose history was being reconstructed was already an acknowledged part of the cultural tradition, or, at least, was politically less harmful. In addition, the idea of progress was firmly anchored in the history of science. The present reassuringly appeared as the peak of human development, while controversial themes such as the loss of civic virtue or social disintegration did not have to be broached. Moreover, the history of great researchers could be regarded as pedagogically useful, as it could inspire emulation in students.

Stewart's enthusiasm for the 'histoire . . . du petit nombre de grands génies, dont les Ouvrages ont contribué à répandre la lumière parmi les hommes',[74] distinguished him clearly from the older generation of Scottish social historians, who had mostly accorded the individual little significance.[75] But the high value which Stewart placed on great thinkers also had a political dimension. He thus possibly contributed to turning history

72 Stewart, *Dissertation on the Progress of Philosophy*, p. 385.

73 Stewart, 'Account of Smith', pp. 34-5.

74 [Jean le Rond d'Alembert], 'Discours préliminaire des Éditeurs' (1751), in *Encyclopédie, ou Dictionnaire raisonné des Sciences, des Arts et des Métiers*, ed. Denis Diderot and Alembert (28 vols., Paris, 1751-72), i, p. xix.

75 E.g., Millar, *Origin of Ranks*, pp. 5-8.

into a stage for 'great men', in line with the contemporary trend towards rediscovering heroes in history:[76]

> [I] shall study to fix [my readers'] . . . attention on *those great lights of the world* by whom the torch of science has been successively seized and transmitted. It is, in fact, such leading characters alone which furnish matter for philosophical history. To enumerate the names and labours of obscure or even secondary authors, (whatever amusement it might afford to men of curious erudition,) would contribute but little to illustrate the origin and filiation of consecutive systems, or the gradual development and progress of the human mind.[77]

In this way Stewart put a stop to the radicalization of philosophical history as envisaged by younger writers such as John Logan. Logan had attempted to reinterpret the history of civil society as a history of the 'common man' whose natural qualities had developed in the course of human history, and who, in the process, had gradually fought for his rights:

> The arrangements and improvements which take place in human affairs result not from the efforts of individuals, but from a movement of the whole society.
>
> From want of attention to this principle, History hath often degenerated into the panegyric of single men, and the worship of names. Lawgivers are recorded, but who makes mention of the people? . . . Sociability and policy are natural to mankind. In the progress of society, instincts turn into arts, and original principles are converted into actual establishments. When an inequality of possessions takes place, the few that are opulent contend for power, the many defend their rights: from this struggle of parties a form of government is established.[78]

By comparison with Logan, Stewart's marked re-individualization of history can therefore be regarded as further evidence of essentially how 'conservative' he designed his project of conjectural history to be. Stewart and many of his contemporaries established the notion that history was made by great men in opposition to the radical connection between the 'rights of man' and the 'history of man'.

---

[76] Studies of nineteenth-century hero-worship are numerous. Comprehensive views of the subject which may also serve as introductions include the essay collection *Perspectives on Nineteenth-Century Heroism: Essays from the 1981 Conference of the Southeastern Nineteenth-Century Studies Association*, ed. Sara M. Putzell and David C. Leonard (Potomac, MD, 1982); and the article by Ian Ousby, 'Carlyle, Thackeray, and Victorian Heroism,' *Yearbook of English Studies*, 12 (1982), 152-68. Ousby demonstrates the pervasiveness of hero-worship during the Victorian age and considers even Thackery as representative of that turn of mind.

[77] Stewart, *Dissertation on the Progress of Philosophy*, pp. 23-4.

[78] Logan, *Elements of the Philosophy of History*, pp. 14-5.

To be sure, the trend towards rediscovering heroes in history could also have radical consequences if, as was the case later with Thomas Carlyle, rebellious characters were idealized.[79] Stewart, however, did not rate the significance of the individual highly enough to allow his historiography to be used for radical purposes. In Stewart's view, individuals provided important impulses for the progress of knowledge and society, but, as far as he was concerned, it was society that produced great inventors and thinkers, not heroes who shaped society according to their taste:

> [A]lthough it should be allowed that the invention of printing was accidental with respect to the individual who made it, it may, with truth, be considered as the natural result of a state of the world, when a number of great and contiguous nations are all engaged in the study of literature, in the pursuit of science, and in the practice of the arts; insomuch, that I do not think it extravagant to affirm, that if this invention had not been made by the particular person to whom it is ascribed, the same art, or some analogous art, answering a similar purpose, would have infallibly been invented by some other person, and at no very distant period.[80]

Thus, Stewart, along with the philosophical historians of the 1760s and 1770s, still interpreted the modern individual as a socially conditioned phenomenon. Precisely because, in Stewart's view, the individual could achieve great significance in history only for brief periods, he rejected all political utopias based on the intellectual and physical powers of the individual or sectarian groups.[81]

In Stewart's opinion the individual was by no means the 'motor' driving history. He believed that the history of science moved to a different rhythm, one dictated by two mutually interacting forces: 'the natural advances of the mind', on the one hand, and 'the actual succession of hy-

---

79 Whereas older studies usually focused on the alleged proto-fascist nature of Carlyle's concept of the hero, modern research since the 1960s has done much to unveil the radically modern implications of Carlyle's thought. Indispensable studies include Robert A. Donovan, 'Carlyle and the Climate of Hero-Worship', *University of Toronto Quarterly*, 42 (1972-73), 122-41; Philip Rosenberg, *The Seventh Hero: Thomas Carlyle and the Theory of Radical Activism* (Cambridge, Mass., 1974), pp. 188-203; Thomas Culviner, 'Heroes and Hero-Worship: Not so Simple in *The French Revolution*', *Victorians Institute Journal*, 13 (1985), 83-96; John Morrow, 'Heroes and Constitutionalists: The Ideological Significance of Thomas Carlyle's Treatment of the English Revolution', *History of Political Thought*, 14 (1993), 205-23; and *idem*, 'The Paradox of Peel as Carlylean Hero', *Historical Journal*, 40 (1997), 97-110.

80 Stewart, *Elements of Philosophy*, p. 243.

81 *Ibid.*, pp. 232-4.

pothetical systems', on the other.[82] Stewart obviously owed this image to Condillac,[83] who, in similar language, had interpreted language ('arbitrary signs') and cognition as forces which mutually influenced each other, and whose interplay had set off the intellectual progress of humanity:

> L'Usage de ces signes étendit peu à peu l'exercice des opérations de l'ame, et, à leur tour, celles-ci ayant plus d'exercice, perfectionnèrent les signes et en rendirent l'usage plus familier. Notre expérience prouve que ces deux choses s'aident mutuellement.[84]

In Stewart's historiography, the interplay between the operations of the human mind and theoretical systems ensured that the progress of science was represented as a largely self-perpetuating development in which 'inventions and discoveries' followed each other in 'natural succession'.[85]

In my opinion, this concept is at the crux of Stewart's conjectural history. It forms the basis for all the changes which Stewart made to philosophical history: it provided a figure which permitted him, unlike the philosophical historians, not to reconstruct societies within an endless context of anthropological, social, economic, legal, intellectual and geographical conditions, but to concentrate on the analysis of individual strands of development, and to cultivate the history of science as a discipline independent of social and political conditions. This renunciation of the extremely wide horizon of philosophical *histoire totale* is perhaps the most striking difference between Stewart's conjectural history and the view of history advanced by his predecessors. By removing these contexts, however, Stewart eliminated the most strongly politicized areas of historiography, which had repeatedly been used to produce radical

---

82 Stewart, 'Account of Smith', quotation at p. 35.

83 Stewart's briefest comment on his adaptation of semiotic theory is to be found in his *Outlines of Moral Philosophy*, ii, 23 and 33-4. In his *Dissertation* Stewart still referred to Condillac and (mainly critically) to Alembert. *Dissertation on the Progress of Philosophy*, pp. 384-5. Cf. Hans Aarsleff, 'The Tradition of Condillac: The Problem of the Origin of Language in the Eighteenth Century and the Debate of the Berlin Academy before Herder' (1974) in *idem*, *From Locke to Saussure: Essays on the Study of Language and Intellectual History* (Minneapolis, 1982), pp. 146-209, esp. pp. 163-5. Aarsleff, however, concentrates on Condillac's ideas on the progress of language.

84 'The use of such signs gradually stimulated the exercise of the operations of the soul, and this in turn contributed to the further perfection of the signs and made their use more familiar. Our experience proves that these two things promote each other mutually'. Condillac, *Essai sur l'Origine des Connaissances Humaines* (1746), in *Oeuvres de Condillac*, i, esp. I/2/4 (pp. 75-87), this quote at II/1/§4 (pp. 263-4).

85 'Account of Smith', p. 34.

interpretations.[86] At the same time, Stewart transformed historiography from a universal discipline into a type of applied technology, which was capable of dealing with only limited tasks. This restricted discipline could, first, reassure scholars and students about the basis of their knowledge, and, second, provide Political Economy with the empirical data it needed to predict future developments. Beyond this, however, history no longer had a wider function for Stewart, as his *Lectures on Political Economy* (1800-10) clearly demonstrate. Whereas Stewart's plans for his lectures on moral philosophy in 1793 had still contained a section on 'History of Political Society', he reduced the historical part of his later lectures to 'the Rise and Progress of this Branch of Science [i.e., Political Economy]'.[87] Stewart's own historical work, his unfinished *Dissertation on the Progress of Philosophy*, was similarly tailored completely to the development of Political Economy as the most recently conquered peak in social science.

VIII.

To sum up, Stewart's concept of conjectural history did possess undertones of determinism, anti-empiricism and French rationalism which were bound to arouse the distrust of his contemporaries. None the less, there is much to suggest that he himself regarded conjectural history in some ways as the central plank of a Whiggish anti-radicalism. In this way, Stewart tried to arm himself in the 1790s against the critics of the Enlightenment, and to save some of the main tenets of the Scottish tradition for the next century. To those critics who regarded Scottish science as seditious and pernicious, Stewart coolly responded in the manner of a 'Whig aristocrat of science': 'For checking . . . [sanguine and inconsiderate projects of reformation], nothing is so effectual as a general

86 The extent to which Stewart excluded moral philosophical issues from Political Economy is a highly controversial issue. See, among others, Collini, Winch and Burrow, *That Noble Science*, p. 50; Salim Rashid, 'Political Economy as Moral Philosophy: Dugald Stewart of Edinburgh', *Australian Economic Papers*, 26 (1987), esp. 150-4; Richard B. Sher, 'Professors of Virtue: The Social History of the Edinburgh Moral Philosophy Chair in the Eighteenth Century', in *Studies in the Philosophy of the Scottish Enlightenment*, ed. Michael Alexander Stewart (Oxford, 1990), p. 124. Tannoch-Bland, 'Primacy of Moral Philosophy', traces this problem throughout Stewart's *œuvre*.

87 For Stewart's lectures of 1793 see *Outlines of Moral Philosophy*, App. to Pt. 3 (1793), in *Collected Works*, viii, 3-4. The agenda of his lectures in 1800-01 was edited in his *Lectures on Political Economy* (1800-10), reported by James Bridges, John Dow and James Bonar, in *Collected Works*, vols. 8-9 (Edinburgh, 1855-56), viii, p. xvii.

survey of the complicated structure of society'.[88] In the process of accommodating historiography to the needs of his age, he eliminated many elements of the older philosophical history that were susceptible to radical interpretation. A synoptic view of society and reflections on many potentially controversial aspects of politics were given up. Stewart's conjectural history thus amounted to a profound reconceptualization and reduction of Enlightenment historiography.

His critics, however, hardly perceived this more conservative side of Stewart. Instead, they seized upon the terms 'conjecture' and 'conjectural', which for Stewart presumably did not have the connotations that they held for contemporary critics (and many modern scholars). What is more, they did not confine their critique to Stewart. Rather, their rejection of conjectural history went so far as to include even writers who had not advocated this model. 'Conjecture' became a battle cry which was used to brand not only conjectural historians and political economists, but much of the Enlightened *avant-garde*, and to bring them into lasting discredit. Thus, the spectre of conjecturalism overshadowed even the reception of older works of historiography. Biographers of Millar and Kames, for example, could not resist criticizing the propensity of both for conjecture. John Craig worked for Millar's rehabilitation by separating his work as far as possible from conjectural history, and in general, demanding of historians 'accurate observation of the real line of progress'.[89] On the whole, Craig, following the trend of the times, unmistakably condemned Millar's conjectures: 'Mr. Millar paid too little regard to the prevailing taste of antiquarians, and deprived his work of too much of that kind of support, on which they are accustomed, almost conclusively, to depend'.[90] The same applies to Alexander Tytler whose derogatory remark, quoted earlier, on the 'airy, vague and unsubstantial speculations' of conjectural history was directed as much against Kames and Millar as against Stewart.

This stigmatization made it considerably more difficult for historians to continue using conjectural practices. Thus, Richard Sher has pointed out that 'the "conjectural" and . . . philosophical modes of historiography lost ground to the antiquarian and controversial modes, as well as to the quasi-romantic mode found in Scott's historical novels and popular histo-

88 Stewart, *Elements of Philosophy*, p. 238.

89 John Craig, 'Account of the Life and Writings of John Millar, Esq.', in Millar, *Origin of Ranks*, pp. xxxvii, xlv-xlvii, lxxx-lxxxiv; quotation at p. xlvii.

90 Craig, 'Account of Millar', p. lxxxiv.

ries'.[91] Since that time, writers who, bucking the trend, continued to write philosophical history, limited themselves almost exclusively to the history of science and early history. Thus, the characteristic features of philosophical history, such as long-term developmental trends, the postulation of natural laws, universalism, and a belief in progress were generally carefully avoided or interspersed with Biblical exegesis.[92] Ultimately, it seems that by advancing his concept of conjectural history (and by naming philosophical historians such as Smith its originators), Stewart unintentionally contributed to the abrupt decline of the tradition of philosophical history in the 1790s.

Many other reasons for this decline have also been identified. Thus, for example, it has been noted that popular literary tastes changed as the public turned away from philosophical history, which it found too rational. Robert Peel's oft-quoted appeal to the historian, John Wilson Croker, to produce 'not . . . a pompous, philosophical history, but a mixture of biography, facts, and gossip; a diary of what really took place, with the best authenticated likenesses of the actors' expressly confirms this.[93] Moreover, social and religious changes in Scotland were cited as reasons for the decline of philosophical history.[94] Most often, however, political factors were adduced. Many practitioners of philosophical history, such as John Millar, were largely isolated from 1793 because of their political radicalism.[95] Besides, civic humanism, which had still been binding for such historians as

---

91 Sher, *Church and University*, p. 317.

92 The works of the American, James H. McCulloh, *Researches Philosophical and Antiquarian, Concerning the Aboriginal History of America* (Baltimore, MD, 1829), provide a good example of these trends. Cf., for the topic discussed, Donald Winch in Collini, Winch and Burrow, *That Noble Science*, pp. 60-1.

93 John Wilson Croker, *The Croker Papers: The Correspondence and Diaries of the Late Right Honourable John Wilson Croker*, ed. Louis J. Jennings (3 vols., London, 1884), ii, 277. For Croker see William Thomas, *The Quarrel of Macaulay and Croker: Politics and History in the Age of Reform* (Oxford, 2000), pp. 162-209.

94 Richard Sher has pointed out that the milieu of the Presbyterian Moderates was disintegrating, and that history was increasingly becoming the preserve of lawyers, who often approached the past with less comprehensive moral philosophical interests. Sher, *Church and University*, pp. 314-8. Silvia Sebastiani argued that since the late 18th century the authority of the Biblical Revelation was again being more strongly emphasized, which resulted, for example, in a fundamental revision of the historical articles in the *Encyclopaedia Britannica*. Sebastiani, 'Conjectural History vs. the Bible', 51-61.

95 Lehmann, *John Millar*, pp. 67-72 and 145-9.

Millar and Ferguson, was clearly losing its significance.[96] None the less, after almost half a century, philosophical history should have been firmly established in Scotland. For this tradition to be destroyed and no successor to appear for another fifty years required more than political, religious and social reservations on the part of the public. There must have been an internal loss of plausibility which made adherents of philosophical history seek refuge in other historical models.

Belief in progress and in 'abstractness', which had so often been objected to in philosophical history during the 1790s, were certainly not the only causes of this loss of viability. Works which presented 'general views of the progress of the arts and sciences', or applied the tenets of Political Economy, were naturally still widely read in the nineteenth century. Ironically, the very work for which Peel's dictum of 'pompous philosophical history' seems to have been coined – the *History of Europe* by one of Stewart's former students, Archibald Alison (1792-1867) – became the most successful history of the French Revolution in Britain.[97] Yet there were only two things which Alison still had in common with the philosophical historians, namely, an interest in the causes and effects of 'great convulsions', and the striving for 'impartial judgment'. Just as for his contemporaries, so 'moving scenes . . . [and] graphic pictures, which are the life and soul of the highest style of history', were much more important for Alison than abstract reasoning.[98]

Alison's Tory history, closely modelled on Burke's *Reflections*, allows us to conclude, however, which patterns of argument, deriving from the Enlightenment, historians had to give up during the 1790s. These patterns include, in the first place, the idea that, over time, humans had become more perfect beings, and had thus contributed to the welfare and progress of society. Writers such as Burke and Archibald Alison replaced the idea

---

96 Michael Ignatieff, 'John Millar and Individualism', in *Wealth and Virtue: The Shaping of Political Economy in the Scottish Enlightenment*, ed. Istvan Hont and Michael Ignatieff (Cambridge, 1983), pp. 342-3; John Robertson, 'The Scottish Contribution to the Enlightenment', in *The Scottish Enlightenment: Essays in Reinterpretation*, ed. Paul B. Wood (Rochester, NY, 2000), p. 51.

97 Archibald Alison, *History of Europe from the Commencement of the French Revolution in M.DCC.LXXXIX. to the Restoration of the Bourbons in M.DCCC.XV.* (10 vols., Edinburgh, 1833-42). On Alison's *History* see Ben-Israel, *English Historians*, pp. 150-3; Maurice Milne, 'Archibald Alison: Conservative Controversialist', *Albion*, 27 (1995), 417-43; and Michael Michie, *An Enlightenment Tory in Victorian Scotland: The Career of Sir Archibald Alison* (Montreal, 1997), pp. 130-58.

98 Alison, 'British History during the Eighteenth Century', *Blackwood's Edinburgh Magazine*, 57 (Jan.-June 1845), esp. 359-60, quote at 359.

of the perfectibility of humankind with the religious conviction of its fallen nature:

> At the breaking out of the French Revolution, it was almost universally imagined by philosophers, that the extension of knowledge, the humanizing of manners, and the diffusion of education, had provided an effectual antidote to this tendency to decay hitherto always observable in human affairs . . .
>
> The French Revolution affords the most decisive demonstration which the history of the world has yet exhibited of the entire fallacy of this opinion. It was avowedly based by all its authors, both philosophical and political, upon the principle of the perfectibility of mankind: . . . it was the ground on which they at once rested their legislation, and justified their cruelties.[99]

Divergent views about human nature, did not, however, seem to be the main problem. Rather the issue at the heart of the debate was the relationship between individuals/society and God/nature. Many historians during the Enlightenment placed the history of humanity and the natural order in relation to each other, assuming that there were analogous patterns of order in both and reciprocity between the two spheres. These ideas of order were made implausible, or at least, seriously challenged by the French Revolution. Doubts about the idea of a providentially arranged self-regulating order, however, also put philosophical history under pressure. After the September massacres and the *Terreur* in France it was increasingly difficult to understand the history of humanity unreservedly as a unilinear progress of civilization whose patterns of order displayed the workings of a general providence. It was no longer possible to identify unambiguously stable patterns in society and its history. The once far-reaching consensus in Enlightened circles about the existence, and the harmonious character, of providential patterns of order was obviously breaking down. Under these conditions, alternative patterns of thought drawn from religion among other spheres, and in particular from radical versions of Protestant theology, experienced a rapid upsurge. Thus, for example, belief in a special providence or millenarian visions chimed more with the experience of many contemporaries, and gained an increasing number of adherents as substitutes for Enlightened notions of order.[100]

The heated atmosphere of the 1790s forced the decline of philosophical history. Any complex or subtle thinking was quickly suspected of

---

[99] Alison, *History of Europe*, x, 937 and 939.

[100] For a valuable recent summary of early nineteenth-century millenarianism see Tim Fulford, 'Millenarianism and the Study of Romanticism', in *Romanticism and Millenarianism*, ed. *idem* (New York, 2002), 1-22.

breeding disloyalty, and was not always given a second chance. Despite Stewart's incisive, in some ways almost conservative, attenuation of his concept, conjectural history became the *bête noire* of many critics, and this made Stewart's 'Account of Smith' almost an exemplary illustration of the impact of the French Revolution and the nature of political discourse in the 1790s. Alfred Cobban's much cited phrase, 'debate on France', has long nurtured the idea that in the 1790s intellectuals had engaged in a disciplined exchange of views about what was happening in France in a process generally profitable for all sides: 'The discussion of fundamental principles stimulated by the Revolution ... deepened and broadened political ideas'.[101] In recent years, the work of Mark Philp in particular has refuted this assumption. Philp makes clear that the French Revolution did create unprecedented conditions for discourse. News and events which changed every week, if not every day, and the strong polarization of political groups and their spokesmen made an orderly debate impossible and undermined any rational approach to the revolution and the problems associated with it.[102] The reception of Stewart's 'Account of Smith' and his model of conjectural history explicitly underlines this assessment. Even a decidedly non-radical, moderately progressive view of history, which perhaps did not need to have been involved in the debate at all, came under pressure and was so thoroughly destroyed that only fragments survived in the historical works that followed. This demonstrates that firmly established political idioms no longer confronted each other in the discourse of the 1790s, to be modified or exchanged. Rather, the components and deep structures of all political idioms, even those from non-radical traditions, which had any connection, however remote, with revolutionary patterns of argument, were rigorously scrutinized. If any such patterns were detected, the author or the group he represented faced not merely criticism, but exclusion from the debate. In the case of conjectural history, the verdict 'favourable to revolution' was fatal not only for Stewart's view of history, but also for a large part of Enlightenment historical writing.

---

101 'Introduction', in *The Debate on the French Revolution, 1789-1800*, ed. Alfred Cobban (London, 1950), p. 30.

102 Mark Philp, 'The Fragmented Ideology of Reform', in *The French Revolution and British Popular Politics*, ed. *idem* (Cambridge, 1991), pp. 50-77; and *idem*, 'Revolution', in *An Oxford Companion to the Romantic Age: British Culture, 1776-1832*, ed. Iain McCalman *et al.* (Oxford, 1999), pp. 17-26.

Marianne Czisnik

Representations of a Hero
Monuments to Admiral Nelson

Public monuments became extremely widespread across Britain at the beginning of the nineteenth century. Before that, monuments had been produced mainly as sepulchral architecture or sculpture. The most usual exceptions were a few monuments to monarchs. Other monuments, such as the columns to commemorate the duke of Marlborough or the fire of London, were extremely rare. This situation changed with the Napoleonic War which created a novel interest in other public figures than the monarch and an interest in warriors in particular. This public interest in national heroes was particularly intensified by the spectacular naval and military successes at Trafalgar and Waterloo and it consequently focused on the two great heroes of these battles, Viscount Nelson and the duke of Wellington. Using the example of monuments to Admiral Nelson, this essay will examine what motivated people in the first half of the nineteenth century to build monuments to a successful warrior, what influenced them in choosing the form such monuments should take, and finally how these monument were used and regarded by the public, once they had been erected.

I. Preparations for Monuments

When the news of the battle of Trafalgar reached the British Isles in November 1805 a spontaneous monument to the memory of Nelson was erected in Ireland, where a captain in the Royal Navy organized the erection of a crude arch.[1] Three years later ironworkers from an iron-smelting centre in Scotland erected a monolith on a hill to commemorate Nelson.[2] These early monuments were the exception. More common were planned monuments to celebrate the career and achievements of the great admiral.

Although most of the projects for erecting a monument to Admiral Nelson were started in direct reaction to the news of the battle of Trafalgar, they were usually the product of extensive deliberations. This was

1 Rodney Mace, *Trafalgar Square: Emblem of Empire* (London, 1976) [hereafter Mace], p. 51.

2 *Gentleman's Magazine*, 80 (1810), part ii, 461.

necessary because most of the monuments were erected by public subscription. Only two monuments were erected directly at official expense; one, voted for by parliament, was erected in St. Paul's Cathedral, while the other was erected by the City of London in its Guildhall. Both monuments were thus indoors, which made them less accessible to the public. The fact that St. Paul's Cathedral was as much a work of art as a church, and levied an entrance fee, was widely criticized. It encouraged the production of a caricature depicting a sailor with his own monument to Nelson in his garden and a scroll stating: 'Every person who wishes to see the Monuments in St. Paul's must pay Twopence!! Sailors should have a free admission'.[3] Britain did not adopt the French system of extravagant state patronage. Although parliament voted the generous sum of £300,000 in 1816 to pay for monuments to commemorate the battles of Trafalgar and Waterloo, and it opened a competition for the designs of these, it never actually spent the money on any monument.[4] More than twenty years later, when the subscription for Nelson's Monument in Trafalgar Square had just been opened, a designer protested:

> A monument erected by domestic affection, friendship, or admiration, by subscribers, does not become a public or national monument, merely because it is set up in a church or a square, or other conspicuous place. It manifests only the affection, &c. of those who erected it, be their number great or small. A monument raised by the state records the approbation of a whole nation.[5]

But public opinion did not usually agree with this view. A subscriber proudly stated: 'The pillars of Trajan and of Antonine were erected to gratify vain-glorious conquerors, while ours will owe its origin to public gratitude and veneration for the best and bravest of our Admirals.'[6]

---

3 Mary Dorothy George, *Catalogue of Political and Personal Satires, Preserved in the Department of Prints and Drawings in the British Museum* (11 vols., London, 1942), viii, No. 10445, December 1805.

4 J. Mordaunt Crook and M. H. Port, *The History of the King's Works* (6 vols. (London, 1973), vi (1782-1851), 294, fn.

5 Andrew Robertson, *The Parthenon, Adapted to the Purpose of a National Monument, To Commemorate the Victories of the Late War; Proposed to be Erected in Trafalgar Square, or Hyde Park* (Piccadilly [London], 1838) [hereafter Robertson], p. 8. One of Nelson's captains at Trafalgar, Edward Codrington, who had become an MP by the 1830s, protested in a similar vein in parliament (*The Times*, 10 Mar. 1838) and was cheered for this view at a meeting of subscribers to the Nelson Monument in Trafalgar Square (*The Times*, 18 June 1838).

6 John Alfred Langford, *A Chronicle of Birmingham Life* (2 vols., Birmingham, 1868) [hereafter Langford], ii, 305.

The subscription committees indeed did make every effort to show that their projects were supported by the public. They gave 'fellow-subjects of every situation, an opportunity of contributing to the commemoration of a name equally dear to all ranks'.[7] This broad popular approach was also reflected in the processions that were organized to lay the foundation stone or to unveil the completed monument. In such processions local dignitaries and subscribers took part along with groups of ordinary sailors and volunteers. Even when locally influential groups, such as the Freemasons in Glasgow, took part, they were joined by the general public and the 'concourse of people in the Streets, at the Windows, and in the Green was immense'.[8]

There were several reasons for such manifestations of public interest in monuments to Admiral Nelson, the most obvious being the desire to honour the memory of Nelson himself. This motivation was naturally strong in those who had served in the navy. Those who had fought at Trafalgar dedicated a monument of their own on a hill near Portsmouth 'to the memory of Lord Viscount Nelson . . . to perpetuate his triumph and their regret'.[9] It was not only members of the Royal Navy who manifested this kind of personal regard for Nelson; others simply signed the subscription list for Nelson's Column in Trafalgar Square as 'an admirer' or 'a friend to merit'.[10] The desire to do an 'act of justice to his memory'[11] or even to 'strengthen national devotion'[12] was also expressed in the choice of the anniversaries of Nelson's famous battles as dates for the laying of the foundation stone of a monument or for its final unveiling.[13]

Reminding the public of Nelson's achievements could serve to present him as an example to 'encourage those who are entering on the same ca-

---

7 *Nelson's Pillar. A Description of the Pillar, With a List of* Subscribers (Dublin, 1846) [hereafter *Nelson's Pillar*], p. 7.

8 *Nelson's Pillar*, p. 14, and *Glasgow Herald*, 4 Aug. 1806.

9 Inscription, given in: *The Nelson Dispatch*, ii, part 8 (October 1986), 157.

10 *Statement of Subscriptions to the Memorial of the Achievements of the late Admiral Lord Viscount Nelson* (1 January 1841) [hereafter *Statement of Subscriptions*], p. 33.

11 *Statement of Subscriptions*, p. 12.

12 William Wood, *An Essay on National and Sepulchral Monuments* (London, 1808) [hereafter Wood], p. 7.

13 Battle of St. Vincent: Laying of foundation stone in Dublin, 1808; Battle of the Nile: Laying of foundation stone in Glasgow, 1806; meeting to discuss a Nelson monument in London, 1838; Battle of Trafalgar: Laying of foundation stone in Edinburgh, 1806, and opening to the public of monument in Dublin, 1809.

reer'.[14] The often declared aim – 'to stimulate others to emulate his bright example'[15] – could also influence the choice of the site for the monument:

> Whatever plan is adopted, . . . [the monument] will, no doubt, be erected in the most frequented part of the place, the oftener to excite emulation in others . . . being reminded of a character which holds out so many objects of imitation – as a warrior, a Christian, and a man![16]

Others had the more specific aim of using Nelson to encourage other sailors. They maintained that no site was 'better adapted to the monument of a naval commander than a conspicuous station by the sea; where it may both serve as a land-mark, and animate the valour, while it catches the attention of the sailor'.[17]

The monuments to Nelson were also meant to prove that exertions and valour of the kind displayed by the great admiral were rewarded by a grateful nation. One of the declared aims of the monument to Nelson in Glasgow was 'to rouse the youth of succeeding generations, by the view of these lasting honours, that are the reward of distinguished professional genius and heroic enterprise'.[18] It was claimed that 'Honour and renown are what soldiers and sailors fight for, next to the defence of their country'.[19] Prints of designs for monuments to Nelson revealed a more material kind of 'rewards' for exceptional service: some of them showed on the left a list of Nelson's naval achievements and on the right a list of his 'rewards' which listed pensions and, among other prizes, several 'gold box[es]'.[20]

---

14 Matthew Cotes Wyatt, *Prospectus of a Model to the Memory of Lord Nelson* (London, 1800) [hereafter Wyatt], p. 4.

15 Corporation of London Record Office, Misc Mss 207.5 'Battle of Trafalgar', Common Council [hereafter CLRO Misc Mss 207.5], 26 Nov. 1805; see also: Edinburgh City Archive, McLeod Bundle 10, Bay A, no folio number, *Description of the Monument intended to be erected on the Calton Hill, Edinburgh, to the Memory of Lord Nelson* [hereafter ECA, *Description*]; and William Roscoe, *Lord Nelson's Monument, erected in the area of the Liverpool Exchange Buildings* (1813?]) [hereafter Roscoe], one page only.

16 Langford, p. 304, quoting from *Aris's Birmingham Gazette*, 19 Nov. 1805.

17 [Anon., James Elmes], 'A critical Examination of the Architecture of the Nelson Column erected at Yarmouth, 1817-1819', *Annals of the Fine Arts*, 4 (1820), 511-43 [hereafter Elmes] (p. 535). See also Wood, p. 10, who was even more specific in proposing to erect the monument near a 'military seminary from which we may justly expect a long continued emanation of equal skill and bravery'. p. 5.

18 *Glasgow Herald*, 9 Dec. 1805 and again 11 Aug. 1806.

19 Robertson, p. 10.

20 National Maritime Museum [hereafter NMM], PAG 6723 and PAI 5311; see also PAI 5280, where victories and rewards are inscribed on a wall in a niche of which the monument is placed.

More common than intricate didactic considerations was the desire of cities and their citizens to hand 'down to the latest posterity a memorial of their gratitude for his unexampled services to his King and Country'.[21] Such monumental gratitude to Nelson had quite a real significance for some of the contributors. Nelson's pursuit of the Franco-Spanish fleet across the Atlantic and back again, before the battle of Trafalgar, was widely interpreted as achieving the preservation of the British West Indian islands. The 'grateful inhabitants of Barbados' consequently inscribed their monument as 'a tribute of esteem, admiration and gratitude to their illustrious Deliverer'[22] and, in less directly concerned Edinburgh, it was recognized that Nelson was 'our great hero, to whom the Country owes such signal obligations'.[23]

It was sometimes admitted that these obligations were for material gain. A Glasgow newspaper stressed the economic interests that Nelson had helped to protect:

> *We* have shared largely in the benefits procured to the nation by the vigour of his arm, and by the terror of his name. – *We* have had *our* gainings from the established security of the ocean. The panic-stuck inaction, and subsequent flight, of the combined fleets from Martinique, must yet be fresh in the recollection of our merchants; and a tithe of what has been saved to the commercial part of the Island, by the exertions of this man alone, would rear up a more magnificent mausoleum than ever rose at the command of eastern pride.[24]

With similar thoughts in mind, the West India Association subscribed £500 to the Nelson monument in Liverpool, while the corporation of this city subscribed £1000.[25] Business organizations, such as several London livery companies and the East India Company, contributed money even more than thirty years after Nelson's death at the battle of Trafalgar, when subscriptions were collected for the great monument to be erected in Trafalgar Square.[26] Such an economic interest in recognizing Nelson's

---

21 Langford, p. 302; see also: *Statement of Subscriptions*, p. 12, and CLRO, Misc Mss 207.5, 26 Nov. 1805: 'to prove to future ages the very high sense the City of London entertained of his merit'.

22 Robert Herrmann Schomburgk, *The History of Barbados* (London, 1848) [hereafter Schomburgk], p. 246.

23 Edinburgh City Archive, Nelson Monument Committe Minutes [hereafter ECA, NMCM], f. 6.

24 *Glasgow Herald*, 15 Nov. 1805.

25 J. A. Picton, *Memorials of Liverpool. Historical and Topographical. Including a History of the Dock Estate* (2 vols., London, 1873) i, 307.

26 *Statement of Subscriptions*, pp. 34, 55, 65, 75, 125, 128, 57.

achievements was expressed in inscriptions on monuments to Nelson that mentioned loyalty or national pride, and praised the 'unexampled glory [that] confirmed in the eyes of Europe and the world the naval superiority of Great Britain'.[27]

The construction of a monument to Nelson had the attractive side-effect of embellishing a particular place, in some cases with the town's first public monument (as in Birmingham and Montreal). A leading member of the subscription committee in Liverpool promised that the monument would 'do honour to the town . . . as an effort of art'.[28] Such hopes must have been shared by those living close to the proposed site for a monument to Nelson in Dublin's Sackville Street, because the 'Sackville-street Club' and the neighbouring 'Kildare-street Club' subscribed to it.[29] To attract subscribers, the committees made clear that the monument would be erected 'in some conspicuous part' of the town or they praised the 'noble grandeur of the situation' in which it would stand.[30] When the city of Norwich contributed £200 to the Nelson monument of his native county of Norfolk, the corporation sent a speaker to the county meeting to plead for the monument to be erected in a 'commanding situation in or near the city'.[31] The disappointment must consequently have been great, when the monument was eventually erected near the sea in Yarmouth. The strong desire of Norwich to have its own monument to him finally led to the opening of another subscription in the 1840s.

In some places the monuments to Nelson instead of being seen as mere embellishments, formed part of more extensive town-planning projects. In Birmingham the Nelson monument was placed in the market place, which had been 'formerly thronged with mean shops, and butchers' shambles'.[32] In Barbados the subscription committee purchased, with the financial support of the 'Legislature', an area in Bridgetown that was called 'the Green'; and renamed it 'Trafalgar Square'. Shamed by the condition of a place with such a proud name the same Legislature was motivated in

---

27 On the monument on Barbados (*Naval Chronicle* (1806), p. 387) and on monument in Hereford.

28 Roscoe.

29 *Nelson's Pillar*, p. 14.

30 *Naval Chronicle*, (1806), p. 386; and ECA, NMCM, f. 6.

31 Charles Mackie, *Norfolk Annals. A Chronological Record of Remarkable Events in the Nineteenth Century* (2 vols., Norwich, [1901]) [hereafter: *Norfolk Annals*], i, 119 (11 Aug. 1814).

32 *Gentleman's Magazine*, 80 (1810), part ii, 414.

1826 to invest some money in the 'purchase and removal' of 'some unsightly houses [which] obstructed the square'.[33]

The much more famous Trafalgar Square in London was also part of a major town-planning project. This time it was not the subscription committee which influenced the outlook of the place, but, on the contrary, the appearance of the existing square, recently named after Nelson's last and most famous battle, had to be considered in the choice of design for a monument. The area which had been occupied until the beginning of the nineteenth century by the royal stables and poor housing had been transformed into an open space, thanks to the ambitious plans of John Nash. His desire had been to make a previously neglected space between Westminster and the City of London into an elegant part of the metropolis, connecting the two cities. Although his more ambitious plans were not fully adopted, the area was cleared of poor housing, regulations were introduced that excluded 'waggons, carts or other carriage' from remaining in the area, and the passages were cleared of obstructing 'Signs or other Emblems'. In this exquisite setting the monument could not be allowed to obscure the new building of the very broad but low National Gallery by William Wilkins.[34] At the same time the monument had to be big enough not to appear minuscule on the huge square. Another local problem was posed by the sloping ground and the need to consider one of the few existing statues: that of Charles I at the southern end of the new square.[35] An artist, who submitted a design insisted that a 'statue of a subject should [not] be placed looking down upon royalty'.[36] Considering how many different aspects the subscription committee had to keep in mind when planning a monument to Nelson in such an important place, it is not surprising that parliament appointed a select committee to examine the choice of design. This committee discussed the matter only after the building of the monument had actually begun, but it did not change the project.[37]

Such difficulties hampered the efforts of the subscription committees to raise sufficient money. In order to persuade subscribers that the investment would be to their own benefit, they published subscribers' lists

---

33 Schomburgk, pp. 245 and 147.

34 Mace, pp. 29-31, 37, 41, 42, 45.

35 Alison Willow Yarrington, *The Commemoration of the Hero 1800-1864: Monuments to the British Victors of the Napoleonic Wars* (Cambridge, 1980) [hereafter: Yarrington], pp. 282, 283.

36 James Hakewill, quoted in Mace, p. 255.

37 Mace, pp. 69-84, and Yarrington, pp. 318-25.

to give publicity to those who contributed.[38] They also sent out circular letters to stimulate further subscriptions.[39] The circular letter sent out by the Nelson Monument Committee in Edinburgh contained an engraving of a proposed monument on Calton Hill, although the committee had not yet been granted the use of the site and it was not sure whether it would collect enough money for the design (in the event, the committee did not collect enough money to realise the proposed monument in this form). To convey the impression that they were succeeding with their project they decided that 'the Building shall be begun, so soon as the subscriptions amount to a proper sum', but before all the necessary money was raised.[40] This proved to be an unwise decision, because interest in monuments to Admiral Nelson did fluctuate over time.

Shortly after the battle of Trafalgar the feeling of triumph engendered by the victory and the grief felt over Nelson's death had stimulated many subscriptions and civic pride was challenged in a kind of competition as newspapers reported the amounts of money that were collected in Liverpool and that were 'hourly increasing'.[41] Some cautious subscription committees either used only the amount they managed to collect in this first enthusiasm for the project of a Nelson monument (in Liverpool and in Birmingham, for example) or stated that the money that would be collected, after the foundation stone had been laid, would 'be applied towards increasing the height and dimensions of the Monument'.[42] In Hereford the committee was forced to refrain from putting a statue of Nelson on top of a column; they had to content with an urn that proved to be cheaper.[43] A project for a Nelson monument in Bristol had to be abandoned.[44]

The subscription committees for both the Edinburgh and the Norfolk monuments to Nelson hoped for further financial support, because their monuments were meant to serve useful purposes. The committee in Edin-

---

38 *Glasgow Herald*, 16, 20, 23 Dec. 1805 and 3 Jan. 1806; for Trafalgar Square, London: Yarrington, p. 291 and *Statement of Subscriptions*.

39 Public Record Office, WORKS 6.119, Nelson Committee Minute Book, 3 April 1838.

40 ECA, NMCM, ff. 9, 10 (letter), 16, 17 (site agreed on by 'Lord Provost, Magistrates and Council'), f. 18 (design decided), f. 6 (decision about beginning of the building).

41 *Glasgow Herald*, 22 Nov. 1805, before the inhabitants were called to meet and discuss the plan of a monument, 2 Dec. 1805; *The Times*, 26 Nov. 1805.

42 *Glasgow Herald*, 25 July 1806.

43 Flora Fraser, 'If You Seek His Monument', *The Nelson Companion*, ed. Colin White (Stroud, 1995), pp. 129-51 (p. 143).

44 *Naval Chronicle* (1806), p. 111.

burgh had applied at the Admiralty for money, because its monument would replace a flagstaff that was used for signalling in the Firth of Forth. After a project for a Nelson monument in his native county had failed, the new committee in Norfolk hoped for money from the lighthouse authority, Trinity House.[45] Both appeals failed, but the efforts of these committees were assisted by the revived interest in the heroes of the Napoleonic War after the battle of Waterloo and the triumphant end of the war in 1815.

While the reasons for and methods of raising money to build a monument to Admiral Nelson were generally the same, it is surprising that those in London (Trafalgar Square) and Norwich were not erected earlier, in direct response to the battle of Trafalgar. In the case of Norwich, the city leaders and its citizens had hoped that the Norfolk monument to Nelson would be erected in their town and consequently did not open a separate subscription for a monument in Norwich. The case may have been similar in London, where two monuments, in St. Paul's Cathedral and the Guildhall respectively, were being built and people also hoped that a monument paid for by nation-wide subscription would soon be placed in the capital. Such a national subscription failed for three reasons. First, local projects for monuments in the provinces appealed more to those living outside London, because they could enjoy the result more directly. Second, subscribing to a national monument did not seem attractive, since a similar project had failed just four years earlier, when joy at the Peace of Amiens (in 1802) replaced the earlier enthusiasm about the naval victories in the 1790s. When a new subscription was opened after the news of the battle of Trafalgar had reached Britain, several letters to editors of newspapers reflected the dislike of contributing to a new fund for a national monument, without having proof that the earlier subscriptions had been properly used.[46] Third, the fact that parliament voted money for monuments to the victories at Trafalgar and Waterloo in 1816 must have discouraged any project for a subscription for a national monument to Nelson.[47]

Since there is no indication of any opposition to monuments to Nelson, raised by subscription, in either London or Norwich, it appears that both

---

45 ECA, NMCM, f. 11, and Yarrington, pp. 141, 143.

46 *The Times*, 19 Nov., 19 and 27 Dec. 1805, 22 Jan. 1806; *Naval Chronicle* (1805), p. 382.

47 According to *The Times*, 9 Sept. 1824, there were again rumours of plans by the government to erect a 'National Monument' to Nelson or Trafalgar – influenced by the monument to the army in the form of Waterloo Bridge.

monuments were erected to fill the perceived lack of such a monument, with Norwich following the example of London. But why did this happen some thirty-five years after the battle of Trafalgar? Mace has argued that the ruling class wanted to distract attention from its problems with the Chartist movement at the time.[48] But, since the subscription for the monument in Trafalgar Square was initiated by old friends of Nelson or their relatives[49] and was supported by only a few eminent public figures (such as, the duke of Wellington), this argument alone does not seem convincing. Yarrington has claimed that 'the over-riding aim of the committee in its promotion of a national monument to Nelson was to utilize public enthusiasm for the hero in order to resolve the problems of planning the area of Trafalgar Square and its environs'.[50] Although it seems understandable that subscribers to a local monument might think of embellishing their town, it appears hard to believe that people would organize a *national* subscription to a monument for a war hero to solve some planning problems in a newly developed area of London. Considering how much the project was influenced by its surroundings, they may even have regarded the planning problems as a nuisance. Yarrington's idea – that rising interest in national heroes in the 1830s influenced the project of a monument[51] – is more in accordance with the declared wish of the committee itself, to build a monument to the 'glory of Lord Nelson and the Country which he so long and successfully served'.[52]

Whatever the additional reasons for these later Nelson monuments were, both subscription committees (in London and Norwich) overestimated the amounts of money they could collect. While the committee in Norwich – after some delay – somehow managed to erect its statue in 1852,[53] the Office of Woods, Forests and Land Revenues had finally to

48 Mace, p. 57.

49 Namely, T. M. Hardy (Nelson's flagcaptain at Trafalgar) and C. D. Scott (son of Nelson's secretary, John Scott, who was killed at Trafalgar), Mace, pp. 57, 58.

50 Yarrington, p. 281.

51 Yarrington, pp. 280, 281.

52 Quoted in Mace, p. 61. Although it needs to be remarked that sales of biographies of Nelson were only going up after the monument had helped to revive interest in him, Southey's *Life of Nelson* sold well only after Southey's death in 1843 and another work about Nelson was published again, because 'public attention appears again to be awakened to the merits of the Hero of Trafalgar, by the recently declared intention to erect a suitable testimonial to perpetuate the memory of his invaluable public services'. J. Drinkwater Bethune, *A Narrative of the Battle of St. Vincent* (London, 1840), pp. xi, xii).

53 *Norfolk Annals*, ii, 10.

take over responsibility in 1844 for the monument to Nelson in Trafalgar Square. Although this office introduced minor changes,[54] it could not alter the whole design, since the committee – perhaps following the example of the committee in Edinburgh – had already started to realise the design for the whole monument by building the column and putting a statue of Nelson on top of it. The change-over in managing the project did not accelerate the completion of the monument (which included bas-reliefs and lions) and it took until 1867 before it was finished.[55]

It seems that the success of subscriptions to a monument to Nelson depended on more than just the mood of the moment. Thus, the success of the subscription in Liverpool was particularly due to the city's reliance on its extensive trade with the West Indies that Nelson was thought to have saved. Birmingham lacked this direct feeling of indebtedness to Nelson, but its subscription also 'realised only one third of the amount collected in Liverpool'. This was in part because 'one section of the community, the Quakers, who were a particularly rich and influential if small group, was totally opposed to the erection of a monument glorifying war'.[56] On the other hand, the support of some individuals was essential. The widow of Captain Berry, whose husband had served under Nelson at the battles of the Nile and Trafalgar, 'collected from various Ladies at Ipswich', more than £60, whereas Vice-Admiral Page collected only a little over £3 in the same town. No other collection of this kind was made in any other British town. Collections from Jersey (more than £70), Bombay and Calcutta must have depended on similar private exertions as those made by Lady Berry. That the 'ruling class' did not make political use of the occasion may be seen in the fact that only fifteen 'H. M. Ships Companies' contributed; clearly, a successful subscription depended on the personal efforts of a member of the respective ship's company.[57] Other means of support were to dedicate the 'net proceeds of a concert' to the fund for a monument[58] or to publish a sermon whose sales would benefit a Nelson monument.[59]

---

54 Mace, pp. 98-100.

55 Mace, pp. 101-9.

56 Yarrington, p. 104, referring to *Aris's Birmingham Gazette*, 30 Dec. 1805.

57 *Statement of Subscriptions*, Towns in Britain: particularly p. 75; other places: pp. 77, 41, 46; H. M. Ship's Companies, p. 115.

58 *Nelson's Pillar*, p. 37.

59 *The Times*, 2 Jan. 1806, for the Norfolk monument.

II. The Forms of Monuments

Since the subscription committees depended on support from the public for the money raised, they had to consider public opinion in their choice of the style and design of the monument erected. This could even lead to the proposal for a building, to be used for some charitable purpose, that bore scant resemblance to a monument. Thus, the attitude of the Quakers in Birmingham led to the proposal for 'a dispensary and a post-office'[60] as a monument to Nelson in that town. In Edinburgh the subscription committee had decided on erecting a tower, part of which 'should be fitted up into half a dozen of neat cabins, for the gratuitous reception of *deserving wounded Seamen* or *Marines*; the preference to be given to those who have bled with the *Great Nelson*'.[61] This idea was changed into a caretaker's flat in the basement of the monument and this monument to Nelson is the only one that shows any trace of a charitable purpose.

When the subscription committees took purely artistic decisions about the design of their monuments they still had to consider the taste of the day. This was difficult to determine, because public monuments for war heroes did not have a long tradition in Britain. It would have been possible to develop features of sepulchral monuments, especially since Nelson had died so dramatically at the height of his most successful battle. Indeed, the design for the monument in Liverpool bears evidence of such an influence: 'The figures constituting the principal design are Nelson, Victory and Death [in the form of a skeleton] . . . Death lies in ambush for his victim; intimating, that he received the reward of his valour and the stroke of Death at the same moment.'[62] Other sepulchral features are more restrained. William Wilkins added to both of his designs for Nelson columns in Dublin and Yarmouth a sarcophagus 'which is placed on the Pedestal, over [the inscription] Trafalgar, to indicate that he there terminated his mortal career'.[63]

Even sepulchral monuments which had been erected since the second half of the eighteenth century, however, had abandoned any direct references to death, such as skulls and hourglasses. Rugg describes the phenomenon: 'Enlightened theories that removed the terrors from death were in perfect accord with the neoclassical aesthetics that were all-pervasive in

60 Langford, p. 306.
61 ECA, *Description*.
62 Wyatt (after whose design the monument was built), p. 5.
63 *Nelson's Pillar*, p. 17; Elmes, p. 516.

the visual arts of the late eighteenth and early nineteenth centuries.' She points out that instead of the representation of death, the painter Benjamin West demanded 'a monument [to Nelson] that would excite awe and veneration'.[64] Such a monument would have suited St. Paul's Cathedral, if it had been converted – as planned – into a British Hall of Fame. The architect responsible for the fabric of St. Paul's Cathedral had already proposed to erect a statue of Nelson directly over his actual tomb in the centre of the cathedral and he had been supported by sections of the public.[65] This idea was not too much in conflict with the character of the building, if one considers that services took place only in the choir, which was separated from the rest of the building by a wall. This proposal was not realized, however.

Influenced by such ideas about a place for secular worship and by the new character of sepulchral architecture, designs for monuments to Nelson tried to follow examples of classical antiquity and sought to avoid Christian symbols of death. Such symbolism was replaced by national and naval emblems, such as lions, representing Britain (in London on Trafalgar Square and in St. Paul's Cathedral, for example) or anchors, representing the navy (in St. Paul's Cathedral, in Barbados and in Hereford). While a design for the Nelson monument in Trafalgar Square proposed 'piled trophies of Nelson's valour', most other monuments seem to have tried to avoid too many different elements. A competitor simply claimed 'Allegory . . . cannot be tolerated' and a critic of the Nelson column in Yarmouth praised 'chasteness of decoration'.[66] At the same time a critic of the Guildhall monument to Nelson would have preferred a simple statue of the hero to 'a mere profile on a very small medallion' surrounded by figures of Britannia, 'London', Neptune, two seamen and many allegorical details.[67]

Equal simplicity was demanded in terms of the materials to be used. These, according to contemporary taste, should not be artificially coloured and, if combined, should harmonize in their natural colour.[68] The main alternatives in terms of materials chosen for outdoor monuments

---

64 Julie Rugg, 'From reason to regulation: 1760-1850', *Death in England. An Illustrated History*, ed. Peter C. Jupp and Clare Gittings (Manchester, 1999), pp. 202-29 (pp. 204, 208).

65 Yarrington, pp 61-9; *Gentleman's Magazine* (1805), 1202, and 1806, 254; *The Times*, 30 Nov., 7, 26, 30 Dec. 1805.

66 Mace, pp. 257, 246; Elmes, p. 521.

67 *The Times*, 2 May 1811.

68 Elmes, p. 519; Roscoe.

were stone on the one hand and brass on the other. The critics of 'everlasting Brass'[69] argued that it:

> is hardly to be trusted to as a means of communication with posterity, its intrinsic value and easy convertibility rendering it liable to destruction in the event of any foreign invasion or domestic disturbance (this is proved by the fewness of the ancient specimens which have been preserved).[70]

In the end both materials were used and, 'to protect the edifice from the Vandalism of wanton outrage',[71] some of the monuments (in Dublin, Yarmouth and Barbados, for example) were surrounded by fences.

As to the form of the monument itself, there raged a controversy between architects and sculptors. This discussion had started already with an argument between the sculptor John Flaxman and the architect Alexander Dufour at the time of the first subscription for a monument to naval victories in 1799-1801. Both referred to examples from antiquity, but, whereas Flaxman stressed 'how much more sentiment and interest there is in a fine human figure than can possibly be produced in the choicest piece of Architecture',[72] Dufour retorted: 'if we wished to perpetuate his [a hero's] memory, a piece of Architecture is better calculated for the purpose than a Statue . . . It is to the Pillars of Trajan, Antoninus, Pompey, . . . and their inscriptions, which have survived so many ages, that we are indebted for the memory of these great men; while their statues' have been mostly destroyed.[73] Some conciliatory attempts were made to combine the two forms of art and possibly even to include some paintings in a temple.[74] None of these ideas was adopted and ultimately, both main forms, the column and the statue, were frequently used to commemorate Nelson.

A pattern for a monumental column existed in Trajan's column in Rome, which was probably the most famous surviving monument to a Roman warrior. Its shaft is decorated with bas-reliefs which tell the story

---

69 Langford, p. 307; Mace, p. 254.

70 [Anon., 'Stimulator'], 'Hints regarding the expected designs for the Nelson Testimonial', *The Art-Union*, i (April 1839) [hereafter: 'Stimulator'], 46-47. See also Mace, p. 256, and on the subject in general Wood, p. 2; and Yarrington, pp. 43, 44.

71 Elmes, p. 532.

72 John Flaxman, *A Letter to the Committee for Raising the Naval Pillar, or Monument* (London, 1799), p. 7.

73 Alexander Dufour, *Letter to the Nobility and Gentry Composing the Committeee for Raising The Naval Pillar, or Monument* (London, 1800), p. 15.

74 Mace, pp. 246, 266, and 277; B. R. Haydon, *The Autobiography and Memoirs of Benjamin Robert Haydon 1786-1846*, ed. Alexander P. D. Penrose (London, 1927), p. 509.

of Trajan's campaigns in a series of pictures that are organized in a spiralling fashion up to the top, on which a statue of Trajan used to stand. Below the statue is a platform to which visitors were supposed to climb up a winding staircase built into the interior of the column. To imitate such elaborate bas-reliefs was well beyond the means of any subscription committee for a monument to Nelson. They sometimes (in Montreal, for example) placed bas-reliefs on the base of the column, but in the case of the column in London's Trafalgar Square even that proved to be beyond the means of the subscription committee. In any case, this left the question open as to how to design the shaft of the column itself. The Roman architect Vitruvius, whose work was widely known and admired, had divided columns into a 'masculine' and a 'feminine' type. Naturally only the 'masculine' Grecian Doric column and its Roman variant, the plain-shafted Tuscan column, were regarded as appropriate for a monument to a warrior. Consequently, the Nelson columns in Hereford and Montreal have plain shafts, while William Wilkins designed those for Dublin and Yarmouth with Doric flutes and a Doric capital. He had intended a statue of Nelson on top of both of them. This was executed in Dublin, where he did not survey the erection of the monument himself, but he changed his plan for the later column in Yarmouth.

Wilkins seems to have had doubts about simply copying Trajan's column. He might have agreed with the critic, who pointed out at the time that Trajan's column was 'raised by the Romans in degenerate times, when the arts were declining, from a vain emulation to vie in height with the Egyptian obelisks' with 'a round tower in masquerade'.[75] Wilkins, who had travelled for four years through Greece and Italy and was a great admirer of ancient Greek architecture,[76] may well have felt inclined to introduce more Grecian elements. A contemporary observer noticed that he had copied the 'decoration of the lower structure' of his Nelson column from that of the Thrasyllus monument in Athens.[77] The same author admired the platform in Yarmouth with its statue of Britannia, supported by six caryatids on top of the monument, although he was surprised about the number six, as 'original, and extremely elegant'.[78] Wilkins may here again have been in-

75 [Anon.], 'Of the Prevailing Taste for Isolated Columns as Public Monuments', *New Monthly Magazine and Literary Journal*, i (1821), 335-8 [hereafter: 'Isolated Columns'] (pp. 335, 336).

76 *Dictionary of National Biography*, xxi, 267-269 (267).

77 Elmes, p. 525.

78 Elmes, p. 528.

spired by Greek monuments. A Corinthian column in Delphi is surmounted by three caryatids, who carry a tripod, the trophy in a choragic competition. Another choragic monument – the Lysikrates monument in Athens – is decorated with six Corinthian half-columns. The Corinthian column is obviously chosen deliberately, because the Acanthus leaves in its capital represent not only death, but also immortality,[79] an imagery which was known even in Wilkins' day, since the Corinthian column had been frequently used on sepulchral monuments. So Wilkins introduced Corinthian elements of monumental sculpture, symbolizing immortality, while avoiding at the same time the 'feminine' Corinthian column and capital itself.

It has been claimed that the Corinthian order was used for Nelson's Column on Trafalgar Square, because the monument had to harmonize with the Corinthian columns in the front of Wilkins' National Gallery on the northern side of the same square.[80] Here again William Railton, the artist who had proposed the overall design, might have been aware of the Corinthian symbolism of death and immortality. This had been stressed, even in antiquity, by executing the Acanthus leaves in bronze to imitate their naturally green colour.[81] Railton's design was changed several times in several respects and the planned bronze statue of Nelson was finally executed in stone,[82] but the bronze Acanthus leaves of the capital were never questioned. The choice of the Corinthian order may here, again, have been made deliberately to use the symbolism of death and immortality. Some criticized the choice and a representative of the Treasury even wondered, whether the flutes could be altered 'so as to suit a Doric capital',[83] but the column was also praised for its 'lofty and elegant proportions'.[84]

The great disadvantage of a column to a hero was that the commemorated person could not be easily represented. A statue on top, 'raised so high above the natural point of focus of vision, would lose all distinctness of expression . . . unless they [its features] are colossal, and overcharged with expression beyond nature, even to caricature'.[85] When Nelson's statue

---

79 Joseph Rykwert, 'The Corinthian Order', *Arena, The Architectural Association Journal*, 82 (1966), 7-10 [hereafter: Rykwert], (8, 9).

80 Yarrington, p. 295.

81 Rykwert, p. 9.

82 Mace, pp. 73, 89-90; Yarrinton, pp. 308-10.

83 References in Yarrington, p. 297 and Mace, p. 101. The plan to erect a Corinthian column was also criticised in *The Times*, 4 Mar.1839.

84 *The Illustrated London News*, i (1842), 266.

85 'Isolated Columns', 336.

was on show, before it was mounted on top of the column in Trafalgar Square, an observer remarked that the face had 'sharp, angular features, the expression of great activity of mind, but of little of mental grandeur'.[86] To solve such a dilemma, the monument in Hereford, which bears an urn on top, has a portrait-medallion of Nelson on its base. Some proposed designs had included a statue of Nelson in front of the base of a column,[87] but none of them was executed.

The possibility of representing Nelson himself was the great advantage of statues. This, however, posed the question in what kind of dress Nelson should be portrayed as wearing. Only the early monument in Liverpool shows Nelson as a nude with nothing but a cloak over his right shoulder, thus hiding the missing arm, and over the lower part of his body. When the choice for a monument on Trafalgar Square was about to be made, somebody insisted:

> Surely it is not necessary to hand down specimens of the bad taste of a nation – to perpetuate in stone the ephemeral fashions of the times . . . Marble should perpetuate character, not costume – should exhibit the attributes of the mind, not the decorations of the body.[88]

Several designs showed Nelson in 'classical costume', one even intended him to be 'lion-skin habilimented'.[89] A sculptor vehemently protested: 'What is the English tar to say when he sees his beloved Nelson in a Roman petticoat!'[90] Other artists and various subscription committees seem to have agreed with this view and so all other monuments that represent Nelson full-length show him in an admiral's uniform.

Realism in the representation of Nelson posed the additional problem of whether to show him idealized with two arms or to portray him with only one arm. A pamphlet published shortly after the battle of Trafalgar argued that a statue of Nelson in Norfolk should show him with two arms[91] and the Italian sculptor Canova submitted a design for a sarcopha-

86 *The Illustrated London News*, iii (1843) 289.

87 Mace, pp. 246, 252, 253, 255, 261, 266; Langford, p. 307; NMM, PAG 6723.

88 'Stimulator', p. 47.

89 Yarrington, p. 82; Mace, pp. 253, 261.

90 Cockerell quoted in David Irvin, 'Sentiment and Antiquity: European Tombs 1750-1830', *Mirrors of Mortality. Studies in the Social History of Death*, ed. Joachim Whaley (London, 1981), pp. 131-53 [hereafter Irvin], p.135.

91 Referred to in Trevor Fawcett, *The Rise of English Provincial Art. Artists, Patrons, and Institutions outside London, 1800-1830* (Oxford, 1974) [hereafter Fawcett], p. 148.

gus on which Nelson can be seen with two arms.[92] It has been argued that the sculptor instinctively obeyed an artistic law, which made him represent Nelson's body seen from the right. He could easily have presented the image in reverse and hidden the defect of the missing right arm.[93] Considering that it was widely know – even in Italy – that Nelson had only one arm and considering that Canova presented him in Roman dress, it rather seems that he wished to idealize him and not represent him as he was in life. At the same time, the British sculptor Flaxman also worked out how to deal with Nelson's major physical defect: 'in the execution of a statue the loss of his arm might so be indicated yet obscured that it would not injure the general effect of the work, or he might be represented . . . in his perfect figure'.[94] In the event Flaxman was commissioned to execute a statue of Nelson after the design of Richard Westmacott, who had decided to be truthful in his representation.[95] The same Westmacott executed the Liverpool monument (after a design by M. C. Wyatt) and also the statues of Nelson in Birmingham and Barbados,[96] and he thus contributed to the representation of Nelson with only one arm. This does not mean that this approach was uncontroversial. One of the critics of the monument in Birmingham commented indignantly:

> Were a great man, Admiral or General, to have both legs shot off in Battle, should we then put up the mutilated trunk – a statue without legs – in the market place? Can we not imagine ourselves as meeting great men in a future state, whole and perfect?[97]

The subscription committee for a Nelson monument in London's Trafalgar Square, however, would accept only a naturalistic representation of Nelson with one arm.[98] His image by the late 1830s seems to have been too settled to allow for a right arm to be added.

Some statues of Nelson presented him at the top of a conically shaped group of figures and thus could add a certain message to the pure representation of the hero. Hence, a group of allegorical figures was adopted in Liverpool:

---

92 Pietro Verrua, *Orazio Nelson nel Pensiero e nell'Arte del Foscolo e del Canova* (Padova, 1919) [hereafter Verrua], opposite p. 13.

93 Verrua, pp. 24, 25.

94 Quoted in Irvin, p. 137.

95 Yarrington, p. 104; Margaret Whinney, *Sculpture in Britain 1530 to 1830*, revised by John Physick (London, 1988), p. 384.

96 Yarrington, pp. 127, 104.

97 Quoted in Yarrington, p. 113. See also p. 114.

98 Yarrington, p. 290.

> to exhibit, in the strongest manner, the glory and happiness of the hero who dies in the defence of his country; and who, in the act of grasping at another crown, which the Goddess of Victory is placing on his sword, is insensible to the stroke which terminates his glorious career.

Added to the principal figures of Nelson, Victory and Death are 'his country [Britannia], mourning for her loss, . . . her navy eager to avenge it [and] a conquered enemy', all on a lower level.[99] In St. Paul's Cathedral the figure of Nelson stands on a base, which illustrates his three most famous battles and which is surrounded on the right by a lion and on the left by the figure of Minerva (or Britannia) instructing two young midshipmen, who are looking up to Nelson. When a subscription did not raise sufficient money to pay for an elaborate allegorical group, bas-reliefs were sometimes used to convey a certain message. Reliefs on the pedestal of the Nelson monument in Birmingham showed, for example, 'Victory embellishing a ship's prow [and] Birmingham . . . mourning her loss'.[100]

Other types of monuments were less elaborate in their ornaments. The Scottish towers to the memory of Nelson in Edinburgh and Forres have hardly any decorations and the obelisks in Glasgow and Portsdown Hill are also quite plain, although the later contains a small bust of Nelson at its upper end. 'Cleopatra's Needle' on the Embankment in London was given as a present to the British people by the viceroy of Egypt in 1819, as 'a worthy memorial of our distinguished countrymen Nelson and Abercromby'. So the inscription of the 1870s claims, but it has no decoration that specifically refers to Nelson.

Even the major impact on public opinion of Nelson's achievements was not sufficient to justify yet another monumental celebration, at a time when there was more interest in commemorating civil heroes and when public opinion preferred, after the disastrous Crimean War, to commemorate the ordinary soldiers, instead of their leaders.[101]

III. The Later History of the Monuments

Since most of the monuments to Nelson that were erected in public spaces were financed by subscription, they remained private property after they had been completed. Eager to spend the collected money on the realisation of a beautiful design, the subscription committees had often not

---

[99] Roscoe.

[100] Fawcett, p. 148.

[101] Yarrington, pp. 334-336.

calculated the costs of the future upkeep of the monument. An exception in this respect had been the committee for Nelson's Pillar in Dublin, which had considered future costs and had laid so much money aside that it was possible to claim in 1948: 'To-day the Pillar is a thriving business. Last year more than £1,200 was taken at the turnstile and distributed by the trustees among a number of charitable bodies in the city'.[102] The Birmingham committee was lucky that someone bestowed a bequest 'for cleaning the statue and basement'.[103] Other monuments later passed into the hands of their town governments[104] or other public bodies. When the Admiralty took over responsibility for the obelisk on Portsdown Hill – that had been erected by members of the navy, who had taken part in the battle of Trafalgar – a report stated that 'the Nelson Monument . . . is in a very bad state of repair, and that, if it is not practically rebuilt, it will very possibly collapse at an early date'.[105]

The badly planned Nelson tower in Edinburgh on the other hand profited from its attractive position and food and drink were sold in the basement from 1828.[106] It also proved useful for practical purposes: a time-ball was installed in 1853 and the flagstaff was used 'to indicate the days when the London steamers sailed, and arrived'. Notwithstanding its unimaginative exterior, an effort was made to construct a Nelson-site: the ground floor of the monument was used for a small Nelson exhibition and in the 1920s two naval organizations even competed for the responsibility of 'flying Lord Nelson's signal from the Monument on Trafalgar Day'.[107]

Trafalgar Square in London was used for similar celebrations of Trafalgar Day. It was also used for propaganda purposes during the Second World War and later an attempt was made to develop it into a place for naval celebrations in general when the busts of Jellicoe and Beatty were added on Trafalgar Day 1948.[108] The square also became known for dem-

---

102 *Nelson's Pillar*, p.11; Patrick Henchy, 'Nelson's Pillar', *Dublin Historical Record*, 10 (1948), 53-63 [hereafter Henchy], p. 63.

103 Langford, p. 309.

104 ECA, Monuments Catalogue, supplementary file, 32 Calton Hill.

105 Public Record Office, ADM 116/581, 11 Jan. 1899.

106 Edinburgh City Library, John Smith, *The Calton Hill and its Monuments.*

107 *The Nelson Monument, Edinburgh; with The Life of Horatio Lord Nelson by Robert Southey* (Edinburgh, 1882) ix; ECA, Monuments Catalogue, supplementary file, 32 Calton Hill.

108 *The Nelson Dispatch*, ii, part 1 (Jan. 1985) 19 and part 2 (April 1985) 39; Mace picture-appendix no. 50 'National Service is up to YOU' and no. 51, 52; Marcus Whiffen, 'The Story of Trafalgar Square', *The Listener*, 40 (1948), 639-640 (639).

onstrations against government politics, since it offered so much space close to the seat of government and parliament and Mace claims that the fountains were not only introduced to fill the space, but rather to restrict huge gatherings of people.[109]

In other places it was more the monument itself that became subject of controversy. A contemporary critic of the Dublin monument remarked that 'The statue of Nelson records . . . the transformation of our senate into a discount office'. Towards the end of the nineteenth century and again in 1923 attempts were made to get the monument removed, although at least partly 'to suit the modern traffic arrangements'. Eventually W. B. Yeats, who at that time was a Senator, stepped in and declared:

> Nelson's Pillar should not be broken up. It represents the feeling of Protestant Ireland for a man who helped to break the power of Napoleon. The life and work of the people who erected it is a part of our tradition. I think we should accept the whole past of this nation and not pick and choose.[110]

The IRA disagreed. For the fiftieth anniversary of the Easter Rising in 1966, at a time when the group was rather weak, it was 'forced to turn on monuments'. It blew up the statue and the upper part of the monument in Dublin (the rest was later dismantled) as well as the early arch erected to Nelson near Cork.[111]

There have been discussions about removing the Nelson monuments in Montreal, where the French speakers form the majority of the population, and Barbados, where the statue of Nelson is seen as a relic of colonialism.[112] No other monument to Nelson has been destroyed, though the statue on the top of the column in Montreal was so often damaged that it had to be removed to a local museum. It seems that the public in these cities has either adopted Yeats' view to accept these monuments as part of its past or it has decided to include them in their current activities.[113]

---

[109] Mace, pp. 87, 88.

[110] Henchy, pp. 60-2.

[111] J. Bowyer Bell, *The Secret Army. The IRA 1916-1979* (Dublin, 1990), pp. 343, 344. Colin White, 'The Immortal Memory', *The Nelson Companion*, ed. Colin White, pp. 1-31 (p. 4).

[112] *The Nelson Dispatch*, ii, part 10 (April 1987), 191; v, part 11 (July 1996), 386; and v, part 12 (Oct. 1996), 443.

[113] The research for this essay was made possible by a grant from The Carnegie Trust for the Universities of Scotland.

Nelson's Column, Yarmouth, by J. Preston and L. Clark. This print shows the Column designed by William Wilkins in its ideal shape. The sarcophagus was never executed. (National Maritime Museum, Greenwich)

Nelson's Pillar, Sackville-Street, Dublin. Etching and Engraving by R. Winkles after George Petrie, 1829. (National Maritime Museum, Greenwich)

John Flaxman's sketch for a Nelson Monument shows Nelson 'in his perfect figure', representing Nelson with two arms, ca. 1806. (National Maritime Museum, Greenwich)

Statue to the Memory of Admiral Lord Nelson, at Birmingham. From *Gentleman's Magazine*, May 1812, Pl. II, p. 217. (National Maritime Museum, Greenwich)

Nelson's Column, Bridgetown, Barbados. Lithography by W. L. Walton after a sketch by W. S. Hedges. From Robert H. Schomburgk's *History of Barbados*, 1847. (National Library of Scotland, Edinburgh)

Katharina Rennhak

Looks and Language – Performing and Communicating an Ideal Poetics

Shelley's *Prometheus Unbound* and *The Cenci*

> Names are there, Nature's sacred watch-words, they
> Were borne aloft in bright emblazonry;
> The nations thronged around, and cried aloud,
> As with one voice, Truth, liberty, and love!
> Suddenly fierce confusion fell from heaven.
> Among them: there was strife, deceit, and fear:
> Tyrants rushed in, and did divide the spoil.
> (*Prometheus Unbound*, I.648-654)[1]

Prometheus' notoriously bleak vision of what seems to refer to the French Revolution and its aftermath encapsulates Shelley's disillusionment with contemporary socio-political events and conceptions of revolutionary transformations of society. In 1819 the 'poet-legislator' sets out to develop his idealist political poetics of liberation and change in two plays, *Prometheus Unbound* and *The Cenci*, convinced that '[t]he great writers of our own age are . . . the companions and forerunners of some unimagined change in our social condition or the opinions which cement it'.[2]

To understand Shelley's political poetics it is essential to notice that Prometheus' summary of the revolutionary trajectory is misleading in one important point: under the bad influence of the Furies, who provide him with the horrible vision cited above, he wrongly attributes the revolutionaries' failure to effect a lasting change to a mysterious and incomprehensible 'confusion [that] fell from heaven'. After the first act of *Prometheus Unbound* the protagonist – and with him the reader of Shelley's lyrical drama – will have learned, however, that there is nothing either contingent or providential about the seemingly deterministic vicious circle that endlessly perpetuates tyranny and dooms to failure even those revolutions that propagate the right ideals. Rather, as Purinton among others has pointed out, '[h]uman kind is held captive by its own creation' of an ideology that is

1 All references to Shelley's poetry and prose are to *The Complete Works of Percy Bysshe Shelley*, ed. Roger Ingpen and Walter E. Peck (10 vols., London, 1965). References to *Prometheus Unbound* and *The Cenci* (vol. ii) are hereafter cited in the text.

2 'Preface [*Prometheus Unbound*]', in *The Complete Works of Percy Bysshe Shelley*, ii, 173.

based on a 'tyrant/slave dichotomy' and can only conceive of revolutionary change within this system.[3] Although Prometheus initially seems to personify the good force that has pitted himself against his evil other, Jupiter, the first act shows the current slave and rebel to be a potential future tyrant.[4] As long as Prometheus contemplates revenge and only waits for the hour which

> Shall drag thee, cruel King, to kiss the blood
> From these pale feet, which then might trample thee
> If they disdained not such a prostrate slave
> (I.49-52)

he cannot bring about a more desirable world or effect any fundamental change in society, but can merely reverse the power relationship and exchange slave for tyrant and vice-versa.[5] To escape the seemingly endless duality of master and slave mankind has to envision an entirely new system.

Prometheus feels right from the beginning of the play what the 'beautiful idealisms'[6] are that will serve as the basis on which the perfect new model of society can be constructed. Even in his very first monologue he suddenly pauses in the hateful tirade he launches at Jupiter and realizes, 'I hate no more' (I.57). At the end of Act I he is persuaded that 'all hope was vain but love' (I.824). *Prometheus Unbound* obviously does not stage a learning process for its protagonist. Prometheus rather bears the seeds of

---

3 Marjean D. Purinton, *Romantic Ideology Unmasked: The Mentally Constructed Tyrannies in Dramas of William Wordsworth, Lord Byron, Percy Shelley, and Joanna Baillie* (London, 1994), pp. 95ff. Also cf., e.g., Ronald Tetreault, *The Poetry of Life: Shelley and Reform* (Toronto, 1987), p. 132: 'It is thus not just patriarchy which is the oppressive force . . . , but the pervasive conception . . . that all human relationships must of necessity be based on a pattern of dominance and submission.'

4 Cf. the beginning of Prometheus' first monologue (I.1-17), which teems with parallels between 'Thou and I' (I.3), Jupiter and Prometheus, and betrays that the latter is – at that point still – Jupiter's kindred spirit rather than a hero who offers a truly alternative system to his antagonist's tyrannical reign. It is hardly necessary to point out once again that '[t]he intimacy of Prometheus's relation with Jupiter . . . has been noted by almost all critics of the drama'. Michael Simpson, *Closet Performances: Political Exhibition and Prohibition in the Dramas of Byron and Shelley* (Stanford, 1998), p. 250. According to Jean Hall, 'The Socialized Imagination: Shelley's *The Cenci* and *Prometheus Unbound*', *Studies in Romanticism*, 23 (1984), 341: 'Milton Wilson was the first to suggest that the Phantasm of Jupiter is a self-projection of Prometheus.' *Shelley's Later Poetry: A Study of His Prophetic Imagination* (New York, 1959), pp. 63ff.

5 Cf. 'A Philosophical View of Reform', in *The Complete Works of Percy Bysshe Shelley*, vii, 55.

6 'Preface [*Prometheus Unbound*]', ii, 174.

love within himself right from the start. What Demogorgon summarizes in his famous closing words – that 'Gentleness, Virtue, Wisdom and Endurance/ . . . are the seals of that most firm assurance / Which bars the pit over Destruction's strength' (IV.562-64) – is what Prometheus seems to know intuitively from the very first act onwards.

This conception of his protagonist is firmly in line with Shelley's poetics, which is idealist in so far as he never fails to adhere to the belief that man is essentially good: 'a poet considers the vices of his contemporaries as the temporary dress in which his creations must be arrayed, and which cover without concealing the eternal proportions of their beauty'.[7] In her famous commentary of the 1839 'Note on Prometheus Unbound', Mary Shelley is one of the first critics to level the charge of naivety apparently inherent in a theory of social change that is based on such an optimistic conception of man: 'Shelley believed that mankind had only to will that there should be no evil, and there would be none.'[8] While I do not agree with Everest that this is a '*seriously* misleading statement',[9] I will argue that – though Mary Shelley is right in emphasizing the importance of acts of human volition in her husband's theory of change – any charge of fatuity is beside the point. The very fact that the new world does not come to be realized until the last act of *Prometheus Unbound*, although Prometheus knows about the 'beautiful idealisms' right from the beginning, indicates that Shelley's drama revolves around the question of how to make these well-known idealisms come true; it investigates the complex and anything but simplistic mechanisms which have to be enacted to effectively realize a better world. Expanding on Pyle's remark that '[i]n Shelley's Promethean theater of political speech acts, truth is not something to be recognized but that which must be liberated',[10] this essay seeks to explore the mechanisms of liberation envisaged by Shelley.

---

7 'A Defence of Poetry', in *The Complete Works of Percy Bysshe Shelley*, vii, 117.

8 Mary Shelley, 'Note on *Prometheus Unbound* by Mrs. Shelley', in *The Complete Works of Percy Bysshe Shelley*, ii, 269.

9 Kelvin Everest, '"Mechanism of a kind yet unattempted": The Dramatic Action of *Prometheus Unbound*', in *Coleridge, Keats and Shelley: Contemporary Critical Essays*, ed. Peter J. Kitson (Basingstoke, 1996), p. 188, my emphasis. According to Everest, Mary Shelley's statement is 'seriously misleading', because it fails to conceive the fact that the play is 'preoccupied with questions of the relation of individual human agency to great and apparently impersonal processes of change in history'.

10 Forest Pyle, *The Ideology of Imagination: Subject and Society in the Discourse of Romanticism* (Stanford, 1995), p. 114.

I will argue that Shelley develops his theory of how love can be set free, transmitted and realized on the plot-level of *Prometheus Unbound*, while he puts it into theatrical practice and tries to make it work on the intended popular audience of *The Cenci* – a drama that on its plot-level shows why love often (but not necessarily) fails to spread. In the course of this argument I hope to cast some new light on the often discussed peculiar relation between *Prometheus Unbound* and *The Cenci* – the two plays that despite their being written at the same time[11] are so different in form and content that many critics see them as contradicting each other. Last but not least, this will also allow me to qualify interpretations of Shelley's plays and poetics that see him entangled in the Godwinian dilemma caused by the incompatibility of the assumption that man is the product of his circumstances with the simultaneous belief in the (gradual) perfectibility of man. Ulmer, for example, stresses the fact that Shelley addresses *Prometheus Unbound* to 'the highly refined imagination of the more select classes of poetical readers with beautiful idealisms of moral excellence'.[12] He goes on to comment ironically: 'The Shelleyan text either changes viewers by imaging their beliefs, which easily dissipates change in reconfirmation, or fails to change them at all.'[13] My aim is to show that the content of *Prometheus Unbound* and the composition of *The Cenci* point to the poet's relentless endeavour to tackle the question of how exactly the ideal conceptions of the poet can be transmitted. Shelley contemplates and uses various interacting means in order to ameliorate the less imaginative majority, that is, to make them unveil their covered beauty, their love at heart.

I. Speech Acts in *Prometheus Unbound*

While Shelley argues in his essay 'A Philosophical View of Reform' that 'an object . . . is, because we will it, and may be, because we hope and desire it',[14] the plot of *Prometheus Unbound* shifts the emphasis and demonstrates that the object – a better society – *is* the way it is, because we *say* it is the way it is. The analysis of two central scenes of the play – Prometheus' recalling of the curse in the first act and Asia's encounter with De-

---

11 Shelley wrote *The Cenci* between act three and four of *Prometheus Unbound.*

12 'Preface [*Prometheus Unbound*]', ii, 174.

13 William A. Ulmer, *Shelleyan Eros; The Rhetoric of Romantic Love* (Princeton, 1990), p. 112.

14 'A Philosophical View of Reform', vii, 43.

mogorgon in II.4 – will prove the thesis that according to the poet-legislator's theory of political change the new world order, which is based on a concept of love that constantly transcends 'fixed identities' and 'collapse[s] all the differences between the Self and the Other',[15] is liberated not through mere acts of volition, but through volitional speech acts or performative utterances.[16]

To free and realize the true ideals Prometheus must first 'recall' his curse against Jupiter.[17] With his curse, put on Jupiter 3000 years before, Prometheus initiated the tyrant's reign of terror. That is, the oppressive system based on antagonism came into force only because of and at the same time as the enunciation of the curse: 'then my words had power' (I.69), as Prometheus observes. Now, he wishes: 'The curse / Once breathed on thee I would recall' (I.58ff.) – and the action that ensues shows that all the different meanings that the word 'recall' can signify are equally relevant. Prometheus has to *remember* the exact wording of the curse – or rather has to be reminded of what he said. Also, the curse has to be *uttered once again* – not by Prometheus himself, because nothing evil shall 'pass again / [his] lips' (I.219ff.), but by the Phantasm of Jupi-

15 Martin Procházka, 'Titanic Myth and Discourses of Subjectivity: *Prometheus Unbound*, Byron's *Manfred* and *May* by K.H. Macha', in *Romantic Discourses: Papers Delivered at the Symposium on the Bicentenary of the Birth of Percy Bysshe Shelley, Ahrenshoop, October 2-5, 1992*, ed. Horst Höhne (Essen, 1994), p. 116.

16 I draw here on Austin's definition of the 'performative utterance': 'The name is derived, of course, from "perform", the usual verb with the noun "action": it indicates that the issuing of the utterance is the performing of an action – it is not normally thought of as just saying something.' J. L. Austin, *How to Do Things with Words: The William James Lectures delivered at Harvard University in 1955*, ed. J. O. Urmson and Marina Sibisà (Oxford, 1975). The big difference between Austin's performative utterance and Shelley's speech acts is, of course, that Austin holds that a performative utterance is only 'happy', i.e., successfully performed, if it conforms to certain social conventions: 'There must exist an accepted conventional procedure having a certain conventional effect, that procedure to include the uttering of certain words by certain persons in certain circumstances'. (p. 14). In contrast, Shelley endows speech acts with the power to effectively change social conventions. Cf. Angela Esterhammer's excellent study *The Romantic Performative: Language and Action in British and German Romanticism* (Stanford, 2000), which 'delinate[s] parallels in Romantic-period philosophy of language' and J. L. Austin's and Judith Butler's 20th-century theories of the 'performative' (xi).

17 In a different context Angela Esterhammer has recently suggested a reading of the curse scene which is similar to mine. Cf. her 'Romantic Voices, Romantic Courses: Blake's *Tiriel*, Hölderlin's *Tod des Empedokles*, Shelley's *Prometheus Unbound*', in *Romantic Voices, Romantic Poetics*, ed. Christoph Bode and Katharina Rennhak (Trier, 2005), pp. 28-30.

ter which Prometheus calls onto the stage – and which appears as soon as it is called. When Prometheus sees the Phantom, he can recall (that is: remember) the curse, because he sees it '[w]ritten as on a scroll' (I.261) in Jupiter's gloomy, defiant and hateful countenance. Yet, this is not enough, and the curse has to be verbalized, as well: 'yet speak: Oh, speak' (I.261). The verbal repetition of the curse is necessary for at least two reasons.[18] First, Prometheus only fully understands how hopeless and futile his struggle with Jupiter is when his own curse is launched against himself by his archenemy's phantom. Second, hearing the curse once again, Prometheus comes to realize that: 'It doth repent me: words are quick and vain' (I.303). What are we to make of that statement? 'Words are quick' – they are rashly spoken. 'Grief for awhile is blind, and so was mine' (I.304), the protagonist admits. But 'vain'? Does Prometheus suggest that "words" are 'empty' and of no consequence? His original curse certainly was anything but vain. It was nothing less than the foundation of Jupiter's reign. What he means, then, is obviously that words are never final, that actions performed by words, regimes established by a rashly spoken curse, can be 're-called', that is: *renounced*, taken back, cancelled. When Jupiter's phantom launches the curse a second time 'no thought inform[s its] empty voice' (I.249). Thus, it is vain and ineffective, because it is spoken without any intention, without any conviction. The curse, the founding act of a reign of terror, is vain and can be recalled as soon as its words are at variance with the convictions of the speaker. To say it with the 'Preface': If 'the equilibrium between institutions and opinions' is upset, it has to be and can be 'restored'.[19] Words have no absolute power.[20]

---

18 Simpson's analysis of the interrelation of written and spoken words in Shelley's closet drama (which presents the reader with a written text) on the one hand, and in a potential performance of the play (which verbalizes the written words) on the other, adds an interesting third reason. Cf. Simpson, *Closet Performances*, pp. 159ff.

19 'Preface [*Prometheus Unbound*]', ii, 173.

20 It is, thus, obvious that Shelley's speech-act theory locates the force of an utterance at just that point where – according to Austin – it cannot be (solely) placed: in the speaker's conviction or intention. The force of social conventions, without which the Austinian performative utterance is ineffective, can only be put aside in *Prometheus Unbound*, because its protagonist is more than human. The plural of 'opinions' in the quote from the preface, however, points to Shelley's awareness that a volitional utterance of just one human being has no power to establish a new order. It will be shown that he also tackles the problem of how a conviction can spread, how love can be communicated, so that mankind might eventually speak with one voice and thus effect change.

They have great power, however, if they are backed up by strong convictions. In II.4, which stages Asia's encounter with Demogorgon, Asia also learns that social systems are based to a great extent on the verbalization of ideas, hopes and beliefs. After the play has demonstrated how words can be recalled, it focuses on how a new idea can be enacted simply by saying it is real.[21] Demogorgon answers Asia's first question, 'What canst thou Tell?', with the words 'All things thou dar'st demand.' (II.4.8) The ensuing conversation, however, remains unsatisfactory for Asia and reader alike. Demogorgon's answers to Asia's questions – for example 'Who made the living world?' (II.4.9), 'Who made all / That it contains?' (II.4.9ff.) or 'who made terror'? (II.4.19) – remain opaque and enigmatic. In fact, it seems as if – contrary to what he promised – Demogorgon cannot provide any convincing answer. Eventually, however, Asia realizes that his 'All things thou dar'st demand' never meant 'I can provide an answer to every question'. Demogorgon explains: 'I spoke but as ye speak' and 'If the abysm / Could vomit forth its secrets. But a voice / Is wanting, the deep truth is imageless' (II.4.112-116). Apparently, Asia has to learn to conceptualize and to put into words her own desire. She has to verbalize 'the deep truth' which she bears within. Rather than 'gaze / On the revolving world' and try to explain and put into words the bleak reality, that is, she has to give her voice to the image enclosed within her own core. 'What [would it avail] to bid speak / Fate, Time, Occasion, Chance and Change?', Demogorgon asks rhetorically. 'To these / All things are subject but eternal Love.' (II.4.118-120) It is Asia whom Demogorgon 'bids', encourages, to speak instead. She alone is able to initiate the transformation of society by demanding, that is by firmly and hopefully requesting the truth within her. Indeed, she formulates 'her next question as an imperative demand':[22]

> One more demand; and do thou answer me
> As mine own soul would answer, did it know
> That which I ask. Prometheus shall arise
> Henceforth the sun of this rejoicing world:
> When shall the destined hour arrive?
> (II.4.124-128)

Significantly, Asia's verbalization of the 'deep truth' within herself, does not offer a definition or representation (and fixation) of a theoretical

---

21 My argument in this paragraph draws heavily on Simpson, *Closet Performances*, pp. 164-66.

22 Simpson, *Closet Performances*, p. 165.

concept of love, but rather a performative demand. Her demand is couched in terms which bespeak her firm conviction that the sun will rise, that a new society is dawning; and this time she does not receive yet another enigmatic answer. Rather the effect of her 'demand' – 'When shall the destined hour arrive?' – is the immediate arrival of 'the immortal Hours' (II.4.140) on the stage.[23] Only after Asia has had the same experience as Prometheus – that words have the potential to create the reality they envision – can the dream come true. Jupiter will be dethroned and finally destroyed by Demogorgon at the beginning of the next act.

II. The Transmission of Love in *Prometheus Unbound*

What remains to be investigated is – still – the most precarious step in Shelley's visionary theory of the performative power of beautiful idealisms. It has been shown how the beautiful idealisms come true if only love – backed up by hope and confidence – is put into demanding words. What is still unsettled is the question of how love is being transmitted.

Prometheus' task has not been fulfilled in the first act by simply recalling the curse. Not only is he, after Jupiter's Phantasm has disappeared, tempted by Mercury's plea for submission and by the horrible and hopeless visions the Furies set up before him; he also realizes that he cannot effect a transformation of society without Asia's help, without the help of she whose love was never subdued. Asia in turn cannot survive without Prometheus. The Furies explain the dilemma as follows:

> The good want power, but to weep barren tears.
> The powerful goodness want: worse need for them.
> The wise want love; and those who love want wisdom;
> And all best things are thus confused to ill.
> (I.625-627)

The ensuing action suggests that we are to substitute 'Prometheus' for the wise and powerful and 'Asia' for the good and love. At the end of Act I, Prometheus calls for Asia, who has been living in exile in an Indian vale for centuries and whose 'transforming presence . . . would fade / If it were mingled not with thine [Prometheus']' (I.832ff.), as Panthea explains. In the first scene of Act II, then, the audience is shown how love can be communicated from one person to another: it is transmitted not through words, but via the eyes. Not only do the two sisters of love, Asia and Panthea, almost exclusively exchange news and ideas by firmly looking

[23] Cf. Simpson, *Closet Performances*, p. 166.

into each other's eyes – again and again we read sentences like: 'Lift up thine eyes, and let me read thy dream' (II.1.55ff.); but *what* Asia reads in Panthea's eyes is that the same channel of communication worked for Prometheus and Panthea. The latter tells Asia that, in one of the two dreams she had while sleeping at Prometheus' feet, he made the following request:

> Sister of her whose footsteps pave the world
> With loveliness – more fair than aught but her,
> Whose shadow thou art – lift thine eyes on me.

And she goes on to relate:

> I lifted them: the overpowering light
> Of that immortal shape was shadowed o'er
> By love; which, from his soft and flowing limbs,
> And passion-parted lips, and keen, faint eyes,
> Steamed forth like vaporous fire . . .
> (II.1.68-75)

In II.4. a chariot arrives almost simultaneously with the Immortal Hours, which is guided by a 'young spirit / [. . . who] has the dove-like eyes of hope' (II.4.159ff.) and who asks Asia to take her seat next to him. From now on, Asia's presence (of love) is 'unveiled' (II.5.20). '[L]ove, like the atmosphere / Of the sun's fire filling the living world, Burst[s] from [her]' (II.5.26-28). Although this unveiling of the kernel of love is accompanied by sweet sounds and words as well, it is made quite clear that even more important is the radiance which is received through the eyes. Asia is 'The Child of Light' (II.5.54), the 'Lamp of Earth' (II.5.66); she is the image of 'the deep truth'. Love's presence is felt when seen, rather than told or explained.

The radiance of love that communicates itself not through words, but by being seen and felt is also the means by which humankind will be 'infected' with the beautiful idealisms. In III.4, Panthea explains that '[b]efore Jove reigned' the Spirit of the Earth '. . . loved our sister Asia, and it came / Each leisure hour to drink the liquid light / Out of her eyes' (III.4.15-18). Prometheus provides yet another vision about the power of love spreading on earth and among mankind. His vision argues for a gradual transformation of human society – 'veil by veil, evil and error fall' (III.3.62). Prometheus envisions and explains that among mankind works of art – like 'Painting, sculpture, and rapt Poesy (III.3.55) – will discharge their illuminating power not as sign systems, which have to be deciphered, but as

> . . . lovely apparitions, dim at first,
> Then radiant, as the mind, arising bright
> From the embrace of beauty, whence the forms
> Of which these are the phantoms, casts on them
> The gathered rays which are reality . . .
> (III.49-53)

Prometheus' vision is based on the confidence that the light of love which is inherent in every human being, but all too often 'veiled', shines more brightly in some than in others. This confidence is backed by the reports of the Spirits of the Mind, who commented on the condition of the human mind during Jupiter's reign in the first act. Even at that miserable time some people, a sage for example and a poet, at least dream of better times and feed 'on aerial kisses / Of shapes that haunt thought's wildernesses' (I.741ff.). They can create from these '[f]orms more real than living man, / Nurslings of immortality!' (I.748ff.).

Men who feel the love they bear inside more strongly than others have difficulties in transmitting their love, however, since they dream their dreams in loneliness. A single person, be he or she superhuman or human, has no power at all. Even Asia is unable to spread love's power as long as she is exiled. Love only blossoms out into its full magnificence if the loving person finds kindred spirits. Only when Prometheus bids Asia: 'lift thine eyes on me' (II.1.70) can her influence begin to take effect. Accordingly, only if he reaches an audience prepared to receive his message, or rather, ready to watch and look at the beautiful, can the poet-legislator hope to bring about change.

Having finished the first act of *Prometheus Unbound*, Shelley writes to Peacock that he 'shall be content, by exercising [his] fancy, to amuse [him]self, and perhaps some others'.[24] He fears his poetical powers will be wasted unless he addresses his lyrical drama to 'the highly refined imagination of the more select classes of poetical readers with beautiful idealisms of moral excellence'. Those who do not belong to the category of 'more select poetical readers', he will not be able to reach: 'until the mind can love, and admire, and trust, and hope, and endure, reasoned principles of moral conduct are seeds cast upon the highway of life which the unconscious passenger tramples into dust'.[25]

---

24 *The Complete Works of Percy Bysshe Shelley*, x, 21 (24 Jan. 1819 to Thomas Love Peacock). In a letter to Charles and James Ollier (6 Mar. 1820) Shelley's estimate is that, 'if I may judge by its merits, the "Prometheus" cannot sell beyond twenty copies.' (x, 148).

25 'Preface [*Prometheus Unbound*]', ii, 174ff.

As already noted, many critics see the great drawback in Shelley's political poetics as the fact that the poet can only reach an audience which is already enlightened and already participates in the 'great secret of morals [which is] love; or a going out of our own nature, and an identification of ourselves with the beautiful which exists in thought, action, or person, not our own'.[26] Ulmer is not the only critic whom this apparent deadlock causes to comment ironically: 'The Shelleyan text either changes viewers by imaging their beliefs, which easily dissipates change in reconfirmation, or fails to change them at all.'[27] My reading has suggested a different conclusion: Shelley *does* try to imagine how love and moral insights can be communicated.

It is worth emphasizing at this point that Shelley wrote a drama not a poem, after all. In 'A Defence of Poetry' Shelley praises the drama as the genre where 'the connexion of poetry and social good is more observable . . . than in whatever other form'. He gives the following reason: the drama is the form 'under which a greater number of modes of expression of poetry are susceptible of being combined than [under] any other'.[28] The media through which the imagination can be transmitted when a play is performed are manifold. Language, action, music and dance 'produce a common effect in the representation of the loftiest idealisms of passion and of power'.[29] What Shelley is interested in is once again the effect that the staging of poetry produces, rather than the representation itself. That Shelley labelled *Prometheus Unbound* a 'lyrical *drama*' suggests that his poetry can only be fully effective if it is performed on stage. If only his plays were produced, the audience would not only read words, but also see and thus feelingly partake in the radiance of love. If he still addressed his *Prometheus Unbound* to the '*more select* classes of poetical *readers*', he did so, because he realistically assessed the chance of his '*lyrical* drama' being put on stage – never during his lifetime in fact, and hardly ever till this day.

---

26 'Defence of Poetry', vii, 118.

27 Ulmer, *Shelleyan Eros*, p. 112.

28 'Defence of Poetry', vii, 122.

29 'Defence of Poetry', vii, 119.

III. Speech Acts and the Transmission of Love in *The Cenci*

While *Prometheus Unbound* stages a dream, a vision, *The Cenci* is based on 'a sad reality'.[30] The play tells the true story, set in Rome in the year 1599, of Beatrice Cenci, who commits parricide after her evil father has raped her. She is eventually sentenced to death by a society that has never offered any help, but tolerated Count Cenci's crimes.

Critics of the play have for some time realized that by depicting 'a sad reality' *The Cenci* stages the vain struggle of opposing forces that is criticized and overcome in *Prometheus Unbound*. Beatrice, who contemplates and commissions the murder of her father, is anything but an exemplary character. Rather, as the action unfolds she increasingly identifies with the count, her 'apparent opposite',[31] and adopts his 'mentality of oppositions'.[32] By choosing revenge as the only conceivable solution to her inhuman oppression and by justifying her action with reference to God, Beatrice acts in accordance with the very patriarchal principal she seeks to fight.

It is particularly striking that *The Cenci*, a tragedy that presents bleak reality, also focuses on the performative power of language and on the communicative power of looks and facial expressions. It seems as if Shelley was testing the applicability of his theory that is shown to work so well in the dream world of *Prometheus Unbound* by transposing it into 'sad reality'. And, of course, nothing of the theory seems to work here. Or rather, the performative power of language and the effect of looking into each other's eyes is shown to be all too powerful when employed by depraved men.

Count Cenci's curses have an almost immediate effect on reality. Hardly has he uttered the deadly curse against his sons, for whose keep he no longer wants to pay, when the news of their death is announced. Likewise the performative power of words is proven in the revenge plot. Cenci's horrible crime of incestuous rape is never explicitly named

30 'Dedication, to Leigh Hunt, Esq.', in: *The Complete Works of Percy Bysshe Shelley*, ii, 67.

31 Robert M. Corbett, 'The Violence of the Sacred: The Economy of Sacrifice in *The Cenci*', in *Romanticism On the Net*, 4 (Nov. 1996) [10 Oct. 2002]. <http://users.ox.ac.uk/~scat0385/cenci.html>

32 Purinton, *Romantic Ideology Unmasked*, p. 86.

throughout the whole play.[33] The first simile Beatrice uses to communicate what happened is: 'Like parricide' (III.1.35); and these words are the origin of the action that is going to ensue.[34] Words spoken in hate and despair, it can be concluded, are no less powerful than words of love. They, too, create the reality they depict.

Shelley's theory of the powerful look, too, seems to work as well for the evil forces as it does for the good and loving. Thus, while Beatrice pleads with her father to 'hide thyself / Where never eye can look upon thee more!' (I.3.146ff.), she also hopes that his hateful frown will quickly replicate itself in her dead brothers' 'avenging looks' (I.3.152). Moreover, she will soon have the dreadful beam of hate at her disposal, too, as II.1 shows. Cenci's second curse, which among other things pleads that '[a]ll-beholding sun, / Strike in thine envy those [Beatrice's] life-darting eyes / With thine own blinding beams' (IV.1.134-36), has become true even before it is uttered. His hateful looks have long ago poisoned and infected his daughter's. After the rape her 'eyes are full of blood' (III.1.2). The blood in her eyes prevents her from seeing clearly on the one hand, while on the other it obstructs and covers the beam of love Beatrice used to issue. 'Thou art unlike thyself; thine eyes shoot forth / A wandering and strange spirit' (III.1.81ff.), her step-mother, Lucretia, observes.[35] In the end, Beatrice actively uses her newly won destructive power of the evil look. She employs it, for example, to force Marzio, one of the assassins whom she had hired to murder her father and who has confessed the crime, to withdraw his confession – an act which leads to Marzio's painful death on the rack (cf. V.2.80-183).

Faced with the apparent failure of Shelley's theory concerning the communication of beautiful idealisms which will lead to a transformation of society, many critics see the poet-legislator entangled in an insoluble dilemma. If even the initially pure and innocent Beatrice turns oppressor, because – living in a patriarchal society which seems to allow no room for the

---

33 Many critics have analysed Beatrice's reticence and her refusal to put into words the crime she suffered. Cf. e.g. Michael Warton, 'Speech and Silence in *The Cenci*', in *Essays on Shelley*, ed. Miriam Allott (Liverpool, 1982), pp. 105-24; or Stephen Cheeke, 'Shelley's *The Cenci*: Economies of a "Familiar Language"', in *Keats-Shelley Journal*, 47 (1998), 142-60.

34 Cf. Anne McWhir, 'Ab/Using Language in *The Cenci*', *Keats-Shelley Journal*, 38 (1989), 145-61, esp. 152.

35 Shelley traces the process of the clouding of Beatrice's eyes minutely. Even before the actual rape Count Cenci's threats give her 'eyes . . . a chill glare' and a 'cold melancholy look' (II.1.32 and 51).

transmission of love – she cannot conceive of any solution but revenge, then, how can Shelley envision mankind ever escaping from the vicious circle of oppression and achieve change? Some critics are content to notice that the Shelley of *Prometheus Unbound* was not naive after all and 'was wary of too easy a solution to apparently insoluble problems'.[36] Others – like Ulmer – are delighted to have found yet another Romantic poet whose work obviously 'deconstructs its own theory of morally educative catharsis'.[37] In the same vein (and quoting Ulmer in presenting her thesis) Ferriss holds that *The Cenci* calls 'into question the very possibility of poetically restoring revolutionary ideals. The play is in fact a "tragedy of language", making the poet a "cooperative participant in the reconsolidation of oppression"'.[38] Others, like Richardson, hesitate to believe that Shelley (who, after all, writes his 'Defence of Poetry' after he has tested his political poetics in the plays) would cast so profound a doubt over his entire theory. Since I do not find their readings of *The Cenci* quite convincing[39] either, I will suggest a different one, which will show, first, that Shelley's tragedy

---

36 Corbett, 'The Violence of the Sacred'.

37 Ulmer, *Shelleyan Eros*, p. 129; cf. McWhir, 'Ab/Using Language in *The Cenci*', 155.

38 Suzanne Ferriss, 'Percy Bysshe Shelley's *The Cenci* and the Rhetoric of Tyranny', in *British Romantic Drama: Historical and Critical Essays*, ed. T. A. Hoagwood and D. P. Watkins (London, 1998), pp. 209ff.

39 Cf. Donna Richardson, 'The *Hamartia* of Imagination in Shelley's *Cenci*', in *Keats-Shelley Journal*, 44 (1995), 216-39. Richardson concludes that Beatrice's tragic flaw lies in the fact that she does not talk and tell people that her father has raped her, because she 'is afraid public reaction will confirm her fear that power has tainted her'. '[I]f she had confessed to the deed but denied the motives of parricide . . . some of her arguments . . . might have swayed her judges.' (237ff.) Suspicious of any 'if this character had only done that' interpretations anyway, I would argue that if Beatrice had made her sufferings known only to plead for the judges' justice, she would still submit and make herself dependent on the Pope's tyrannical reign. By reverting to the strategy suggested by Richardson, Beatrice might save her life, but would not achieve any transformation of patriarchal society. Gold tries to save Shelley's theory from deconstructive readings by differentiating between the 'tyrannical use of language' and the poet's use of language. The former involves 'the disjunction of meaning and expression for the purpose of controlling others'. The latter also entails 'linguistic deception': 'Shelley must also use language manipulatively to cloak his instructive intentions and . . . to disguise the fact that, rather than having rendered the manuscript history faithfully, he has infused it with his own ethical considerations'. His deception differs from the tyrant's in so far as it 'has not for its purpose the tyrannical imposition of his will over the reader'. Gold's defence of the poet as 'the custodian of language', however, obviously and inevitably becomes entangled in the deconstructive dilemma. Elise M. Gold, '*King Lear* and Aesthetic Tyranny in Shelley's *The Cenci*, *Swellfoot the Tyrant*, and *The Witch of Atlas*', in *English Language Notes*, 24 (1986), 59, 64, 59.

offers a less deterministic view on the plot-level than is often suggested; and which, second, will take into account the poet's insistence that *The Cenci* should be staged and presented to a wide and popular audience.

I definitely agree with all those readings that stress that Beatrice becomes entangled in the patriarchal system and is not conceptualized as an exemplary character. Shelley himself makes it quite clear in the preface that 'Revenge, retaliation, atonement, are pernicious mistakes. If Beatrice had thought in this manner she would have been wiser and better'. Beatrice is doomed to failure, because '[t]he crimes and miseries in which she was an actor and a sufferer are as the mask and the mantle in which circumstances clothed her for her impersonation on the scene of the world'. I find it equally important, however, that Shelley's tragic protagonist is also said to be 'one of those rare persons in whom energy and gentleness dwell together'.[40] It is essential to note that Beatrice is also a character who, like Asia, radiates love and has the potential to spread beautiful idealisms among mankind[41] – at least at the beginning of the play. Cardinal Camillo comments in a dialogue with the Count:

> Where is your gentle daughter?
> Methinks her sweet looks, which make all things else
> Beauteous and glad, might kill the fiend within you.
> (I.1.43-45)

The Cenci offers several reasons for the failure of Beatrice's mission of love. First, she is 'barred from all society' (I.1.46), locked in by her tyrannical father and thus prevented from finding or infecting any kindred spirit. To find an accomplice in love, however, is – as the analysis of *Prometheus Unbound* has shown – vital for the success of any transformation of society. Second, when Beatrice gets the chance to meet others – as during the feast that her father organizes to celebrate his sons' deaths – she has to realize that 'no one [dares] look on [her]' (I.3.132). Apparently, the presence of her father – and only in his presence does Beatrice have contact with others – is overpowering. Third, there is one character, of course, who initially profits from Beatrice's loving looks and is a kindred spirit to the female protagonist: her step-mother Lucretia. The latter, however, obviously does not qualify as the energetic male principle that complements 'female' love. She, who lacks any transformative energy, can hardly be compared to Asia's partner, Prometheus.

40 'Preface [*The Cenci*]', ii, 71, 73.

41 Cf. Hall, 'The Socialized Imagination', 341.

All this still seems to point towards an interpretation that sees humankind forever determined by miserable circumstances. Unlike Asia, one might even add, Beatrice does not even have the chance to go into exile and hide until her Prometheus appears. She can either perish or lose her innocence in the struggle against tyranny.

The end of the play, however, offers a glimpse of hope for a better future. It does so in the form of the character of Beatrice's younger brother, Bernardo, whose importance is often overlooked. Bernardo is not only as innocent as Beatrice (IV.1.41), he even says: 'I am of my sister's mind' (II.1.98) – a statement the wording of which points to a deeper similarity between sister and brother than its context might suggest. Moreover, he is the only member of the Cenci family who is not involved in the revenge-plot at any stage and thus remains untainted throughout. He is also the one who shares Beatrice's dream of paradise in the very last scene of the play. His words 'Dear, dear sister, / Would that thy dream were not a dream!' (V.3.13ff.), on the one hand, certainly deplore his sister's current situation and show that so far Beatrice's vision of paradise is nothing but a dream. On the other hand, however, they also betray his own ardent desire for change. For the time being, Bernardo is definitely not the partner with whom Beatrice could join forces as Prometheus and Asia do. He is simply too young and too weak to provide the energetic, male counterpart to Beatrice's love and gentleness. He has, however, seen Beatrice's love:

> To see
> That perfect mirror of pure innocence
> Wherein I gazed, and grew happy and good,
> Shivered to dust! To see thee, Beatrice,
> Who made all lovely thou didst look upon –
> Thee, light of life – dead, dark! . . . (V.4.129-134.)

Of course, everything we might conjecture about Bernardo's fate after the curtain has fallen on *The Cenci* is mere speculation. The play itself, however, offers two alternative prospects as both, Cenci and Beatrice, are concerned about Bernardo's future in their last wills. The count bequeaths all his dark deeds, hoping that '[t]he memory of these' will '. . . make his youth / The sepulchre of hope, where evil thoughts / Shall grow like weeds on a neglected tomb.' (IV.1.52-54) Beatrice's legacy sounds more promising:

> Farewell, my tender brother. Think
> Of our sad fate with gentleness, as now:
> And let mild, pitying thoughts lighten for thee

Thy sorrow's load. Err not in harsh despair,
But tears and patience. One thing more, my child,
For thine own sake be constant to the love
Thou bearest us; and to the faith that I,
Though wrapped in a strange cloud of crime and shame,
Lived ever holy and unstained. And though
Ill tongues shall wound me, and our common name
Be as a mark stamped on thine innocent brow
For men to point at as they pass, do thou
Forbear, and never think a thought unkind
Of those who perhaps love thee in their graves. (V.4.142-154)

Beatrice puts all her trust in Bernardo's capacity to keep his love alive; and, after all, it is she, not her father, who has the last word. The play thus clearly suggests the possibility that Bernardo might grow to be a kind of human Prometheus. The desire for a better world does not perish with Beatrice. Bernardo bears the seed of love, which was unveiled by his gazing into his sister's eyes while she was yet pure and unspoiled. And he has the potential to pass it on to posterity, where he might eventually find a kindred spirit.

IV. The Transmission of Love: *The Cenci* – A Play to be Performed

In a famous letter Shelley tells Peacock that *The Cenci* is anything but another closet drama. It is 'eminently dramatic' and Shelley hopes for 'the greatest degree of popular effect'.[42] And, indeed, the tragedy proves that Shelley knew how to cater to a wider audience.[43] He taps his contemporaries' preference for Gothic plots and settings,[44] succeeds in avoiding elaborate images and only uses 'the familiar language of men'.[45] For all that, *The Cenci* ties in nicely with Shelley's poetical and political theory developed elsewhere; although it is written for the masses Shelley does not give up the main points of his theory as far as the communication of an ideal po-

42 *Complete Works*, x, 60 (July 1819 to Thomas Love Peacock). Shelley insists again and again that the *Cenci* is 'calculated to produce a very popular effect' (78; 6 Sept. 1819 to Charles and James Ollier) and that it 'is written for the multitude, and ought to sell well' (148; 6 Mar. 1820 to Charles and James Ollier).

43 For an interpretation which holds that the opposite is true and claims that '[t]he play is deeply insecure about its theater, its audience, its style and its language' consult Cheeke, 'Shelley's *The Cenci*', 159.

44 Cf. Michael Gamer, *Romanticism and the Gothic* (Cambridge, 2000).

45 'Preface [*The Cenci*]', ii, 73.

litical poetics is concerned. He stays true to his abhorrence of 'didactic poetry'[46], which is based on the assumption that even the most beneficial doctrines can be distorted and turned into instruments of despotism.[47] Moreover, he does not present his audience with a 'reasoned system on the theory of human life'[48] which would curtail the all-important productive process of the imagination. With Beatrice he does not present a character who can easily be categorized as either good or bad.

Critics who have tackled the question of just how Shelley tries to reach and improve his audience have rightly focused on two authorial statements in the preface to *The Cenci*:

> The highest moral purpose aimed at in the highest species of the drama, is the teaching the human heart, through its sympathies and antipathies, the knowledge of itself; in proportion to the possession of which knowledge, every human being is wise, just, sincere, tolerant and kind.

And:

> It is in the restless and anatomising casuistry with which men seek the justification of Beatrice, yet feel that she has done what needs justification; it is in the superstitious horror with which they contemplate alike her wrongs and their revenge, that the dramatic character of what she did and suffered, consists.[49]

From these quotations many conclude that Shelley tries to achieve his moral purpose and to prepare his audience for the concept of social change by triggering a mental process.

> Caught up in the emotional dialectics of the predicament, the imagination of the reader is propelled back and forth between two sets of ethical imperatives in the effort to establish some preponderance between them, in the attempt, that is, to justify the one enormity by the other, only to find the task impossible.[50]

Richardson, to quote just one more example, similarly claims that 'the play finally makes an appeal to rational analysis and detached judgment by treating Beatrice's beliefs ironically, in order to teach the audience that people

---

46 'Preface [*Prometheus Unbound*]', ii, 174.

47 Cf. 'A Philosophical View of Reform', where Shelley holds that even the ideas propagated by Christ were deformed and reduced to dogmas, 'were employed as symbols of domination and imposture; and a system of liberty and equality . . . was perverted to support oppression' (vii, 5).

48 'Preface [*Prometheus Unbound*]', ii, 174.

49 'Preface [*The Cenci*]', ii, 71.

50 Stuart M. Sperry, *Shelley's Major Verse: The Narrative and Dramatic Poetry* (Cambridge, Mass., 1988), pp. 137ff.

have some responsibility for their actions despite the inevitable limitations of human weakness and social tyranny'.[51] To agree with Sperry, Richardson and all the others[52] who argue in the same vein would mean to agree with an interpretation that eventually backs deconstructive readings of the play by identifying yet another inconsistency in Shelley's argument. For how can the 'human *heart*' of the spectator be taught, if the mind gets lost in restless casuistry? And how is it to be explained that the Shelley of *Prometheus Unbound* and 'The Defence of Poetry' invests a lot of energy to differentiate between 'two classes of action of the human mind which are called reason and imagination',[53] only in order to then emphasize the single importance of the former in his conception of *The Cenci*?

While I agree that it is certainly one important effect of Beatrice's tragic fate to make the recipient aware of the vicious circle in which Shelley finds himself caught, I would argue that setting off a mental process in the audience is not Shelley's only aim. Writing *The Cenci* he is still 'aware that until the mind can love, and admire, and trust, and hope, and endure, reasoned principles of moral conduct are seeds cast upon the highway of life which the unconscious passenger tramples into dust'.[54] He does not retract this claim made in the preface to *Prometheus Unbound*. The sheer fact that the term 'knowledge' looms large in Shelley's preface to *The Cenci* does not necessarily imply that 'the highest moral purpose [which is] the teaching the human heart . . . the knowledge of itself' entails the audience's rationality. Rather, here as elsewhere in Shelley's prose and poetry, to know one's own heart is to realize that its essence is love. Love, however, cannot be communicated through words or transmitted by (rationalist) discourse; it has to be seen and felt. The only hope for a better society lies in the spreading of the 'light of love'; only after love has been spread, after the heart has knowledge of itself, can the seeds of reasoned principles fall on fertile soil. To reach that goal it is absolutely vital that the tragedy is performed on stage and that, moreover, only the best ac-

51 Richardson, 'The *Hamartia* of Imagination', 329.

52 Cf., e.g., Earl R. Wassermann, *Shelley: A Critical Reading* (Baltimore, 1971), pp. 119ff.; Purinton, *Romantic Ideology Unmasked*, p. 101; Scrivener tries to show that Shelley's 'drama will effect a harmonizing of [mind and emotions], thus removing the negative features of intellect'. But his claim that Shelley reaches this aim by employing a 'Brechtian kind of alienation effect' again stresses the primary importance of the intellect. Michael Henry Scrivener, *Radical Shelley: The Philosophical Anarchism and Utopian Thought of Percy Bysshe Shelley* (Princeton, 1982), p. 188.

53 'Defence of Poetry', vii, 107.

54 'Preface [*Prometheus Unbound*]', ii, 174ff.

tress, specified by Shelley as Miss O'Neil,[55] stars as Beatrice. Only by actually looking into Beatrice's innocent eyes (at the beginning of *The Cenci*) will the tragedy become a 'mirror in which the spectator beholds himself, under a thin guise of circumstance, stript of all but that ideal perfection and energy which every one feels to be the internal type of all that he loves, admires, and would become'.[56] Only then will love be transmitted to the spectator. For love to achieve its effect in people who are not yet aware of Shelley's beautiful idealisms, not yet kindred spirits of the poet, it has to be a radiating presence on the stage.

But is this effect not destroyed, if one takes into consideration the force of the evil count's looks, which the audience feel on themselves – just as much as Beatrice's ameliorating gaze – and more permanently? According to 'The Defence of Poetry', this is not necessarily the case. With reference to the 'tragedies of the Athenian poets', Shelley claims that in the theatre the spectator's

> imagination is enlarged by sympathy with pains and passions so mighty, that they distend in their conception the capacity of that by which they are conceived; the good affections are strengthened by pity, indignation, terror and sorrow; and an exalted calm is prolonged from the satiety of this high exercise of them into the tumult of familiar life: even crime is disarmed of half its horror and all its contagion by being represented as the fatal consequence of the unfathomable agencies of nature, error is thus divested of its wilfulness; men can no longer cherish it as the creation of their choice.[57]

In the theatre, 'the good affections' are even strengthened by the display and reception of 'indignation, terror and sorrow'. Count Cenci's evil looks induce fear and terror and are therefore repellent. In the theatre, Count Cenci's looks are not contagious, because nobody (who is not immediately involved in the destructive plot) would voluntarily choose the evil count's concept of hate and destruction. Crime may be an inevitable part of nature, but it is not what men willingly embrace; especially if they are provided with the alternative of love. Beatrice's radiance inevitably tri-

---

55 'What I want you do is, to procure for me its presentation at Covent Garden. The principal character Beatrice is precisely fitted for Miss O'Neil, and it might even seem to have been written for her.' *Complete Works*, x, 62 (July 1819 to Thomas Love Peacock).

56 'Defence of Poetry', vii, 121. That Shelley does not consider his theory of the loving look to be merely symbolic is made clear in 'A Philosophical Reform', where he expresses his belief in the power of passive resistance: 'it is not to be believed that they [English soldiers] would massacre an unresisting multitude of their countrymen drawn up in unarmed array before them, and bearing in their looks the calm, deliberate resolution to perish rather than abandon the assertion of their rights.' (49)

57 'Defence of Poetry', vii, 121.

umphs since it falls on fertile soil. The female protagonist's loving looks trigger an intuitively positive response, since they have the effect of enlightening the hidden core of love, which is always present, though all too often veiled, in every human heart.

To conclude: As with every elaborate theoretical system Shelley's political poetics is based on an act of faith. We may not share Shelley's belief that man is essentially good and that, consequently, political progress can be initiated by a poetry that involves the recipient in the enlargement of the imagination. We might, rather, want to argue that, if we consider man to have made some progress since the end of the eighteenth century, this is due to the enlightened and reasoned ideas propagated by the radicals of the 1790s and put into political practice by the revolutionaries in France and America. We may hesitate to share Shelley's belief for different reasons. Perhaps we have learned to put our faith in the all-pervasive power of a deconstructive philosophy and, thus, delight in detecting the inevitable inconsistencies that can be found in Shelley's political poetics (just as well as in any other philosophical system), rather than read the poet-legislator's poetics on its own terms. We may or we may not believe in Shelley's theory – this is not the point. What this essay set out to show is that Shelley's political poetics as developed and realized in *Prometheus Unbound* and *The Cenci* relentlessly tries to find a way out of the Godwinian dilemma. By focusing on the power of looks and language, the poet-legislator can, on the one hand, acknowledge that man is the product of his circumstances, but, on the other, still conceive of a set of means that lead to the perfection of man and also a profound transformation of society. To share the poet-legislator's basic assumptions (that man is essentially good, that there are always some in whom the light of love is not completely veiled, and that love can only spread when seen) might be easier for the happy few who have had the chance to experience the effectiveness of loving looks, because they have seen either *Prometheus Unbound* or *The Cenci* in the theatre. But this I cannot judge, since I do not belong to that tiny group 'selected' not by Shelley, but by generations of theatre managers and stage directors who have all too often decided not to produce his plays (because, for the most part, they have no knowledge of their hearts?).

Kai Merten

Excursion and Seclusion

William Wordsworth in the French Revolution – the French Revolution in William Wordsworth

It is often overlooked that of those William Wordsworth's texts that directly refer to the French Revolution only a single one, *Descriptive Sketches*, was actually published during the key events of the 1790s. Encountering this text in the Cornell edition raises a series of questions. It juxtaposes two versions on facing pages and dates them 1793 and 1836 respectively.[1] The later text appears to be massively revised as it is more than 120 lines shorter than the earlier version. More complicated, however, is the fact that the earlier version bears no authorial date of composition, whereas the 1836 version shows the date of '1791 & 1792'.[2] It is clear that much less of it was actually written at that time than of the version published in 1793 that bears no composition date. Both versions refer to the French Revolution but they do so in completely different ways, dependent both on their contents and their reception. What is more, reading a text that, in its two versions, is both contemporaneous with, and more than forty years removed from, the French Revolution should make us aware of the problem of historicity and chronology in Wordsworth's work and of the status of historical events in his texts. If we face the later version alone we have to ask ourselves if and how a text can be from 1791-1792 – the composition date the later text bears somewhat misleadingly – and from 1836 at the same time. Can the later text be said to belong to both the spheres of 1791-1792 and of 1836? Or does it belong to yet another dimension of time constructed within the work itself? As we shall see, these questions lie at the heart of Wordsworth's self-fashioning as an author. Wordsworth emerged as an author only in the course of events that are contemporaneous with, and some of them directly connected to, the French Revolution. As shall appear, it is especially the two versions of *Descriptive Sketches* that bear witness to this development. Apart from the differences in their wording, what we have to understand is that the two versions are essentially different texts, written by two different kinds of writer.

---

1 *Descriptive Sketches*, ed. Eric Birdsall (Ithaca, 1984).

2 *Descriptive Sketches*, ed. Birdsall, p. 119.

Descriptive Sketches, in its first version, was composed in 1792 and published in January 1793, only a week after the execution of Louis XVI. The text refers to events during Wordsworth's walking tour through the Alps in 1790, also described in Book 6 of *The Prelude*. He crossed France to reach the Alps in the summer of 1790, but returned to France late in the following year. He spent a short time in Paris and moved on to Orleans and then to Blois where he wrote *Descriptive Sketches* in the first half of 1792. Apparently, Wordsworth participated in the revolutionary politics of Blois. What is more, in Orleans he had met a young French woman, Annette Vallon, who became pregnant by him. Wordsworth went back to Orleans in September 1792, only, however, to arrange for a representative to be present at the baptism. He then moved on to Paris, where he stayed for six weeks, and left the country late in 1792. He offered the text of *Descriptive Sketches* to the London publisher, Joseph Johnson, who brought it out in January 1793, together with Wordsworth's earlier poem *An Evening Walk*.[3] The revisions in the later version were due to an important reissue of the text in a new six-volume edition of *Poetical Works*, published in 1836 and 1837, that Wordsworth undertook with his new publisher, Edward Moxon.[4]

My comparative reading of the two versions of *Descriptive Sketches* will focus on their respective endings as these are the points where they most strongly diverge. In the basic sequence of events described, the two versions stay virtually the same. *Descriptive Sketches* is conceived as a series of impressions on a journey across the Continent. Both versions are preceded by an 'Argument' which contains a list of the stations touched on the tour. The poem, however, is not actually written in the style of a versified travel narrative focusing on the spatial progress of its characters, but rather as a sequence of impressions of famous spots and significant scenes. This links it to the tradition of the loco-descriptive poem, a popular genre throughout the eighteenth century, with James Thomson's *The Seasons* (first published in 1730) as its starting point. The loco-descriptive poem is not so much a narrative as an expanded lyrical genre that describes pictorial elements of landscape and rustic life, and combines it with 'historical retrospection, or incidental meditation', as Samuel Johnson writes in an influential definition from 1779.[5] After the *Grand Chartreuse* as one of the first stations, the poem moves on to Italy, with the most

---

3 Cf. Stephen Gill, *William Wordsworth: A Life* (Oxford, 1989), pp. 56-69.

4 Gill, *Wordsworth*, pp. 388-9

5 Quoted after *The New Princeton Encyclopedia of Poetry and Poetics*, ed. Alex Preminger and T.V.F. Brogan (Princeton, 1993), pp. 286-7

significant spot being Lake Como, and then it enters Switzerland, where geographical destinations become less important. Instead, the poem examines the way of life of Swiss peasants. From Switzerland, the poem returns to France with a description of the aspect of Mont Blanc. The next station touched on is Savoy, which appears as a region in utter subjection to Italy. After the description of a cottage community, the poem turns from the past of the tour to the present of composition, located in the Loiret region. A depiction of the Loiret landscape presumably set in 1790 is juxtaposed with an evocation of its present state of war. At this point, the two versions go in different directions. The significant section runs as follows in the text published in 1793:

> Oh give, great God, to Freedom's waves to ride
> Sublime o'er Conquest, Avarice, and Pride,
> To break, the vales where Death with Famine scow'rs,
> And dark oppression builds her thick-ribb'd tow'rs;
> [...]
> Where Discord stalks dilating, every hour,
> And crouching fearful at the feet of Pow'r,
> Like Lightnings eager for th' almighty word,
> Look up for sign of havoc, Fire, and Sword;[6]

The scenery is described as virtually infested with personified vices. The text appeals to God to unleash an equally allegorical Freedom as a force to fight against Conquest, Avarice, Pride, Death, and Famine. The conception of 'Power' is included in this cursing of the evils as the supreme force with all the other vices in its service. If we decode this very extended image, it appears that inequality and oppression are attributed to widespread consciousness of – and obedience to – power. In linking this scene to contemporary discourses and media that refer to the French Revolution, we find several points of connection. On the one hand, the text addresses the same rejection of power to be found in Godwin's *Political Justice* (1793) and his novel *Caleb Williams* (1794). On the other hand, the imagery of this scene associates it with political caricature during the 1790s that equally used personifications of 'vices' and often gave them the appearances of the actual personalities to be scorned.[7] Poems appearing in politi-

---

6 *Descriptive Sketches*, ed. Birdsall, p. 116.

7 Although in the course of the eighteenth century the allegorical and the emblematic had fallen out of favour in caricature, they once again enjoyed great popularity in political prints of the 1790s, especially those designed for the 'lower orders'. Diana Donald, *The Age of Caricature: Satirical Prints in the Reign of George III* (New Haven, 1996), pp. 44-74; at p. 74.

cal magazines of the time used a similar strategy of visualizing and elucidating conflicts between value systems, such as 'To a Young Lady, With a Poem on the French Revolution' by Samuel Taylor Coleridge, published in the first edition of his miscellany, *The Watchman*, in 1796. Coleridge employs imagery of a violent struggle for liberty quite similar to that Wordswort has used.

> When slumb'ring FREEDOM rous'd by high DISDAIN
> With giant fury burst her triple chain![8]

Wordsworth's poem, then, is made to be read as a current political statement in that it resorts to elements of textual, and indirectly of pictorial, media of political debate. It is meant to be placed in the debate about the French Revolution that took place in the time when it was published. Thus, when the 1793 version goes on to envisage a king drowned in a flood to be triggered off by the God invoked in the text, this is meant as a statement on the question of regicide, which became especially topical in Britain after the execution of Louis XVI in January 1793, the same month that *Descriptive Sketches* was published. The scene goes on to echo the famous story of King Canute as an exemplum of regal modesty, but Wordsworth gives it a negative turn by invoking a king convinced of the boundlessness of his powers:

> And grant that every sceptred child of clay,
> Who cries, presumptuous, "here their tides shall stay,"
> Swept in their anger from th' affrighted shore,
> With all his creatures sink–to rise no more.[9]

If we compare the whole section just analysed to the parallel scene in the 1836 version, we find that there are significant changes. The relevant section starts off by setting a frame for an examination of the struggle in the Loiret in very different terms:

> – All cannot be: the promise is too fair
> For creatures doomed to breathe terrestial air:
> Yet not for this will sober reason frown
> Upon that promise, nor the hope disown;
> She knows that only from high aims ensue
> Rich guerdons, and to them alone are due.

---

8 *The Watchman* No. 1, 1 Mar. 1796, reprinted in *The Collected Works of Samuel Taylor Coleridge*, general editor Kathleen Coburn, *The Watchman*, ed. Lewis Patton (Oxford, 1970), pp. 27-9; at p. 28.

9 *Descriptive Sketches*, ed. Birdsall, p. 118.

> Great God! by whom the strifes of man are weighed
> In an impartial balance, give thine aid
> To the just cause . . .[10]

Both versions address God in mankind's struggle for freedom. In the earlier version, however, the power of God is called down to earth in an act of self-consecration that aims to give humans godly strength. The later version checks its own progress at this point ('Great God!') and invokes a wholly reliable and detached Good Lord. Whereas the earlier version calls *down* to earth the powers of a vindictive god, the later text calls *out* to God who is implored to watch over the strivings of man with benevolence and 'impartial balance' ready to intervene, it seems, when necessary but not to give his power away uncontrolled to human beings. In addition, the later version reflects a laborious reworking of the imagery of a violent invasion of nature. In exchange for the depiction of a vice-infested nature, it goes on to extend the image of the flooding to include positive elements. The stream is supposed to give water to the dried-out land instead of flooding it with a destructive force:

> So shall its waters, from the heavens supplied
> In copious showers, from earth by wholesome springs,
> Brood o'er the long-parched lands with Nile-like wings!
> And grant that every sceptred child of clay
> . . .
> May in its progress see thy guiding hand,
> and cease the acknowledged purpose to withstand;
> Or, swept in anger from the insulted shore,
> Sink with his servile bands, to rise no more![11]

As opposed to the stream of revenge in the earlier version, the later text calls for modesty and firm belief. What the terms 'guiding hand' and 'acknowledged purpose' also imply is a change in the idea of historical agency. Whereas in the earlier poem only human beings are conceived as agents of historical events, 'Freedom's waves'[12], in the 1836 poem the stream of history is watered by both God and Man. This implies that God has full knowledge of the historical process and that monarchs can be guided to the good through their faith. The latter aspect especially is an expression of belief in the 'progress' of the world through the combined action of Man and God. It is in this sense that we have to understand the

---

10 *Descriptive Sketches*, ed. Birdsall, p. 117.

11 *Descriptive Sketches*, ed. Birdsall, pp. 117, 119.

12 *Descriptive Sketches*, ed. Birdsall, p. 116.

Christianity of Wordsworth's voice at this point. In detaching himself from the immediate historical process by handing it over to God, he is in a position to see the world through God's eyes and speak about it with a God-like superior voice. If we hear the sentences, 'All cannot be: the promise is too fair / For creatures doomed to breathe terrestrial air', we are invited to imagine the Lord himself speaking. 'All cannot be', contains a verbal tense not to be found in the parallel passage in the earlier version, the present of timeless sententious truth, the so-called gnomic present. By using this tense, the text refers, one could say, to the timeless sphere of godly transcendence. The speaker's 'sober reason' is divine because he seems to be able to judge the justification of human 'hope' and 'promise' with full knowledge of the outcome of the events. We have to bear in mind that this voice is dramatized to be contemporaneous with these events, which gives its assessment of human action tremendous superiority as in: '[s]he [sober reason] knows that only from high aims ensue / Rich guerdons, and to them alone are due.'[13]

The very last section of the poem is again strikingly different in the two versions. It forms a return to the basic communicative situation of the poem, with the poet addressing his fellow wanderer, Robert Jones. The 1793 version closes with the speaker in distress about the world's injustice, whereas 1836 ends with confidence and '[w]ith a light heart'.[14] In 1793, the very depiction of a gigantomachia of vices becomes a burden that prefigures 'the dead load of mortal ills'[15] at the end of the text. In this version, the poem conjures up a country infested by monstrous vices and presents as inescapable a situation which, due to the poem's signalling of its political topicality, would be related to the historical situation in Europe at the time of its publication. The later version removes the personifications and instead develops an optimistic vision of steady progress. It opens up a realm of detached and superior overview unimpeded by struggles in worldly time and place, a space where knowledge of the future is written into the gnomic present of the text. I would argue that what is implied by these revisions is not so much conservative religiousness, but rather a different speaking position associated with the transcendent power conjured up in the text. The poem still refers to political events, but now with a much more detached voice that presents the process of history as being both in the hands of God and in the knowing of the poet.

---

13 *Descriptive Sketches*, ed. Birdsall, p. 117.

14 *Descriptive Sketches*, ed. Birdsall, p. 119.

15 *Descriptive Sketches*, ed. Birdsall, p. 118.

The text loses a considerable part of its urgent topicality, but gains the ability to refer to the future and thus obtains absolute foresight. The poem's futurity gestures towards progress in history and makes the turmoil of the French Revolution appear as already over and gone through, as bearing its own pastness inscribed.

In order for us to understand what made it both desirable and possible for Wordsworth to introduce a position of God-like overview into the later version of *Descriptive Sketches*, I want to examine the development of Wordsworth's poetical stance in two steps. First, I want to extract some information about it from one of Wordsworth's most important textual instances of poetical self-fashioning, the 'Prospectus to *The Recluse*' and to find out when it was that Wordsworth invented himself as a poet. This examination will throw some light on the the speaker's position in the second version of *Descriptive Sketches* just analysed. We will, however, also find that it is a strategy of Wordsworth's poetry to present the development of the poet as an event happening exclusively inside his mind and inside his work as a dramatization of the mind. That means that in a second step, in order to understand fully the speaking position of the second version, and indeed also of the first version, of *Descriptive Sketches*, we shall have to turn to the discursive conditions of both these positions.

According to Jonathan Wordsworth, one of the first things that Wordsworth did when he arrived in Grasmere was to sit down and write a 'Prospectus' to the project of his life, *The Recluse*.[16] Wordsworth's self-fashioning as a poet who keeps himself away from the cultural centre geographically and sees his main duty as the meditation on, and mediation of, a philosophy developed in close contact with the nature that surrounds him is widely known. Using Wordsworth's own terminology, this speaking position could be called that of 'seclusion' and could be defined, again in Wordsworth's own words, this time from the 'Preface' to his poem, *The Excursion* (1814), as 'the sensations and opinions of a Poet living in retirement'.[17] In the 1800 version of the 'Prospectus to *The Recluse*' reconstructed by Jonathan Wordsworth, William gives a second dimension to this 'seclusionist' position. The 'Prospectus' is worth quoting at some length:

---

16 According to Jonathan Wordsworth, the text was written between January and March 1800: 'Prospectus to *The Recluse*' in Jonathan Wordsworth, *William Wordsworth: The Borders of Vision* (Oxford, 1982), pp. 388-90; at p. 388.

17 William Wordsworth, *The Excursion*, selected and intr. Jonathan Wordsworth (Oxford, 1991), pp. viii-ix

Paradise and groves
Elysian, blessed islands in the deep,
Of *choice seclusion* – wherefore need they be
A history, or but a dream, when minds
Once wedded to this outward frame of things
In love, find these the growth of common day?

Such pleasant haunts *foregoing, if my song*
Must turn elsewhere, and travel near the tribes
And fellowships of men, and see ill sights
Of passions ravenous from each other's rage,
Insult and injury and wrong and strife,
Wisdom be thou my guide, and if so tasked
I hear humanity in fields and groves
Pipe solitary anguish, . . .
Do thou give meaning more akin to that
Which to God's ear they carry, that even these
Hearing, I be not heartless, or forlorn.
Come thou prophetic spirit, soul of man,
Thou human soul of the wide earth, that hast
Thy metropolitan temple in the hearts
of *mighty Poets*; unto me vouchsafe
Thy *foresight*; . . .
. . . that my song may live, and be
Even as a light hung up in heaven to chear
The world in times to come.[18]

In the first third of this section, the poet describes himself as living in a 'choice seclusion' directly in contact with nature, a paradise that is neither historically detached nor limited to the imaginary ('but a dream'). The section then goes on to conjure up worldly anguish and ends with the poet's wish for 'foresight' to be able to assess adequately the events just evoked. The hymnic invocation at this point ('Come thou') suggests that the poet attempts to conjure up his 'natural human soul' to act as a prophet to history. On one level of the text, the poet seems to be brooding over the human race in seclusion and to be invoking his own soul to lend him the ability of foresight. In the meantime, however, the problem of how to become a prophet is solved on a different level. The solution lies in a temporal double exposure that the text suggests with the word 'foregoing'. The meaning of 'forego' here is 'abstain from, go without', but a hint of the word's second meaning, 'precede in place or time', is also present.[19] Implied in leaving

18 'Prospectus to *The Recluse*', p. 389, my italics.

19 *The Concise Oxford Dictionary of Current English*, ed. J. B. Sykes (Oxford, 1976), pp. 412-3.

behind 'the choice seclusion', then, is also a turning back of the clock to the '[i]nsult and injury and wrong and strife' of the French Revolution in the 1790s. The poem returns to the past yet stays in the present of the poet's contemplation. The events are revisited while the voice doing so does not even use the past tense. Thus, the present is being written back into an account of past events, making it possible to conjure up a past (as) present. The 'mighty Poet's' plea for 'foresight', then, is accompanied by a textual performance of the reverse process. Only turned around, as the making present of the *future*, would this be the demonstration of foreknowledge. A mode of foresight, however, is made available insofar as, by revisiting accounts of the past, the past is actually invested with knowledge of the future. Of course, this does not work, because the past cannot *really* be revisited. Or can it? After all, there are texts of the past. They could be revisited and invested with hindsight knowledge. '[P]assing events' could be transformed into historical process and the 'existing state of things'[20] could be brought into contact with its own future. This ability would indeed be divine, and the poet's ear, listening to the noise of present events, would become 'God's ear' as the 'Prospectus' has it. By investing the past with the present, Wordsworth's 'Prospectus', I wish to argue, performs a temporal movement that simultaneously suggests an intertextual strategy: revisiting earlier texts with hindsight and writing into them the superior 'wisdom' of what is to come. Wordsworth's 'seclusion', then, contains the seed of a very specific 'excursion': the journey back into his own texts. This is exactly what happens to the 1836 version of *Descriptive Sketches*. How Wordsworth comes back to write the future as present into the text has been analysed at some length above. Future knowledge of the outcome of historical events is written into them in the gnomic present. Wordsworth's excursion back to his earlier excursion to the French Revolution serves the purpose of investing the earlier text with foresight of the outcome and with the eventual processuality of the events described. There is a further dimension. His foreknowledge, Wordsworth hopes at the end of my quotation from the 'Prospectus', also secures the future importance of his texts in the '[w]orld in times to come'. The futurity inscribed in the texts is meant to provide for their real future relevance.

The absence of a prophetic stance in the earlier version becomes explicable now. In 1792, this stance was simply not yet available to Wordsworth as it was created only at the end of the same decade. Wordsworth's

---

20 *The Excursion*, ed. Jonathan Wordsworth, p. vii.

rewriting, then, assimilates a text that escapes – because it antedates – the functioning of a discourse in which he wishes his texts to be set. *Descriptive Sketches* was meant to survive not as a contribution to a current debate by an altogether unknown writer, but as a poet's excursion to the 'tribes of man' enlightened by his prophetic spirit. As a textual event, it constitutes Wordsworth's excursion in the 1830s back to a text of the 1790s. Wordsworth, however, was careful not to let his poetical propheticism be associated with literary stasis, a lack of development. The *œuvre* he shaped for himself was supposed to combine prophecy with constant progress. Hence, even if there was the opportunity of complete revision, Wordsworth made *Descriptive Sketches* stand out as not yet perfect – albeit already prophetic. Even in 1836, it was positioned as a still somewhat immature work of youth, qualified and to some extent supplanted by later texts.[21] *The Prelude*, in both the 1805 and the 1850 version, refers to *Descriptive Sketches* as the product of 'a youth undisciplined in verse'.[22] This qualifies the earlier text, but it also fixes its status in the poet's *œuvre*. On the one hand, Wordsworth's 1836 revisions reshape the poem in order to make it seem to have already contained the seeds of a poetical stance that he in fact developed only much later. On the other hand, the revisions reaffirm the sense of the poem's 'earliness' in the interior chronology of Wordsworth's *œuvre*, and thus reinforce its function as an indirect index of the 'growth of the poet's mind'.

By gathering such information from the texts themselves we could now complete our reading of the two versions of *Descriptive Sketches*. The time structure that organizes Wordsworth's works, we could conclude, changed from a response to exterior events to an independent temporal structure interior to the *œuvre* of William Wordsworth. This would imply that the meaning and the frame of reference of his texts came to depend on the author's own categories and on their relationship to other of his texts even in those poems that mention historical events. We could also, of course, trace the well-known story of political disappointment and withdrawal from the political sphere. We would find evidence for it in the 1799 version of *The Prelude* which was written at about the same time as

---

21 In the introduction to the 'Juvenile Pieces' in the 1836 edition, Wordsworth writes: 'The corrections [to the *Descriptive Sketches*], though numerous, are not, however such as to prevent its retaining with propriety a place in the class of Juvenile Pieces.' Quoted in *Descriptive Sketches*, ed. Birdsall, p. 18.

22 1805: vi, 600; 1850, vi, 670: see e.g. *The Prelude: The Four Texts (1798, 1799, 1805, 1850)*, ed. Jonathan Wordsworth (Harmondsworth, 1995), pp. 244-5.

the first version of his 'Prospectus'. In *The Prelude* Wordsworth tells about his flight into Nature from the 'indifference and apathy / And wicked exultation . . . in this time / of dereliction and dismay'.[23] We could even back up our findings with evidence from the later version of *Descriptive Sketches* and explain the mode of detachment as political disappointment. Wordsworth's turning away from the French Revolution has often been read and accepted as the starting point of a private and autonomous poetical project, not concerned with, or connected to, the immediately contemporary. We have been presented with a Wordsworth in withdrawal, relentlessly working on, and revising, his texts and forming a poetry for the future, exactly by ignoring the demands of most of the public of his own time.[24]

Wordsworth's futurity, however, was in many senses a matter of his present. A project of poetical seclusion and interiorization can only work if, as a cultural practice, it is negotiated and acknowledged in public. 'Public' here does not imply a Habermasian model of enlightened negotiation, but the specific discourse, or set of discourses, that a literary text is set in through its publication. In this sense, the conception of a 'public sphere' is dependent on discursive construction and negotiation by, among others, the very texts that project a retreat from it into privacy. If we do not take this into consideration, if we were to analyse Wordsworth's interiorization solely from within his works, we would in a sense *fall into* Wordsworth's texts instead of analysing what it was that allowed the author to shape his texts according to a chronology[25] he had himself invented and

---

23 *The Prelude 1799. Second Part*, ll. 480-1 and 486-7, see e.g. Jonathan Wordsworth's edition, p. 34.

24 The position is summed up approvingly by Michael Gassenmeier: '[I do not] wish to indulge in juxtaposing contradictory images, visions of the millenium [*sic*] blazoned from the heights of revolutionary hope against revisions conceived in the vales of disenchantment with the French course. We've known them all . . . And we all know that the original concept of renovating the world by external means, by a political and social revolution was replaced by various concepts of transforming the world by internal means, by a revolution of consciousness.' Michael Gassenmeier, '"'Twas a Transport of the Outward Sense": Wordsworth's Own Account of his Visions and Revisions of the French Revolution' in *Beyond the Suburbs of the Mind: Exploring English Romanticism. Papers Delivered at the Mannheim Symposion in Honour of Hermann Fischer*, ed. Michael Gassenmeier and Norbert H. Platz (Essen, 1987), pp. 116-136; at pp. 116-7.

25 'Chronology' here implies not only the temporal order of events in an ontological sense but also the specific perception of time that Wordsworth wrote back into his earlier texts, i. e., his epistemology of time.

that enabled the texts, in turn, to discursivize their own author as their main frame of reference. I want, therefore, to sketch out briefly the set of discourses that facilitated the emergence and maintenance of the discourse that Wordsworth created for himself.

The rejection of the public sphere became an option of self-presentation in the 1790s. Several genres, such as Romantic poetry, Gothic novels, and even political theory, such as Edmund Burke's writing on the French Revolution or John Thelwall's self-styled 'politico-sentimental' texts gained their author or reader positions from a gesture of withdrawal from the public.[26] Wordsworth's story of an alienation from the politics of the French Revolution can be seen as a story that worked in that context, particularly given the fact that a year before his withdrawal to Grasmere late in 1799, *The Anti-Jacobin Review and Magazine* was founded, a journal that virtually set out to hunt down insubordinate poets and expose Jacobin poetry. Quietism, self-referentiality outside the field of poetry considered immediately *political*, became a quiet option in that it provided for *long-term* estimableness and was therefore also potentially lucrative. Whether Wordsworth's a-politicalness played into the hands of 'political indoctrination' and 'ideological manipulation' of the British public, as McCann warns with regard to the movement of 'sentimental retreat' in the 1790s in general,[27] or could be seen as part of a counter-public of political alternatives, as he claims with regard to John Thelwall,[28] lies beyond the scope of this article. What should have become clear nevertheless is that Wordsworth's withdrawal from the public had to be public in itself.

If we look further at the reception of Wordsworth's earliest work in the context of the literary market and the literary criticism of the time, other reasons appear why the gesture of retreat became both an option and a *desideratum* at the end of the eighteenth century. In 1792, Wordsworth asked his friend, William Mathews, 'to form an acquaintance with some of the publishing booksellers of London, from whom [he] might get some hints of what sort of works would be the most likely to answer', because 'the field of Letters is very extensive, and it is astonishing if we cannot find some little corner, which with a little tillage will produce us

---

26 Cf. Andrew McCann, 'William Godwin and the Pathological Public Sphere: Theorising Communicative Action in the 1790s', *Prose Studies*, 18 (1995), 199-222; at 201.

27 McCann, 'William Godwin', 201.

28 Andrew McCann, *Cultural Politics in the 1790s: Literature, Radicalism and the Public Sphere* (New York, 1999), pp. 101-106.

enough for the necessities, nay even the comforts, of life'.[29] At that time, Wordsworth was writing the *Descriptive Sketches*, a poem which, as I have tried to show, was indeed supposed to meet the demands of the market of topical political poetry while simultaneously signalling its adherence to the familiar genre of the loco-descriptive long poem. The contemporary reception of the text, however, was rather negative. Reviewers such as Thomas Holcroft complained about the very fact that the publication of the poem meant even '[m]ore descriptive poetry'[30] and attacked it as lacking innovation. The poem did not sell very well at all, and Wordsworth started reworking it soon after its publication. In another letter to Mathews in 1794 he worried about the sales figures and told his friend that he had decided to withhold another poem he had written,[31] unless he could be sure 'to derive from it some pecuniary recompence'.[32] If this statement does imply a turn away from the quick market of current political debate it also endorses the exploration of a long-term market organized around authors and their work, where the *author* 'create[s] the taste by which he is to be enjoyed', as Wordsworth wrote in 1815.[33] What are the factors that facilitated the development of this new market?

One of the fields where the idea of a unified, coherent *œuvre*, consisting of original works stemming from a poet's imagination was first propagated was the debate about the copyright and the proprietorship of literary works. The conception of poetry as an emanation from an independent mind could be pitched against those voices that considered writing in any case as the contribution to current ideas and thus as common property for which the author could expect no payment. Copyright legislation in 1710 had provided for some copyright for new works of literature,[34] but had actually strengthened the booksellers who usually acquired complete copyrights from the authors for a single fee. Wordsworth fought for the cause

---

29 William Wordsworth, *The Letters of William and Dorothy Wordsworth: The Early Years 1787-1805*, ed. Ernest de Selincourt, rev. Chester L. Shaver (Oxford, 1967), p. 76.

30 *Descriptive Sketches*, ed. Eric Birdsall, p. 11.

31 The poem was to be published as *Guilt and Sorrow* in 1842.

32 *Early Years* (1967), p. 120.

33 William Wordsworth, 'Essay, Supplementary to the Preface' in *The Prose Works of William Wordsworth*, ed. W. J. B. Owen and Jane Worthington Smyser (3 vols., Oxford, 1974), iii, 62-84; at 80.

34 The term of copyright in new works was limited to 14 years, to which could be added another 14 years if the author was still alive: see Richard G. Swartz, 'Wordsworth, Copyright, and the Commodities of Genius', *Modern Philology*, 89 (1992), 482-509; at 493-4.

of a long-term copyright owned by the *authors* from about 1800 onwards and presented his own texts as a main argument for his position in the debate.[35] To discredit the idea of literature as public property, then, also served to keep the financial control of one's texts in one's own hands. The second half of the eighteenth century had contributed to the strengthening of authorship by facilitating the emergence of a new type of writer: the great English poet. Samuel Johnson's *The Lives of the Poets* (1781), accompanying his anthology of English poetry, established the frame for a cultural interest in national poets. This anthology, together with Thomas Warton's *History of English Poetry* (1774 to 1781) and especially the complex of Shakespeare veneration, criticism, and publishing made available a national heritage of poetry, both as a corpus of works and as a model of literary self-fashioning.[36] *The Collected Works* became a site where the development of the 'poet's mind' could be presented and where texts could be ordered – and marketed – under a single famous name. The copyright legislation from the eighteenth century onwards had also made it possible to publish cheap editions of an author's work in a competitive system. Until Wordsworth's time, however, *The Collected Works* of a great author was a profitable item mainly for the publisher. In 1836, then, we catch Wordsworth at an important point in his career as an 'English poet', about to publish a complete edition that he expected to be profitable for himself not least because he was to own the copyright completely.[37] Wordsworth had turned from a young author eager to contribute to current debates to a poet interested in publishing his own name and genius. For this edition, he saw an occasion for 'the revisal of so many of the old Poems, to the re-modelling, and often re-writing whole Paragraphs'.[38] It was at this point that Wordsworth in-

---

35 In 1814, the copyright for new works had been extended to 28 years or to the remainder of the author's life if he outlived that term. Wordsworth, however, kept on arguing for an extension into the 1840s, until in 1842 the Copyright Act, which granted a copyright of either 42 years after publication or seven years after an author's death, ended the debate. 'Introduction General' to William Wordsworth, 'The Law of the Copyright' in *Prose Works*, iii, 303-306; at 303. Cf. Lee Erickson, *The Economy of Literary Form: English Literature and the Industrialization of Publishing, 1800-1850* (Baltimore, 1996), pp. 49-69, and Susan Eilenberg, *Strange Power of Speech: Wordsworth, Coleridge, and Literary Possession* (New York, 1992), pp. 192-212.

36 See for an admirably concise account of this development John Brewer, 'Histories, Exhibitions, and Collections: The Invention of National Heritage in Britain 1770-1820', *Aufklärung*, 10 (1998), No. 2, 11-22.

37 Erickson, *Economy of Literary Form*, pp. 58-9.

38 *The Letters of William and Dorothy Wordsworth: The Later Years*, ed. E. de Selincourt, rev. Alan G. Hill (4 vols., Oxford, 1978-88), iii, 353.

scribed into *Descriptive Sketches* the superior and detached perspective of a 'mighty poet' that he had sketched out in 'The Prospectus' – together with the very strategy of this re-inscription – 36 years earlier. In 1836, he saw an occasion to incorporate it in his earliest work and, what is more, to publish in what was a single moment an *œuvre* reshaped to express a 'unity in progress'.[39]

Indeed, connected to the idea of a history of English poetry was the idea of a progress of poetry and cultural achievement in general. This idea, developed throughout the eighteenth century, was well-established in Wordsworth's time and could now be conceptualized as, and exemplified by, a series of biographies of individual poets and their contribution to the progress of literature. Again, these progenitors provided role-models for writers who could successfully relate themselves to a national literary tradition and thus effectively ignore day-to-day politics. In Wordsworth, we find the conception of the historicity and progress of literature interiorized as the development of his own work. We have to understand his concern about the future of his *œuvre* also in this light. His activity in the copyright-debate was also focused on the expansion of *post-mortem* copyright.[40] He wanted to make sure, one could argue, that through a controlled edition of his texts his *œuvre* could stay a unity under his name, organized in the temporal structure he had himself laid down. The effect of futurity introduced into *Descriptive Sketches* depended on its reception as one of his early poems. On the quality of foresight in these texts, it seems, was in turn dependent another mode of futurity: the ability of his texts 'to chear / The world in times to come', as Wordsworth had written in the 'Prospectus'. Both modes of futurity, then, are clearly interdependent. Wordsworth had realized that the futurity of his *œuvre* was a matter not only of its interior structuring but also of the affirmative reception of this quality in the future. *Descriptive Sketches*, however, could only keep its prophetic quality if it continued to be received as one of Wordsworth's juvenilia, written in '1791 & 1792', as the 1836 version has it. Wordsworth introduced the early date at the end of the poem only in 1836, aiming, as Eric C. Walker writes

39 The 1836 edition was not the first edition of *Poetical Works* that Wordsworth published. (Re-)Shaping his *œuvre* was a project that occupied much of his time from the 1810s. He had revised *Descriptive Sketches* both for a two-volume version of *Poems* (1815), where it appeared in extracts, and for a four-volume edition of *The Miscellaneous Poems of William Wordsworth* from 1820. The actual rewriting of the ending of the poem, however, occured in 1836. Cf. *Descriptive Sketches*, ed. Birdsall, pp. 16-8, and Gill, *Wordsworth*, pp. 336 and 389.

40 See e.g. Wordsworth, 'The Law of the Copyright', pp. 318-9.

about an 1815 edition of his works, 'at unity in the shape of the life's work'.[41] The biographical arrangement of his *œuvre* was imperative to the functioning of the discourse of William Wordsworth.

Wordsworth, then, fashioned himself very much like an *auteur* in terms of Foucault's theory of authorship.[42] Instantiating Foucault's 'author function', the category of the 'English poet' emerged in an interrelation between acts of self-positioning of writers, of marketing of dead and living authors through their publishers and of the emergence of a new conceptualization of Britain's literary past. *Descriptive Sketches* bears witness to Wordsworth's development into an 'English Poet' in two ways. In its failure as an intervention, it represents a starting point to Wordsworth's poetical self-fashioning. On the other hand, the second version testifies to the moment when Wordsworth was in a position to provide for his own poetical future in several senses. This version could have been read in the light of the well-known history of Wordsworthian enthusiasm, disillusion and withdrawal from the spirit of the French Revolution. I chose, however, to focus on the emergence of the discourse of William Wordsworth in the course of the 1790s and on the effect this discourse had on the poem of Wordsworth's most closely connected to the Revolution. The earlier text bespeaks the status of the French Revolution as an event ruling the literary market and a young author responding to it. The later version, however, shows us a reversed discursive functioning and warns us how sharply we have to differentiate between Wordsworth in the French Revolution and the French Revolution in Wordsworth.

---

41 Eric C. Walker, 'Wordsworth's "Third Volume" and the Collected Editions, 1815-20', *Papers of the Bibliographical Society of America*, 80 (1986), 437-453; at 444.

42 See Michel Foucault, 'What Is an Author?', trans. Josué Harari, in *Textual Strategies: Perspectives in Post-Structuralist Criticism*, ed. Josué Harari (Ithaca, NY, 1979), pp. 141-60.

Index